A Woman Doctor's Civil War

Esther Hill Hawks as a young woman.

A Woman Doctor's Civil War
Esther Hill Hawks' Diary

Edited with
Foreword and Afterword
by
Gerald Schwartz

University of South Carolina Press

To my Mother
and to the memory
of my Father

Copyright © University of South Carolina 1984

Published in Columbia, South Carolina, by the
University of South Carolina Press

First Edition

Manufactured in the United States of America

Library of Congress Cataloging in Publication Data

Hawks, Esther Hill, 1833–1906.
  A woman doctor's Civil War.

  Bibliography: p.
  Includes index.
  1. Hawks, Esther Hill, 1833–1906. 2. United States—
History—Civil War, 1861–1865—Medical care. 3. United
States—History—Civil War, 1861–1865—Personal narratives.
4. United States—History—Civil War, 1861–1865—Women.
5. Sea Islands—History. 6. Afro-Americans—Sea Islands—
History—19th century. 7. Physicians—United States—
Biography. I. Schwartz, Gerald, 1932–   . II. Title.
E621.H36 1984   973.7'75   84-11998
ISBN 0-87249-435-7

Contents

Introduction and Editorial Policy

The original diaries of Dr. Esther Hill Hawks comprising three 6½ inch by 7¾ inch bound composition books were salvaged from papers and trash discarded from an apartment in the process of renovation in Essex County, Massachusetts, in 1975, by Mr. and Mrs. Eldon Porter. The Porters, who now reside in Long Beach, North Carolina, are still in possession of these volumes.

There is reason to believe that Dr. Hawks wrote a fourth diary volume, which very likely covered the years she lived in Florida prior to her permanent resettlement in Lynn, Massachusetts, in 1870. It was with considerable anguish that the present editor decided to temporarily abandon his search for the possible fourth volume and to publish the existing diary volumes at this time.

The Hawks papers at the Library of Congress were of great help in editing the Diaries, particularly the correspondence between Dr. Esther Hill Hawks and her husband Dr. John Milton Hawks from the time of Milton's departure from Manchester, New Hampshire, in January 1862, to the time of the Hawks' reunion several months later on the South Carolina Sea Islands.

Much significant and fascinating background material on Dr. J. M. Hawks was found in these papers, in the holdings of the Edgewater Public Library in Florida, and at other repositories in that state. Since that material *ipso facto* pertains to and clarifies the life and career of the author of the diaries, it has been incorporated extensively into the Foreword, Afterword and Footnotes of this volume.

The reader will detect that Dr. Esther Hawks at times devoted much space to personal trivia and comparatively little to details about her important medical and other achievements. The present editor has sought to amplify her accomplishments where possible through footnotes.

Like Mary Boykin Chesnut, Dr. Hawks wrote two versions of some of the events she described in her diaries. Unlike Mrs. Chesnut, Esther

Hawks did not distort the past, nor seek to appear omniscient by extensive modifications a generation after her initial jottings. Presumably with a view toward eventual publication, she did sometimes seek to correct and improve her grammar and syntax, clarify her prose style, and add a few previously missing details when she wrote her second versions of events. These revisions were likely written mere weeks, or at most months, after the original diary entries and were composed in secure and quiet comfort rather than in hospital tents or makeshift quarters.

Where there is redundance the editor has chosen one version over the other on the basis of greater clarity and felicity of expression. Readers are assured that nothing of historical substance has been changed during the course of the selection.

The handwriting of Dr. Esther Hawks was clear most of the time, though it bordered on the illegible when she wrote either hurriedly or under an emotional strain. Even at its clearest, Dr. Hawks' handwriting is interspersed with dashes and stray marks. Her spelling and punctuation were erratic. Moreover, Dr. Hawks' style of writing dates and her use of upper case letters and quotation marks is inconsistent.

Accordingly the present editor had to make several decisions pertaining to editorial method and procedure. An effort has been made to assure consistency of format and style. Only a few changes have been made so that the essential flavor of Dr. Hawks' writing, flaws and all, may be preserved. Where Esther Hawks' writing was modified, the following editorial guidelines and rules were established:

Clarifications deemed necessary by the editor have been inserted in brackets.

Words inadvertently repeated as at the end of one page and beginning of the next have been deleted.

Some loose fragments inserted in the diaries have not been used. Others have been incorporated directly into Dr. Hawks' narratives, or used as footnotes.

Letters torn off or blotted out from the diaries have been supplied in brackets.

In lieu of chapter titles Dr. Hawks' random section headings have been preserved inasmuch as these headings constitute natural breaks in the narrative. Some repetitious references to the month, however, have been deleted.

Dates flush against the margin but not raised have been indented.

Changes of pen, ink, or writing style are, where appropriate, presented as new paragraphs.

Where a new paragraph is needed and a dash appears, the dash is construed as Dr. Hawks' intention of starting a new paragraph. Where a diary entry date follows a sentence, a new paragraph is also begun.

Dr. Hawks' spelling inconsistencies are maintained. Where a seeming misspelling might be a function of faulty penmanship, the correct spelling is supplied.

Some letter inversions are retained. Others, where the inversion would change a word's meaning, or confuse the reader, have been corrected.

Some dashes and other random marks have been eliminated, as have insignificant punctuation marks penciled in by Dr. Hawks after the original diary entries had been made.

All signs replacing the words "and" and "etc." have been rendered as ampersands.

Raised letters have been dropped.

All emphasis of Mrs. Hawks is indicated by italics.

Unnecessary parentheses penciled in after a diary entry written in pen earlier have been deleted.

Every effort was made to identify accurately all individuals mentioned in the text. It was, however, impossible to locate information on very obscure persons. Where extensive research failed to reveal the identity of an individual of more than passing significance the word "unidentified" appears in the footnote. Where the identity of a person was likely but less than certain, the word "probably" was inserted before his name in the footnote.

Exceptionally famous individuals and events were not identified in footnotes.

Where a salutation on a letter or the document has special significance, it has been used in place of a standard footnote abbreviation such as EHH for Dr. Esther Hill Hawks, or JMH for Dr. John Milton Hawks.

The editor assumes all responsibility for the accuracy of the transcription of the diaries of Mrs. Hawks and all other manuscript sources. Lacking familiarity with the nineteenth-century handwritings of diarists and correspondents other than the Drs. Hawks, however, the editor cannot claim to have been quite as precise in transcribing every dash, ampersand, abbreviation or the like of such writers.

Acknowledgments

Contributing substantially to this work have been William Copeley, Phillip Currier, Joe Ginn, Cary Graham, Ludovine Hamilton, Gail Harmon, C. H. Harris, Barbara Miller, Alice Strickland, Jerry Tate and Estelle Williams. My wife Molly was very helpful throughout the eight years between transcription and publication, as were Alva and Eldon Porter.

And most of all my appreciation and respect to Earle Jackson whose guidance was invaluable.

Gerald Schwartz

Cullowhee, N.C.
October, 1984

Foreword

When the will defies fear, when duty throws the gauntlet down to fate, when honor scorns to compromise with death—this is heroism.

Robert Green Ingersoll, *Speech in New York, May 29, 1882*

Dr. John Milton Hawks in 1864.

Heroism abounded on the battlefields of America's internecine Civil War. Not infrequently, as Stephen Crane depicted in *The Red Badge of Courage*, this heroism was predicated upon random chance, and was displayed by such fellows as Crane's Henry Fleming who was devoid of consciousness as to the great issues of the conflict.

Every now and again a generation of cynics needs to be reminded that there were also other participants in the national tragedy who were not merely swept along by the tide of events, but who were thoroughly conscious of the war as a struggle to enhance human freedom and human dignity. Such a person was the heroine Esther Hill Hawks, born Esther Jane Hill, in Hooksett, New Hampshire, on August 4, 1833, the fifth of eight children of Parmenas and Jane Kimball Hill.[1] Her New England ancestory went back several generations and included a paternal grandfather, John Hill, who fought in both the American Revolution and the War of 1812.

Esther Hill was educated in the public schools of Suncook and Exeter, at the high school in Manchester, and the academy in Kingston, all in the state of her birth. Later, she taught school in East Kingston, Merrimack, and Thornton's Ferry, New Hampshire. In addition to being intelligent and studious Esther was physically attractive, if not strikingly beautiful. She had hazel eyes, and an abundance of flowing, curly black hair. Her "quiet, serene, and good looks," were made all the more striking by her height. Esther was five feet, seven and a half inches tall, which is to say taller than most of her contemporaries of either sex.[2]

There is reason to believe that Esther Hill had had several suitors as of the day in 1850 that she accompanied her friend Helen Hawks to visit the combined office and drug store of a young Manchester physician, Helen's brother, Dr. John Milton Hawks.[3]

We do not know as much of Esther Hill's early life as we do of that of her husband-to-be Milton. Fortunately for posterity, casualties and other patients were few at the camp of the Twenty-First United States Colored

---

1. "Esther Hill Hawks, M.D.," *Lynn Historical Society Register* (1906–1907): 40.
2. The quotation is from the unpublished and untitled tenth wedding anniversary reminiscences of Dr. John Milton Hawks, October 4, 1864, Milton and Esther Hawks Papers, Library of Congress, Washington, D.C., as is part of the physical description. Esther Hawks' height, hair, and eye color are from an undated military pass issued to her during the war. Hawks Papers.
3. Hawks, anniversary reminiscences. All information in this introduction, pertaining to events prior to the Civil War are from this source unless otherwise noted.

Troops, at Morris Island, South Carolina, on October 4, 1864, the eve of the Hawks' tenth wedding anniversary. The occasion prompted a decennial taking of stock by John Milton Hawks, the regimental surgeon, not merely of his marriage, but of his life up to that point.

That life, at least in it prepubescent phase, was repressed, even by the standards prevailing among those descendants of the Puritans, who inhabited nineteenth-century New England. Milton was born to Colburn and Clarissa Hawks, in Bradford, New Hampshire, on November 26, 1826. He summed up his melancholy childhood as follows:

> I have been young but was never a boy—like other boys. Was not like other youths, am not like other men, it seems to me. I never played at marbles, ball or kite. I never sang or played an instrument of music. These latter methods of expressing the soul were not allowed me. And I was not of ready speech; and often when I felt the most—had most to say—from joy or sorrow, could find no utterance but in tears.

Milton attended school in his hometown, "tugging away" at such subjects as algebra and chemistry. His great loves were his studies, his mother and his sister, until he met "B" shortly before he completed his preliminary education at age fifteen. Already he had a "premenition of fleeting time," and engaged in maudlin weeping. "Yes," Milton Hawks vowed, "I must do something in the world." That something initially was clerking in his uncle's grocery store in Massachusetts, an employment he described as his "highest ambition."

In the Fall of 1842 Milton when still only fifteen taught school in Warner, New Hampshire,[4] and became enamored of another young lady who was "prettier than B, knew a hundred times as much." Affairs of the heart though did not prevent him from moving on to Schenectady, New York, to both teach and further his own education, or from sailing for Savannah, Georgia, in September 1844.

When Milton left for the South, he did so with forty dollars in gold in his pocket. After nearly two years of itinerant teaching in Houston County, Georgia, he returned home with the small fortune of three hundred dollars, recommenced his courting of "B", and commenced the study of medicine with Dr. George H. Hubbard. Neither situation proved satisfactory for very long. While "B" was employed at the cotton mills in Lowell, Massachusetts, Milton wrote to her, and got a reply which "almost chilled me, it was so badly written." Milton's sensitive soul was compara-

---

4. William Richard Cutter, *Genealogical and Personal Memoirs Relating to the State of Massachusetts* (New York: Lewis Historical Publishing Co., 1910), p. 358.

bly wounded when he was privy to a "falling out," between Dr. Hubbard and his wife pertaining to an appropriately New England subject, blueberry pies. "Brute," thought Milton Hawks, as he vowed never to forgive the doctor for his cruelty to his pretty wife.

Whether prompted by his loathing of Dr. Hubbard, his desire for more sophisticated medical knowledge, or both, young Hawks left and enrolled at the Medical College in Woodstock, Vermont.

At the close of the term he took a roundabout way from Vermont to New Hampshire by way of Lowell in order to visit "B." So profound was his shyness though, that knowing full well that he was at the Lawrence Mill where "B" worked, he feigned confusion, asking if it was the Merrimack Mill and went away too bashful to confess his mission. When Milton finally tracked down his lady love in her well-chaperoned boardinghouse, he was so taken with her loveliness that he reproached himself for having once been so upset by her bad writing.

In the Spring of 1843 Milton Hawks, while visiting his home, decided that farm labor meant hard work and poor wages and that he could do much better by teaching school. Accordingly, having set aside his medical studies, he traveled to New Jersey where employment as a teacher awaited him. While in New Jersey, what Milton would describe as one of the great turning points of his life occurred. He met Dr. Churchill of Lowell, who invited him to return to that city and to join him in his medical practice. Milton was elated to learn that Dr. Churchill would not charge him tuition, would turn over much of his business to him, and would pay his board. That board was, by coincidence, at the home of an uncle of "B's," and Milton saw a great deal of her. It was not long though before a rift occurred between the two lovers. "B" took to attending religious meetings and became increasingly pious. "I," Milton explained, "talked young infidelity—I mean scepticism."

One evening "B" timidly confided in Milton that she feared they differed too much to be happy together. "What did I do?" Milton wrote years after the event:

> drop on my knees before her and plead, and promise to make
> that difference less? did I embrace her and kiss her and tell how I
> loved her——Not a bit of it. I sat unmoved, and might have been
> mistaken for a judge passing sentence on a criminal.
> In two minutes I was standing with her hand in mine bidding her
> farewell, without the slightest show of regret or sorrow or
> affection.

There followed other emotional involvements, in the midst of which Milton Hawks went west to pursue his final formal course of medical training, graduating from the Eclectic Medical College of Cincinnati in 1847. He then practiced medicine in Illinois with an affluent physician who had a "marriageable daughter." Milton tried to like her, but could not quite summon up any real affection.

Worse, be became deathly sick and returned home to New Hampshire. Friends and family expected him to die at any time because of his coughing day and night and chronic diarrhea that had almost reduced him to a skeleton. His beloved sister Helen nursed him back to health while she lifted his spirits with her wonderful sense of humor. "I was not afraid to die," Milton wrote, "But didn't want to—so I didn't."

In the Fall of 1848 after he had recovered from his illness, Dr. Hawks moved to Manchester and opened an office on the second floor of the Museum Building. No patient save for members of his own family found him there until one of the city's well-established physicians, Dr. D. C. Collins, offered to take him in as a full partner. Milton accepted the offer enthusiastically, buying half of Dr. Collins' stock and moving into his house to board. Quickly Dr. Hawks began enlarging his circle of acquaintances. One of his new acquaintances, incidentally, was Dr. Collins' daughter Nancy, whom he described as "pretty and smart though cantankerous." The competition for Nancy's affections included a fellow boarder, an actor who took her to the theater almost nightly. Against such a romantic rival, the young doctor had virtually no chance, though he would later admit, "If she had given me any encouragement I should have loved her." Instead, Milton Hawks became if anything more bashful than ever, rarely attending parties or even sewing circles.

His bashfulness, however, pertained only to his relationship with women. There was little trace of it in his professional life or in his increasingly active political life. Milton Hawks had by the late 1840s become a proponent of numerous reform causes. He devoted much energy to women's suffrage, and as early as 1848 he advocated both in the New Hampshire press and on the lecture platform the granting of women's suffrage.[5]

Such was the fellow to whom Esther Jane Hill was introduced in 1850. If it could be reported that love at first sight resulted from that introduction, this narrative would be rendered both more romantic and dramatic. That, however, was not the case. Dr. Hawks continued his quest for love elsewhere.

He attended church regularly, motivated not by faith but by a desire to look over the field. He began frequenting sewing circles for the same rea-

5. *Makers of America,* Florida Edition (Atlanta: Florida Historical Society, 1909) vol. 2., p. 386.

son. And when Esther Hill's sister Hattie called at his drug store and admired the botanical specimens he had fastened against the wall, he admired *her*, though she was engaged to another. Milton confessed that he was "liable to *damage of heart* from exposure."

Esther meanwhile was apparently smitten by young Dr. Hawks. When a classmate of hers at Kingston Academy came to Manchester, she went to Milton's office at Esther's request and told him that Miss Hill was anxious to receive a letter from him. Soon a brisk correpondence developed, including a letter in which Esther learned that since his business was declining Milton was determined to go to California with his new friend James H. Fowler. She accordingly received him in proper Victorian fashion at her boardinghouse in Boston. It was a snowy day, but Esther's smile and gracious ways were more captivating than the falling flakes.

Torn by ambivalence, Milton Hawks sailed, not for California, but for Savannah. Several months went by before he again wrote Esther, though she remained paramount in his thoughts. Of this period Milton would write, "I feared to have any girl fall in love with me on account of my uncertain prospects." But he "gradually became more reckless, and at last got so that I didn't care if Ett loved me outright."

Throughout the Summer of 1851 Milton lived in Augusta, Georgia, boarding with a family of Jews. Predictably, there was a daughter Helen who was "the queen of beauties." This Helen, to Milton's astonishment and delight, was "a liberal minded Jewess," who read and appreciated Voltaire! Despite lingering memories of his Ett back in New England, Milton enjoyed the company of Helen, until the combination of a misunderstanding with Helen's mother about an invitation to a party and his old wanderlust drove him still farther south to Florida by way of Charleston. He traveled to Jacksonville, Palatka, and elsewhere, going broke in midpassage. Desperate, Milton swapped a volume of Shelley's poems to the captain of a steamer for passage part way to St. Augustine, and got into debt for a ride by stagecoach the rest of the way.

In St. Augustine, Hawks started a school, and while boarding at a hotel met a Castillian "rouge and chalk beauty," who *sent him* a bouquet of flowers. Any romantic notions he harbored toward her were dissipated when he learned that she was "a very loose, grass widow."

Milton Hawks did not earn enough teaching to meet his expenses and moved on to Jacksonville where he became infatuated with an eleven-year-old girl, and later with Julia whose wealth and beauty prompted him to fantasize that he "had her and E. set before me to choose from." His choice was the distant Esther who won out too in his frequent mental comparisons between herself and virtually every new woman he saw,

A Woman Doctor's Civil War

most of whom were (at least according to Milton's standards) both rich and beautiful, and not infrequently smart as well—as in the case of the South Carolina lady who was most "perceptive about the sectional crisis impending."

His continued wanderings included a brief return to Augusta where he resumed his earlier partnership in a medical practice. Sister Helen meanwhile had written advising "plump and plain" that he return home and marry Esther Jane Hill. Milton had at last grown tired of his peripatetic way of life and had come to regard himself as an exile. Accordingly in June 1852, he began his return trip northward, stopping en route for a week at a Fourieristic Phalanx in New York to savor the utopian communal life. By August Hawks was reestablished in his medical practice in Manchester, sleeping on the floor of his office with nothing between him and the floor save sheets of newspaper.[6]

It was not long thereafter that Esther Hill took time off from her teaching to come to Manchester where she received Milton at the home of the mother of his friend, Fowler. Dr. Hawks had a "fluttering sensation" as he went to see Esther for the first time in nearly two years. Though the effect of the visit on Milton was merely pleasant and satisfactory and not "thrilling," he felt from that time on that his "path was clear." He later recalled:

> "How dear were the visits of Esther to my office to get some problem in Algebra solved. How I longed to be alone with her. —my eye glistened, and my pulse beat quicker, when her gentle tap at the door called me to open it.
>
> When I visited her home, how pleasant every thing was—what a kind mother, smart brothers—how fine the country—how pleasant the neighbors—everybody, and every thing in that region was about right. ——The blueberries we picked, tho few were sweeter; the roads we traversed pleasanter than any I had seen before.

Esther, who had earlier taught in East Kingston, had by now moved on to a new position in Merrimack. She received not only frequent letters but also frequent visits from her increasingly ardent suitor in Manchester. When tragedy struck through the death of her father, Esther traveled to Manchester for solace. Milton pressed her to his heart unable to speak, but presumably quite able to express his anguish and support silently. A real bond was being established between the two.

6. Dr. John Milton Hawks to Dr. Esther Hill Hawks, June 17, 1862, Hawks Papers, Library of Congress. Unless otherwise noted all letters to and from the Drs. Hawks, regardless of salutation will be henceforth identified solely by EHH and/or JMH and will be from the Hawks Papers, Library of Congress.

The stronger that bond though, the stronger became Milton's doubts and suspicions, particularly about Esther's chastity and loyalty. These doubts and suspicions turned into dark brooding paranoia when a mutual acquaintance hinted to him that Esther had arrived in her current school district with "unfavorable reports about her." Against this backdrop, rationalizing that he had had a premonition that Esther was sick, one Saturday Milton went to the Manchester train depot and took "the cars" to Merrimack to pay her a surprise visit. His heart sank when he found her out blackberrying with the fellow who earlier had played Iago to his Othello, and whom he now concluded was actually a rival for Esther Hill's affections. The matter was resolved however, and subsequently Esther and Milton began to make plans to marry.

To implement those plans she arrived at his boardinghouse in Manchester, on October 4, 1854, and they stayed up late packing their trunks for a long honeymoon journey to Florida. Early on the following morning, with the frost still whitening the dead grass, the two started on their rail journey to East Kingston where they took Esther's family by surprise with the announcement that they intended to wed that very day. "No flummery there," Milton proudly recalled. "No weeks of preparation, shown in the wedding cakes—or white satin dresses." The stern, practical business of life, would start in practical fashion. "I shall always respect Mr. Mellish——He it was that pronounced us one—a thing that we had done long before for ourselves," Milton later reminisced, then added rhetorically and not a little wistfully, "Was it too stern?" At the close of the short, simple ceremony, witnessed by her brothers Sylvester, Warren and Eddie, Esther burst into tears.

A few days later, Esther and Milton Hawks left for Boston and then New York from which they sailed for Florida. They would spend most of the winter in Manatee, south of Tampa. Here, while Milton investigated the feasibility of investing their meager capital in orange cultivation, Esther taught a private school in the Methodist Church.[7] Foreshadowing her later career she also taught a small school for black children, even though in so doing she risked imprisonment for violating the law if any complaint were lodged.[8]

For recreation, the newlyweds traveled up the Manatee River and Braden's Creek and went on shell-hunting excursions on nearby islands and

---

7. Ellen M. Patrick, "Address," *Tributes of Respect and Love From Associates and Friends, Read at the Remembrance Service Held at the Friends' Meeting House on Silsbee Street, Lynn, Mass. May 30, 1906, In Honor of the Late Dr. Esther H. Hawks* (Lynn, Mass: Boy's Club Press, 1906): 7.

8. Mrs. Wm. Lummus, *Tributes of Respect*, p. 26.

on the dividing line between Tampa Bay and the Gulf of Mexico. Esther Hawks also devoted considerable time to studying Milton's medical books. Indeed, she absorbed the contents of these books so rapidly and so thoroughly that on their return trip home in the spring of 1855, sailing up the Mississippi River from New Orleans, Esther delivered public lectures on physiology in Vicksburg and St. Louis.[9] The Hawks traveled eastward by rail from St. Louis, topping off their extended journey in typical honeymooner's fashion by viewing Niagara Falls.

The trip, however, was not without its moments of awkward, and even painful confrontation. It was often embittered by a shortage of funds. Even though Milton had liquidated most of his belongings before their departure, he had but little money. Esther's provision of most of their meager funds created an emotional strain; the honeymooners were forced to practice rigid economy "inconsistent of all times with connubial bliss; but especially at the very outset." "Five hundred dollars more," Milton sadly recollected, "would have given us in our new station the material basis to sustain a happy union." The trip, he concluded, "was a sure trial for the affections."

Once settled into "the little cosy quarters," the Hawks occupied in Manchester where Milton resumed his practice, harsh scenes yielded, if not to connubial bliss, then at least to a more pleasant mutually satisfactory relationship. And now, in the midst of her housekeeping, Esther Hawks resumed her informal but intense study of medicine, reading the medical volumes in Milton's office, clerking in his drug store, and even frequently visiting his patients.

By the Fall of 1855 Esther had become so determined to join the nation's small but growing ranks of women physicians that, with her husband's acquiescence, she abandoned her *ad hoc* medical training in favor of a formal course of study at the New England Female Medical College. This institution had been founded in Boston in 1848 by Dr. Samuel Gregory, a year before Elizabeth Blackwell became the first woman to graduate from an American medical school by receiving a degree from the Geneva Medical College in upstate New York. Gregory was strongly opposed to the practice of obstetrics by male doctors. His objections to what he sneeringly called "male-midwifery," were that it detracted from female delicacy, and was a temptation to immorality, "tending to lead women down the paths of prostitution, and inducing young men to go into medicine because of their curiosity about women."[10]

9. Myra Allen Ruppel, M.D., *Tributes of Respect,* p. 15.
10. John B. Blake, "Women and Medicine in Ante-Bellum America," *Bulletin of the History of Medicine* 39 (March–April, 1965): 118.

However preposterously prudish its founder's motivations and however primitive its initial facilities, lacking even a skeleton to use for instruction in anatomy and a permanent building, by 1855 the New
England Female Medical College was on a reasonably secure footing.
There was a faculty of seven who no longer were compelled to move
from one private home to another for lectures. Esther and the other
thirty-seven students attended both lectures and clinics in such subjects
as chemistry, toxicology, physiology, hygiene, materia medica and thera-
peutics, anatomy and surgery, as well as obstetrics and diseases of women
and children. The school by that time owned not merely a skeleton but
also separate skeletal bones, Auzoux manikins, models of the eye and ear,
obstetrical manikins, refined drugs, apparatus for laboratory demonstrations in chemistry, and both normal and pathological specimens in alcohol, along with numerous charts and a substantial medical library.[11]
Among the lectures Esther attended were those given by the German-
born pioneer of women physicians, Dr. Marie Zakrzewska. This student-
teacher relationship would later blossom into a lifelong friendship.[12]

In accordance with the New England Female Medical College's regula-
tions Esther Hawks attended two full seventeen-week sessions in two
successive academic years, graduating along with six other New England
women in 1857.[13]

In the interim between sessions, Esther spent considerable time nursing Milton's sister Helen, in Hopkinton, New Hampshire.[14] So great was
her devotion to Helen that she forewent her usual Fall visit to her mother.
Milton was no doubt properly grateful; but for all his commitment to
women's suffrage Milton Hawks had apparently harbored resentment
over the breaking up of his home, however temporarily, occasioned by
Esther's enrollment in medical school. Years later he would proclaim, "I
wish Ette had never seen a medical book, or heard a lecture. It is not a
business man-like worker that a husband needs. It is a loving woman."

This should not suggest that Dr. Hawks' life was uneventful while his
wife was attending school in Boston. As his own medical practice grew,
so too did his zeal for reform. Milton had, by the mid-1850s become
deeply devoted to the abolition of slavery, as had countless thousands
throughout the North, and particularly those among the educated classes

11. This composite description is drawn from *Seventh Annual Report of the New-England
Female Medical College* (Boston: Published by the Trustees, 1856) and from Frederick C.
Waite, *History of the New England Female Medical College 1848–1874* (Boston: Boston
University School of Medicine, 1950), pp. 79–81.
12. Ruppel, *Tributes of Respect,* p. 16.
13. *Eighth Annual Report of the New-England Female Medical College* (1857): 4.
14. EHH to JMH, August 17, 1862.

of New England. Always an activist, as opposed to a mere theoretician, J. M. Hawks was a member of the American Anti-Slavery Society, indeed so prominent and active a member that it was he who was called upon to organize a meeting in Manchester, when that organization's renowned orator Stephen S. Foster visited the city.[15] Milton spoke publicly on behalf of the abolitionist cause as well, at one time sharing a platform with William Lloyd Garrison, fiery editor of the antislavery journal, *The Liberator*.[16]

As busy as Dr. Esther Hawks was in establishing her own medical practice when she returned to Manchester, she too actively supported abolitionism. And yet she never quite, in the pre-war period at least, summoned up the intensity of zeal for the cause displayed by her husband. For example, while the two were enjoying an idyllic holiday at Hart's Lodge in Conway, New Hampshire, Milton, ever ready to proselytize, handed a young man they met an antislavery tract. Esther became enraged, angrily demanding, "What does he know or care for such reading?" Milton was plunged into several hours of morose silence, and when Esther walked round and up to the top of the huge perpendicular rock that constituted the resort's chief attraction, he silently hoped she would fall off and kill herself.

There were other conflicts too. Some were grounded in Milton's self-confessed pedantic tendencies, combined with Esther's fierce intellectual independence, others stemmed from his more rigid sense of propriety and her freer, less restrained mannerisms. And there were impediments to a quiet home and marital joy which stemmed from Milton's "eternal desire to make a hotel of our house." "People for whom neither of us cared," he would confess, "have lounged about our house for weeks. Somebody always there—adding to the work—assisting none—throwing a restraint around our actions—looking on when we desired to pledge anew our love in a kiss."

It is a safe assumption that most of these "loungers" were proponents of one reform cause or another, still a safer one that fellow abolitionists were numerous among them. As the sectional crisis worsened the Drs. Hawks devoted more and more time and energy to abolitionism. Along with her activity on behalf of relief movements for the local poor in Manchester, Esther remained active as "a pronounced anti-slavery agitator."[17]

In the mid-1850s, shortly after the Hawks' had returned from their honeymoon in Florida, Esther had served on committees for raising money and sending relief to the famine stricken victims of the mini-civil war

15. Jos. A. Hoviland to JMH, November 17, 1856, Hawks Papers.
16. Cutter, *Genealogical Memoirs,* p. 359.
17. Lummus, *Tributes of Respect,* p. 26.

that was "Bleeding Kansas."[18] It was during this period that Esther and Milton Hawks made the acquaintance of James Redpath. A British-born journalist, editor and lecturer, Redpath was an early convert to the antislavery cause, and he too raised funds for victims of the fighting between proslavery and antislavery forces in Kansas. He also had recruited antislavery New Englanders to move to Kansas and had raised guns and money in the churches and town meetings of New England to support the slave-freeing plans of John Brown.[19]

Redpath's own plan incorporated more than merely attaining freedom for slaves. It also involved a determination to resettle them in Haiti on the Caribbean island of Hispaniola. In 1859 Redpath became Haitian Commissioner of Immigration in the United States. He established the Haitian Emigrant Bureau, with offices in Boston and New York. James Redpath's message was that "In Hayti—the colored race—can develop itself in freedom; there, exhibit its capacity and genius. Nowhere else is there such an opportunity presented, absolutely nowhere in the world."[20] Several thousand free American blacks bought Redpath's argument. So too did various white abolitionists, among them the Drs. Hawks.

Milton Hawks did not limit himself to lending moral support to the Haitian resettlement movement. He signed on with the Bureau and in February 1861, in the midst of the secession crisis, sailed from Boston to Haiti. Thousands of free American blacks had already emigrated to that nation, which had undergone another revolution in 1859. A multitude of problems confronted them however. Allotments of land from the Haitian public domain promised the newcomers were being delayed, and when granted were devoid of water when irrigation projects were abandoned before completion. Unsanitary conditions at the immigrant receiving station in St. Marc and elsewhere contributed to a high mortality rate. And Haitian officials were given to appropriating the newcomers' belongings, while on a less official level native peasants plundered their remaining goods with impunity.[21] Dr. Milton Hawks' mission was to urge the alleviation of such conditions upon officials of the Haitian government including President Nicholas Fabre Geffrard, and to arrange for the absorption of more freed emigrants from America.[22]

18. Ibid.
19. Ludwell Lee Montague, *Haiti and the United States, 1714–1938* (New York: Russell and Russell, 1966), p. 74.
20. James Redpath, *A Guide to Hayti*, 1861 edition; (Boston: Haytian Bureau of Migration, 1861), p. 174.
21. Montague, *Haiti and U.S.*, p. 75.
22. JMH to EHH, February 25,27, 1861. JMH to R. Saxton, Brig. Gen., U.S. Army, August 4, 1862, Hawks Papers.

A Woman Doctor's Civil War

Back in Manchester, Esther Hawks continued her struggle to gain acceptance as a physician against still prevailing prejudice, the pain of which was only partially relieved by her splendid sense of humor.[23] She also busied herself by conducting business at the Hawks drug store, to which she repaired daily from 12:00 NOON to 2:00 P.M. and from 6:00 to 8:00 P.M. to fit women up with shoulder braces, supporters, trusses and the like.[24] And she looked after home and property, and continued her charitable work, more and more of which was connected with the war effort as the months passed.[25]

At length Milton returned to Manchester, his enthusiasm for Haitian colonization undimmed.[26] The rebels had fired upon Fort Sumter. The secession crisis had turned into a full-scale war. For several months Milton Hawks continued his practice of medicine while continuing to work for abolitionism. Not the least of this work consisted of urging in the press that the war be changed from a mere effort at national reunification to a crusade against slavery.

It was in this spirit that in August 1861, Dr. Hawks wrote what some maintain was the first letter to appear in a secular newspaper advocating the arming of blacks. His appeal, published in the Manchester *Daily American* read in part:

> Let us liberate the slaves; take them into our service and place weapons in their hands. . . . Let us join the War for the Union and the Constitution, and make it also a War of Emancipation. Let us once more unfurl the Stars and Stripes over all the territory from the Potomac to the Ohio, and from Fort Sumter to the Rio Grande. And when our banner shall again float in the Southern breeze, the sons of Africa will no longer curse it, for not a slave shall be left shackled beneath its folds.[27]

Meanwhile, Dr. Esther Hawks, determined to make a contribution to

23. Ruppel, *Tributes of Respect,* p. 17.
24. *The Daily American* (Manchester, New Hampshire), August 27, 1861.
25. Esther Hawks undated appeal "To the Women of Manchester," which she signed as secretary of the Women's Aid Society, proclaiming the need for 2,000 shirts and urging readers to "meet at Smyth's Hall armed and equipped for service," with "scissors, thimble and needles," is a good example. Hawks Papers.
26. Enthusiasm for Haitian emigration was far from universal. At a well-attended meeting in Brooklyn's Jay Street Church black clergymen and others "Resolved, That we firmly, flatly, uncompromisingly oppose, condemn, and denounce as unfair and unjust, as unwise and unchristian, the fleeing colonizing efforts urged by James Redpath, the white, seconded by George Lawrence, Jr., the black, who is employed by him." *The Liberator* (Boston), May 17, 1861, p. 79.
27. *The Daily American* (Manchester, N.H.), August 27, 1861.

the war effort, left for Washington for medical service, hoping to be employed as a physician, or, failing that, as a nurse.[28]

The Federal government was not hiring female physicians however. And Dorothea L. Dix, the reformer of insane asylums and prisons who had been commissioned as the first Superintendent of Army Nurses, perfunctorily rejected Esther's application for appointment as a nurse. Miss Dix, in true Victorian fashion, would approve for such service only middle-aged women of plain appearance.[29] Dr. Esther Hill Hawks was neither.

Nonetheless Esther remained in Washington for several months as a volunteer worker in the hospitals. It was during this period that the disastrous first battle of Bull Run was fought. Mrs. Hawks later recalled in her journal:

Washington was under marshal law and panic reigned. The night after the defeat of Bull Run the city was full of our forces, who had been driven back by the enemy.— The measured tramp of Regiment after Regt. like the distant beat of muffled drums, stirred the still night, and woke us to a realizing sense of the needs of many of the poor tired "boys in blue," who were too exhausted to keep in the ranks and so fell to the rear, and we spent the entire night furnishing them with tea—coffee—and such provisions as could be procured.

Many escaped slaves followed in the wake of our army and had also to be provided for. It was about this time that Gen. Butler hit upon the novel method of settling the vexed question of how to dispose of these runaway slaves by declaring them "Contraband of war."[30] The name was immediately adopted, particularly by the negroe's themselves. I remember with what scorn the Washington negroes, looked at and spoke of these nondiscripts.

Dr. Nichols,[31] who went from some part of Mass. had already established what was known as "Contraband Camps, where great numbers of the wretched creatures, were poorly fed and housed— and to these 'camps' we often went for 'help'. Aunt Phillis, our general factotium had great contempt for their abilities and we found her estimate about right when she declared "dat dem concubine niggers in date are camp no count for sure."

28. Esther Hill Hawks, "War Reminiscences—1861," unpublished journal.
29. Ibid. See also Richard Harrison Skyrock, "A Medical Perspective on the Civil War," Medicine in America: Historical Essays (Baltimore: The John Hopkins Press, 1966), pp. 103–4.
30. Maj. Gen. Benjamin F. Butler who was in command at Fortress Monroe, solved his own labor shortage as well as the new status of blacks by this designation.
31. Rev. D. B. Nichols.

In December 1861, two months after Esther had returned to Manchester, Milton Hawks partially liquidated his business. The Hawks spent Christmas together, then in January Milton departed, leaving Esther in charge once again of home and what medical and drug business remained.[32] His goals as he headed for Washington were twofold: to help however possible, to crush the rebellion and end slavery and to exploit prevailing conditions so as to increase his personal fortune.

Upon his arrival in the capital Milton played the tourist and continued to do so throughout his stay, visiting the White House, the Smithsonian, and the like.[33] He also tried to use what influence he could muster to work for American recognition of the governments of both Haiti and Liberia.[34] Hawks volunteered to go south on a spying mission, but a representative of the Provost Marshall's office refused him, laughingly explaining that Milton's thick accent and very facial features would quickly betray his New England origins.[35] At Fortress Monroe, Hawks also volunteered his services, this time for the more feasible mission of caring for the wounded on Roanoke Island, but he was again rejected.[36] He had no greater success in seeking a counselship to Haiti or Liberia, despite the efforts on his behalf of New Hampshire's Senator Daniel Clark. Even a well-paying if mundane government clerkship was elusive.[37]

Milton was growing desperate, especially after a pickpocket relieved him of his wallet containing seventy-five dollars in gold and twenty-seven dollars in paper currency while he was in line waiting to get into the gallery of the House of Representatives.[38]

But Dr. Hawks did have one good source of income. He had long since concocted a stimulant, which he sometimes preferred to label a relaxant, out of rum or other diluted alcohol, bitters, and pulverized lobelia seed. These ingredients were permitted to stand for fourteen days. They were shaken with regularity, the dregs poured off, and an equal quantity of

32. JMH to EHH, January 17, 1862. Additional references to these changes in the Hawks' medical and pharmaceutical practices appear throughout their correspondence in January 1862.
33. JMH to EHH, February 21, 1862.
34. JMH to EHH, February 7, 1862.
35. Ibid.
36. JMH to EHH, March 4, 1862.
37. JMH to EHH, February 26, 1862. Several of Milton Hawks' letters home from Washington substantiate this. In addition he was ambivalent about a clerkship even when one seemed in the offing: "But what good is money to do me!" JMH to EHH, February 7, 1862.
38. JMH to EHH, February 23, 1862.

simple syrup of sugar and water added.[39] Milton undertook sale of this bottled elixir to federal troops, initially at wholesale, but soon was involved in direct sales on a single bottle basis to individual soldiers. Before long, Dr. Hawks' stimulant was being sold by several agents, and he contemplated manufacturing it in Washington or Baltimore to save the freight on glass bottles from Philadelphia to Manchester and on the shipment of the product to the Virginia front.[40]

In the midst of this flurry of activity Milton found time to make inquiries on Esther's behalf about possible openings at the Hospital Department. "A female physician could do well after a few years here," he wrote home.[41]

Presumably, Dr. Esther Hawks contemplated such a contingency with interest, or even enthusiasm. But she was far from bored or idle back in Manchester. From all indications Esther's medical practice was growing considerably. Her accomplishments were being increasingly acknowledged and appreciated too, as when she received word from Boston that she had been elected *in absentia* one of the officers of the Ladies Medical Acadamy at that organization's first meeting.[42] Esther also served as Secretary of the Manchester chapter of the Soldier's Aid Society,[43] which provided the troops with clothing, hospital linens, and other items not furnished by the government. The Society also helped needy dependent families of soldiers. In addition Esther managed the Hawks property, dealt with matters pertaining to insurance and banking, and directed the bottling of the stimulant. "You are a capable woman of business," Milton wrote her.[44]

Late March 1862 found Dr. J. M. Hawks in New York, where he attended a meeting of spiritual reformers at Clinton Hall, and Professor Louis Agassiz's lecture on natural science at Irving Hall, in addition to less uplifting attractions such as Barnum's Museum. He was much taken by some of the exhibits at the latter, but suspected the snow-white hair of the Al-

39. JMH to EHH, June 6, 1862. The stimulant was advertised as "the best remedy that can be carried into camp for the colds, diarrhea and rheumatism which occur there in consequence of sleeping on the ground." *The Daily American* (Manchester, N.H.), August 27, 1861. Dr. Hawks' Drug Store also blended and sold "Restorative Bitters, Canker Drops, Catarrh and Headache Snuff, Nervine, Vermifuge and Cathartic Pills."
40. JMH to EHH, March 4, 1862.
41. JMH to EHH, February 10, 1862.
42. Mrs. Abell, Treas. to EHH, March 25, 1862.
43. Undated appeal "To the Women of Manchester," signed by Esther Hawks as Secretary of the Women's Aid Society. Hawks Papers.
44. JMH to EHH, April 1, 1862.

bino man, woman, and child he saw was artificial. "That's the only quarter I've thrown away," he reported to Esther.[45]

Milton's chief business in New York though was not his own edification or entertainment. It was to offer his services to the National Freedman's Relief Association as a superintendent of Union controlled plantations on the South Carolina Sea Islands.

This offer was cordially accepted by that agency, which proffered the doctor not merely a three-month contract such as is commonly signed with plantation superintendents, but rather one that was binding for "the season."

A violent snowstorm delayed the departure from New York of the steamer *Oriental*, but by April 9, the vessel was on its way—its destination, Port Royal, South Carolina.[46]

What were the circumstances under which a ship loaded with Northern uplifters, many of them such as Dr. John Milton Hawks ardent abolitionists, set sail, even as the Civil War raged, for the very heart of rebel country? An understanding of these circumstances is essential to any who would hope to understand Milton Hawks' mission, and the subsequent mission of Dr. Esther Hill Hawks, an account of which constitutes the essence of this volume.

The Sea Islands stretch along the Atlantic Coast from Charleston to Jacksonville, the South Carolina island group lying from the Charleston area to the Tybee River, close to Savannah. These low, flat islands are characterized by soil containing considerable pale yellow sand, including particles of disintegrated coral. Abounding with semitropical vegetation, the islands were famous throughout the world for the cultivation of the finest, silkiest long-fiber cotton grown anywhere. They were also famous throughout the cotton belt as the home of some of the antebellum South's most cultivated and aristocratic planter families, including the Barnwells, the Rhetts, the Fripps, Elliotts, Trescotts, and Coffins.

In the early months of the war, when these planters, most of whom had been fire-eating champions of secession, conjectured about a possible Union assault on the South Carolina coast at all, they assumed that such an assault would be against Charleston.[47] On November 7, 1861,

45. JMH to EHH, March 27, 1862.
46. JHM to EHH, April 12, 1862.
47. The foregoing information pertaining to the Sea Islands is drawn from personal observation and from the following: George Linton Hendricks, "Union Occupation of the Southern Seaboard, 1861–1865" (unpublished Ph.D. dissertation, Dept. of Political Science, Columbia University, 1954); Guion G. Johnson, *A Social History of the Sea Islands* (Chapel Hill: University of North Carolina Press, 1930); Willie Lee Rose, *Rehearsal for Reconstruction* (Indianapolis: The Bobbs-Merrill Co., Inc., 1964); Katherine Smedley, "The Northern

these conjectures ceased when Commodore Samuel F. Du Pont's federal fleet attacked, not Charleston, but Port Royal Sound. "I have seen a big battle," Dr. Esther Hawks' brother, private Edward O. Hill of the Fourth New Hampshire Volunteer Infantry, wrote home, "but did not take any part in it."[48] There was no need for army personnel, commanded by Brigadier General Thomas W. Sherman, to do so. The navy's big guns were sufficient. "It looked kind of careless to see the old frigate *Wabash* pour in broad side after broad side into that little fort," young Eddie added.[49] After receiving more than four hours of devastating naval bombardment, the Confederates were forced to abandon Fort Walker and, within a few hours, Fort Beauregard. This fateful day was for generations to be known among Sea Island Negroes as "the day of the gun-shoot at Bay Point."[50]

The Northern forces found that virtually the entire white population of the Port Royal area, including that of the town of Beaufort where many planters maintained seasonal homes, had fled to the mainland. They left behind an enormous, unpicked crop of valuable long-staple Sea Island cotton. And they left behind as well thousands of blacks. Soon cotton agents began arriving from the North to arrange for the harvesting, baling, and shipping of the cotton, their efforts being directed by a special agent of the Treasury Department, Edward L. Pierce of Massachusetts.

Pierce was concerned not only with the state of the current cotton crop, but also with seeing to it that another crop was planted for the ensuing year, and implicitly he was concerned with the well-being of blacks in the region. These blacks, while no longer enslaved, were not legally "free" as yet either. They were designated as "contrabands," the term coined earlier by General Benjamin F. Butler. While they were overjoyed to be free of their master's rule, these contrabands had many desperate needs, not the least of which was their need for clothing and other supplies, and the rudiments of an education. Accordingly, Edward Pierce urged friends in New England to proffer some assistance. These friends in turn promptly organized the Educational Commission for Freedmen in Boston. Soon similar organizations were at work in Philadelphia and New York, recruiting and paying plantation superintendents, teachers,

---

Teacher on the South Carolina Sea Islands" (unpublished Master's thesis, Dept. of History, University of North Carolina, 1932) and *Letters and Diary of Laura M. Towne Written from the Sea Islands of South Carolina 1862–1884,* Rupert Sargent Holland, ed. (Cambridge: Riverside Press, 1912).
48. E. O. Hill to "Brother Warren," November 12, 1861, Hawks Papers.
49. Ibid.
50. Rose, p. 11.

doctors and the like, while the Federal Government paid them a supplementary allowance for transportation, subsistence, and housing.

One of the earliest arrivals among those sent out to aid South Carolina blacks by the National Freedmen's Aid Association of New York was Dr. John Milton Hawks.[51] His ship, the *Oriental*, reached Hilton Head on the morning of April 13, 1862. It was an ecstatic Milton Hawks who stepped ashore, for he had been laid up in his berth, violently seasick throughout the voyage.

Within days Hawks was assigned outside of Union military lines to Otter Island, a small island on the north side of St. Helena Sound, where he was ordered to "take care of the persons of color under authority of the Treasury Department," by Edward L. Pierce.[52] Soon he crossed the South Edisto River to Edisto Island where in the first cabin he visited he found a sick black man lying on the floor, and administered the only drug he had available in his carpet bag, paradophyllin.[53] Dr. Hawks also administered a pep talk to a group of twenty-two blacks in the area urging them to plant all the corn they could, though the blacks had planted three acres of sweet potatoes and were already planting corn with the aid of a wild colt they had caught and broken for plowing.[54]

On another trip to Edisto Island some days later Milton had what he told Esther was a "wonderful streak of luck." The recently paid troops of the Ninety-Seventh Pennsylvania were on board the *Delaware*, on which he made the crossing. By nightfall he had sold them thirty-six dollars worth of stimulant at twenty-five cents a bottle, and had sold his gold watch at a substantial profit as well. Milton was elated, but no more so than he was over his observation that blacks were willing to work, that the "experiment of freedom" was a great success, and that thousands of dollars worth of cotton would likely be raised by free black labor on Edisto alone![55]

By May, Hawks' achievements included his organization of a school for over thirty freedmen, only one of whom, a woman, knew the alphabet. Milton appointed her as teacher.[56] He laid plans to organize a normal school to train black teachers,[57] and he was increasingly active as a physician. In this capacity, he delivered several babies and introduced the in-

51. JMH to EHH, April 1, 1862.
52. Directive from Edward L. Pierce, Special Agent of the Treasury Department, Port Royal, April 17, 1862 (Library of Congress, Hawks Papers).
53. JMH to EHH, April 23, 1862.
54. Ibid.
55. Ibid.
56. JMH to EHH, May 9, 1862.
57. JMH to EHH, May 17, 1862.

novation of maintaining birth records, giving new mothers a card containing the child's name and date of birth. "In this way, the next generation of negroes will be able to tell how old they are," Hawks proudly explained.[58] Other medical labors were less prone to induce joy in the doctor. He encountered one case of complete prolapsus, the woman's uterus protruding as large as Milton's fist. He prescribed ointment and tonic and was horrified to learn the cause of this condition: The woman's master had forced her to work in the fields until she dropped from exhaustion.[59] Another former slave had burned his feet off to the ankle years earlier. No doctor had ever been called, and the stumps had never healed properly. Dr. Hawks applied ointment and castile soap to the raw sores, and planned to "bring Mother's snuff and test its virtues."[60]

Milton also engaged in less noble labors: the confiscation of furniture, including a piano, which had belonged to departed rebel residents.[61]

Life was challenging; life was rewarding and good! "Come on down," Milton urged Esther. "I can keep you on boiled rice, blackberries and strawberries and milk."[62] And the while he encouraged his wife to come south and join him, Milton urged his superior, Edward L. Pierce to request either the Boston or New York Freedmen's Aid Society to send Esther down to the Sea Islands.[63]

Mere weeks away from Esther, Milton had written that he regularly kissed her picture and remembered "how sweet the sustance was, of which this is but a beautiful shadow."[64] His love letters from South Carolina remained impassioned. Some people at Port Royal, including a fellow physician and a certain lady from Philadelphia who believed in "affinities" had been living together, but there were no such temptations for him, Milton declared.[65] And yet there was a certain degree of ambivalence about his encouragements to Esther to join him on the Sea Islands. Come, and bring honey-scented soap, linen, a New England style bean pot, a side saddle, and "oh! bring a cradle!", Milton wrote in July.[66] But prior to that, in May, he had suggested, "If you can't come here by the middle of June you had better not come till October." This was a refer-

58. Ibid.
59. Ibid.
60. Ibid. Another medication used by the eclectic Dr. Hawks was a linament made of prickly ash bark in vinegar. JMH to EHH, May, 1862.
61. JMH to EHH, May 17, 1862.
62. Ibid.
63. JMH to EHH, May, 1862.
64. JMH to EHH, February 28, 1862.
65. JMH to EHH, August 3, 1862.
66. JMH to EHH, July 27, 1862.

ence to both the miseries of heat and mosquitoes with an attendant threat of malaria during that season and to the rampant rumors of an impending Confederate counterattack on Federally occupied coastal areas, perhaps by "a formidable iron clad" sailing out of Savannah in conjunction with a rebel land assault.[67] And in August, Milton again voiced concern about Esther's safety should she travel by steamer through stormy seas generally prevailing in late summer.[68]

Lacking most of Dr. Esther Hawks' letters to her husband, we can only conjecture as to her attitude, but on the strength of Milton's correspondence it appears that Esther was most anxious to come south. She was not only occupied professionally, but assuming she carried out Milton's instructions, she was also managing their property, arranging for fence repairs and the planting of ploughed acreage, and preventing the cutting of green trees.[69] She continued to conduct the Manchester end of the stimulant business, presumably heeding in this connection Milton's advice that she never let anybody think that cayenne pepper was one of its ingredients![70] And of course, Esther continued her good works on behalf of the war effort, chiefly in preparing and forwarding hospital comforts to sick and wounded soldiers.[71]

But it was Dr. John Milton Hawks who was in the midst of the action, now conveying blacks to more secure locales,[72] now teaching a Sabbath School,[73] here conspiring to arm black civilians in his charge,[74] there striving to help pupils who were utterly devoid of prior knowledge. "Their minds are blank, and readily receive such impressions as you see fit to make," Milton wrote to Esther of a class of older children who knew not even the names of the months or seasons, nor in which direction the sun rose or set.[75]

Milton Hawks, while he "found it eminently proper to take care of number one,"[76] was ever ready to help unfortunates. While managing a

67. JMH to EHH, August 3, 1862.
68. JMH to EHH, August 27, 1862.
69. JMH to EHH, May 9, 1862, June 6, 1862.
70. JMH to EHH, June 6, 1862.
71. Identification Pass from City of Manchester, Mayor's Office, October 27, 1862 (Library of Congress, Hawks Papers).
72. JMH to EHH, April 30, 1862.
73. JMH to EHH, May 22, 1862.
74. At Milton Hawks' request an assortment of firearms and ammunition were landed at the wharf for distribution by him to freed blacks, but consent for such distribution was not received. JMH to EHH, June 15, 1862.
75. Ibid.
76. JMH to EHH, April 12, 1862.

plantation he gave away to dependent blacks most of the clothes he had brought south with him in his trunk.[77]

He wrote Esther, in an especially poignant letter, "I pray for the chance to stay at a good salary, so I can afford to live away from other business, then I will get you here, and we will have a fine time, (not) because it is all pleasure and no trouble, but because notwithstanding the heat, the sand, the insects, the lassitude produced by the climate, we can do a vast amount of good."[78] And later, he wrote, "It is a growing conviction with me that the enjoyment of mortals is in proportion to the good they do their fellows."[79]

In mid-July Hawks' trunk was broken into aboard a steamer, and such things as shirt dickies and handkerchiefs were stolen.[80] Stealing was rampant, he complained, and he was laughed at for advocating honesty.[81] But John Milton Hawks was increasingly given to advocating more than honesty. Some of the positions he voiced in his correspondence would prompt Willie Lee Rose a century later to call Milton Hawks, "perhaps the most fanatical missionary at Port Royal."[82]

After Brigadier General Rufus Saxton had replaced Mr. Pierce as administrator of the Port Royal operation, Hawks wrote,

You are aware that the Government of the United States in its attempts to crush the rebellion is only half in earnest, and consequently cannot be very certain of success.

"Slavery first; afterwards the country" is the principle on which things have been, and are likely to be managed.

In view then, of the uncertain fate of the people of color who are now within your jurisdiction I would recommend that an opportunity be offered them to emigrate to the Republic of Hayti.[83]

Within a couple of days after receiving "full approval," from General Saxton,[84] Milton rode some ten miles to urge an audience of blacks on St. Helena Island to emigrate to the Caribbean republic.[85]

77. JMH to EHH, June 15, 1862.
78. JMH to EHH, June 30, 1862.
79. JMH to EHH, August 3, 1862.
80. JMH to EHH, July 16, 1862.
81. Ibid.
82. Rose, *Rehearsal for Reconstruction,* p. 185. For all his fanaticism Hawks found the physical condition of slaves on Edisto Island satisfactory, their cabins comfortable, and their hours of work in the fields not overly long. *National Anti-Slavery Standard,* June 14, 1862, p. 3.
83. JMH to Rufus Saxton, Brig Gen., U.S. Army, August 4, 1862, Hawks Papers.
84. Endorsement to JMH to R. Saxton, Brig. Gen., U.S. Army, August 4, 1862, by R. Saxton, Brig. Gen., August 6, 1862, Hawks Papers.
85. JMH to EHH, August 15, 1862, August 18, 1862.

Fortunately for our own Republic, Milton Hawks did not act as readily to implement some of his other rhetoric. "So Washington is probably burned to ashes and the President and Cabinet moved to New York as Philadelphia would be unsafe," he wrote after rumors of a federal defeat in Northern Virginia. "Just between you and me, I hope the rebels will burn Washington. It would wake up the Government which has been asleep. W. is full of Secesh and ought to be cleaned out. Then again it is not fit for the Capital of the Nation."[86]

And he wrote still later: "My belief is the same as on the first day of the war: our policy toward slavery must be changed or the south will establish its independence. . . . The greatest kindness that a man could do his government today would be to assassinate Pres. Lincoln—He stands directly in the way."[87]

Following the issuance of Lincoln's preliminary Emancipation Proclamation, Hawks would, however, do an abrupt about face and proclaim that the "name of Lincoln in spite of all his follies, must stand forever emblazoned in letters of living light."[88]

In May 1862 the ranking military commander of the Department of the South, comprising federally occupied islands off the coasts of South Carolina, Georgia, and Florida, General David Hunter, had boldly but prematurely issued an emancipation proclamation freeing all slaves under his jurisdiction. Hawks had earlier written to Hunter urging him to organize a black regiment and reminding the general that Negroes had made excellent soldiers under Toussaint L' Ouverture in Haiti.[89] Within days after "emancipation" Hunter began raising, through both enlistments and conscription, a regiment of black troops on the Sea Islands.

President Lincoln, fearing to alienate those border slave states which had not left the Union, countermanded Hunter's emancipation proclamation. The War Department refused to sanction the Hunter regiment, prompting the General to disband all but one company in August.

Meanwhile, the status of the entire Port Royal experiment had been undergoing considerable change, as had that of Milton Hawks. In June 1862, War Department control over the federally occupied Port Royal area had superseded control by the Treasury Department. General Rufus Saxton took command and established his headquarters at Beaufort.

86. JMH to EHH, September 3, 1862.
87. JMH to EHH, September 11, 1862.
88. JMH to EHH, October 2, 3, 1862.
89. John M. Hawks, "The First Freedmen to Become Soldiers," *Southern Workman,* Winter 1909, p. 107.

Plantation superintendents earlier selected by the freedmen's aid associations were, to Hawks' delight, to be retained by General Saxton. That delight was based partly on a substantial pay increase (to one hundred dollars per month, the same salary as that paid to assistant military surgeons) and partly on Milton's appointment by Saxton as a physician in the recently established hospital for blacks in Beaufort.[90]

"You will please take your precious self here as soon as may be," Milton now wrote to his wife. "The prospect, Dearest Ette, never seemed so fine for the future as now."[91]

It was grand, Milton reported, to be sleeping now on a feather bed replete with clean white sheets and with easy access to a bathtub.[92] It was grander still to be able to "meet surgeons as a brother surgeon, of no particular 'party' or 'ism' but as a physician."[93]

But Milton's empathy with suffering blacks remained his paramount emotion.

I will not ask of the Soldier's Aid Society anything for the Blacks as it might lessen the zeal of some of the sisters, and I should be sorry to do that. But if they could see the old half palsied woman in the hospital, who had before we took her involuntary discharges from bowels, and no change of clothes, they would be willing to send at least one dress and shirt.[94]

Dr. Hawks performed amputations and other surgery in the Beaufort hospital, but complained about too little work and too much leisure.[95] Presumably it was a gnawing feeling that his contributions to "the cause" were not quite great enough that led him to terminate his civilian status in favor of a commission as a U.S. Army Acting Assistant Surgeon on General Saxton's staff in mid-October 1862.[96]

One of Dr. Milton Hawks' important duties during this period was administering medical examinations to men who were enlisted in what was to become the first black regiment ever mustered into federal service, the First South Carolina Infantry Regiment.[97] Hawks would be the first medi-

---

90. JMH to EHH, July 10, 1862.
91. Ibid.
92. JMH to EHH, July 16, 1862.
93. JMH to EHH, August 3, 1862.
94. Ibid.
95. JMH to EHH, August 4, 1862.
96. Military Service Record of John M. Hawks (National Archives).
97. The designation of this regiment was later changed to Thirty-Third United States Colored Troops.

cal officer attached to the regiment.[98] This unit, earlier officially authorized by the War Department, was organized by General Saxton shortly after he returned from a leave in the North. Members of the remaining company of the "Hunter Regiment" were quickly joined by numerous black recruits who both liked and trusted Saxton as they had never liked or trusted Hunter.[99]

Milton enthusiastically wrote Esther about his new military status, urging her still again to join him at Port Royal. But his letters do not appear to have arrived in New Hampshire before Esther's departure from home.

Following a brief visit to kinfolk in Bradford and other New Hampshire towns, a visit which featured fresh air, long walks, wholesome food and "no pork, not ever!",[100] Esther Hawks had returned to Washington.[101] She spent several weeks attempting to find a suitable position as either healer or teacher in the capital. Frustrated, Esther ended her efforts in early October and returned to Manchester. En route home she paused in New York to file an application for an appointment as a teacher of freedmen with the National Freedman's Relief Association, which had some months earlier sent a small group of women to the Sea Islands as teachers.[102]

She was at home for only a short while when a message arrived for her. It is with this message that the present editor yields to the pen of Dr. Esther Hill Hawks.

98. JMH to Brig. Gen. Jos. Barnes, Surgeon General, U.S. Army, December 18, 1865 (J.M. Hawks, Military Service File, National Archives).

99. William H. Pease, "Three Years Among The Freedmen: William C. Gannett and the Port Royal Experiment," *Journal of Negro History*, XLII (April, 1957), 113–14.

100. EHH to JMH, September 26, 1862. Dr. Esther Hawks' strenuous objections to the eating of pork had been ignored by Milton who, when she "couldn't see him," ate boiled ham for breakfast and dinner. JMH to EHH, September 29, 1862. Apparently it was not merely the eating of pork which brought about the illness. "Above all things," wrote Milton, "bring a *seive* we eat bugs in our batter cakes, if the cook hasn't time to pick 'em out of the flour."

101. Hawks, "War Reminiscences."

102. Ibid.

Esther Hill Hawks, M.D.

South Carolina coast from Charleston to Savannah during the Civil War.

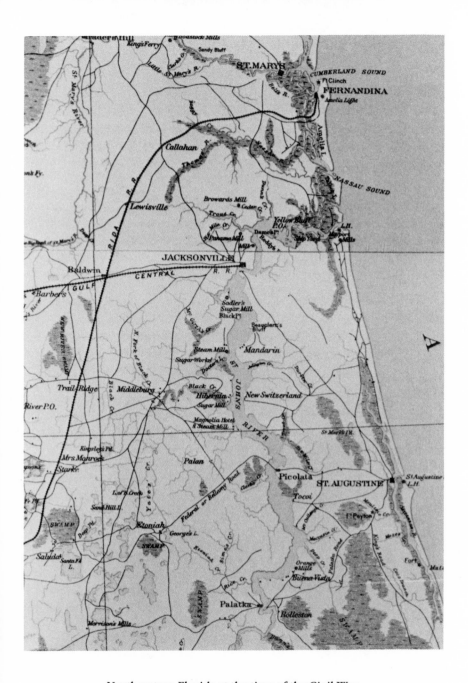

Northeastern Florida at the time of the Civil War.

[The Sea Islands]

Be ready to leave New York on the next boat which leaves the — inst. This was the substance of a note I received just at tea time on Sat. Eve, and in order to take the boat indicated I must be in N. Y. on the following Tuesday and to do that must leave home Monday morning. Having heard nothing definite from the So. [Society] in regard to my application to be sent out as a teacher among the Freed men the time allowed me for preparation seemed short—however having firm faith in the belief that I was born to be a missionary, I decided that the time had arrived for me to sacrifice myself, so I answered accordingly—and on Tuesday Morning at 6 o'clock stood alone on the pier in the great city of N. Y. I knew not which way to turn and for the first time doubts as to my fitness for the mission work I had undertaken crowded my mind. I consulted my tablets to learn the next move, for in the confusion I had forgotten the Hotel to which I was directed. Just then a kind-hearted cab-man offered to [d]eliver me from the care of my baggage which I allowed him to do saying in as polite and humble a tone as I could assume—I wish to go to Lovejoys' *Hotel* please; to which he replied, "Sure marm' and its there we take all the immigrants." This was all dutch to me but I learned its significance in the two days I was obliged to wait there. Rooms that smell of tobacco smoke and beds that show an innocence of any recent acquaintance with water, are always indicitive of the class which occupy them. During the day several other women arrived who, I soon learned were bound for the same missin [mission]. Most of them had been out before and walked over the disagreeables in our position as trifles to be expected and not minded. There presence was a great support to us who were new to the business. Our little band only numbered nine women, and there were also many men passengers aboard who were going, some in a spirit of adventure others to be employed as Supt. [Superintendents] among the freedmen.

Our boat, an old river steamer, quite unfit for ocean travel[1] was heavily loaded having several companies of a Me. Regt. and their camp stores aboard. When off Cape Hatteras we encountered a heavy gale, and for 48 hours the Capt. never left the Pilot house. The great waves broke over, pouring down the gangway extinguishing the fires, so that no cooking could be done—and the floor of the salon and of our state rooms were often (several) inches under water—Measles broke out among the soldiers who were crowded into the least possible space, and for a time all the enthusiasm and romance was washed out of us. Mrs. Gen Hawley,[2] occupied the state room with me and we were both to awfully seasick to take much interest in the result of our venture.

Among the passengers, was one of the Vanderbilts: and his terror was most pitiable: he would walk the cabin imploring every officer he met to put him ashore! We were a week going from N.Y. to Hilton Head a distance which should have been covered in 62 hours, and it was a most grateful party, tho' very limp and forlorn looking, who gathered on deck as we steamed up the harbor to Hilton Head, just as the sun was sinking— and all joined in singing a hymn of thanks giving. Words are inadequate to express what discomfort and misery we endured on board that little, close dirty boat, and on our arrival I felt more strongly than ever, that I had mistaken my mission. —The *Delaware* had been reported as wrecked so our safe arrival was most warmly welcomed. We spent the night on the boat and early next day our sturdy band of pioneers, was taken on a gay little tug-boat—very much bedecked with flags and bunting, up the beautiful river Beaufort—to the little city of the same name. We got off the boat, the wharf was crowded with vehicles of every discription. There was a long row of us and the pile of baggage which answered to our names was quite appaling. I looked on in dismay. What was to be done with us? Presently a very pleasant faced, beardless young fellow came up to us and with a most comical expression of conntenance announced that he was Mr. —— and was to take us in charge. I looked at the boy, then at the core of resolute looking women and the pile of bag-

1. The *Delaware* was indeed small and unseaworthy and the voyage induced much seasickness in Esther. She was thankful though that she had not sailed on the only other vessel to leave New York for Port Royal, S.C., during her seventeen day wait in the city. That ship, the *George Peabody*, was feared lost at sea. Esther H. Hawks to Mrs. Secretary and Ladies (of the Soldiers Aid Society), November 25, 1862. Milton and Esther Hawks Papers, Library of Congress, Washington, D.C.

2. Harriet W. F. Hawley, who was en route to join her husband (future Connecticut Governor General Joseph R. Hawley) at Beaufort, S. C., where she would begin her work as a Union army nurse. Years later she would nurse many of the survivors of Andersonville Prison Camp.

gage—and my thoughts ran something in this wise—Oh, what a big thing it is to be born a *man*! We all meekly followed his directions—two ambulances and a cart were in waiting into which we were *packed*—and we started for the 'Home'—where we soon arrived, were counted and left on deposit 'till called for. This 'Home' is a great institution—built after the style of a very poor barn. It is quite roomy and very airy—and we had the freedom of the house. There isn't a shrub or tree anywhere in its vicinity, only sand, sand, and when the wind blows it would be filled but for the fact that cracks in the house are so large that the sand is blown clear through and piled up at the back side. We were all too tired to be very critical on this first day of our arrival and when night came were glad of anything for a bed—but I must confess to a few cold shudders running down my back, when I took a contemplative view of our camping ground it looked so like one of the soldiers' 'burying grounds' I had visited—and the line of some body's poetry about the 'Little graves ranged in a row" kept running in my head long after the rest were quietly sleeping—and my head would come off the apology of a pillow and my eyes take a survey of the quiet mounds! What a miserable night that was! How the great rats ran over us and scrambled over the pile of ghostly looking boxes in the corner. How the sick—[3]

Beaufort S.C. Oct. 16th 1862

The 'city' of Beaufort, as it was called by its former inhabitants must have been a very beautiful place previous to its occupancy by our Soldiers. It is finely located on the Beaufort river—which forms a graceful curve somewhat crescent shaped, very inviting to the eye, as we approach the place. The principal street 'The Bay' as it is called, lays along this bend; its palatial mansions facing the water. The streets are narrow and but few of them have even an apology for a sidewalk and what there is, are too n—— for two to walk abreast with ea—— Pr—— ious to the landing of our tl—— —ere well k—— ardens, full of rare flowers—— magnificense ——whole l—— le place con-tained everyt—— e. It was one of the spots o—— ut our crazy solderly [sold—— —uty and its wealth. Much of the rich furnit—— —— by officers and sent north to friends—more of it was wantonly destroyed by the soldiers—apparently for the mere

---

3. This section which trails off after the word "sick" was written on a loose fragment inserted in the original diary.

love of destroying—Private libraries, which would have been such a blessing to them now, were *brutally* troden under foot. The churches were robbed of all ornament—the keys torn from the organs to make letters for their caps—the fences and out buildings torn away to build fires or make tent floors—and even the brick wall enclosing the dead, torn away to build chimney—and after a few months of military occupation Beaufort's left only in name. If our soldiers had been content with destroying the rebel property—there might be found excuse for them—but every indignity which human ingenuity could devise was heaped upon the poor negroes, who had hailed their coming so joyfully—and during the first year of our soldiers coming the blacks probably suffered more from their tyrany and insults, than ever in their lives before. It is a sad comment on humanity, but I believe in *this* case, a true one! No colored woman or girl was safe from the brutal lusts of the soldiers—and by soldiers I mean both officers and men. The 55th Penn. Reg would, no doubt bear off the palms in these affairs, if they could have their just dues. The Col. (White)[4] for a long time, kept colored women for his especial needs—and officers and men were not backward in illustrations of his example. Mothers were brutally treated for trying to protect their daughters, and there are now several women in our little hospital who have been shot by soldiers for resisting their vile demands. One poor old woman but a few months since, for trying to protect her daughter against one of these men was caught by her hair and as she still struggled, shot through the shoulder. She is still in Hospital. No one is punished for these offences for the officers are as bad as the men. Many such instances have come to my knowledge—but such open atrocities as were commited at first, are now quite rare—. Men in power, bitter proslavery men, whose influence was all used against the negroes—have been, many of them removed from The Department, and their removal gave great satisfaction to the Supt. in charge of the affairs of the Freedmen—. Gen Saxton, our present commander, whose long-tried faithfullness to the cause of freedom is well known, has made it somewhat disgraceful to be caught abusing women and little children!

Beaufort, from a military point of view is of no great importance to us. There are no forts within the limits of the city—only the remains of one of sand built by the rebels on the bank of the river. It was never completed and is now almost obliterated. Two and a half miles out towards the 'ferry' on what is known as the "Shell" road, entrenchements have been thrown up and strong fortifications created and our troops have been at

---

4. Col. Richard White.

work on them all Summer—guns have been mounted for a long time. The work is now nearly completed. This point is considered the only one necessary to fortify, to protect the place; beyond—at the 'ferry'—across which, is rebeldom—a company of Mass. Cavalry is picketed. It is but a short cut across to the mainland and the rebels frequently come across in small numbers to spy out our doings. Sometime in Aug. a small party came over to Barnwell's Is.—(where we have no pickets stationed but the island is inhabited by negroes) and succeeded in carrying off quite a number of colored people—and but a few days since a negro reported to our picket that three rebs had landed on a small island near. The story was not credited—but to be sure about it the Cavelryman took two negroes in a boat with him and went to reconoirter. As they were about to land the Soldier was shot dead and the two men taken prisoners.

Port Royal Ferry where the pickets are stationed is twelve miles distant from Beaufort. A long 'causeway' has been built out from this side—and standing on that it is easy to converse across with any one on the other side. It is here that all "flags of truce" are received by us—and this is the way of land communication with Charleston and Savannah.

There is a fine road leading from Beaufort to the ferry known as the "shell road" and was, probably one of the best ever made in the South—covered with oyster shell—hard and smooth as a floor the entire distance—protected from the sun by grand old live oak and magnolia trees whose branches covered with mistletoe and draped with the long grey moss, in many places quite reach across the road forming beautiful arches and noble avenues over which clambers in riotous confusion the vigarous Virginia Creeper, now in full bloom—the sweet yellow Jassamine, and the mottled leaved, Bigonia—with a great wealth of lesser vines and shrubs whose acquaintance I have not yet made—but all this loveliness is fast disappearing and already the road is much mistreated by the axes of our soldiers who are cutting away the foliage in order to remove so good an ambush for a foe. Two Forts, Duayne and Stevens are nerely completed, and we feel secure against any ordinary force. This beautiful "shell road" is quite a thoroughfare, for all pleasure seekers—parties of equestrians ride gaily over it daily giving little heed to the momentous causes which have turned into a military depot all this 'leafy luxurianse'.

Scattered over the island, at every desirable point for a location—looms up the grand mansion of the 'massa." Some of these buildings are as well constructed as the more stately city residence—and were occupied as permanent residences by their (other) owners—while others had less pretentious houses—simply furnished, 'the family' only living in them during a part of the year. —I have visited but few of these planta-

tions but two of these deserve particular notice. The Barnwell plantations a little this side the "Ferry"—on the banks of the river, deserve
especial notice. Approaching the house which is entirely hid from the
road—you pass through a wide avenue, bordered on either side with
magnificent live oaks whose lofty branches, meeting together over head,
like some templed arch, [so] richly frescoed with the parasite moss and
air plants, that only an occasional sunbeam ever penetrates the shade.
Another plantation of the same name, a little beyond this plantation, has
an avenue a half mile in length very like this only that the trees are much
smaller and on this place stands the monarch oak of all the islands—eighteen feet girth and sending its long arms out over a third of an acre!—
thickly hung with moss its shade forms a temple fit for gods to worship in
and even our lawless soldiers have, so far, respected and spared it. The
name of Barnwell is one of the most common here and must belong to a
very wealthy family. —Sad stories are told of some of them by their poor
bondsmen!—but it is a fact worthy of notice, that slaves very seldom re-
fer to their old owners or the manner in which they were treated by them
and what they do say voluntarily is usually in their praise. There are two
reasons for this; first their pride—which revolts at the idea of being punished—this is very strong—and particularly so with such as have been
house-servants—the more intelligent they are, the more revolting the
idea of corporal punishment. The other reason is due to their natural
cunning—and is more frequently used by the lower class of blacks! —
They wish to impress you with the idea that even as *slaves* they were not
worked so hard as now—and will occasionally speak of the amount of
money *given* them for holidays by "ole massa ———"; but this is merely
a subterfuge with them and you will find it hard to find an adult among
them so degraded as to be really willing to return to their old lives——but
their gratitude for what you do for them is like the gratitude of children—
—they are pleased, but look upon it as a matter of course—and that you
are spending your time and money in their interests doesn't seem to
strike them as anything remarkable. This applies to them as a whole; but
there are many noble exceptions—many who seem sensible of all that is
being done for them and are willing to help in the work—many who remember little personal favors and try to return them in their way. —I am
of the opinion that all this parade in the papers, of their great appreciation of the benefits conferred on them, as told by the Superintendents
and others connected with the Freed man's Association is more for *effect*
than as a true estimate of the character of these people; and where this is
not the case—and writers of this sort are sincere in what they say—their
opinions are based on the low estimate which they really have of their
abilities—not looking at, or judging them as *men* and *women*—capable

of great improvement, but rather as a strange kind of anomaly neither brute or human——and when they exhibit strong feeling or emotions of any kind—it is siezed upon by these superficial observers, as something wonderful!! It is a difficult thing to give a clear synopsis of the peculiar characteristics of the negro after even a years study into their habits and disposition!—— They have certain notions in regard to religion which is quite detrimental to their moral character—and the system of religious instruction adopted by the Freedmen's Ass. tends rather to encourage this state of things rather than to eradicate it by teaching a truer code of morality. They have little or no, idea of *practical religion*. The "Golden rule" has never entered very largely into their every day life. For instance, one of their people, having no special claim upon their sympathy may die for want of a little care and nursing or a few of the commonest necessaries of life and no one think of supplying them—then they would get together in large numbers and spend a half day in funeral exercises lamenting and singing in a manner to convinse one that their community had met with a very calamitous bereavement. So in the hospitals where they are employed as nurses. They do what you tell them providing you keep an eye on them—but if you ask or expect them to help each other they will probably tell you that they came to Hospital to get well and not to work—and no amount of *talk* will induce them to admit that they ought to do anything for the comfort of each other—unless they are *hired* as *nurses*; many times indeed *always* they would do a thing to oblige me because they liked *me*—but not because they felt any moral obligation to do it. Their perception of duty towards each other is very obtuse! —I am speaking of them as a *whole* and I am speaking of them as I have found them—as soldiers—as families—as patients—Nurses—and as pupils——and it is pleasant to remember the many noble exceptions to the rule! I could mention many noble instances of self sacrifice connected with the time the wounded men came from Morris Island—but of that in its place.

The 1*st* S.C. Volunteers——Col. Higginson[5]——Regiment and with which I became connected as teacher early in Jan./63 is made up entirely of Volunteers, and of course contains the best of the colored men in this

5. Col. Thomas Wentworth Higginson, long an abolitionist and friend of John Brown. A scholar and author, Higginson had been Captain of a company in the Fifty-first Massachusetts Infantry when Gen. Saxton offered him command of the black troops of the First South Carolina, on the recommendation of Dr. John Milton Hawks. John M. Hawks, "The First Freedmen to Become Soldiers," *Southern Workman* (1909) vol. 38, pp. 108, 109. Higginson was as amazed, he later wrote as "had an invitation reached [him] to take command of a regiment of Kalmuck Tartars." Thomas Wentworth Higginson, *Army Life in a Black Regiment* (Boston: Beacon Press, 1962) p. 2. Recovering from his shock, Higginson proceeded south immediately to assume his new duties.

viscinity, though the South Carolinians are in the minority—there being more from the mainland—from Georgia and Florida, obtained on expeditions for recruiting purposes—this gives to the regiment a greater per cent of shrewdness and intelligence then the others have for it is an undeniable fact that the negroes of these Sea Islands are of the lowest type—— the flatest nosed and thickest lipped—accompanied by the numbest sculls, any where to be met with in America. The reason for this seems to be largely their environment—cut off as they are almost wholly from any intercourse with a higher intelligence, there has been no mental food for them any more than for the swine and cattle with whom their lives are shared and the wonder is that we find them so nearly human so teachable—and the little undeveloped scared looking 'pickaninies' are improving their chances. They are already saucy—scream—fight and cut up didoes very like other children! which is all very encouraging!—for a passive, undemonstrative race of children, will surely make but poor *men* and *women*——But to go back to the Regiment—.

I find Dr. H. [J. M. Hawks] has gone with an expedition down the coast—and instead of being in charge of freedmen, he has entered the military service as Surgeon—so I go with Dr. and Mrs. Durrant[6] who are to occupy the same house with us and we have spent the past week in trying to make the house habitable under the disadvantage of an almost absolute lack of materi[als]. We have a whole family of servants—Joshua, the 'maid of all work', does the cooking and general housework. Eve, his wife splits the wood and takes care of the horses: while Venus and Appolo, the children, are supposed to run of errands and do the 'chores,' but their chief work seems to be rolling in the dust and standing on their heads, in which they are experts. Our location is very pleasant—facing the little park, in the center of which stands the Library—and back of us is the river; near by a Co. of Regulars under command of Maj. Langdon[7]— all the other Regts. are outside the city limits—with the exception of a NY. Regt. Col. Van Dyke's,[8] which is stationed near the Bay, at Hd.qtrs.

The place is crowded with colored people, and they are all eager to go to school, books being the one thing denied them, they have a frantic desire to get possession of them; yesterday a couple of half grown boys, came to see if I would teach them to read. The book they brought was a

6. Dr. and Mrs. Henry K. Durant (also spelled Durrant) of New York. Durant was Medical Director at Port Royal.

7. Maj. Loomis L. Langdon, who doubled during his long professional military career as a newspaper correspondent and author and following retirement from the army was a banker and philanthropist in Brooklyn.

8. Probably Col. Charles H. Van Wyck of the Fifty-sixth New York Volunteers.

fine vol. of Virgil which they had rescued from the wreck of the Public Library! —There are several schools already established. The one in a church near us I have visited. There are about 300 pupils, and only two teachers—one at either end of the large room, surrounded by a crowd of children, hearing them read one at a time, while the noise and din of voices made such an uproar that it was impossible to hear yourself think! These teachers are to go to one of the Islands and I am to take charge of this school. For two weeks I struggled with the problem of how to make one teacher do the work of six and was then obliged to give it up, not because I had exhuasted my resources, but for the time being my stock of articulate speech had become exhausted, and you may try to imagine the effect of a *whisper* on a class of 300, who were all studying aloud!

We have at last got our house keeping arraingements settled. The family consists of Dr. & Mrs. Durrant and Dinah a little Marmasett Monkey, the pet of the Dr's wife, Dr. H. [J. M. Hawks] and myself with Joshua Eve, Venus and Appollo—as servants. Dr. Durrant is a great sportsman, so when we are tired of military rations, he has only to use his rifle, on the sand peeps at the back door—and Joshua serves them on toast in fine style—shrimp are also plenty, and an occasional feast of deviled crabs—cheers and strengthens us for the inevitable 'hard tack' which must form the basis of government rations! It is curious how many appetizing dishes can be made out of nothing if one only knows how to do it.

We have noticed all day that some unusual interest is going on with the colored people. Joshua and Eve have long confabs with the hospital attendants and other servants in the neighborhood. My curiosity is aroused (got the better of politeness) and I enquire of Joshua "What is going on!," —Ah! nothing much Missis' only we all's has 'pinted a praise meeting", down in Aunt Chloes cabin. Joshua glowed with pious ferver, rolled up his eyes and drew down the corners of his mouth after the most approved method, and Eve solemnly informed me that Joshua was the leader of the meeting. As the time for the meeting drew near Mrs. D. [Durant] and I begged permission to be present, and as soon as the pitch knots were lighted, we went to the cabin and were given standing room outside the band of *shouters*. Soon, Joshua stept into the middle of the room opened the meeting with prayer, and began singing in a minor key with a nasal drawl as accompaniment "Sister Mary's sitting on the tree of life— Roll Jording, roll". I wish I was in jubilee, ha—Jubilee, Roll Jordin roll." The whole company take up the chorus and repeat it over and over, with infinite variations, until exhausted. Then Joshua makes a new start, with "Brudder Tony's sitting on the tree of life"—and so on until the names of all the members have been called—and every one is on their feet shuffling and swaing from side to side keeping time with their whole bodies, and putting in the emphasis with an occasional unexpected screach—followed by a groan from the whole company. This is kept up until they were all to exhausted to keep on their feet, and fall in heaps on the cabin floor. We went to the house by ten o'clock but, it was past midnight before the "Shout' was sufficiently subdued to give us a chance for sleep.——

This regiment has been the especial care of Gen. Saxton. The first attempt at organizing negro troops was made by Gen. Hunter early in the spring. He succeeded in raising about half a regt. They were kept hard at work on the entrenchments for about 4 months and then the Government refusing to pay them, the organization was broken up—but two companies were kept together by Capt. James[9] and Capt Trowbridge[10] and these became the nucleus of the present reigment—It was with great misgivings and fears as to its ultimate success that Gen. Saxton permited this second attempt at equiping negro troops—and not till Government had pledged itself for their pay. The men were suspicious and reluctant—and not till after they received their first wages did they feel confidence in the good intentions of Government towards them. This occured early in Jan./63 nearly three months after their organization—and was due to the liberal kindness of Gen. Saxton, who borrowed the money, and paid the soldiers at his own risks. This had the effect of satisfying the men and restoring confidence to the regiment.

The first expedition undertaken by this Regt. left Beaufort, somewhere about the middle of Nov./ 62 just before our arrival, under the command of Col. Beard[11]—this being previous to Col. H's [Higginson] connection with it. The object of the raid being to obtain lumber, known to be at a certain saw-mill, Blew & Joddy Mills,[12] near Darien, Ga., up the St. Mary's river, on the coast of Georgia. It was in every sense, a brilliant success! A valuable lot of lumber, rice, and other articles was obtained beside a *brisk* encounter with the enemy in which the men showed a reckless bravery which elicited warm praise from the officers—proved themselves well qualified to bear the title of *soldier*. Several of the men were wounded. While the Surgeon Dr. H. [J. M. Hawks] was dressing the wounds of one of the men—another came up with his arm badly shattered—when the

9. Capt. William James of Pennsylvania who recruited more freedmen for military service than any other officer on the Sea Islands. Hawks, "The First Freedmen," p. 108.

10. Capt. Charles T. Trowbridge of New York, Commander of Company A of the First South Carolina Volunteers.

11. Lt. Col. Oliver T. Beard, detached from the Forty-eighth New York Infantry.

12. Described elsewhere as "Blew & Todd's Mills." Hawks, "The First Freedmen," p. 109.

first man stepped back saying "fix him first, boss he's worse than I is." How few are the men of any color who could have been more unselfish!

This little expedition was a great thing for colored soldiers, and from it we date the first dawning of tolerance and respect for them, from either officers or men. Col. Beard who commanded the expedition, is a coarse, and intensely pro-slavery officer, but even he commended the men most heartily for their brave conduct.[13] Soon after their return Col. Higginson took command of the Regiment and commenced a thorough and systematic coarse of Military discipline. The regiment is stationed four miles down the river from Beaufort on the Smith Plantation and have christened their Hd. Qts. as Camp Saxton. Col. H. [Higginson] arrived here about the middle of Nov. Preparations were already going forward for the celebration of the 1st of Jan. in anticipation of the Presidents confirming his emancipation proclamation. In the regiment, Chaplin Fowler,[14] is at work for that end, and Mr. French[15] is stimulating the freed people of Beaufort and the adjacent Isles, to participate in it. —The colored people have had their confidence so often abused, that many of them are timid and suspicious. They do not understand the object of the meeting—and the white soldiers, in many instances encourage this feeling by telling them that Gen. Saxton is going to get them all together and then deliver them up to their old masters! so that, when the day arrived—some of the Superintendants found that their people had absented themselves, and were nowhere to be found. —This prevented there being so large a company of colored people present as there might otherways have been. Still the day, Jan 1st 1863, was a day long to be remembered, bright and beautiful; and a very large concourse of people, officers, teachers—and citizens were early gathered in the beautiful grove, near Camp Saxton, where the ceremonies of the occasion were to take place. The order of exercises consisted of speaches from Gen. Saxton, Col. Higginson Rev. Mr. French Chaplin Fowler, Mrs. Frances D Gage,[16] and a poem read by

13. Col. Beard reported to Gen. Saxton on his return that the "colored men fought with astonishing coolness and bravery. For alacrity in effecting landings, for determination, and for bush fighting I found them all I could desire,—more than I had hoped. They behaved bravely, gloriouosly, and deserve all praise." In addition to destroying salt works, wagons and the like, and confiscating lumber and rice the expedition returned with ninety four more black fighting men than it had started with. *War of Rebellion Official Records*, 1 ser., XIV, 191–92, Beard to Saxton, Nov. 10, 1862.

14. Milton Hawks' old friend James H. Fowler. Educated at Dartmouth and Harvard, Fowler was an ordained Unitarian minister who served as Chaplain of the First South Carolina.

15. Rev. Mansfield French, who had come south on behalf of the American Missionary Association and later helped organize freedmen's aid missions.

16. Mrs. Gage was an abolitionist and missionary who encouraged blacks to enlist as soldiers.

Prof. Zachos,[17] written for the occasion a quartette, sung several songs, written by Mr. Judd, Sup. [Superintendent] of the colored people.[18] Then a beautiful stand of colors was presented to the Regt. from the members of Dr. Cheever's church of N.Y.[19] through Mr. French. Several of the colored soldiers made short speaches, and then, Col. H. [Higginson] invited the crowd to partake of the *feast* of roast beef—bakers bread and molasses and plenty of lemonaid prepared for them on some tables near the camp. A *bar-becue* I think he called it. Ten beeves had been cooked whole,—or nearly so. This is done by digging a deep pit, and burning oak wood in it till a great bed of coals results, then suspending the animal over it to cook with frequent bastings and turnings. I think, by the quantity of *raw* beef I saw leaving the grounds, in women's aprons the *cooking* was rather a failure! No provision was made for feeding white folks, so at the close of the exercises we rode wearily home, fortifying ourselves as we often needed to, with the reflection that if the occasion had been earlier tedious it would be pleasant to remember, in the future that we were present at the first celebration of the indipendence of the freedmen in South Carolina. May it *never* be *less*!!

Two weeks later I enlisted in the Regt as teacher. Chaplin Fowler had already prepared a school-house by driving some poles into the sand and covering them with canvass. This gave us a shelter and the soldiers were eager to learn——a box containing 500 primers arrived from the Freedman's Aid Associa., and we commenced operations. Things went on finely 'till a great wind came and tore our old canvas house into *strings*. It was wholly demolished and we were school-houseless! but our indomitable Chaplin immediately set to work to replace it with a more substantial one, and in a very short time we had one with a capacity for seating two hundred—circular in form built by driving posts into the sand and nailing round poles to these to a heght of ten feet—then the roof built up in the same manner—coming to a point at the top, and supported by a pole in the center, then this rib work was covered with fresh palmetto leaves.

Seen from the river our house made a pretty picture, and was christened, the Pagoda". It was one of our *show* places, for the many visitors who came to Camp Saxton. —Smiths' Plantation, on which our Camp is built has quite a history. —It has one of the most magnificent groves of live-oaks in the country, covering several acres, and every tree a mon-

17. Professor John C. Zachos, born in Constantinople of Greek parents, had taught literature at Antioch College in Ohio. He was an official at Parris Island.
18. Mr. H. G. Judd, who was in charge of Freedmen on Port Royal Island.
19. Dr. George B. Cheever's Church of the Puritans. Cheever was a zealous advocate of prohibition and abolition.

arch. The long grey moss, which Nature uses so lavishly for drapery, covers the trees so thickly that only the tinyest ray of sunlight penetrates the foliage, and a soft twilight rest in the grove at all hours. The plantation house stands on a slight elevation, facing the river, which at this point is deep and wide an avenue of fine large Magnolia" trees leads from the house to the waters' edge, and on either side are great beds of flowering shrubs and roses in the greatest profusion. At the left of this garden are the ruins of an old Ft said to have been built by the Spaniards more than two centuries ago.[20] The walls, built of Coquina, are over-grown with tall bushes and cedar's. In the rear of the house a very large live-oak is pointed out as the whipping post—the rebel owner of this plantation is represented by his 'sable' furniture, (not always transportable!) as an old darkie explained, with an evil flash boding no good to "Massa Smith," should he show himself "Dat's where ole massa used to string we'n up and put on de lash" — and in one of the out buildings they show us a strong iron ring to which refractory chattels, when erring, were chained! The cabins on this plantation are quite superior to any I have seen. They are so arrainged that a person standing on the back piazza of the planters house can see the front and back enterance of each cabin and no one could go in or out unobserved. A large vegetable garden, enclosed by an impenetrable fence of Spanish bayonets (Yucca Grande' flora) is now used as coro-yard [courtyard]—not even a dog, can get through this fence.

Early in Feb. an expedition in charge of our Col. was sent down the coast, Its destination St. Marys, at the head of the St Mary', river in Fla. On landing, (it was evening) our soldiers under the charge of Sargt. Robert Sutton who, when a slave, had lived there—took quiet possession of the place: It was a proud moment for Robert when he placed a guard of colored soldiers around the house of his former owner, "Madam Alberti" and one of the great rage to the good dame when she discovered the outrage, and heard her own nigger, "our Bob," give the order to shoot anyone who attempted to leave the house without his permission![21]

It was great fun to hear Sutton tell the story, on his return to Camp. The Regt was absent ten days and Col. H. [Higginson] seems well satisfied with the expedition. March 6th the Regt. with the exception of those, to

20. Smith's Plantation was sometimes called Old Fort Plantation. The fort was originally built by the French Huguenot colonizer Jean Ribaut in 1562.

21. The intelligence and competence of Sgt. Robert Sutton have been well chronicled. The ironic adventure described herein appears as well in Higginson, *Army Life*, and Sutton is praised by Charlotte Forten, "Life on the Sea Islands," *Atlantic Monthly*, 13 (May, June, 1864), 587–96, 666–76, and by Edward L. Pierce, "The Freedmen of Port Royal," *Atlantic Monthly*, 12 (September, 1863), 291–315.

ill to be moved, left "Camp Saxton," has again started south for Jacksonville, Fla. leaving Dr. H. [J. M. Hawks] in charge of the hospital.

They took possession of the place meeting but a feeble resistance from the rebels—but found their force insufficient to hold it and sent back for reinforcements the 8th Me and 6th Conn. have been sent to reinforce them. Col Vinning[22] of the 6th being ranking officer, takes command of the Post. They were frequently—annoyed by the rebels but no serious causalities occurred. Capt. Whitney[23] of Co. G. took his men out on a raid into the enemies country and came suddenly on a squad of rebel Cavelry. Capt. W's [Whitney] men are all young, and quite a reckless set so they immediately gave battle in good earnest and as a sample of their coolness, Capt W. relates that one of the men, after discharging his gun saw a fine large goose, gave chase, captured it, and held it between his knees while re-loading. There was no damage to anyone but the goose on this occasion. Our Chaplin distinguishes himself by his reckless daring and bravery. He does most of the confiscating of rebel property and is very successful in this branch of the service. So while Col. Higginson, commanding, is busy establishing Hd. Qtrs., and Lt. Col. Billings[24] is 'administering the oath' [of loyalty to the Union] to certain tow-headed individuals, known as "loyal Floridians," the Chaplin, with a squad of men, is out in pursuit of adventures and generally returns well laden with spoils. The soldiers are always ready to follow his lead—they appreciate this trait in his character more keenly than they do his sermons, as was illustrated by one of the men enquiring of an officer What for Mr. Chaplin done preach adding gravely, he's the fightenest man in de Regt and he swear like de berry debble". Poor 'Jim' he's where he won't be able to do much more fighting with 'carnal weapons!'"[25]

Just previous to the arrival of the order to evacuate the place, Col. Montgomery,[26] with the few men under his command went Seventy miles up the St. John's to Palatka [Fla.], and on arriving at the wharf, see-

---

22. Col. Marcellus Vining.

23. Capt. H. A. Whitney of the First South Carolina Volunteers, afterwards Thirty-third U.S.C.T.

24. Lt. Col. Liberty Billings of the First South Carolina Volunteers, afterwards Thirty-third U.S.C.T.

25. At the time of this entry, "Poor Jim," Chaplain James Fowler, was imprisoned at Columbia, S.C. after being captured by the Confederates while intercepting telegraphic dispatches between Savannah and Charleston. John Milton Hawks, *The East Coast of Florida* (Lynn, Massachusetts: Lewis and Winship, 1887), p. 69.

26. Col. James Montgomery, commanding officer of the Second South Carolina Volunteers. Montgomery, a veteran of the "Bleeding Kansas" guerrilla campaigns, was a deeply committed abolitionist, who years before Sherman's March to the Sea was determined to bring the war home to Southern civilians.

ing no signs of life prepared to land. Chaplin Fowler, first landed, ran up the wharf, looked about and returned, reportin, nothing in sight, and just as the whole side of the vessel was swarming with eager soldiers and officers, a volley of musketry was poured into their midst, from a concealed foe, wounding Col. Billings, who with both hands elevated, in the act of climbing down the side of the boat, presented a good mark. A ball passed through *both* hands; no bones broken. A poor old man, John Quincy, belonging to our Regt. and who had gone up in search of his family was fatally wounded. Strange to say, the party reembarked and returned without making any effort to ascertain the strength of the enemy—reaching Jacksonville just in season to leave with the rest of the expedition—— A miserable failure productive of nothing but evil![27] On leaving Jacksonville, the soldiers destroyed everything within reach of their hands, and then made an attempt to burn the place—which was only partly successful. Our Regt. returned to "Camp Saxton" the 1*st* week in April. The men have a great many wonderful adventures to relate but I do not think the Offices felt very highly elated over the expedition. During the absence of the Regt. we lived quietly at Smith's plantation—moving into the house, soon after they went away, which was occuped by Mr. Hawks and Sought, Supt's—and also, in part by our Surgeon as hospital. On a little knoll by the river's bank stands the rude plantation Chapel, dum witness of many a scene of agony where master and slave used to worship. The building one of the rudest being mearly of rough boards without finish of any kind—only a little porch over the door and surmounted by a cupula in which once hung a bell, gives it a quaint not unlovely picture strangely in harmony with its surroundings, and adds much to the picturesqueness of the view as seen from the river! Close by, within sound of the murmur of the wave Our Chaplin marked out a new Cemetary for the soldiers, and about 20 poor fellows were laid in it, during the six months, we occupied the Camp. It had been used by our Q.M. for Comissary stores and was very dirty but by turning over the boards and a little cleaning it was rendered usable and here I opened school for the plantation children and such of the soldiers, left behind, who were able to come. About forty children attended with commendible regularity and promptness, and made creditable progress, but my most remarkable pupil is one of our soldiers, too old for active service, he has been detailed as nurse and make a

---

27. Captain J. J. Dickison, C.S.A., who directed the ambush at Palatka, reported that the fifty men under his command inflicted between twenty and thirty casualties while suffering but one man slightly wounded. Had the federal troops advanced as expected, Dickison added "we should no doubt have had a close and desperate engagement." *Official Records*, 1 ser., XIV, 237–39.

very efficient one. He is in his 76th year, is very eager to learn and never seen without his primer when off duty. It seems quite impossible for him to tell which side up his book is but if perseverance is worth anything he will master the alphabet in time: his face lights up with pride and joy when I praise him! He is a native of Georgia and long a resident at St. Simons' Island, from which place he was taken by our soldiers on the first expedition of our Regt. to the Island; two sons were with him;—one fell by a rebel bullet, while trying to escape, the other has since died in camp, and all the rest of his numerous progeny are still in rebeldom. His age exempts him from military service but he has no desire to leave the Regt., he says, "I know I can't do~~~~ ~~~~ can do something, and I'se bound ~~ " ~~~~~~ ~~e thoroughly polite, gentle- ~~~~~~ Dear old York Brown! may ~~~~~~ ssed pleasantly and quietly ~~~~~~ ...occasional visitor. Gen. Saxson, one of the teachers his brother, ~~~~~ ~~~~, ~~ives called on us once formally and several times rode up to the door for a few minutes chat—nothing pretentious about any of them!

Mean while a new Regt. to be called the *3rd* S.C. was organizing and Dr. H. [J. M. Hawks] was busy examining the recruits brought in by our indefatiguable Capt. Bryant[28] whose hopes and prospects were good for the colonilcy.

All of the men who came in for examination were either hopelessly lame and come hobbling along with (new) sticks cut for the purpose not many rods from Camp or they have some mysterious disease which has baffled the skill of all Drs' way back to "ole massa's time," and the amount of suffering such men will bear and the stubborness with which they persist in shaming disease, in order to escape 'soldiering' is truly wonderful! The examinations are very ludicrous. York Brown (my old pupil) tries to shame them into being men, but most of them are incorrigable and he would leave them in great disgust. It is funny to see the change, when they find soldering inevitable and but few keep their canes or their limp after they get into the new uniform—then these men are the loudest in laughing at and exposing the tricks of the others.

Even these unwilling men make good sentinels as was proved one night just before the return of the Regt. when one of them attempted to run guard; and being stopped threatened to shoot the guard if he didn't let him pass but the man stood firm at his post, when the other raising his

28. Capt. Oliver E. Bryant, who died of disease in Jacksonville, Fla., July 13, 1865.

musket, snapped it in his face it "hung fire,' when he run to his tent got a
new cap, came back and shot the guard; Poor Dick was brought immediately to hospital—the bright arterial blood making a pool whereon they
paused. We feared at first he would bleed to death before any measures
could be effectual in stopping it—the ball had entered the fore arm, frac-
turing it, passed through the axilla and out over the shoulder. —There
was no one to assist the Dr. but me, everyone seemed panic stricken but
the poor fellow bore it like a hero; not a word of complaint not even a
groan escaped him during the painful process of ascertaining the extent
of the injury.

The colored soldiers are beginning to receive some attention from Military Hd. Qts. and it is decided to open a hospital for them in Beaufort.[29]
On the 12*th* Apr./63. Dr. H. [J. M. Hawks] was put in official charge of the
hospital—tho' the house had been selected and some arraingements
made some days previously—but at that time the first patients were received. Our Regt is to leave "Camp Saxton," which grieves us all, but
they are to go to do picket duty at the Ferry and this is considered quite
an honor as it is a post of importance and some danger and is the first recognition we have received from the Post Commander Col H [Higginson]
is delighted and promises the Chaplin and other offices plenty of oppor-
tunities for cultivating the acquaintance of their rebel neighbors across
the Ferry.

One little event occurred in Feb. at Camp Saxton, which I failed to
cronicle in its right place. This was the marriage of our Adj: Geo. W.
Dewhurst to a lady from Me. who came all the way out here for this purpose. The Regt. formed a "hollow square" and the ceremony was performed inside—by the Chaplin—and witnessed by many curious eyes,
who came down from B [Beaufort] to be present at so strange a performance. The groom was in a delightful state of military precision and the
bride pale and interesting as was becoming to the occasion.

In Hospital—

The first General Hospital established in Beaufort for colored soldiers,
was opened on the 12*th* of Apr. 1863 under the charge of Dr. [J. M.]
Hawkes. The first patients admited being the sick and wounded men

---

29. General Hospital Number Ten for Colored Troops, the first such hospital sanctioned
by the War Department. "I am happy to say," wrote Dr. Seth Rogers, Surgeon of the First
South Carolina Volunteers, "that at least we have a hospital with a look of permanence, and
about as good as the others. Dr. and Mrs. Hawks and one hospital steward have worked
hard to get it in order." "Letters of Dr. Seth Rogers," *Massachusetts Historical Society Proceedings*, vol. 42, 1910, p. 388.

brought back by Col. Higginson from the Jacksonville expedition! This was another step for colored soldiers as heretofore they had been confined to regimental hospitals which being on a limited scale must necessarily exclude many who need constant care and nursing, besides not having all the appliances for the comfort of the sick, to be found in a large establishment.

It was great fun to witness the extreme reluctance, not to say positive disgust with which the patients went through with their innitiatory. The first thing to be done when a patient is admitted into hospital is to make him thoroughly acquainted with soap and water, and their pitiful pleadings to be let off from this exercise would have been pathetic if they had'nt been so rediculous. Failing to soften the obdurate hearts of wardmaster and Steward, I would be appealed to with all the pathos of negro eloquence. One poor fellow exclaimed with tears in his eyes I know you ai'nt gwine to do it if you can help it—praise de Lord—for I'se done killed foreber if you puts de water all ober me. I neber could stan it in ole massa's time! Surviving the first washing the next was easier tho' they never could be brot' to see the luxury of the thing! The next great difficulty to be overcome, was to get them to sleep between sheets! Poor fellows! they stared aghast on being told to get in between such immaculate whiteness! Of course it *had* to be done, but when those who were able, made their beds, the sheets of some were carefully folded and lain on the outside of the beds, while others spread them out over the blankets, and got into bed, upon the bare mattress—I have found that it takes a great deal of persuasive teaching, with many practical illustrations to enable a *negro soldier* to *make* a *bed*. We were for some time without bed steads—had to wait for them to be made. It took so long to do the smallest job—that I would sometimes almost despair of ever having the house put into decent order for a hospital. The house was one of the Barnwell mansions—and when our troops came here, magnificently furnished but 18 months occupation by soldiers leaves nothing but a filthy shell; Mrs. Strong, wife of our Maj. was appointed nurse by Mrs. Lander,[30] and she and I went about for weeks with a *soaped* rag in hand, overseeing and instructing in the cleaning. We already had between 20 and 30 patients—and this, with getting things in order kept us very busy!

From my first connextion with these people, I have felt quite at home among them, and there is nothing repelant to my feelings about them any more than there is to all dirty people—but here in Hospital we could keep

30. Mrs. Jean Margaret Davenport Lander, a former actress, who was in charge of nurses in federal hospitals at Port Royal.

them as clean as we chose, so I circulated among them with the greatest freedom—prescribing for them, ministering to their wants, teaching them, and making myself as thoroughly conversant with their inner lives as I could. I do not think, at this time, without a degree of inhumanity, a hospital for colored, could be conducted on the same rigid principles, as for white troops. These negroes are like ignorat unformed children, and the difficulty of reasoning them out of an opinion or ideas when it once takes possesion of them, can never be known 'till tried. You talk to willing listeners—they assent heartily to what you say but—they are of the same opinion still.

They are not thoughtful for each others comfort, and I never cease wondering at their indifferance to the death of their comrads and even of near friends. There is seldom any display of feelings and in but few instances have I seen sufficient emotion visable to look upon it as grief at the loss of a son or brother. No doubt their religious belief has much to do with this as one of the strongest articles in their creed is, that "no one dies before his time." To return to the Hospital from which I seldom allow myself to be absent so long, I do not think this, Hospital was admited to the brotherhood of hospitals on quite an even footing. Favors were a little grudingly bestowed. White soldiers near us were hardly respectful to our patients and little annoyances, such as throwing bits of old iron at them, got for the purpose at a blacksmiths'—shop, calling names and other impertenances were of frequent occurance. These troubles came mostly from a Co. of regulars whose camp was quite near, and as the buildings were not very well suited for hospital purposes, it was thought best to change the location, and so run away from many sources of anoyance.

Dr. H. [Hawks] has been taken from the hospital detailed by Gen. Hunter, to accompany a secret expedition to the coast of Florida. Meanwhile no Surgeon being sent to take charge, of the hospital, I am left manager of not only the affairs of the Hospital, but have to attend Surgeons' call for the 2nd [S.C. Volunteers] and without a Surgeon—so every morning at 9 o'clock the disabled are marched down to the hospital in charge of a Sergent and I hold surgens call, for hospital and Regt. and with great success; on the back piazza sending some to duty and taking into the hospital such as need extra care. An occasional chronic 'shirk' will complain to the Col. that, "dat woman ca'nt do me no gud, she ca'nt see my pain" but he gets no sympathy from the Col. and is obliged to go on duty if I so mark him. So for three weeks I performed the duties of hospital and Regimental Surg. doing the work so well that the neglect to supply a regular officers was not discovered at Hd. Qrtrs. I suppose I could not have done this if my brother[31] had not been hospital steward—or if the patients had been white men—but these negroes are so like children that I feel no hesitancy in serving them!

The last of May Dr. Greenleaf[32] assumed charge, and I returned to my teaching, (having had the experience of two months hospital life), with many feelings of regret expressed by the patients and felt by my self. As the patients were removed to another building I continued to occupy the same house, and as the Fates ordained, I went into the old school where I first commenced teaching on my arrival here. The school was large and I exhausted so five weeks trial closed it by prostrating me with fever, and in two weeks more the schools were all closed by, most of the buildings being wanted for hospital uses and the teachers such as did not run home on the first alarm, as nurses.

July 18*th*! never to be forgotten day! After many days of anxious waiting the news came, "Prepare immediately to receive 500 wounded men," indeed they were already at the dock! and before morning we had taken possession of the building where our first hospital was started. I had been carried, a few days previous to Dr. Durrants to stay with Mrs. D. during the absence of her husband in Bermuda so the house was soon cleared. 150 of the brave boys from the 54*th* Mass. Col. Shaw's Regt.[33] were brought to us and laid on blankets on the floor all mangled and ghastly. What a terrible sight it was! It was 36 hours since the awful struggle at Ft. Wagna [Wagner][34] and nothing had been done for them. We had no beds, and no means even of building a fire, but the colored people came promptly to our aid and almost before we knew what we needed they brought us buckets full of nice broth and gruels, pitchers of lemonade, fruits, cakes, vegetables indeed everything needed for the immediate wants of the men was furnished—not for one day but for many (Then too the Sanitary Com. [Commission][35] blessed us with its ready aid. Every-

---

31. Edward O. Hill.

32. Dr. Arthur W. Greenleaf, Assistant Surgeon of the Thirty-fourth U.S.C.T.

33. The Fifty-fourth Massachusetts Infantry was the first black military unit enlisted by any Northern state during the Civil War. It was commanded by Col. Robert Gould Shaw, a member of one of New England's most prominent abolitionist families.

34. Fort Wagner, S.C. On the evening of July 18, 1863, the Fifty-fourth Massachusetts Infantry assaulted Fort Wagner which guarded the entrance to Charleston Harbor. The black troops were tired, wet and hungry as they charged across a narrow strip of sand directly into a terrific volume of fire. The men of the Fifty-fourth would not be daunted. They charged the parapets and swarmed into the fort itself, fighting desperately on until it became apparent that the white regiments in support of the attack would not arrive in time, and a general retreat was ordered. Luis F. Emilio, *A Brave Black Regiment: History of the Fifty-fourth Regiment of Massachusetts Volunteer Infantry, 1863–1865* (Boston: Boston Book Co., 1894), Chap. V.

35. The Sanitary Commission, organized by Fredrick Law Olmsted, was the forerunner of the American Red Cross in providing care and comforts for soldiers.

thing for our immediate wants was furnished and in 24 hours the poor fellows were lying with clean clothes and dressed wounds in comfortable beds, and we breathed freely again) before setting about creating a hospital: no one, unless they have had the experience can, imagine the amount of work and worry needed in setting one of these vast military machines in motion! and in this case humanity demanded that the poor fellows who had fought so bravely, should be first attended to. The colored people still continued to supply delicacies and more substantial aid came from the citizens and Sanitary Com. (It was a busy time, and the amount of work done in that 24 hours, by the two surgeons, and one sick woman is tiresome to remember! The only thing that sustained us was the patient endurance of those stricken heroes lying before us, with their ghastly wounds cheerful & courageous, many a poor fellow sighing that his right arm was shattered beyond hope of striking another blow for freedom! Only a few weeks before we had welcomed them as they marched so proudly through our streets with their idolized leader Col. Shaw, at their head! —How all the colored people cheered and gloried in their fine appearance—and now the people are so eager to show their pride in them that they constantly deny themselves in order to bring gifts to the hospital!)—

Several severe cases of gangreen poisn'd the air and had to be removed outside—out breathing the tainted atmosphere and overwork caused me a relaps and disheartened, I prepared to be sent North—but God had more work for me here and after a week of pain I returned to my post and the hearty "God bless you we are glad to see you back with us" compensated for much weariness.

We now have a small hospital fund to supply us with the many little comforts necessary to our patients—and most of them are easily satisfied. Many have died, several cases of gangrene have been provided for in tents: Two severe amputations today neither surviving but a few hours. One of these, a boy hardly 20 years old, Charley Reason formerly a slave, but of late years resident in Syracuse N Y., I have taken a great interest in; he is such a noble looking fellow, and so uncomplaining—so grateful when I bathe his head and face, as I sat by him holding his one poor hand! O yes! he said in reply to my question of why he came to the war! I know what I am fighting for, only a few years ago I ran away from a man in Maryland who said he owned me and since then I've worked on a farm in Syracuse but as soon as the government would take me I came to fight, *not* for my country, I never had any, but to gain one—My mother died years ago, And your father—I thoughtlessly asked, forgetting the peculiar relations between father and child in this part of our country. The hot blood throbbed up into his face, but he only said "My mother was all I had to love me, and she has gone home, sweet home: I shall see her soon—I'm glad to go home." The majesty and the mistery of death stole over his face, fading the eager look from his great mournful eyes, and clinging close to my hand, with a whispered "pray with me," he sank into unconsciousness, to be roused no more by the loud roar of the cannon or the low voice of sympathy—and kissing his *white* forehead I went to minister to other sufferers needing me more.

I find many of these men have been slaves, but by far the greater proportion were born and bred in the free north—A few are from Canada. Some few well educated—three are graduates from Oberlin.[36] They are intelligent, courteous, cheerful and kind, and I pity the humanity which, on a close acquaintance with these men, still retains the unworthy prejudice against color!

Three brothers, noble, stalwart men, lay side by side severely wounded! The fourth who had left home with them fell and was buried with his Col. at Ft. Wagna [Wagner]![37] They had left home, giving up useful and lucrative employment, with no idle thoughts of pleasure, nor yet from mere recklessness, but with an earnest, hopeful purpose in their hearts that they too, might help win for themselves and their race a *country* God forgive the Nation's weak and wicked policy which withholds from such its fullest protection! —"We offered to go when the war broke out," they told me, "but no one would have us, and as soon as Gov. Andrew[38]

36. Oberlin, in Ohio, was the first American college to admit black students.
37. Col. Shaw's death in the attack on Fort Wagner received much publicity and made of him a legend, particularly in Boston. The Shaw Monument on Boston Common contains the following lines by James Russell Lowell:

Right in the van on the red rampart's slippery swell
With heart that beat a charge he fell
　　　　Foeward as fits a man.
But the high soul burns on to light men's feet
Where death for noble ends makes dying sweet.

Shaw, an object of ridicule to the victorious Confederates, was stripped of his uniform and buried in a common grave with the black troops he had commanded, which inspired the following anonymous verse:

They buried him with his niggers!
　　　A wide grave should it be.
They buried more in that shallow trench
　　　Than human eye could see.
Ay, all the shames and sorrows
　　　of more than a hundred years
Lie under the weight of that Southern soil
despite those cruel sneers.

38. Governor John A. Andrew of Massachusetts, who authorized the raising of the Fifty-fourth.

gave us a chance all the boys in our place were ready, hardly one who could carry a musket stayed at home." An elder brother of theirs, who had a family to provide for, remained at home: but when the 55*th* [Mass. Vol. Inf.] came out he was with them (Their name is Crunkleton [Krunkleton]). Another, a young man from Cincinnatti, educated at Oberlin, of ability and good mental capacity—An orderly Sergt. in Co. A has a promise of promotion for his brave and gallant conduct at Ft Wagna [Wagner]—has the real worth and material for a good officer, but he is a very trying patient, chafes and frets because he cannot be with his Company— he is not so patient and uncomplaining as the others—is more ambitious. He is very neat about his person and any disorder about his bed or the room frets him.

O, Mrs. Hawks, he exclaimed one day, when I had been talking to him of that higher courage which enables us to bear the defeat of cherished hopes and ambitions, "It isn't that I can't die if necessary; I'm not afraid to die, I came to die fighting for the rights of the black man What I want is to go back to my regiment and go with them wherever they are called to go, but I cant stay here, inactive, and not know what has become of my Col. or my Co [Company]! I know the Dr. tells me I cannot do anything for months. I wish he exclaimed passionately, the ball of that miserable traitor had ended my life rather than made me a miserable cripple! and the strong man wept such bitter tears as I hope never to see again. My heart went out to the noble fellow and I comforted him as best I could thanking God for the rare boon of ministering to such spirits My brave Sergt. is not greatly beloved by those under him, he is arbitrary and a little tyranical but a good disciplinarian. He received the injury to his spine after being wounded and thrown from the parapet by a cannon ball passing so close to him as to carry away his cartridge box and shiver his musket. In writing to his friends he asked me not to say he was injured in the back. "They would'nt understand he said," and I cant bear to have them think for a moment that Sergt. Morgan's[39] back was to the rebels!"

One young man, Jonny Lott, one of my especial pets a handsome boy, a mere boy, who had come from the far west to bear his part of suffering, had his right arm shattered and his life was, for many days, despaired of, and in the long days of weary restlessness I learned the brave spirit of the boy well. He was well educated—had taught a term in a colored school. One day I had been reading beside his bed I said to him, Johny do you ever wish that you had been born white? He kept quiet a few moments, his eyes covered with their long silken fringes, then with a quick nervous

39. John Morgan, First Sergeant of the Fifty-fourth's Company G.

movement, looking up with a dewy moisture in his great beautiful eyes, he said "I always felt glad to be just what I am, a black boy with no drop of white blood in me There is a chance now to do a great deal if one has the heart for it and I am ready to give my other arm, or my life if necessary, for my race!" Was'nt that a noble answer for a boy of seventeen black or white. How proud I was of him! God grant that his days may be long and full of usefulness![40]

The love which they all bear their young commander Col. Shaw has something of the divine in it. And for several days their first eager question to me as I passed from one to another in the early morning would be "Do you hear any news from Morris Island? Anything of our Colonel! They never tired of talking about him.

Said Sergt. Morgan, in speaking of his death, "I suppose his friends will consider it a great disgrace for him to lie buried with a lot of niggers but if they know how all his men loved him, they would never wish to take him to any other resting place"! I read him the noble words of Col. Shaw's father in his letter written to Mrs. Childs [Child][41], which pleased him very much and after a few moments silence he said "no wonder Col. Shaw was such a good man, with such a father!" That has done me more good than all the praise which has been bestowed on the regiment."

I might use all the time allowed me in recounting such incidents in connection with the 54th Regt. but I have perhaps already tired you of my black heroes. Hardly one, out of the seventy under our care but won golden opinions from us all by their patience in bearing the petty annoyances and deprivations to which all must be subjected—and during the two months that I went in and out among them no difficulties occured which my presence and word could not settle. I endeavored with my whole heart, to make this dreary hospital life, as home-like as possible—and I was richly rewarded by their grateful thanks.[42]

40. A random note at the top of this page in the original diary must have been one of the most difficult entries Esther Hawks wrote: "Poor Jonny died on the 30th of March in Gen. Hosp. in David's island poor boy he never got to see his dear old father as he longed so much to do."

41. Lydia Marie Child was an abolitionist author, editor, and lecturer and a close friend of the Shaw family.

42. These thanks were expressed repeatedly and often eloquently by soldiers of the Fifty-fourth Massachusetts Infantry and other black units in letters to Dr. Esther Hawks, several of which have been preserved in the Hawks Papers, Library of Congress. For example: "Sorry to have you go for you or minds me of the Saviour when he left high heaven and com down on earth to Save our lost and blind race when he went a way his disippels were Sorry to have him go you lady's left your homes and come here to teach our lost and blind race were have bin [kept] from all larning and lost from all of the enjoyment of this life and you are a lady to have left your home and come to teach us . . ." Freeman Pugh, Third U.S.C.T., to EHH, June

About the middle of Sept. the hospital having passed into other hands, I left it—much to my own and the patients regret—and well they might regret me, as the Surgeon into whose charge they fell was a young, ineficient disipated negro-hating tyrant—Dr. Mead of N.Y.[43]—and the Steward with which the hospital was but recently supplied—was a low-German—fit associate for the Dr. They were both most heartily hated by the men—and during his reign nearly all of the men had the chance of a few meditative days in *jail*—put there for the most trivial offenses. Both Dr. and Steward had a pretty colored girl to minister to their private wants. Mrs. Adams[44]—white nurse; was insulted on the first evening of his arrival at No 10 and on her complaining to the Medical Officer Dr. M. [Mead] excused himself by saying that he was under the influence of liquor—*and was excused*—but poor Mrs. A. [Adams] was so persecuted by him that she was obliged to leave the hospital. The fowl which I had obtained for the sick were all eaten by those in the Office. *Not* one was ever cooked for a patient, during his stay—but they all *disappeared*! A box of luxuries sent out to the 54*th* wounded—by the friends in Boston—consisting of fruits, jellies wines and some clothing was disposed of in the same way—the Steward wore the comfortable clothing and the edibles went on the office table! It looks hard to believe so poorly of human nature but *seeing* is believing, sometimes.

Dr. M. [Mead] soon ran his course in the hospital, but not before almost every patient in it had served a few days in the jail for some trivial offense. The men were constantly coming to me with complaints. I could do nothing but comfort them with my sympathy—and hopes of better times.

Being now at leisure, Dr. H. [Hawks] with his regiment and I still at Dr. D's [Durant's], I turned my attention to raising a class, in the colored hospitals nos. 6 & 10, and found not difficulty in doing so. My health not being fully established and the heat so oppressive, kept me from going into camp with Dr. [J. M. Hawks]. All of the teachers and most of the other northern ladies had left, and not yet returned. Dr. D. [Durant] returned from Bermuda about the middle of Sept.

23, 1864. ". . . soldiers Friends who admire you so much and who think that the only Friend in this Department were you who took such good care of us while we were at Beaufort in the Hospital. . . . I says (to a companion) While I was at Beaufort and had the Headace I used to have a friend who used to come and put her magic hand on my Forehead and it leaves me directly." Burrill Smith, Company A, Fifty-fourth Massachusetts Infantry, to EHH, November 3, 1864.

43. Dr. Charles Mead, Assistant Surgeon of the 112th New York Infantry who was put in command of General Hospital Number Ten.

44. Identified in the Hawks Papers only as nurse L. Adams.

Early in Oct./63 Dr. H. [J. M. Hawks] was transferred from the 1*st.* to the 3*rd* S. C. Regt.[45]—which was stationed at Hilton Head—and on Nov. 4*th* I again went to live in Camp, anticipating a dreary life from my experience of the previous winter at Camp Saxton. My first day was one of considerable excitement in Camp. The men had just been informed that they were to recieve but $7 per month instead of the full pay of soldiers. They were told by the Col. on dress-parade—he explained as clearly as he could the reasons given, at the same time making it clear to them that all the officers felt that it was a wrong which could be righted in time and he had no doubt they would, in time receive the balance of their pay, whether they accepted the seven dollars now offered or no—but the men had no confidence in the promises of the offices—there was sullen looks and a spirit of insubordination was evident—but no overt act occurred that night. Earley next morning a large number of men from the different Companies marched up in regular order to Col. Bennett's tent, and stacked their arms. Col Bennett,[46] talked kindly to them, showing them the foolishness of such a course, and urged them to return to duty. Many of them did so, but a few of the leaders refused to take up their arms or to return to duty and resisted the officers ordered to arrest them. A serious struggle seemed pending, the officers went about armed. The leaders of the meeting were sent to the Provo-Guard house—and a strict watch kept on the other men to see that no revolt was attempted. It was a long time before the men went cheerfully to their duty and who can blame them!

Life in camp was monotonous but pleasant. The officers all treated me with the greatest kindness. They seemed like brothers—and all anxious to contribute to my happiness and comfort. My school was large and flourishing—the men were eager to learn, and more constant in attendance than they had *seemed* to be in the 1*st* Regt.

Our Camp is pleasantly located facing the harbor and only a short distance from the smoothe hard beach which streatches for miles away, making of the finest highways for horseback exercise ever seen—and every day we gallop over its hard surface, 'Brownie' and I meeting nothing worse than an occasional sentinal—who takes no more notice of us than as if it was a most common occasion—whereas if the truth was known, their isn't half a dozen women on the whole island! Once, while cantering along we were halted by a sentinel and our 'pass' demanded. We stopt so suddenly that the saddle turned and I rolled off at the soldiers feet—he

---

45. This transfer was accompanied by a promotion of John Milton Hawks from Assistant Surgeon to Surgeon. *Official Army Register*, Vol. VIII, p. 204. The Third South Carolina was later designated the Twenty-first U.S.C.T.

46. Lt. Col. Augustus G. Bennett, commander of the Twenty-first U.S.C.T.

tightened the saddle—remounted me and away we went without a word having been spoken! —The first of Feb. a large number of troops were brought to the Post—those from Morris Is. were moved down, and encamped outside the entrenchments. It was evident that a large force was to be sent somewhere soon and our officers were all anxious that our Regt. be included in the move. The 54*th* Mass. and 2*nd* S.C. Regts are encamped near us and I had the pleasure of meeting many of my old friends from the hospital.

[Florida]

All is activity and bustle but no one seems to know to what end. At the end of a week, the troops have started south, for the "third annual conquest of Florida." Our Regt has recieved orders to be ready to move at an hours' notice. This was on Friday, the 11*th* of Feb./64. Simultaneously with the order the teams come into camp to move such things as are to be taken. I begged the Col. to take me, and he consented. In spite of all the precautions taken many of the men succeeded in getting out of Camp, so as to avoid going on the expedition—so that the Regt. that was marched on board the *Charles Houghton* was a small one, and I was counted *one of* it.

We made the trip without incident, in about twenty hours. Col. Littlefield,[47] whose fragment of a regt. had lately been consolidated with the 3*rd* (ours) was in command. Nothing unusual occurred on the passage but both officers and men kept an eager lookout as we neared the bluffs at the mouth of the St. John's, and felt a little disappointment that no enemy "blazed away" at us from some of the many convenient places along the river shore, but a Sabbath stillness reigned, with naught but the song of birds the whirr of the water fowl as they passed us, to disturb it.

As we neared the wharf at Jacksonville the place had a most deserted look: All of the upper part of it, comprising the wealthiest portion had been burned, and the tall chimnies alone, stood to mark the spot and tell the tale of what had been on and near the wharf a few soldiers of the 54*th* Mass., no other appearance of life was visible, were idling about the streets, which are filled with obstructions to prevent a surprise from the rebs. The best part of the city was burned by our soldiers last year—only one of the many fine houses remains and that is used as Hd. Qtrs.

---

47. Col. Milton S. Littlefield, whose postwar financial career, primarily as a manipulator of railroad securities, would inspire Jonathan Daniels to entitle his biography *Prince of Carpetbaggers* (Philadelphia: J. B. Lippincott, 1958).

It was 4 P.M. when we reached the wharf—but the sun had set before I went ashore. Dr. took me to the "Taylor House"[48] while he attended to his duties in seeing to the hospital affairs and stores. The Taylors' have so timed their sentiments as to remain undisturbed in the town through all the many convulsions which have agitated it and are now as ready to take the oath of allegiance to the Gov. as they doubtless have ever been to support the rebel cause! —My accommodations at this hotel were rather primative and the prospect of spending the night there anything but agreeable. The room given to my use was absolutely destitute of every appearance of furniture, save one broken chair—the window was broken which I didn't mind, but the door wouldn't *shut* and *that* I *did* mind. My bedding had been brought from the boat and lay on the floor—but the prospect for the night was not cheering—but soon after tea Dr. [J. M. Hawks] came in with the joyful intillegence that he had found a chance fully equal to this one, for us to spend the night. It was in the Fla. House. The Surg. of the 2 S.C. had taken possession of it for Hd. Qrs. and we might have *half*. My spirits arose immediately. A hard bed and hard *fare* was nothing in comparison to being alone in that secesh house.

Our Stay in Jack.-ville was short the Regt being ordered out to Camp Finnegan [Finegan], about 14 miles from the city—where we are told, a "Camp of instruction" is to be started. —We find Camp Finnigan has only been vacated by its rebel occupants a few days before we take possession—and their is every evidence that they left in a hurry. The next day being Sunday was spent in writing letters for the men—to their wives and sweet-hearts left behind. One of the officers, Capt. Poppy [Poppe],[49] enjoyed the fun with me and such vigarous love-letters as we wrote, must have quite astonished the young ladies of color to whom they were sent. Here are the views of one of our soldiers on love, "Arter you lub, you lub, you know boss! You cant broke lub, Lub. stan—'e' aint gwine broke! Man hab. to be berry strong and smart for broke lub. Lub is a ting dat stan jes like tar, arter he stick, he stick he aint gwine move: he cant move less dan you burn him. Hab. to kill all two arter he lub, fo' you broke lub! —You can imagine the warmth of the letters dictated by such sentements.

The men are very busy cleaning up the grounds and making the Camp habitable. The sudden change in the weather causes great discomfort. Their is a thin crust of ice over the little puddles of water left by yesterdays rain, and the blossoms from the peach trees and the dainty yellow

---

48. The Taylor House was a hotel at the corner of Market and Bay streets in Jacksonville.
49. Capt. John L. Poppe of the Twenty-first U.S.C.T.

Jessamine which the boys brought in great arms-full to decorate my cab-in—are already turning black—as the sun melts them.

Instead of tents the offices all have cabins, of logs, pearched on four tall posts which are driven into the sand—the cracks between the logs are roughly covered by small rails, leaving ample openings for the most thorough ventilation—the roof is covered with palmetto leaves,—on one side their is a rough chimney built of sticks and morter, there are no windows, or doors, but army blankets swing gracefully before the opening and give an air of cosiness and warmth very grateful to our half frozen bodies! The floor is of loose boards and being so far from the ground, the wind has a fine chance at us, so I have talked down another blanket for a carpet.

The weather continues very cold and there is great discomfort among the men. —The guard-house is just in the rear of our cabin, and some unusual excitement has kept up a constant talking through the night. This morning, seeing the Provo-Marshal, Capt. Willoughby,[50] standing near the guard-house, I enquired if there was any trouble, and he pointed to three boyish looking prisoners belonging to the 55th Mass., who were under guard. —They had been arrested about mid-night, taken directly before acting Brig. Gen Littlefield, tried and condemned, to suffer death by hanging on the afternoon of the same day. —They had committed an outrage on a white woman. At the time appointed 3 p.m. our Regt and the 2.S.C. were drawn up in line and the poor fellows, launched into eternity. They showed no sign of emotion of any kind, but our soldiers sobbed aloud and were all greatly affected. Gen Seymore [Seymour],[51] who had come from J.ville to witness the execution, after it was over turned to the men, and said, loud enough for them all to hear "Served them right, now let any other man try it if he dares." The bearing of the Gen. and his manner of speaking left an impression on our offices of his utter heartlessness. If the same measure had been meted out to white offices and men who have been guilty of the same offense towards black women, Gen. S. [Seymour] might have grown hoarse in repeating his remarks. This dreadful affair has spread a feeling of gloom over our camp.

19th   The Provost has recieved instructions to lay out a garden for the Brigaid, and our officers are all busy beautifying Co. Hd. qtrs. It is evident that we are expected to remain here for some time.

50. Major Richard H. Willoughby of the Twenty-first U.S.C.T., later to be appointed Provost Marshal General of the Charleston Military District after the surrender of that city.
51. Brig. Gen. Truman Seymour, a controversial commander of federal troops in both South Carolina and Florida.

20*th*   This morning there are rumors of an engagement of our forces under Gen Seymore, at the front, near Lake City and that our soldiers are driven back. Maj. Gen Gillmore,[52] who has command of the expedition, has Hd. qts. at Fernandina which keeps the need at a long distance—from the scene of the action, especially as we hav'nt force enough to keep the road open between Jacksonville and Lake City a distance of 80 miles—and our soldiers are already suffering for supplies. At 5 p m an order came for the Col. Commanding the Post for the Regt. to be ready to march forward at a moments notice. Hamiltons Battery is entirely destroyed, the guns falling into the hands of the enemy, and that we have lost a thousand killed and wounded and as many taken prisoners: Our Regt was under arms waiting for the order to march when an order came for the men to be provided with 3 days rations—this throws us into a state of anxious expectation. The men in hospital are cooking rations, as we have no "hard tack" flour has been served. This they mix with water and fry in bacon fat—in masses about 10 in. across and 1 1/2 in. thick. 6 of these will be furnished each man of the hospital staff. If they could be worn as armor, it would make the men invulnerable! how it will affect them as rations remains to be proved! Our horses stand saddled, all night at the door. I shivered with terror at every sound, expecting the order to march, but the long hours dragged slowly on and morning came with no change. At noon the 2nd S.C. were ordered back to Ja-ville, and our Regt was left alone in charge of Camp Finnegan [Finegan]. The air was heavy with forebodings of evil. Our officers go about with anxious faces. Stragglers from the front tell terrible stories of our defeat and losses. The rebel forces are under the command of Gen Hardee,[53] and we have been most disasterously out-generaled—our soldiers are retreating as rapidly as possible, leaving their dead and wounded in the hands of the enemy. At dark we recieved the order to fall back to Ja-ville as rapidly as possible. The retreating army was only ten miles ahead—so all our baggage and Regimental stores, had to be left, in Camp under charge of a small guard—with slight prospect of our ever seeing any of them again! —It was 7 p.m. when we got started. I rode at the head of the column with the Col.—The surgeon being obliged to ride in the rear to see that no [one] falls by the way. It is a warm moonlight night and considering that we are retreating

---

52. Maj. Gen. Quincy A. Gillmore. At this time he was commander of the Department of the South and the X Corps.
53. Lt. Gen. William Joseph Hardee, C.S.A.

before the enemy, we had a very jolly march. The men sang most of the way, "John Brown's being changed to "Hang Jeff Davis on a sour apple tree" being the most popular air. We reached J. [Jacksonville] at about 11 o'clock. —The men camped on the ground and we found a welcome at Col. Montgomerys Hd. Qtrs. 500 wounded had arrived—and the Surgeon went directly to the hospital to assist in their care. —After a few hours rest, I went to a church near, where I found 50 wounded men who had come in during the night and had entered the church for shelter they had not been attended to so getting some men to bring water: and sending another to the Sanitary Com. [Commission] for rags and bandages, we commenced work on such as most needed immediate care.

The S. Com. also sent me some coffee and a fire in the yard soon gave us plenty of warm water for bathing and a drink of hot coffee all round for the half famished boys: Soon Dr. H. [J. M. Hawks] and an assistant came in and the work of repairs went bravely on—and by 1. p.m. the wounds are all dressed. The men fed and supplied with clean shirts and clean straw to lie in. Most of the wounds are comparatively light—but many of them may prove severe from the fatigue and exhaustion of their long march. Many touching instances of friendliness occurred, among our patients, who were a mixed company of black and white, in very close quarters the black Regts. had borne the fiercest onslaught of the enemy, and the white soldiers were loud in their praise and when I saw white soldiers sharing their tobacco with the black ones, I concluded that the end of the war was near for the millennium had begun!

As I was carefully removing the pieces of clothing carried by a spent ball through the fleshy part of the arm of a colored soldier, I saw that he took unusual interest in my work—his admiring eyes followed every movement, and as I finished, he said "Is you Mrs Hawks," there is'nt only one woman in dis world who could do that, S. I know you is. My brudder told what you did for the 54*th* soldiers in the hospital. —On enquiry I learned that this was the brother who had stayed at home of the those who were wounded at Ft. Wagner—and he had come out with the 55*th*.

Our force is entirely routed, we had but 5000 men, while the enemy brought 20,000 against us, but the officers say even this might not have been so disastrous if only there had been a Gen. in command—but with our superior offices 80 miles away the disaster was inevitable! —and why the rebels do not follow up their victory and bag the whole of us is very strange *and* gratifying. Our loss is estimated, at 1400. The Col. of the 3.U.S. Ct. was killed—and many other officers but we cannot know the whole extent of our loss yet. The men especially the the colored troops

A Woman Doctor's Civil War

fought like demons—the white soldiers say this of them.[54] A great many troops have come in today and our army surrounds the city, they are drawn up in line of battle and expect an attack at sunset but no attack was made and in a few days many of the troops were withdrawn and sent to Morris Is.

[1864]

                                                          Sunday Eve. Apr. 24*th*
   Alone! The day has been very long! The morning warm and rainy. — couldn't sleep—the noise of the men and teams, who, not-withstanding the rains, were busy in removing the boards timbers and other things of any value, left by the 24*th* Mass. in their camp—when they broke up housekeeping last night, and went on board the *Dictator* 'en rout for Fortress Monroe! Strange how much I miss them—especially when I remember that I had hardly a speaking acquaintance with a single officer or man in the Regt. but they were so quiet and gentlemanly that I felt a sort of protection in their nearness which I now miss!

   No, Sunday-school—the children were all too late—kept from getting ready by the rain perhaps! Read a little—looked over my trunk, arrainged a few flowers to send in letters to friends. —Col. Beecher[55] came in; lay down on my lounge, and complained of fatigue gave me a graphic description of his efforts in manging an unruly horse, in which he was two hours in getting him to the gate to let the Col. dismount; last night between the hours of eleven and three—. He admired my flowers, of which I have a great profusion, just now, talked nonsense, for half an hour then went away in quite a happy mood.

   54. The events described constituted the Battle of Olustee, the only major engagement fought in Florida during the entire war. Esther Hawks' estimate of Confederate strength was vastly exaggerated, her assessment of the magnitude of the Union defeat was not. Gen. Truman Seymour's division of X Corps, which had earlier secured Jacksonville as a base, hoped to break up rebel communications between East and West Florida and to capture the Confederate supply base at Lake City. Seymour's force marched inland and was reinforced by Gen. Quincy A. Gillmore's troops, after proceeding some twenty miles. Scattered Confederate forces were driven back to the main body of troops commanded by Gen. Joseph Finegan. Finegan then attacked and routed both the Seventh New Hampshire and Eighth United States Colored Infantry. The Fifty-fourth Massachusetts Infantry held until the night of February 20, 1864, when Seymour withdrew with extremely heavy losses. Among the several sources consulted the most useful was Samuel Jones, Maj. Gen., C.S.A. "The Battle of Olustee or Ocean Pond Florida: and comment upon it by Gen. Joseph R. Hawley. Robert Underwood Johnson and Clarence Clough Buel, eds., *Battles and Leaders of the Civil War*, IV (New York, Thomas Yoseloff, Inc., 1956), pp. 76–80.
   55. Col. James C. Beecher, who served as both a chaplain and a commander of black troops. Son of Congregationalist minister Lyman Beecher and brother of Henry Ward Beecher and of Harriet Beecher Stowe, James had been a missionary in China at the start of the war, and later returned to the ministry. He committed suicide in 1886.

+ + + +. Those four crosses stand for four little colored boys who have been in to read Jeff Chism—Henry Walker—Will Anderson, Alfred Walker—each has a history which would be worth writing if one had the right threads, a good story would be the result. Its too late to write about it tonight.

25th.   The days are sadly alike, and its rather queer that I am taking such a fancy for scribbling when there is nothing of interest to attract one. Arrainged my flowers, and went to school. Soon after my return. Col.B. [Beecher] came in like a great boy to "look after me" he said—did not stop to sit down, but joked a few minutes in his hearty irrisistable way and left as abruptly as he came. In a short time Dr. M. [Marcy][56] came in to enquire after my health. Told me the Regt. with the exception of three Co's which are to be mounted, had been ordered to Tampa, on the western coast, to be absent ten day- marching across the county, mearly to *take observations*, and anything else to be taken! I'm sorry to have them go. I shall miss Col. B. "too much" — besides it leaves us with very little protection. If there are any 'rebs' near, they'll catch us, sure!

'Will' and Jeff came as usual to say their lessons! On returning the church key to its nail behind my front door, Mr. Henry, of the 'Christian Commission'[57] stopped and chatted a few minutes. Expressed his surprise at my having the courage to live here all alone—and departed, no doubt, with the idea that I must be a "strong-minded' female!

26*th*   Warm weather has farely set it. This week is like July—Roses are at their prettiest—and mosquitoes ca'nt get much thicker!

Col. B. [Beecher] came round to say good bye; he is not very sanguin of the success of this expedition and feels a little depressed. Left some letters, one to his 'fiancee' Miss Johnson, for me to put in the P.O a few days after he has gone, so, he remarked, 'They will not have so long to worry, after hearing I am away before I can write again." Good man! I like him better every day! Dr. Marcy also came and I took his wife's address in order to write to her should he not return in due season He was in fine spirits! I shall miss him very much! Indeed I've not a soul left to wish me 'howdye' but my black children! No great chance of intellectual growth

---

56. Dr. Henry O. Marcy. After helping to prevent dysentery by supplying Federal troops with fresh food and helping to prevent the spread of contagion in Charleston, Marcy was appointed medical director of Florida during the last year of the war. He would later become the first American student of Joseph Lister, the father of antiseptic surgery. One of the earliest bacteriologists in the United States, Marcy was elected president of the American Medical Association in 1891.

57. There is no further identification of Mr. Henry available. The United States Christian Commission was organized by the Young Men's Christian Association to improve the moral and physical well-being of Union soldiers.

A Woman Doctor's Civil War

under such circumstances. My girls brought me a charming great bunch of roses to-night.

27*th*   I am of the opinion that this is a foolish waste of paper. No letters no nothing but my class of boys this eve! I miss Col. Bs visit today. Went down to Mr. Dodge's[58] and stayed to tea—had cold rice, and molasses, and bread and butter! We should feel pretty poor to sit down to such fare in N.E.!

28th   Sick-head-ache-all day—didn't sit up after coming from school—wove sick fancies and dreamed.

29th   The day has been cool and windy: an agreeable change from the oppressive heat of the just past days. Have felt better to-day than for many days. 'Ben.' one of our Regt. left here in hospital came to see me—told me of three other of my boys who are sick here so I went over to see them—the first time I have been in a hospital since the wounded from Olustee were sent away. The boys were very glad to see me, and begged me to come again. Went from there to P.O. found letter from Dr. [J. M. Hawks]—and by his description of Morris Is. I think a further residence in this place more desirable.

'Ben' has been round again this evening to see me, and we have been talking about old times and how he got to the Union men. He is from Savannah,—has been here about 16 mo's; and if I could tell his story as he tells it, it would'nt be bad, as I can't do that I will say nothing about it. He is quite anxious to go back to the Regt.

Mr. Henry came in when he brot' the key, and we have been talking about 'Ben' a little—he also told me that our pickets were driven in this afternoon by the rebs—no harm done!

Apr 30*th*   Quite too hot to go out today till late this evening—been very quiet—no callers but little Mabel Dodge, too[k] her with me to P.O. also called on Dr Roberts[59] to get him to look up Dr's [J. M. Hawks] lost property. Called at Mr. Oak's to see Mr. Robinson who has been ill with fever. Wrote to Milton—and this evening wrote another letter. Today one of my little school boys came and 'brot' me his 'picture' he is a drummer in the 3*rd* U.S.C.T. and lives in Phill. was always free. His name is Frank Hawkins and a bright little fellow he is.

A 'flag of truce' came in to-day and at the same time, from another point on our lines, our pickets were again driven in. It seems that yesterday two of our men were captured. The rebels are evidently testing our

58. Mr. J. G. Dodge.
59. Dr. Nathan S. Roberts, Assistant Surgeon of the Twenty-first U.S.C.T. under Milton Hawks.

strength—Tho' I presume they have definite knowledge of our force here. Gen. Birney[60] and some of his staff went to Pilatka [Palatka] with this expidition which has started for the interior. It is not known that he or any of them are to go any further.

Our Camps.

Previous to the withdrawal of the troops from this post many of the Regts had beautified their camps exceedingly. Our Regt was encamped on the rising ground beyond the 'Creek', about a half mile distant from the city—and, since the trees were cut away to give wider range for the guns, in full view of it. The men exhibited great ingenuity in the construction of their "domicils" as their tents were not used here. The camp, but for its location, was most unsightly—no attempt at ornament was made by officers or men—and it more resembled an irregular grouping together of *pig and chicken pens*, than anything to which I could liken it. Still the boys had made them quite comfortable with boards, sticks, turf and mud, and no filth was allowed to accumulate The 2nd S.C. was close by and no better in appearance. To the left, and a short distance from these was the camp of the lst N.C. Col. Beecher's Regt—which he, and all his officers had taken much pride and pains in beautifying[.] The men had no better quarters than ours but the camp was laid out regularly, with Co. streets regularly laid cleared out and graded—and the unsightly huts which serve instead of tents entirely hidden from view by the wealth of evergreens surrounding them—and with which the streets are lined. At the head of each street appears the Company letter interwoven with moss and vines, making an arched entrance to the street picturesque and pleasing to the eye. The officers tents are all ornamented in the same manner with moss and shade trees. The men exhibit great skill in making their cook house and dining-rooms attractive. The Col's tent under a beautiful live oak just large enough to give an agreeable shade was temptingly comfortable with its soft carpet of pine boughs in the outer room made by the tent—'flis,' and good board floor in the tent with a nice little chimney at the back part. Alongside and similarly arranged was the Dr's. Near by a commodious building, is in process of erection, for school purposes, and the general appearance of things would indicate an indefinite stop in this encampment, but before the school-house was completed the Regts were

60. Brig. Gen. William Birney, son of Liberal Party anti-slavery presidential candidate James G. Birney. After the Union defeat at Olustee Gen. Birney was appointed commander of the District of Florida.

A Woman Doctor's Civil War

ordered to move down just outside the entrenchments—and now our advance picket-line runs through those pretty old camps!

Jacksonville Fla.
Sunday May 1st 1864
    What can be sadder than to pass through life with nothing to love. To live though the long, weary months and years with an ever increasing yearning in the heart for some object dearer than all the world besides, on which to lavish the strong pure heart love. The *mother love*—dearer than all other!

    I have longed for this, prayed for it with all the passionate entreaty of a desolate nature. Why am I denied. Why can no softening purifying influences be sent to lead me through life's tangled pathway. Am I less worthy, less capable of such high trust—than the many I meet who do not even realize their blessedness? I *do* need something to love. I grow selfish and hard externally until I am sometimes tempted to think there is no *love* in my heart, but I will not believe it. I *have* the power to love earnestly—passionately. O God! give me something to break through the bonds which chain it ! Give me something to love.

    May 1st   A new month! but it brings none of the happy hopeful feeling of a N.E. may-day! It seems like mid-summer. The day has been hot and sultry. Sunday-school was large this morning. After school had the children come in and sing for half an hour. They were very much delighted. Mr. and Mrs. Dodge and Mabel came up to tea and we have been to church to hear Mr. Henry preach! A mild young man—not particularly powerful—though perhaps I ought not to say that after such a pretty compliment as he paid me last night as I stood in the door to say good-night he enquired if I had ever seen the picture of 'Evangeline.' I said a beautiful thing" because, he added, "as you stand there your *head* reminds me of it." —I felt very 'gracious' and have been particularly "*sweet* on him" ever ever since. Chaplin Gregg[61] of the 7*th* U.S.C.T. called tonight and we all walked up to his tent with him- had a pleasant chat. *Sat in a rocking-chair*—a novelty worthey of remembrance!

    2nd   School very large to-day—also had quite a number of visitors. The colored soldiers come about the door very much—and I invite them in for a lesson. One from Manchester named Henry Long, came and joined the school to-day he belongs to the 3*rd* U.S. enlisted in Phil. is quite a good scholar—used to go to the 'Intermediate.' This evening yelded to the entreaties of the children and had a 'spelling school.' Thirty

---

61. Chaplain James Gregg.

of my best scholars, and several soldiers present. Let them "choose sides" with which they were particularly delighted; then I let them 'spell down' and one of my boys, Sam Muncy and a soldier, from the north, gave each other a 'hard try' after out-spelling all the others—they then both missed the same word—a word of four syllables. After an hour's spelling we had a sing. The boys are most of them fine singers and they enjoyed it exceed- ingly. Lt. Knight[62] called—informed me that we have been given, by Gen. Anderson[63] 48 hours to remove women and children from the city. This eve. my boys have been in singing the "Year of Jubilee to me. These boys are great friends of mine. Lt. Knight and a Lt. from the 3.rd U.S. came in and we have passed a pleasant evening. It is a real pleasure to *see folks* once in awhile!

One of the four, reported as captured from our pickets, there was but *one* taken and he has been given up as he was captured during the time of a business interchange by 'flag of truce'—so Gen. A. [Anderson] prompt- ly gave him up, accompanied by a polite note of apology.

3rd

Cool enough to-night to make it pleasant sitting by a fire. 'Henry' brought me some great Magnolia buds this morning, one is nearly blos- somed. Ripe blackberries and green pears are in the market—vegetation is, at least, six weeks in advance of Port Royal.

A colored soldier, Henry Long, from Manchester has joined my school. He is a bright, smart young man and quite a good scholar. The school is very large and new ones come in every day. The children make good im- provement—and are well behaved. I love some of them very much. There is one 'Topsy' among them who, I think, might have sat, to Mrs. Stowe for her picture.[64] She is apparently, about fourteen—quite black, good features—bright and keen—belonged to a Mrs. Brooks, living six- teen miles beyond Lake City at the time we came here. On hearing that the Yankees were so near, after night set in the locomotive property of said Brooks journeyed northward and were all safely brought in by our soldiers, or rather they brought themselves in, coming the whole eighty miles on foot—the women toteing the babies. Sarah shows more bitter- ness in speaking of her old mistress than I have ever seen in any of them. She says—"I'll always hate her 'cos she never give me 'nuff to eat, not till

62. First Lt. Alva Knight of the Thirty-fourth U.S.C.T.
63. Maj. Gen. J. Patton Anderson, C.S.A., who commanded Confederate troops in the District of Florida.
64. Topsy was the wild but captivating black child in Harriet Beecher Stowe's novel *Un- cle Tom's Cabin.*

it 'spile when she done had 'nuff'—" and the greatest incentive which she has to learn is that she may be able to write to her old mistress to tell her that she "have bacon and homony and rice too, all I can eat, and if you come here I'd like to see you starve." —She chuckles over the way they all left her rolls up her eyes and "tinks ole missis wait good while in the morning, she call Delia loud den me but she never get none our breakfast dat day!"

4*th*   Been out all the afternoon visiting among the colored people. They are evidently a better class than most of those we meet at Port Royal. One woman by the name of Foster, who is the mother of ten children, and sends several of them to school, was living between here and Camp Finigan [Finegan] with her husband, who is a free man—but, she said, he chose to go with the rebels so she took all the children she had with her and came with our soldiers leaving him to go his way—and she has not seen or heard of him since. Another, a woman taken by Col. Montgomery when here a year ago and who has been, with her husband, in that Regt. ever since—found, on returning here, her two children a girl and boy, the girl comes to school but the boy ran away and she thinks, returned to his rebel masters because, she says, he was afriad our folks would make a soldier of him. As I passed the house, she came out and with an air of great concern enquired if I thought "they would *vaccinate* this place". Not understanding her, I told her I didn't think there was much small pox here but I would vaccinate Sarah if she cared to have one. That was all very well but she wanted to know if the *soldiers* would "vaccinate the place," I began to see through this and made haste to assure her that I had no fears of such an event!

Called at 'Sanitary Com.' to get some books, talked a half hour with Mr. Day[65]—who is a man with an excellent opinion of himself—but of no special merit, and a decided 'bore.'—Mr. Henrys has gone to Beaufort. I miss him very much.

There is evidently a violent working of the 'spirit' in the Camp of the colored regt. close by, if the noise and shouting is to be credited. I never heard such a noise! something unusual must be going on—Taps—I hope that will stop it !

5*th*

Been sewing—had nothing but 'contraband' thoughts.

65. Unidentified.

6th

School pleasant today. Didn't get home till 2.P.M. Quite a class of Col. Beechers' men come to school since the Regt. came inside of the lines. They are very eager to learn and take hold with a hearty good will encouraging to see. My first class I am trying to initiate into the mysteries of writen Arithmatic, and they do *credit to* their *teacher* (!). I think they begin to have an idea of the *whys* of addition. They are delighted with the practice.

Been over to call on some of the children who are sick with measles. Made a little dress for 'Cloe' and carried her—too small. If I had'nt had considerable experience in *getting along* I should wonder how they manage to live with hardly the bare necessities of life—still they are cheerful and happy. Gave me some great sour oranges which the 'father' had bought. They seem so delighted to have me call. I carried the oranges over to my 'boys' in hospital—who were very grateful—promised to carry them something to read—Francis McKinny, one of my scholars has just been in to say good bye. She and her mother are going to return to St. Augustine—brought me a plate of cakes from her mother—nice and warm. I am sorry to have her leave school. She is a dear girl. I love her very much.

7th Saturday night!   Another seven days gone and not much to add to the record! —I often wonder if it is my *duty*, really to live in this way—if I am doing just as *much* good as I might be in some other sphere—if I am wasting time which should be devoted to my profession. Shall I ever resume its duties—sometimes I say *no* to the question, in my own mind. There is a feeling of *dread* connected with my experience, which I cannot shake off. I never wish to go through the same scenes. Shall I go home this Summer and return again—Blessed be the veil which hides the future!

Very busy this entire morning in fixing the old lounge over—made it quite comfortable. Went by invitation, to dine with Mrs Dodge and have spent the day there—found 'Pattie' quite disconsolate, on my return, she was just starting in search of me. Got a letter from Dr. [J.M. Hawks] and one from Fowler for him. —Dr. wishes me to come to Morris Island. Wonder if I shall go?

May *8th*   Sunday-school well attended—and the duties of 'Superintendent' devolving on me! I wonder what I sha'nt be placed in position to do while in the Army! Got along very well—quite a number of soldiers in—got two of them to hear classes of boys. The children sang finely. — Went to hear Chaplin Gregg preach—after setting a little while, just be-

fore services commenced who should come in to church but Mr. Purdie,[66] Miss Ireston[67] and Miss Kendal,[68] Ladies from Beaufort—with
whom I have but slight acquaintance but it was a great delight to see a familiar face. Came home with me and stayed a short time. Came in again
this evening, with Capt. Hodges[69] and we have had a pleasant social time.
Mr. and Mrs. Pillsbury[70] also arrived on the *Boston* to-day and are at Mr.
Dodge's. I did'nt know how lonesome and down-hearted I was till the
sight of these good friends brought to mind the dear old times of last fall
and winter before coming here, when I was near them. After all I 'sorter'
like it!

May 9*th* Monday.

Sick all night but arose early to see Mr. & Mrs. P. [Pillsbury] before leaving, as they were determined to do, for St. Augustine, this morning—got
a cup of coffee at Mr. Ds. [Dodge] then we went on board the boat with
them. It was crowded with passengers, a great many ladies from Beaufort
on a pleasure trip—and many leaving here for Port Royal. Spoke with
Mrs. Severance[71] and several others, but there were only a few that I
knew—joked Mrs. P. [Pillsbury] on the dangers of the boat being blown
up, little thinking what a narrow risk they were to run—for a little this
side of Yellow Bluff, the *Harriet Weed* which was just in the wake of the
Boston, drawing less water went nearer the shore, and was blown into
too many pieces ever come to-gether again. It must have terrified the other boat very much. I hope poor Mrs. P. will not come to the conclusion
that I am in league with the rebs, because I proved so near a prophet! —
After returning to the house, as I lay on the lounge, weaving sad homesick fancies and just ready to cry over my loneliness—with mind fully
made up, that no one on earth cared for me Dr. Marcy, like a sunbeam
popped in. Bless his homely ph'q! how good it looked! He was so kind
and anxious about me—it was "to much" after so many long days of waiting for a friendly face and 'woman like' I had a *good cry*. Well, the show
over, I listened with great interest to his adventures—but had to leave in
the midst, to go to school. He came around this evening about five and

66. Mr. G. A. Purdie, a friend and later business associate of John Milton Hawks.
67. Probably Helen M. Ireston of Lynn, Mass.
68. Unidentified.
69. Capt. Thorndike D. Hodges of the Thirty-fifth U.S.C.T., who would later serve as Assistant Adjutant General, Dept. of South and City of Charleston.
70. Gilbert and Antoinette Francis Pillsbury of Ludlow, Mass.
71. Mrs. Carolina M. Severance whose husband was collector of the custom house on Hilton Head Island and with whom the Hawks had once boarded.

we have been out riding horeseback. So kind in him for it could'nt have been any pleasure to him after riding from ten to thirty miles a day during the past two weeks. He has been in and spent the evening. We have had a pleasant one. I shall not forget it. He brought me a bottle of wine and says I must go home by 1*st* June or I shall be sick. O how pleasant it seems to have someone *appear* to feel an interest in one's welfare! At 10:P M. he left to go on board the boat for Picolata where Col. B. [Beecher] and the Regt. are stopping!

10*th*   Been lying down all the afternoon, got up about sunset and went to P.O. then to Mr. D's [Dodge] where I have but just come from. Mr. D. goes to the Head to-morrow, and I shall probably stay with Mrs. D. and Belle, nights of his absence. Called to see Miss Kendal and the other ladies but did'nt find them.

11*th*   Mr. Dodge and also the ladies left this morning for the 'Head'. Gen. Birney and Staff have also gone. The *Mary Benton* takes them to the 'bar' where they expect to be transfered to the *Boston*. Mrs. D. is very nervous about the torpedoes in the river.

12*th*   Nothing!

13*th*   Went to ride with Capt. Hodges—enjoyed it very much. Tried to go out beyond the picket but couldn't pass without a 'pass' signed by the General—very good as we, nodoubt should have very foolishly gone into danger. Visited Battery 'Frebly'. The men of the different Batteries have been, practicing, to get the range of the guns—for a few days past. Shelling the woods. The whirr of the shells through the air, gives us an occasional start in school. Been in school alone, as Mabel is sick. 32 'Contrabands' came up from 'Augustine to-day!

14*th*   No change for the better in Bell—been there all day.

Sunday 15*th*   Got home late this morning from Mrs. D's [Dodge]—found the children all waiting, for me, to go to Sunday-school—went as soon as possible and was just getting underway when Mr. Robinson the elected Superintendant, made his appearance for the first time, since his election, and relieved me of the duties pertaining to the opening of school much to my relief and gratification—before we got through, the long line of soldiers from the 7th Reg. C. T. came in filling the church to overflowing so we sang our closing song, and retired. Some of the colored boys came to read. Then I did a little reading for my own pleasure, then went back to Mrs. D's. —Had a little thunder shower in the eve.

16*th*   Had a very heavy thunder shower this evening came over home between the showers—Soon after coming over, Capt. H. [Hodges] came in and I shall never tell even here all the *pretty things* said and did, because, you know, *I promised not to*[72] —On returning to Mrs. D. met Mr. Henry. Real glad to see him—had only been there a few minutes before Mr. H. returned and called for me, presented me to *Miss Barcalow*[73] as a teacher come from the Head, to my assistance. Mr. D. [Dodge] also came!

17*th*   Capt. H. [Hodges] came for me and we went to ride—enjoyed it very much as I always do horse-back exercise. H. took tea with us and spent the eve. with Mis. B. [Barcalow] and myself. Miss B. sang songs.. Capt. talk sentiment—he is *fond* of *ladies*—but has, I think, the same idea of them as all men of the world have—namely that they only *differ* in *degrees*. All are accesibl only pay their price. Perhaps I mis-judge but certain little indications lead me to think so. After taking a few of his conceits out of him, I shall like him well enough!

Had a large mail to-day—no sastisfactory news from M. [Milton Hawks]. I shall probably remain here to the end of the term if my health permits.

18*th*

My throat is very troublesome again. I must go home and recruit, this summer. Lost my watch chain somewhere about the School to-day—cant find it. This eve soon after coming from school Dr. Marcy came in; just down from Picolati [Picolata], he and Col. B. [Beecher] came down in a small row-boat and were out in all the terrific thunder shower which we have had—so they are thoroughly drenched. Dr. [J. M. Hawks] anxious and uneasy, has applied for leave of absence. Col. B. [Beecher] as blue as he can be and dissatisfied with everything—expecting his lady-love and cant be at the 'Head' to meet her! Spent the evening with us.

19*th*   Capt. H. [Hodges] came to go to ride but I did'nt because I was expecting Col. B. [Beecher] and Dr. M. [Marcy] to tea then Dr. came with a wee bit of a 'Secesh' pony and I went. The pony is one which they took on the old St. Mary's and is, apparently about half grown, though really of full size. He is a 'stiff-necked' little fellow and goes like the wind. Found the Col. waiting on our return. They have just departed, and to-morrow morning go back to Pelatka [Palatka]: A new mail in to-day brings us news of the fierce conflict between Grant and Lee, still raging, probably now decided. God grant on the side of the Right!

72. The words "and I shall never..., *I promised not to*," were lined out by Dr. Esther Hawks.
73. Unidentified.

20th.

My hoarseness is so bad that I only stayed a short time in school, then left in Miss Barcalow's care, and went to execute some shoping commissions for Mrs. Dodge, and on reaching her residence, learned that the *Mary Benton* left for 'Hilton Head' at 1.o'clock She decided to be in readiness to go on it and we were very busy until then in getting her and Mabel ready to go. At noon a salute, fired in honor of the victory, startled us into thinking there was an *attack* for a moment.

Went on boat with Mrs. D. and M.—Two Secesh ladies occupied the upper deck and were holding 'court' with about a dozen officers around them.

Soon after reaching home Col. Beecher came in. He was in excellent spirits owing to news from his 'Franky'[74] that she would start for this Dep. [Department] on the 24*th*. He is to be at the 'Head' [Hilton Head] to meet her; go on board the 'Boat with such friends as he desires and a clergyman, have the 'parson' "fire away" as long as he chooses" to use the exprssive words of the Col. then go to Beaufort, and return here at the first opportunity of bringing his *wife* along. He is restless and uneasy, fearing something will transpire to balk all this fine plan, but I cheered him and petted him into faith and confidence that all will come about just as he desired and he confessed that I was "the dearest little woman in all the Dept." and he liked me "better than anybody else only Frankie"—went away with the promise to come in for a game of whist in the evening. Came with Dr. M. [Marcy] and Dr. de Grass. (colored) Asst. Surg.[75] who has just returned from the North. A pleasant gentlemanly and intelligent man. Col. B. [Beecher] returns to Pilatka [Palatka] in the morning. God bless him! He is one of the *best* men He ever made.

22*nd*   Had a new experience today, been acting 'Commissary Sergt,' 'rationing' the 'people' for Mr. D. [Dodge] during his absence. I think now, the only thing remaining to fit me for some important *Military* position, is to have command of a Company or Regt for a short time. I have no doubt in my *ability* to command them—providing they be *colored* troops. Went to ride with Capt. H. [Hodges] on Dr. M. [Marcy's] little pony—had a long quiet talk with him—on the relations with and deport-

74. "Franky," was the bride-to-be of Col. James C. Beecher. Years after his death, remarried and writing as Frances Beecher Perkins, she would relate her Civil War experiences in "Two Years with a Colored Regiment," *New England Magazine*, 17 (January, 1898), pp. 533–43.

75. Dr. John V. DeGrasse of the Thirty-fifth U.S.C.T.

ment of men and women towards each other. He has a fine generous nature, frank and confiding—evidently has always been "Mother's boy." — is consequently very susceptable to woman's influence, and is for the time, whatever they make him. —A character pleasant to meet! Pony did'nt behave well coming home .Insisted on going to the stable, so twisted and turned till the saddle and I *turned*—had it adjusted and remounted and with much coaxing arrived safely at the *gate*—but rather provoked at such a display of mulishness on the part of so small a *beast*.

As we sat quietly conversing—no, I was reading a letter just handed me, from M. [Milton Hawks] by Chaplin Gregg—a knock at the back-door apprised me of visitors and Corp. Tucker, doffed his hat, with a "good evening school-mistress, our boys have been forming a band and would like to seranade you if you do'nt care," but I do care, I said, and should like it above all pleasures. Will the boys come into this room or stay outside? they concluded to come in, and my little dining room was filled to overflowing. The banjo and 'bones' touched by skillful fingers accompanied by their rich voices charmed us for more than an hour with patriotic and other songs—then one they called 'Archie' gave us a specimen of his dancing. A curious scene! I enjoyed very much, and was so lucky to have on hand some cakes with which to '*treat*' them. They belonged to the 3*rd* U.S.C.T. they left apparently very much delighted with their entertainment, and with the promise of a repetition of the performance.

23*rd*

Sunday school poorly attended; Went to church to hear Chaplin Gregg's Thanksgiving sermon, in accordance with 'Uncle Abe's'wish— (not my going but the thanksgiving). I have'nt heard anything which could begin to compare with it since coming into the Dep. It was noble words, bravely said—and I could'nt help thanking the Chaplin for the good they did me. 'Communion service' in the evening—furnished table, pitcher, glass etc. but not my presence. Stayed at home and Capt. H. [Hodges] read us one of Beecher's sermons. Dr. M. [Marcy] came for me to go to church and was quite surprised to learn that I was not a "professor" wished I was then I would'nt "play *cards*". Asked me to promise not to play anymore. I asked if he thought there was any more harm in spending an evening with cards than in gossip, or that it would hurt a church-member, quoting the example of Col. B. [Beecher] He said he thought so—he thought Col. B's influence with his officers was really *pernicious*, and that they did not respect him as they otherwise would but for certain habits of this nature. I agreed with him, but was'nt quite ready to promise abstinence, and this evening about sunset, went over to his hospital quarters to have the talk out—he walked home with me and we discussed the subject thoroughly. I am convinced that he is right—still I did not give the desired promise—but I did promise to *try myself*—and see if I can do so, and I have no doubt of *success!*

Dr. M. [Marcy] has a strong religious nature and is one of the few I have met who, I feel, lives up to his highest Christian light. I like him heartily—and wish I might always be blessed with the near presence of such a friend!

24th _____

25th   Just before the close of school an orderly from the Provost. Marshall came in to enquire who had charge of Mr. D's [Dodge's] business during his absence—because, he said, there were thirty contrabands at the guard-house who needed seeing to; I told him I could 'ration' them and would be at Mr. D-s for that purpose at 2.P.M. Went and worked hard all the afternoon, in dealing out food to the poor creatures, who seemed happy with ever so little. They had come from up the river near 'Magnolia'—got to the bank and raised a white flag, were taken on board a steamer and brought here. None but the women and children came for rations the men being all furnished work. These Florida slaves are certainly far superior to those of the Sea. Islands. They are intelligent and active—and many of them have picked up a little book learning. It is not uncommon to find a *fair* reader among those who have always been slaves.

26th   An expedition left here to-day at noon commanded by Col. Shaw[76] of the *7th* [U.S.C.T.]—and comprising most of the force of the place. They have gone towards "Camp Finegan"—probably to ascertain the position and force of the enemy in that direction. Have taken two days 'rations'—Dr. Marcy has gone with the mounted men of the *1st* N.C.

This eve Corp. Tucker announced that the 'boys' were coming to serenade us if agreeable—so at about 9 1/2—just as we were ready to step into bed, a rush of many feet on the back porch indicated their arrival. We had inadvertantly left the back door open, so they came directly in supposing it all right. We soon got into boots and wrappes and were ready to receive company—but the rediculousness of our position thru us into a great glee—which lasted long after the boys had sung their songs, drank their beer, and gone. About 11 o'clock the (probably) accidental discharge of a musket startled us, and soon after, eager voices and hurrying feet in-

76. Col. James Shaw, Jr.

creased our perterbation. I got up and on reconnoirtering, saw a long line of troops marching quietly to the Camp of the 7*th*, just above us. I knew it must be that Regt and that the expedition had returned. Soon all was quiet and we fell asleep.

27*th*   Dr. M. [Marcy] Mr. Henrys and Mr. Day have been in to spend the evening. Dr. M. gave us a graphic description of the 'raid'. He went in sight of Camp Finegan. They found more of a force to oppose than anticipated and dared not to go forward leaving this place so defenseless, so Col. Shaw, ordered a bivouac for the night at 'Ceda Kure,' but sharp firing by the rebs on our right induced him to draw in his pickets and return to J. [Jacksonville] that night.

28th.   Col. Beecher came in from Augustine, where he has left his regiment, to-day, en route for Port Royal to meet his 'Franky' and make her his wife—spent the afternoon and evening here. Capts. H. [Hodges] and Weld[77] the district Provost, came in, and soon after, my seranaders made their appearance and gave us a regular 'Christy' concert.

29*th*   To-day has been very hot,—Dr. M. [Marcy] came in this morning to enlist my sympathis in behalf of a pretty, *white*, colored girl, who, it seems has lately been brought here, from the north, where they have been for a year, she still held as a slave. While in N.Y. she was kept very secluded, never allowed to go to church or mingle with those of her color and her mind filled with all manner of alarming stories to keep her contented and being really well treated she seemed to have no desire to change her condition Soon after coming here, 'Moses' or Aunt Harriett[78] as we call her here, found her out and learned these facts concerning her, but as she was young and very pretty thought it best that she remain with her Misstress, rather than to break loose from all restraint and be floating about subject to the control of no one, feeling that in such a state she would soon be ruined. 'Aunt Harriett' interested Dr. M. in the story and he promised to provide a home of safety for her, and the object of his visit to-day was to ascertain if I would take her into my home and care for her till he goes north, when he will take her and place her among his friends and have her educated, to all of which I readily agreed; After his departure I went to visit the many sick children who are out of school, with measles. O the misery, the degredation and dirt in which these poor children are lying is enough to *almost* make one forget them human—Four and five in one family, sick upon the floor, of one little room. Its a wonder how they live! I tried what I could to clean them up a little and came

---

77. Capt. Lewis L. Weld.
78. Harriet Tubman, who had for years before the war been chief conductor on the underground railroad leading escaped slaves to freedom.

home tired and heart sick. Just before 'sun down' Dr. M. [Marcy] came over with the little pony and we went to ride. Moses [Harriet Tubman] had promised to come round with Priscilla at dark so we hurried home but not finding them, took a smart run up to the Battery and back. Dr. came in to tea and Capt. H. [Hodges] came in after and we spent a pleas'nt, social evening. Dr. M. [Marcy] gave me a short history of his connection with the Regt. and its officers. Good little man! if the army could boast more like him, there would be less to fear for the moral condition of its offices. Strongly religious—and temperate in all things, united with a warm, genial heart—his influence is sure to be felt, wherever he may be placed. We had a long talk on religious subjects while out riding—he told me his *experience*—and why he had joined a church.

30*th* A cool *shady* day,—been to church—Chaplin Gregg preached..He is just the sort of man for a chaplin, and is especially adapted to the needs of a colored regiment—active energetic, and enthusiastic—he carries everything before him. He has a school, of two hours everyday at which all the non.commissioned officers not on duty are required to be present. The Chaplin is about fifty but looks much younger!—

31*st*

Monday morning! Just three months ago to-day I commenced the first free school in Florida! Three months! They have been short, but I look with pride and pleasure on the work done! I have a large, orderly and intelligent school; The scholars love me and I love them, most of them have made excellent improvement. They are easily governed—and generally disposed to obey. I have had no cases of 'discipline' no 'revolts' or 'desertions', I feel that I can look upon my labors here as successful.[79]

79. In this paragraph Dr. Esther Hawks tentatively summarized a most important achievement of her Civil War years. Her accounts elsewhere, pertaining to her conducting of what was not only Florida's first free school, but also its first racially integrated one, are at variance with her claim in this diary entry that there were "no 'revolts' or desertions' ".

During the federal occupation of Jacksonville which commenced in February 1864, Esther began this school at the Odd Fellows Hall, which her husband Milton had earlier cleaned out and furnished with seats. The school, stocked with textbooks contributed by the Christian Commission, opened on Monday, February 29, 1864, with thirty pupils, only one of whom was black. On the second day of classes sixteen new black scholars enrolled. At day's end, Esther was informed by one of her white pupils, Miss Mary Magdalin Lamee, that her mother had made it clear that she could not continue attending if black children were taught there. "O very well," Esther replied, "if your Ma rather you wouldn't learn you must stay away, but the school is free to all." The school record indicates that Esther was saddened by this turn of events. "Said Mary is as ill looking a cub as there is in the lot—but not to blame for Ma's prejudices," she wrote.

Actually, Esther Hawks had good reason to bemoan the loss of Mary. She and her brother Frank were apparently the only two pupils of either color, advanced enough to read "read-

The northern mail brought me sad news! Eddie was in the battle under Butler and is 'missing'[80]—God grant that it be 'missing' to be found again! Another expedition leaves here today for 'Camp Finigan' or farther on: The 1*st* N.C. a part of the 17*th* Conn. and some other troops came in to join the expedition, last night Col. B. [Beecher] has not yet returned—he seems fated to be absent whenever his boys go into a fight. A letter from M. [Milton Hawks] says that Miner[81] is coming this way to look after me!

June 1*st*   The months of birds and roses—but our roses are all gone, and the birds are always making it June here.

School is smaller to-day—the expedition has taken my soldiers. There has been rapid and heavy firing by our gun boats this evening. A part of the troops went by water and a part by land—in order to surround, surprise and capture the rebs.

2*nd*.   No news from "the front" Mr. Henry and Chaplin Gregg rode out this morning to join them.

---

ily." Some, including one white, who was twenty-two-years old, did not even know their letters.

Racial tensions increased among parents, despite cooperation and friendliness among pupils of both races. The white children, according to Esther were, if anything, more poorly dressed and dirtier than the colored ones, but there was "an evident disposition among white noses to turn up at the colored ones." Esther Hawks, despite a New York *Tribune* article which quoted her as saying that the races were pursuing studies "harmoniously," anticipated declining white attendance. She was not mistaken. One parent violently withdrew her child who had come to school without permission, threatening to "break his bones."

At the end of six weeks, but one white child remained, though many had made "creditable improvement" in the first chance most of them had ever had to enjoy schooling. Parental opposition among whites, according to Esther Hawks,

> was greatly augmented by many of our officers, who thought
> it was quite shocking to have white and black children sent
> to the same school, encouraging the idea that if kept from
> this, a free white school would soon be started for them.
> This has not been done, though the need of such a school is
> very great. The streets are full of white children, who
> out of school hours, are the friends and playmates of our
> pupils, and I confess that I dislike to have them exposed
> to such *demoralizing influences!* The white children come
> about the door looking wistfully in, but if I ask them to
> come in, they invariably say, "Ma won't let me come."

Ellen M. Patrick, "Address," *Tributes of Respect and Love From Associates and Friends, Read at the Remembrance Service Held at the Friends' Meeting House of Silsbee Street, Lynn, Massachusetts, May 30, 1906, In Honor of the Late Dr. Esther H. Hawks,* (Lynn, Mass.: Boys' Club Press, 1906) p. 12.: School record of Jacksonville; Hawks Papers, Esther H. Hawks "Freedmen's School in Florida,"; New York *Tribune*, April 1, 1864.

80. Esther Hawks' brother Pvt. Edward O. Hill was captured by the Confederates on May 16, 1864, at the Battle of Drury's Bluff, Va., and confined in Richmond. Memorandum From Prisoner of War Records, Military Service Record of E. O. Hill, (National Archives).

81. Dr. John Milton Hawks' brother, Capt. Miner Hawks.

3rd   Gen. Gordon got frightened[82]—feared a 'flank' movement on the part of the enemy cutting off his retreat to Jacksonville. Saw a few rebel Cavelry and had a little skirmishing. Dr. M. [Marcy] estimates that about a hundred mounted men, drove back our brave *3,000*. It is evident that our General *ran*, and that he is a timid old woman who ought to be 'cuddled' with herbs and flannel, instead of leading brave soldiers! The men are very much exhausted by their long and rapid marching through the excessive heat of two days—and many fell out by the way and were picked up by the ambulances.

5th-Sunday.

The morning is very cool and cloudy, It rained through the night. Col. B. [Beecher] returned last evening *without* a wife. She, for some unexplainable cause connected with *passes* not being able to get passage. The Col. is of course very miserable over it—is a *little* afraid of being laughed at. Spent the evening here with Dr. M. [Marcy] and went home quite cheerful. It was late when we retired then Miss B. [Barcalow] had one of her 'hysterics fits' which kept me awake till after two this morning—then of course I must wake at *five* so I anticipate a *'greivous'* day.

June 19th Sunday—

The days glide by, so much alike that there is no mark to put on them. As I draw near the close of school my labors are increased, as I wish to have a little exabition for the children's friends and we are as busy in preparing as the weater will permit. Sunday School flourishes and I have every reason to feel glad that I have been able to do this work—tho' as Col. Beecher, said to me last evening "It has been a *thankless* work—no one *knows* or *cares* anything about it or appreciates the amount of labor or of good you have done here." —but I feel an inward consciousness of duty faithfully performed and I *know* it is not all in vain. My scholars love me and they have made great improvement in every direction!

This is the *'rainy* season'—and during last week the sun did'nt shine but on one day—constant and heavy rain with a heavy sultry atmosphere—its hard breathing!

June 29th

Just four months to-day since I commenced the first free school in this place! and every school-day, since then I have been in it! It has been to me

---

82. Brig. Gen. George H. Gordon, who in the books he wrote after the war put forth a more heroic interpretation of his military career.

A Woman Doctor's Civil War

a labor of 'love' and of great interest—and I feel amply rewarded for all
my pains-taking in the good improvement of the children—and in feeling
that I have so great an influence over such a wide circle of children's
hearts. I know they love me, because *I love them!*[83]

Examinations passed off quite satisfactorily. The school behaved admirably, said their lessons, sang their songs and recited their 'pieces' to the
delight of every one; Several officers were present and addressed the
school. The house was well filled with the friends of the children. An orderly Sergt. from the 54. Mass. here in hospital made the *best* speach of
the occasion—forcible and right to the point. I felt proud of him! The
children looked bright and clean and some of them were beautifully
dressed!

Today has been the great day for them. I have long promised them a
pic-nic—so great preparations have been on foot for it—and they have all
enjoyed themselves till *tired*. The table of refreshments was abundant
and looked as nice as any I ever saw. It was spread in the gallery and beautifully decorated with flowers. A soldier with his violin soon made his appearance and little feet and older ones too, danced till weary. Capt.
Spaulding[84] of the 7*th* U.S.C.T. came in and soon after I got a match started, he leading off with little Carrie Williams, I next with Julia and Charley
Murry. The children were delighted! —Then after another dance three
little children aged 5: yers, sang 'John Brown," all joining in the chorus.
— After refreshments—they played and danced till dark, a refreshing
shower having given us all new vigor. It has been one of the hottest days
of the season.

June 31*st*   Spent the day at Picolati [Picolata]—with Col. B. [Bee-
cher]. He and Regt. returning on boat with us. Eventful day to me.

---

83. The enthusiasm of the black pupils at this school "would inspire even the dullest of
teachers," Esther Hawks wrote. The children were not only prompt and regular in attendance but were quick to learn. At the close of school she reported that a class of twenty-four
could recite the entire multiplication table fluently. Some could perform written examples
on the slate or black board through the first three rules in *Adams' Arithmetic* and explain
the rest intelligibly. Progress had been made in spelling, geography, and other subjects. "Do
not forget that these are black children, lately held as property, and quite as unfamiliar with
arithmetic and writing as their masters' other 'beasts of burden'," explained Esther.

The Jacksonville school was not attended exclusively by children. Fifty soldiers from different regiments attended regularly. Other men, exempt from military duties and employed
as laborers, cooks and waiters, would hurry in and eagerly urge "please Miss, hear my lesson right soon, I must go in an hour." School Record of Jacksonville; Hawks Papers; Esther
H. Hawks, "Freedmen's School in Florida," *The Commonwealth*, (Boston), September 9,
1864, pp. 1, 2.

84. Capt. Harlin P. Spaulding.

July *6th*

It has seemed like Sunday all of the week! The *4th* was one of the quiet-est days I ever spent. Only a national salute fired at noon broke the Sabath stillness—quite a party of officers and citizens left here on Sunday for St. Augustine, where some demonstrations of a patriotic character were an-ticipated. We remained in doors until evening. Had several callers—and about 4 P.M. the "Drum Corps" of the *3rd* USC.T. (many of whom were members of my school) attended by a crowd of 'friends and admires, halted in front of my door, honoring me with a 'Serenade'. It was an un-expected delight and I appreciated it highly. They played well, a number of patriotic airs, then gave three cheers for their friend and teacher and departed in high good humor. This was the only *noise* I heard through the day. Just at night being disappointed in our anticipation of a boat ride (could'nt obtain the loan of a boat) Col. Beecher brought horses and we took a gallop out to the picket posts and through town just escaping a violent shower which came pouring down in torrents in a few minutes after we reached home. Col. B. Provost *Marshal-Sherman*[85] and *Judge Advocate* Hodges spent the evening, "far into the night" with us, in pleasant chat. Thus quietly passed the usually noisy day and now Miss B. [Barcalow] and I, are anxeously waiting transportation to Hilton Head— on our way to home and friends once more!—

85. Probably Capt., later brevetted Lt. Col. George R. Sherman.

[The Sea Islands]

Morris Island. —Camp of 21*st* U.SCTs July 22*nd* 1864.[86]
Left Jacksonville on the 17*th* inst. in company of Miss B. [Barcalow]
who has been sick with fever ever since last writing, making my labors *almost* "greater than I could bear—for my duty to the destitute and sick
must not be neglected. The weather has been excessively hot. Mr. Dodge
has gone north—leaving many of his duties devolving on me, besides taking our '*bread order*' with him, so that for some *ten* days I was *litterally*
reduced to '*begging* my *daily bread*', as there is an order prohibiting the
sale of bread or flour to any but officers—so 'Provost Marshall' has sent
us some, daily.

Tus. July 19*th*
On Sat. morning of 16*th* Lt. Sherman sent us word that the *Canonicus*
would leave for Hilton Head at 'M' [?]. We had about three hours to make
all necessary preparations in—and by the the timely aid of Hosp. Steward
of 55*th* we succeeded in being on board at the appointed time—attended
by quite as *long* a *train* of *officer friends*, as usually surround the 'Secesh'
ladies when they make temporary absences. I felt badly to leave the little
"Parsonage" where I have been so happy! during the past five months!
Happy days, dear, kind friends! pleasant toil—all now labeled "things
that were!"

We were obliged to lie inside the bar until Monday morning it being
considered to rough outside for our little boat. Got news, while there
that the expedition which left Jacksonville under command of Gen. Birney on the morning of 15*th* were on or near Nassau river—had captured a
number of horses and cattle and a few prisoners and had sent out for reinforcements from 4*th* Reg.

---

86. Hawks' regiment, the Twenty-first U.S.C.T. had been at Morris Island, S.C., since February 1864.

Reached Hilton Head Monday evening between nine and ten—only stop'd a few minutes but went to Beaufort to unload the "Sanitary" [Commission] goods, which have all been removed from J. [Jacksonville]. Went on shore Tues. morn. and got Miss B. [Barcalow] cared for then went to Dr. Durrants; but returned to the 'Head' on same boat before noon. Met Mrs. Dewhurst and two other ladies on board on their way to Morris I. On landing, went directly to Q. M. Moore,[87] who was very kind and gave me all the aid he could in getting here. Spent the night with Mrs. Pillsbury and Wed. eve. at ten o' clock the *Peconis* left the wharf, with us ladies on board bound for "Lighthouse Inlet"—where we arrived at eight next morn—had no trouble about landing, our 'passes' being all-sufficient—and here I am all safe at last.

While eating dinner, one of the most violent thunder storms I ever witnessed, came up. I expected we should all be blown into the sea. The "Signal Station"—built of timbers—and about eighty ft. high was blown down—a man was on top at the time but escaped without serious injury. The rain continued to fall at intervals all the afternoon, and as night set in "the winds blew and the rains' fell" till not a dry spot could be found in our tent—and it seemed to me, we should all blow away to-gether—but we did'nt!

Sunday July 24*th*. Morris' Island Hd. Qtrs. 21*st* U.S.C.I.

Since my arrival, the storms which usher'd in my coming, has continued with unabated fury—and I have only been out of the tent to go to my meals. It has been to cool for comfort. I *have suffered* for the want of *winter clothes*. As I sit in our tent, the door opens to-wards the sea. Three 'Monitors' like faithful sentinels lie are in view just a little way from shore—all silent and Stationary. A little farther down rises the head of the ill-fated *Keokuk*,[88] and all about are the other vessels of the fleet—all stagnant. The Navy is getting into rather poor repute here. Its "masterly inactivity" is being set down to *cowardice*, rather that strategy. An attempt was made two nights since to blow up Fort Sumpter [Sumter], but the exceeding roughness of the weather prevented the carrying out of the proposed plan, which will be again attempted in a few nights.

The incessant roar of the sea as it dashes its huge waves against the shore almost at our feet, makes a mournful music like the low-minor keys of some wind instrument touched by skillful fingers.

---

87. Captain John H. Moore, Chief Quartermaster, Department of the South.
88. The *Keokuk* was an experimental ironclad steamer sunk by Confederate guns fired from Fort Sumter during an attempted naval assault on Charleston in April 1863.

July 27*th* Morris' Island So. Ca.

My impression of Morris' Island, before seeing it—was of a long low sand bar, similar to some of those in Tampa Bay, with not even a blade of green grass on it—and I am pleasantly disappointed in that I find it larger and greatly diversified with *hills* of sand and covered with grasses, among which the tall 'sea-oats' is very conspicuous and abundant. The various regiments, of which there are five or six besides detatchments of artillery etc. are ranged along the beach facing the open sea—giving the Island the appearance of a thickly populated city, as we approach it from the water—besides securing to the soldiers — the constant, fresh sea breezes—and very fresh they have been since I came here. A thin *woolen dress* has'nt been uncomfortable and the mouslins which I wore in Florida most certainly would be.

Our Reg. is located in about the centre of the troops—and within reach of rebel shells when they choose to send them. The camping ground is much pleasanter than at Hilton Head and the Officers have taken greater pains in fixing up their quarters than ever before.—The men have new uniforms with leggings. The 'drum-corpse' has been enlarged-drilled and uniformed so that the regiment presents a much finer appearance than ever before. There is considerable sickness just now—tho' but one has died since coming on the Island. Seventeen, from one Company were drowned on the night of the 2*nd* July, while on the 'James' Island' Expedition—occasioned by the carelessness of the Capt. of the 'Steamer' which attempted to tow them across the river. This cast a gloom over the regiment, which would not have resulted had they fallen in battle. — The men are eager for me to recommence school. Many of them have made good improvement during the five months that I have been out of the Reg.

Yesterday, 26*th*   The day being fine we rode in an 'Ambulanse' up to the 'front'—driving the whole way along the smoothe hard beach with ocean's majestic hymn sounding in our ears—while a note of deeper bass and more portentious meaning, peled from the iron throats of [Fort] 'Gregg' at regular intervals! We pass the ruins of a house which stood near the beach when our forces first came here. Two small, new houses, with grated windows next caught the eye—looking like a couple of large bird-gages. These are the residences for the rebels prisoners in retaliation for the exposure of our men by the rebs in Charleston. In speaking of it, the Lt. in command at Ft. Putnam nee Gregg—hoped they would'nt be brought their—it was "so barbareous". Poor sniveling fool! how quick to compassionate when rebels are to be endangered!

We stopped first at Wagna [Wagner] historic name—and I felt that here surely I trod on sacred soil. At first view, I was disappointed. Everything about and in the Ft. was in such perfect order. The little strip of garden in front of the Comdg officer's tent door—the flowers in all the apparent security of their native homes, the Magazines turfed over with grass—and even the monster guns which have sent dessolation into so many homes, looked peaceful, basking in the hot sun. But as we traversed the different parts—visited the Magazines—then under all the "bomb-proofs', like vast subteranean vaults, I confess that my ideas, as to the area of Wagner had to expand. I had a curious picture in my mind of a 'bomb-proof' —do not remember of ever hearing a description of one. I imagined them cavities behind some projection walled up and large enoug to hold two or three—into which the men run on seeing a shell coming—instead—I find great chambers roofed with hung logs —capable of holding *regiments*. A smaller room with boards ranged on the side for offices to sleep on—and everywhere most perfect order and neatness. Most of the work was done by the rebels —tho' the Capt. told us it was in the filthyest condition possible when it came into our hands. Two large, guns taken with the Ft. like the leaders of the rebellion have traitorously turned against their former friends—and now *bark* as loud and as willing for us as they did for them. I gathered N.E. "barn-grass" and the sweet red clover so common to our hills, from the spot where our Putnam,[89] brave and honored name, fell— and right across, on the other corner of the paraphet—another consecrated spot, the gallant—the heroic Shaw—led on his 'black avengers', and fell for a hope worth fighting for and a Country worth *dyeing* for! May she prove herself worthy of the sacrifice! My mind went back through the short year that has passed, to the eventful 18*th* of July /63, when the whole country was thrilled with the daring charge on this most formidable Fort: and I remembered how the torn-and mangled bodies were brought into hospital to us; —how brave and patient the men who had dared and *lost* so much—and it was hard to realize that my feet stood on the soil soaked through and *through* with our Countries' richest blood! I should have taken off the shoes from my feet and with head uncover'd, trod with silent reverence over such hallowed earth! —but all the excitement of actual *war* is about us. Cannon, not with *blank car-*

---

89. Lt. Col. Haldimand Sumner Putnam, a regular army officer from New Hampshire killed in the charge on Fort Wagner, July 18, 1863.

tridges—belching forth destruction and death—pegging away at old 'Sumpter' [Sumter]—which, to the naked eye, looks like a great rough sand or clay heap very much battered by time and hard usage! but all our battering of the past ten days, with 'two-hundred pounders' has'nt made any visible impression—only to make the dirt fly! It being a clear day, Charleston lay, like a fine picture, visibly before us, and with the aid of a glass, laborers on the dock and on the Forts could be seen. It *looks* as though it might be one of the easiest things in the world to go into Charleston—and their is nothing visible on either Moultrie or Sumpter to prevent taken *peacable* possession—however, I would'nt care to be *one* of a party to make the attempt unless very anxious to "shuffle off this mortal coil."

Sullivan's Island smiled back to us showing her teeth of batteries all along the beach. All along the beach too, below Charleston are visible rebel batteries. To the right of the city lies Jame's [James] Is. the scene of our last military exploit. Yesterday morning four deserters were discovered in the marsh—naked and almost dead from exhaustion. They were brought in by one of our Lt's, on duty at Ft. Gregg and they report that if our fource, on the occasion of the last expedition had gone on instead of retreating, they would have taken the batteries of that Is. as the rebel force there is quite small—but this is what we always hear after a *failure!* —As we passed Ft. Seymore, we caught a glimps of the monstrous 300 lb. gun just mounted there—and just as we were opposite the mortars in "Chatfield' a huge shell from one of them, went tearing through the air, making us all jump and 'duck' our heads, and the concussion of the air was very sensibly felt. All along the road which we were now traversing, lay cannon balls, and unexploded rebel shell—sometimes we could count a dozen as we rode along. As we rode into the Ft. at Gregg we were saluted by thirty *pounder*—so close as to make us all jump again. The only guns fired from this Ft. just now, are these two 30 lbs. the 200 lbs guns being both disabled one burst the day before we were there. We went into the magazine and bomb proofs which resembled those at Wagna [Wagner]—only much smaller. Around the flag-staff is ranged rebel shells and pieces—with cannon ball piled one above another making quite a show. Things at "Gregg" are in rather a *loose* state just now, and if the rebs knew it we might "hear of something to *their advantage!*" We had a charming ride along the beach—which in some places, is full of roots and stumps of trees showing that, not long since, all this part of it was *dry land*, also illustrating the encroaching disposition of old ocean. Reached home just in time not to lose our dinner.

Morris' Island July 28*th* 1864

A fitful, April day; Through the fast coming drops of one of its showers, beamed in at our door the geniel Scotch face of Dr. Brown,[90] from the 55*th* Mass. Stationed on Folly Is.—How good it seems to meet such friends—how it brings back the old college days at Boston—skipping lightly over the years of bloody war intervening! —He spend most of the day with us—and have just returned from our walk on the beach with him on his return—rested at the Christian Com. [Commission].

Sunday July 31*st*   But for the refreshing breeze from the sea, it would be intensely hot to-day—and even this breeze sometimes seems so hot and dry as to almost burn.

Had a funeral in Camp yesterday—one of the men died of pneumonia—went to the burial. —This island, in going over it a little back from the beach, is just one great grave-yard! How many a poor fellow, who with hopeful, patriotic hearts, have left their homes; burning with zeal to do something for their Country—has found a grave in these marshes and sands! —It must be a sad spot to the sick and lonely soldier! Cut off almost, from the world, with none of the usual excitements accompanying a Military Post, on the mainland, not in direct communication with the mails. —kept on poor fare, that is, with but little chance for fresh food, and harder then all, constantly at work at such labor which to the soldier is most irksome—"fatigue duty". For the amount of work necessary to be done here, the number of troops is inadequate without overworking. I have heard the Adj. and several Capts. say that many of their men had been on duty *every* day for ten days——and this is likily to continue unless more troops are brought here. —

This evening we anticipated having "divine service" but just before the time to commence the rebs. sent us a couple of *shells* by way of showing their affectionate remembrance of us—and the meeting is defered much to the relief and satisfaction of Chaplain Jones[91] who is a great coward—and whenever there is any noise of shells near he is taken with an intense desire to visit the P.O. or 'Christian Commission,' both of which are situated out of the reach of rebel *compliments*! —The peculiar noise of a shell tearing through the air is enough to upset the *nerves* of a *novice*, but we old *campaigners* get used to them! (ahem!)

There comes another shell. —It burst over the camp just above ours and some of the pieces struck on the beach close by. I heard the fall—and

90. Dr. William Symington Brown, Surgeon of the Fifty-fifth Massachusetts Infantry, who had taught Esther at the New England Female Medical College.
91. Chaplain Erasmus W. Jones of the Twenty-first U.S.C.T.

Lt. Jacobs[92] says looked a little *pale*. —I did'nt feel so Five shells have passed over and about us this afternoon.

Morris' Island. August—1864.

3rd   There has been but little shelling since Sunday. A couple of shells came near the camp on Monday—and last night there was very heavy firing on both sides—but not directed towards the camps. It was the heavest firing, and the most rapid, I have yet heard.

Last night it being dark and everything propitious we went into the surf—bathing right in front of our tent. The great heavy waves dashed me about so that I found it difficult keeping my feet. I enjoyed it very much—but it is too rough to learn to swim. I had all I could do to keep from being dashed up on the beach by every wave that advanced.

Capt. Pope [Poppe] was here in the evening and told us that this morning at 10 o' clock an exchange of prisoners would be effected, in the harbor. These are the same for whom these three prisons on the uper end of the Island were built but they have never occupied them—and on the other side, they are the ones exposed by the rebels, in Charleston, to the fire of our guns. There are some forty offices on both sides. Three Generals—Gen. Seymore [Seymour] of the Florida Campagn is among the number. We could see both boats very plainly—as they approached each other but not near enough to see any of the transactions. Our boat was the old *Delaware*, the same which brought me into the Dep. [Department]. They lay alongside for some time and no doubt glorified the event over a little iced champaigne. —It must be a happy day for the prisoners! —A Captain and Lt. escaped prisoners, came in last night. They belong to some Ohio regt., and escaped by jumping from the cars during the transfer of prisoners up in Georgia. —There has been but little firing to-day. It is exceedingly hot and the glare of the sun on the white sand is blinding. I am longing for Northern breezes.

August–5*th* 1864.

One of the most difficult things to 'have a *realizing sense*' of, in this climate, is the *change* of *seasons*. April and August are so much alike it is hard knowing when one ends and the other begins—but *birthdays* will come round, and ones mirror is a more faithful friend than memory. If *mirrors* could be abolished I could not believe that I am *growing old*—but with these faithful friends present, before me I cannot forget the rolling years even if I would. The weather is intensely hot. Murcury at 7 ½

92. First Lt. John E. Jacobs of the Twenty-first U.S.C.T.

this morning stood at 80°. There is a constant sea-breeze or we should be great sufferers and the glare of the sun on the sand is very trying for the eyes. —Towards evening yesterday Capt. Pope [Poppe]—'Chief Inspecter' came with his horse and a two wheeled contrivance—called "the buggy"—and we rode up the beech to the old "beacon house" ruins. On our return who should we meet but Gen. Schimmelfenneg[93] he looked astonished—and no doubt concluded that I must be a *'mermaid* as what woman would *dare* be on this Island contrary to his order! I shall look for a polite invitation to leave!![94]

Aug. *6th*

Last evening Col. and Adj. came in—had a gay time. Soon after retiring—the rebs commenced shelling the camps, firing at intervals of twenty minutes all night causing a general state of uneasiness among the soldiers. Every few minutes some one would sing out *'cover'* then there would be a grand rush and immediately the whirr and explosion of the shell would be heard! Every fresh *arrival* would wake us—but we were as safe in our tents as any where so I did'nt get up. Several pieces of shells were found in camp in the morning.

    7th   Shelling continued again last night. A piece of shell fell and was picked up quite near our door. I have it as a *'relic* to take home with me. Boat leaves this morning for the 'Head' and on it go Col. B. [Beecher] and I enroute for N.Y. Dr. [J. M. Hawks] goes to the Head with us—so farewell to Morris' Island!

    Arrived at home on the 27*th* Aug.

---

93. Brig. Gen. Alexander Schimmelfennig.
94. Gen. Schimmelfennig's banning of women from Morris Island was explained by Milton Hawks, "His wife I believe wants to come, and he don't want her. She is a great scold, so the Genl. shuts down on all feminines." JMH to Sister Helen, June 14, 1864. Letter in possession of Mr. Philip Courier, Herkimer, N.H.

Editor's Note

Home was of course, New Hampshire, not merely Manchester, but Bradford, Brentwood, and other towns where Esther and Milton Hawks had family. The while Esther alternated between visiting, resting, and supervising repairs on the Hawks' house, she received mail from friends and colleagues in the South, some urging her return. Dr. H. O. Marcy wrote from the Jacksonville Headquarters of the 35th U.S.C.T., "Wish you were here. I would give you a *contract*. We are very short of Medical Officers."[95]

Milton, meanwhile, used his abundant spare time on Morris Island to brew up a keg of beer for the hospital, and to make a pint of his favorite ink, which he used in writing his letters to Esther.[96] That spare time became somewhat less abundant when six hundred rebel prisoners were brought to the newly constructed stockade on the island.[97] With his fellow physician, Dr. Durant, gone to Beaufort for several days, Dr. Hawks was left to attend to these prisoners, many of whom were suffering from diarrhea or dysentery.[98] For all his loathing of rebels, Milton was sympathetic to their plight, and applied successfully to his superiors for increased and improved rations for the prisoners in the form of tea and soft bread.[99] Hawks' frustration was great though, when on a trip to Hilton Head, he went to the office of the Medical Purveyor and found that a requisition which he had made weeks earlier had not arrived.[100]

It was during this period of Esther's absence in New England that Milton Hawks, the veteran abolitionist, wrote a letter which expressed his then current attitudes toward freedmen and their status:

Don't ask for any more aid for the Freedmen in this Department. They are all employed at good wages. It is almost impossible to get a servant or cook—everybody among the colored people seems to have enough to do. They ought to be taxed to pay for their schooling. It is well enough to give them a start when they first escape from Slavery, but as soon as they can be made self sustaining they should be.[101]

95. H. O. Marcy to EHH, August 31, 1864, Hawks Papers.
96. JMH to EHH, August 25, 1864.
97. JMH to EHH, September 7, 1864.
98. JMH to EHH, September 18, 1864.
99. JMH to EHH, September 28, 1864.
100. JMH to EHH, October 8, 1864.
101. JMH to EHH, September 22, 1864.

A Woman Doctor's Civil War

In late September Dr. Hawks' regiment received several months worth of long overdue back pay.[102] Within days thereafter he applied for a thirty-day leave, reminding the hesitant Medical Director to whom he submitted his application, that he had never before requested leave in over two years of military service.[103] Dr. Hawks was proud too, as one who placed great stock in preventive medicine, that not a single officer or enlisted man in his care was confined by sickness to tent or hospital.[104] In late October, Milton was granted his furlough, and joyously informed Esther, "I shall hasten to your arms," which he did aboard the *Fulton*, out of Port Royal.[105]

The Hawks rested and recuperated together for some weeks, then prepared to return to their duties in the South.

102. JMH to EHH, September 28, 1864.
103. JMH to EHH, October 8, 1864.
104. JMH, Surgeon Twenty-first U.S.C.T. to Assistant Surgeon Ramsey, U.S. Army Act'g Medical Director, Department of the South, October 14, 1864. Military Service Record of John Milton Hawks, National Archives.
105. JMH to EHH, October 25, 1864.

Hilton Head S.C. Nov. 1864

Left N. E. on the night of 21*st* one of the darkest I ever knew. There was some doubts about our being able to go across the 'Sound' it was so dark and rainy but on arriving at New London the boat was in readiness and we started going slowley, arriving in N.Y. somewhat late but in due season. Dr. met me at the boat, and reported all ready for starting at 10. A.M.—The morning was warm and sunny and the mud made the streets *almost* impassable—such mud! seen no where out of N.Y. after a rain!

Came on the *Fulton*. The weather was most delightful the entire voyage. Went into Ft. Monroe—so that we were out five days arriving here—on Sunday the 26*th* Went up to Mr. Pillsbury's where they had 'Thanksgiving dinner' in waiting for us. Learned that the troops from Fla. and other Posts were expected in, going on an expedition no one knew where or for what purpose. That night and all next day, the harbor and wharf presented a busy scene. Went down on wharfs to see if there was an opportunity to go to Beaufort. Met Col. Beecher (whose regt had arrived during the night, and lay out in the stream) and Dr. Marcy, God bless him, and several other offices from the 34 & 35 regts. but found no boat for B. [Beaufort]. Met Dr Durrant, who told me he was going on the expedition and wished I'd go up and stay with his wife which I promised to do at the first opportunity.

The expedition is under command of Gen. Hatch,[106] so nobody expects very much of it.

28*th*   Dr. [J. M. Hawks] is ordered to go to the Front where there seems likely to be some hot work.

29*th*   *Cosmopolatin* [Cosmopolitan] came down today bringing 70 wounded[107] and reports of a terrible blunder on our part resulting in a defeat of object in view namely, to destroy Lacolatiage [?] bridge—but our troops have a foothold on the mainland and seem determined to hold it.

29*th*   The air is full of rumors—of [Gen. William T.] Sherman's proximity; of our dead and wounded;—The citizens here are all on guard, scarce a soldier being left in the place. Last night five of the rebel prison-

---

106. Brig. Gen. John Porter Hatch. Though he was twice brevetted for gallantry during the Mexican War, Hatch's subsequent military career was spent at dreary stations in Oregon and Texas and as acting chief commissary in New Mexico. Early in the Civil War he led cavalry in the Shenandoah Valley but with little distinction. After being seriously wounded Hatch performed duties on courts-martial, in command of cavalry rendezvous, and in garrisons throughout the Department of the South.

107. The *Cosmopolitan* was a small transport that drew little water and was able to navigate the Broad and Beaufort rivers. It was fitted up for hospital service in 1863.

ers at the Provost, escaped and have not yet been retaken. There is much excitement about town.

Went up to Hospital to-day, along the beach with Mrs. P. [Pillsbury] and Jenny—another lot of wounded brought in. Hear that Col. B. [Beecher] is badly wounded and Col. Marple[108] a prisoner.

30th   Offered my services to Surgeon in charge at Hospital and am to go up to-morrow to assist among the wounded—the white soldiers are all brought here and the colored go up to Beaufort. Mrs. P. [Pillsbury] has been sick during the week and I have been in school everyday. The school is not as pleasant as mine at Jacksonville[.] It has averaged about 20. per. day. The children are more difficult to manage—don't mind as readily— perhaps I'm a partial judge. It is not over pleasant being here and I am homesick to get away.

Beaufort December, 1864

On the evening of the 30th Dr. [J. M. Hawks] came down on *Cosmopolitan* in charge of 50. wounded; Found a little boat going up to B. [Beaufort] and about nine in the evening we went on board expecting to wake up at the wharf in B. but no such good fortune awaited us so at dawn Dr. [J. M. Hawks] went ashore, to be ready to take a boat for the 'front' at the earliest opportunity while I awaited the "course of events" with such fortitude as I could on board boat. We were long in starting and it was noon when we arrived here. Mrs. D. [Durant] was very glad to see me, and I feel more at home, than at Hilton Head.

Sunday went to church—and Sabbath school—met many old friends. The children and colored people here all know me. It is good to be remembered!

Dec. 2nd   Went to see Col. Beecher at officer's hospital—not so badly wounded as represented—will not loose his limb. But quite some ball still in the leg. He is cheerful and spicy as usual—and quite as *lively*!

Dec. 7th   Have spent the week among the wounded at the different hospitals. Found many old friends-and plenty to do in writing letters reading, and comforting such as need it. Col. B. is doing well. Mrs. B. [Beecher] arrived from Jacksonville on Tuesday eve, She is a dear little woman—no one can resist loving her! Col. Hartwell of 55th[109] and Col. Gurney of 127th N.Y.[110] are wounded and in the same room with Col. B.

---

108. Col. William W. Marple, commander of the Thirty-fourth U.S.C.T.
109. Col. Alfred S. Hartwell.
110. Col. William Gurney.

[Beecher]. A great many officers have been disabled. Many new hospital are being fitted up, and to-day I have had charge of the fitting of a large building on Bay St., to be used for officers as the one now in use is quite full. It is cold and I am very tired.

Last Monday Mrs. Cooley,[111] Mrs. Durrant and I rode out to the Ferry to see our fleet and hear if possible what was going on over the river. We prepared a nice lunch and made up our minds for a fine time. The other ladies went in a buggy and just *I* on horseback—but Mrs. D's little pony is so easy that I arrived there with but slight discomfort. We could learn nothing but a repetition of the rumors rife in town so after wandering about, for an hour or so under those magnificent oaks, and partaking of refreshments we started for home, where we arrived at about dark I quite satisfied with horseback exercise. This is the longest ride I have ever take —(the distance twenty miles) and I expected to suffer severely from it but have been able to do my duties in hospital every day though I must own to considerable *stiffness*.

Wednesday about Midnight Dr. [J. M. Hawks] came in to our *sleeping room*—having just arrived, with 50 wounded—and had to return in the morning.

Sat. spent the day on board the *N. Y.* with the return prisoners, who have just been exchanged and are on the way north; Stopped here for coal. Spent the night at Mrs. Strongs' with Mrs. Fowler; (who came with Chaplain on boat *Arago*)[112] and learned that a boat would go to the Head in the morning and one leave then during the day, for Jacksonville and I determine to go on it.

---

111. Mrs. Jane Cooley, a teacher from Massachusetts.
112. The *Arago* was a government steamer that served as a shuttle between New York and Hilton Head.

[Florida]

Jacksonville Fla. Dec. /64

Left Hilton Head on Monday eve about sunset, on the *Mary A Board-man*. There were eight other ladies passengers—the cabin small and accommodations none of the best,—was sea-sick all night. Went into Fernandina next day about noon where we must stop as this boat returned immediately to P.R. [Port Royal] but as good fortune would have it the *Collins* lay at the wharf ready to go to J. [Jacksonville] the next morning so we left the boat in excellent spirits. Mr. Dennett[113] went with me up to the 'Asylum' where we met a cordial welcome from Miss Merrick[114] and all the household. They are a pleasant family. Fernandina is a far prettier place than I expected to find and the "Finnegan [Finegan] house" the finest located-at-quite an elevation from the water, the prospect from it is charming. Then it is a great roomy house, surrounded by verandas and hemmed in with trees which enclose a beautiful yard. The house is comfortably furnished and has now 18 little orphan children residents—they all looked neatly dressed and contented. Great preparations were going forward for Christmas so the house was like a bee hive. Four of the teachers live there, fine intelligent ladies with hearts in their labors. Left next morning at 8 o'clock on the *Collins* a "*love* of a *boat*" and it is said of her that "she *rolls* when tied to the dock'! so we had a "sweet" time after getting over the bar. She pitched forward and rolled sideways in a most fearless and astonishing manner! We had gone to the forward part of the boat on first starting—and had to remain there clinging to the ropes and each other to prevent being rolled into the water. After several hours of most

---

113. N. C. Dennett, a superintendent appointed by Gen. Saxton to look after freedmen who had gathered in such Florida east coast towns as Fernandina and Jacksonville.
114. Chloe Merrick of Syracuse, N.Y., who had bought the Fernandina home of Gen. Joseph Finegan for a fraction its worth and had converted it into an orphanage for black children in 1864. The orphanage was supported and operated by the New York Branch of the Freedmen's Union Commission. It was ultimately moved to Magnolia, Fla., when Gen. Finegan was permitted to redeem his home,

unhappy postures until I ached in every joint, two gents assisted me over to the pilot house, but it soon commenced raining so we were obliged to go below. I lay down in somebodies berth. The cabin was full of men, smoking and playing cards—wasnt much sick, only enough to keep my head on the pillow. Made the acquaintance of Maj. Hatch, Pay Master, very kind. Arrived at the wharf at dark and proceeded directly to Mr. Dennetts. (the house formerly occupied by Mr. Dodge). Found a pleasant welcome, a good supper, (of which I stood very much in need having fasted since morning) a poor night's rest and miserable headache next day. The weather is cooler—so cold as to be uncomfortable without a fire.

Dec 23*rd*   Went into school this morning and said 'hodye' to the children. There were great exclaimations all over the house as I went in. "Miss Hawk has come" I heard on every side and their bright eyes glistened with delight as I went to speak to each one. It is pleasant to find ones self so fondly remembered even by poor little black children. I go along in the street and from every house and yard I am greeted with the delighted exclaimation "Thers Miss Hawk." and occasionally one rushes out, gets hold of my dress or hand and before I can extricate myself, I am surrounded by my dusky admirers—then they come by the dozens to the house to see me. It is all very pleasant, but I miss my little home up in the "Parsonage" and the kind friends who blessed it by their frequent presence!

Sat. 24*th*   Christmas Eve—spent it at Mr. Lt-Col Willards[115] with the other ladies. Several offices present—Sang and played 'children's games'! very dignified! It was past midnight when we reached home. To complete our childishness—hung up our stockings in the chimny-corner and found them well filled next morning with sugar-plums &.

25*th*   Went to church and Sunday school. Mr. Swaim[116] the preacher is one of the stupid kind. His sermon was merely *words* no soul—no sense in them—nothing for a hungry soul or heart. It was the most expressionless discours I ever listened to—and this is to be our spiritual aid here! He has a strong desire to please the white inhabitants yet does not wish to loose the colored—so in the morning his words are turned to fit white ears, and in the afternoon black ones are to be accomodated. Two

115. Lt. Col. Ammiel J. Willard of the Thirty-fifth U.S.C.T.
116. New Jersey born Rev. John S. Swaim, who would later be appointed first pastor of Jacksonville's Trinity Methodist Episcopal Church.

Sabbath-schools are also run. I am afraid that, between the two *horses*, he may "come to *grief.*"

26*th*   Went to a party-given by Capt. Hart[117] — enjoyed it right well—quite a large gathering. Had dancing—no objectionable people present. On Wednesday Eve we all went up to Mrs. Willards to another party. Had singing and dancing and games—the whole winding up with a grand "negro minstrel performance" very laughable and so we all laughed—our hearts content, and came merrily home after midnight. Sat. afternoon was going to assist in the entertainment given at the school for white children but Capt. Hodges came in—just arrived from the north on the last boat, so I prefered his company to theirs and stayed at home.

In the evening the singing class and several others were here to watch with us the coming of the new Year. We had trimed our rooms, so they look charmingly, and also provided refreshments, so we had a '*jolly*' time. Sang songs—played a few games and acted foolish generally. Sorry ending for /64.

Jacksonville Fla. January 1865

1*st*   All through the pleasant sunny day, we have been busy triming our rooms for a 'happy New Year' at night a pleasant company gathered here. Mrs. Lt. Col. Willard, Maj. Bodwell[118] Capts. Hodges & Gates[119] and Lts. Barber Marcellus and Turner;[120] all fine singers and good principled young men—officers of the 3*rd* U.S.C.Ts. We had refreshments at ten. Some of the company stayed till after the old year had departed. We spent the time in singing and recitations and pleasant chit-chat. The *Delaware* came in and left in the evening for Savannah—only staying here a few hours—so we were all busy preparing mail matter.

Capt. H. [Hodges] came and went to church with me. Yesterday I thought him unchanged by his home visit—but today, I see that he *is* changed and to-night he goes, without regret, on the *Delaware* to be A.A.A.G. [Acting Assistant Adjutant General] on Gen. Fosters'[121] staff. "Requiescat" Wrote to Dr. H. [J. M. Hawks] and that was the only letter I succeeded in getting off. Mrs. D. [?] sent me a bundle of letters from Beau-

---

117. Probably Capt. George D. Hart of the Third U.S.C.T.
118. Probably Major Frederick W. Bardwell, Third U.S.C.T.
119. Capt. Jaalam Gates, Thirty-fifth U.S.C.T.
120. Firsts Lts. Issac R. Barbour, Jr., Samuel S. Marseilles, and Pierpont C. Turner.
121. Maj. Gen. John Gray Foster who commanded the Department of the South in the last year of the war, and later the Department of Florida.

A Woman Doctor's Civil War

fort, by Capt. Bennett, one, among them from Mrs. Stevenson,[122] informing me that I have been 'adopted' by a branch society in Boston, which
would soon communicate with me, but there has been no letter yet.

Jan. *8th*   No mail yet! Not a boat at this Post. School flourishes. We
have about 50 in the afternoon, of the advanced pupils and they are making good progress.

The week has passed about as all the others. I have been housekeeper
but the duties are not severe. Resigned my sceptre this morning into the
hands of *Bottsy*[123] who will make a most notable 'housekeeper'. — We
have had the usual amount of visiting Spent one evening at Mrs. Willards
and last eve, as usual, they were all here to sing. Today been to church
and Sunday-school as usual. Last eve called at Mr. Swains [Swaim]. Met
Mr. Robert[124] and Mr. Reynolds[125] of N.Y. there and had a long discussion
on the condition of the poor people, both black and white "in this Dept.
On my mentioning my desire to start a sewing school among the children
but that I could, not for the want of funds, Mr. Robert asked how much I
needed to start with, I thought if I had even ten dollars, I could make a beginning—he immediately drew out his wallet, saying "Well Mrs. H. I'll
start the sewing school if that amount will do it." It is quite a donation
and we must make it productive of good. I am to report to him its results.

Jan. *15*

Another week gone! The weather has been to cold to do anything
about our sewing school. Have visited most of the people, find them
much improved in their physical condition since last Summer. The general health is good—and all seem to be industrious. I meet happy greetings
wherever I go.

Monday eve. Mrs. W. [Willard] Maj. B. [Bardwell] Lts M. [Marseilles] &
B. [Barbour] spent here, had 'charades', singing &—and on Wed. eve all
went up to Mrs. W's [Willard]; had *fun* and *frolic*! —We do not get many
invites from the *natives* here, nor do do they honor us by calling, as they
do on other northern ladies. We are evidently *unpopular* even with our
northern ladies and most of our officers tho' there are only officers of
colored troops here—Amen.

122. Hannah E. Stevenson, who was Secretary of the Boston Educational Commission
which later became the New England Freedmen's Aid Society.
123. Fannie J. Botts of Syracuse, N.Y.
124. Christopher Rhinelander Robert, a New York financier and member of the American
Union Commission. A philanthropist, Robert founded Robert College in Constantinople
and a school in Chattanooga for "mountain whites," and was much given to spontaneous
contributions such as the one described by Esther Hawks.
125. Unidentified.

Mr Reynolds preached for Mr. Swaim to-day and it is the first preaching I have listened to since my return. He said nothing new nothing I hav'nt known for years but he talked as though he felt what he said and had'nt been a *fossil* for centuries.

The *Comet* has come in from Fernandina and goes to the 'Head'—leaving here this eve. About a hundred present at Sunday School after it was over, Miss B. [?] and I went up to camp of 35*th* to see some of my old friends among the soldiers, on the sick list—talked, and read a few chapters in the bible to them—then went into the church where there was a 'colored meeting'—after went into Mrs. Willard's stop't to tea and spent the evening. Maj. B. [Bardwell], Lt. M. [Marseilles] & Barber [Barbour], in, sang chants &—came home at 9'o'clock.

Went to two horseback rides last week with Maj Bodwell [Bardwell] — the first, on Thursday got up by Mrs. W. [Willard] was rather *disasterous* —and came near being a *tragedy*. The party consisted of, Maj. B. and myself. I mounted on a *powerful chargers* of the Maj's'. Miss Botts of Mr. Dennetts 'Nelly' Capt. Johnson, and Mrs. Willard on Mrs. Martell's horse. In starting "Nelly" run with Miss Botts, the styrup broke and all came to the ground, with no injury save a few scratches on poor Bottsy, again mounted, the Maj. and I rode off, leaving her to the care of the Capt. My horse got the spirit of mischief in him, so *he run* and such a dash as we must have cut! on arriving at Mrs. W's [Willard] we left the Capt. to get another horse for poor Bottsy and took a little ride outside the entrenchments—but Mrs. W's horse *balked*—refused to stir a step—but with much pulling and coaxing was induced to take a *small* canter then came to a dead halt again and so on—meanwhile, Botts, splendidly mounted dashed by—then we left the Capt. and Mrs. W. [Willard] and went on— but soon finding they did not come went back to them, then Mrs W. and Capt. J. [Johnson] changed horses, then after a little Mrs. W. and Miss B. [Botts] changed and my saddle turned for the *third time*, and we got started again. My horse run again and everybody was most generally uncomfortable. I was glad to get home, lame and sore as if I had ridden twenty miles.

Sat. Maj. [Bardwell] came and invited me to go again, I did'nt feel much like it but offer of a ride was too tempting so I accepted. The party consisted of Mrs. W. & Lt. Mc.Corng [?] Mr & Mrs. Day, [?] Maj. & I, and we had a most charming ride—no disasters, no unpleasantness!! —In the evening the sewing class met here with the addition of Mr. and Mrs. Day.

15*th*
Our Sunday-school is large and very interesting. To-day there were a hundred pupils present. I have a large class of soldiers—about fifteen in

all—good readers bright—and quick. We take a chapter in the Testament have it read then *talk* it over; I find them very ready with answers!

16*th*   Spent the morning with Mrs. Reed, wife of Q. M. who is sick with fever. She is a little childish thing and clings to me as though I was her mother; She is quite a tax upon our kindness. Went up to Mrs. Willards after Sunday school. On our way, called at the camp of the 35*th* to see some of my old friends who were left behind, sick. Read a few chapters for them—for which they were duly grateful then went into the church, where the soldiers were having a meeting—reached Mrs. W. s about five—stayed to tea and spent the evening in singing. Maj. B. [Bardwell] Lt. B. [Barbour] and Marcellus [Marseilles] were there. Came home at 9-o'clock.

Jan. 20*th*

It has been cold or rainy all the week The morning schools has been interupted very much but mine is always present so I have kept the usual hours not withstanding the inclemency of the weather.

Wednesday eve we all went up to Mrs. W.s [Willard]; She gives 'receptions' once a week—elegant little affairs. She understands getting up entertainments. Had music—dancing, charades, and refreshments Maj. [Bardwell] came home with us, as *usual*! It was proposed that the party meet at our house on Thursday eve. and have *reading* as part of the entertainment, but last night was so rainy—it was postponed indefinitely.

26*th*

On the morning of the 22*nd*, by invitation of Q. M. [Quarter Master] Moore, I joined a party of pleasure seekers on board the Steamer *Delaware*, destined for St. Augustine. Gen. Scammon[126] and several of his staff offices were of the number. The morning was rainy and a heavy fog hung over the river. In trying to get off, the boat got aground and it was ten o'clock before we were farely started. This delayed us in reaching the bar, at the mouth of the river. The time was enlivened with *singing, puning* and other nonsense. When near the bar we got aground but got off without difficulty. The Gen. thought we had better not go over the bar, but stay there 'till next high tide, but it was finally decided to go on, and, the Gen. not feeling in *good appetite* dinner was delayed 'till we should cross the St. Augustine bar. A pilot was signaled—but by some stupidity the boat did'nt stop for him quick enough and we soon found that the

126. Brig. Gen. Eliakim P. Scammon who commanded the District of Florida during the closing months of the war.

boat was fast on the bar and the tide runing out. There was small hopes of getting her off. The breakers dashed her from side to side fearfully—and everything movable danced about the cabin in a lively manner—espied by the *passengers*. The Gen. got nervous and went hurrying about and at last coming up to where a group of us ladies were clinging to a post and one another to keep from falling, he said, Ladies I think I had best send you all to the shore—it will help lighten the boat—so please get ready immediately—"Ah; there was hurrying to and fro." and we were soon ready—the small boat was launched, the steps got out on the side of the boat where the breakers were dashing against her with great foarce. It was next to impossible to keep her alongside, or the steps on the boat. — A great wave would take her, and it required all the skill and strength of the men to keep her from being dashed against the steamer It required some skill and dexterity to get us into the boat all rightside up. The ladies, as a general thing behaved admirably. Six ladies and three children, with Mr. Hyatt[127] in command were in the first boat and before we could get clear from the *Delaware* she was a third full of water. The rain fell steadily. As our little boat passed round the stern of the steamer a huge wave lifted us so that our heads were brought on a level with her upper deck— but no collission followed and we got off in safety—the fog was so dense that, in a few minutes, we lost sight of the steamer. Our oarsmen were some soldiers so the only sailor on board was Mr. Hyatt and he totally unacquainted with the coast—we were fast losing sight of the last buoy— the ladies were very fearful, and no sight of the coast—only the dreadful roar of the breakers dashing somewhere in the dense fog but beyond our sight. It was a moment of suspense and terror to all on board. I confess that my heart sank when Mr. Hyatt gave the order to turn about and try to find the steamer—we might be going right out to sea for all we knew, but just then the Good Father lifted the veil and the coast, like a dark line on the edge of the water, appeared—with the surf beating angrily against it, while a little farther to the left the breakers dashed sullenly. The men now pulled with a hearty good-will, and the boat was thrown as far as possible up the beach but before we could be taken out a huge wave dashed over her and us, giving us all a most thorough drenching, but we were so thankful to feel the firm earth again under our feet that we made no complaint of the waves. We found ourselves on Anastasia Island, six miles above St. Augustine and three miles above the light-house, the rain falling fast—the night setting in everything so wet as to preclude all hopes of a fire still we set about trying to make one, for a beacon light to the steamer

127. Unidentified.

—after much effort we succeeded in getting a fire started and, when the next boat came ashore with the sick men, some, with the assitance of the offices, went out and got a lot of light wood and we soon had a great blaze. We tried to make the sick men as comfortable as possible by spreading their blankets, overcoats &—down by the fire and letting them lay down. It did'nt rain quite so hard and they got quite comfortable. The night was warm so we did not suffer from the cold. The Gen. [Scammon] came ashore with the other ladies in the second boat—which was launched on the other side of the Steamer and got off without difficulty. After such passengers as chose to come, were landed there was no further need of a fire [at] that point, but up at the Light-house so as to be seen from the town that they might send small boats to our relief—many had already gone to the light house. It was about ten o'clock when we reached there. The walk seemed very long in the darkness, with our wet clothes clinging about us, and the timid ray from the poor little fire looked very friendly when it first greeted us, but on arriving at the house we found it a mere shell, without doors or windows—a poor fire on the hearth, round which our fellow pleasure seekers were huddled. The prospect was not cheering. The Gen and some of the offices succeeded in building a fire on the beach and also sent a messenger to the town for boats, meanwhile we were most thoroughly uncomfortable—cold—tired—wet and hungry. Mrs. Hyatt and I got a blanket and lay down on the floor—there was no place to sit down. I was so tired that, in spite of the discomforts, I fell asleep as did also Mrs. H. but we had not lain long when the Gen, announced that small boats had come for us from town and we must go on board directly. It was'nt pleasant to think of taking another boat ride that night but the best that could be done, the rain had ceased and the stars were out not a breath of wind stiring. We embarked without difficulty and reached the town without further adventure at about 2.A.M. Went to Buffingtons Hotel, no one up but the house was soon astir and we had the promise of our yesterdays dinner—which in due time we received then went to bed with thankful hearts and very tired bodies. Monday morning we were cheered with the grateful intelligence that the *Delaware* was safely off the bar and would soon be at the wharf. The rain fell in torrents all the morning untill about eleven o'clock. Several of the passengers came on shore, in a small boat—and were thoroughly wet, but we succeeded in keeping *merry*. Mr. Dodge, who has been in town for several weeks, came round and I went about town with him. It is a quaint old place with streets so narrow that the piazass on the houses came out entirely over the side walls and were they not arrainged so as not to come opposite each other they would come so near that any one standing in them, might easily shake hands across the street. We visited the "oldest building" supposed to have been built more than two hundred years ago-by the Spaniards. It is built of 'Cocena' as is most of the other buildings of the place, as well as the streets which are now much worn.

In the afternoon Capt. Moore got an ambulance and took us about town. Called first on a pretty 'Morroccan woman, who makes the most beautiful baskets and other fancy articles, from the palmetto imaginable our company bought about $25,s worth of her and we ladies were each presented with a lovely basket from Capt. Moore. We then called on Mrs. Eaton who is keeping a large boardinghouse, and from this, rode to the old Fort, in company with Capt. Moore, Dr. Applegate, Capt. Tilton and Adj. Chatfield[128] of the 17*th* Conn. which is stationed here—he is a very gentlemanly officer and showed us all about the fort,[129] explaining what was of the *old* and what had been newly built Took us into all the dungeons and by places. The Chief Engineer Lt. Turner,[130] came on the boat with us, to open the other three dungeons, which have been accidently discovered by one of them caving in.

We spent a very pleasant hour in examining this 'relic' of a past age—got a few blossoms from its sides and a *bone* from the blackest dungeon, probably it belonged to some poor victim of Spanish tyrany. —Returned to the Hotel. It seems strange to me to wander about these quaint old streets, meeting so many colored people and here none of them say "howdye Miss Hawk," but I have no acquaintances among them here only one little girl who came down from N.Y. with us—and another who came here last winter and attended my school. Called on the teachers—the Misses Smith, Miss Harris & Conant.[131] They live very prettily and comfortably in the family with the Methodist located at this Post.

The General ordered that the boat be got off by the early tide on Tuesday morning so we all went on board in the eve. played whist and euchre and spent the evening far into the night, very pleasasntly. The boat did not get over the bar 'till six next morning very much to the Generals annoyance and disgust—indeed he was quite *wrathy* over it and stormed

128. First Lt. H. Whitney Chatfield.
129. Fort Marion, first called Castle of St. Mark.
130. First Lt. Pierpont C. Turner.
131. Cornelia J. and Eliza J. Smith, both from New York State, Mary M. Harris and Kate D. Conant.

A Woman Doctor's Civil War

about considerably, but old Johny the pilot knew what he was about and did'nt mean to have the boat on the bar under his hands This delayed us so that we did not cross the St. John's bar 'till after two, in the evening Reached the wharf at Jacksonville just about sunset, tired, and very glad to be once more at home. Mrs. Hyatt was quite ill from the efficts of the fright so I went home with her and made her comfortable before going to my own home. Thus endeth my first pleasure trip in this Dept.

January 25*th* 1865   It is good to be at home and comfortable again! I feel the effects of our exposure somewhat, but not as much as I expected. Mrs. H. [Hyatt] continues sick, I am attending her.

We are agitating the subject of a "sewing circle, to aid the miserable whites who are suffering greatly at this time and as soon as Mrs. H. is sufficiently recovered we shall visit the Gen. [Scammon] and ask his cooperation on the matter.

30*th*   By desire of the Gen. expressed in a polite note through his Adj. Mrs. Hyatt and I visited him this morning—were received with great affability and he enters most heartily into our idea of a sewing circle and promises to aid in any way we may desire.

Called on several poor families where there is sickness. We are to have our first meeting on Friday afternoon—meanwhile we notify all who ought to be interested to be in attendance. I do not anticipate a great '*rush*'. It wont be a *popular move*.

February 1865

3*rd*   Our meeting met as proposed. *Six* ladies present—four northern ones and two residents however we organized—chose offices and proceeded to business—with Mrs. *Hawkes* in the chair. Mrs. Swain was chosen Pres. Miss Eveleth[132] V.P. Mrs. Hawkes Sect. Treas. with Miss Decosta[133] as Asst. Sect.—with a long list of visiting committee. Then we discoursed on ways and means—allotting to each her duties and adjourned to meet again in one week. Company in the evening. Gradually the troops are being withdrawn from this Post. The 21. US [C.T.] has been ordered to Morris Is. and I am left to look after the freedmen and organize schools for the children as fast as it can be done. The colored people are crowding in to the city and there is already much sickness and destitution among them. There are also many of the "poor whites who are in even more desperate conditions. These Fla. Crackers are much less human

132. Miss E. B. Eveleth of Long Island and Brooklyn, N.Y.
133. Unidentified.

than the negroes, more ignorant, dirty and lifeless—many of them look as if they had already been buried for months—their hair and skin and dirty, faded butter-nut clothes, look all of a piece. Even the negro's have great contempt for them.

4th   Gen. Scammon our Post-Commander desired to see us so we went to call on him this morning. He shows unusual interests in our efforts to improve the sanitary condition of the refugees—He said that he had been "forced to the conclusion that these 'poor whites' were inferior, in every respect to the colored population of the place." A view of the case with which I perfectly agreed. He then went on to say that the most intelligent scout and the most effective one at this Post, was a colored man, a former slave—and that he sent in the best reports—in proof of which he read us a long, well-written report in regard to the movements of the rebels in this vicinity—adding that this scout never came in without bringing in prisoners. He also told us that he had written a letter asking for this man a Lieutenancy—for said he—"he richly deserves it—though I pay him $100 pr. month but he is worth five times that amount to me, indeed he is invaluable"—High testimony for the poor slave. The rebels have offered three thousand dollars for him—so they know his worth. The Gen. asked him how he had learned to write: to which he replied, "I stole it sir little by little, when I was on the plantation".

The Gen. told us it would be doing good service if we ladies could visit these poor families, and ascertain their condition who needed rations and who were imposing upon the government; We promised to do what we could in the matter—and took leave. He gave us authority to say in his name, that all who did not clean up their quarters and send their children to school should be sent to the guard house. Thus armed we started and through the day visited forty families. It is impossible to describe the squalor and filth and indolence in which we found most of these "low down" crackers! It is a great shame that our government should be hampered with the support of such a miserable set of vagabonds! I 'reckon' there is less *dirt* in their houses to-day than there has ever been since their occupancy for every one began to *dig* about before we were well out of the house. —I venture to say that they were never so clean as they are to-night. We stood by and obliged them to use soap and water on their children and their own, hands and faces, and it was surprising to see how much more human they looked after the operation! and this we did twice a week for a long time!

On Friday evening we also commenced our sewing-school, among the women, and a Sunday-school for the children. The sewing class, only numbers 25, and the women mostly bring their own work. Those that do

A Woman Doctor's Civil War

not, are working on some clothing for some *destitute white* children. The Gen. has given us money from the Post fund, for the purchase of material![134]

5*th* Sunday

Today we have commenced our sabbath-school at our school-house under very favorable auspices. 140. children were present—all with clean, happy faces.—We all enjoyed it very much indeed. It is the first warm Sunday we have had, since I came here. The whole week has been warm and pleasant and, in consequence, school has been better attended and more comfortable for us all. Last night, at about ten o' clock while the singing class were here—Maj. Bardwell was called out, and the news communicated that 'Dickinsons' [Dickison][135] band had made another capture of a small force of our men and that his force of about 200 cavelry were on the other side of the river, close by. It created quite an excitement in town as it was reported that Capt. Hart our depot Q.M. was among the captured—*but that*, is reported false this morning. The sad news is brought us that the ten government teams which left St. Augustine, under escort of about forty men and the Lt. Col. of the 17 Conn. were captured, after a desperate resistance from our men, by Dickinsons' [Dickison] band of 200 cavelry. Col. Wilcoxson[136] was seriously wounded as was the Adj. who was most brutally murdered, and burried on the spot. It was only four miles out from the city-and since, the body has

---

134. Esther Hawks elaborated on this phase of her work in a letter published in *The Freedmen's Record*, I (March, 1865), p. 39, reading in part:

Our Schools are in a flourishing condition; we have an average attendance of one hundred and sixty. I have organized a sewing-school,—the children bringing such work as they have,—and we teach them to mend, and patch, and the older ones to cut by patterns, which we prepare for them. It is an interesting sight to see my sewing-school; and the delight of the smaller ones, who are being initiated into the mysteries of making rag babies, is comical to see. It is the best I can do, we have so little to do with besides. I have great faith in the knowledge which comes to children through their dolls.

Last Saturday, I visited thirty-seven different families, white and black, in town. I wish I could give you some idea of the difference between the two,—equally poor, equally dirty and destitute! The whites, have a hopeless, listless appearance; and no words of encouragement or cheer seem to reach them. They do not hesitate to beg, and are full of complaints. There is no elasticity in them; with the blacks, it is just the opposite: they are cheerful, willing to work, do not beg or complain, and are far more hopeful objects to labor for.

I ought not to have said they are equally dirty; some of them are; but we have many colored families here who are patterns of neatness; and I make them all "clean up," once a week, or as often as I go among them, which they do cheerfully, and are improving much in this respect. The health of the place is remarkably good at this time.

135. Capt. John J. Dickison, led Confederate light cavalry in several raids on Union work details in the vicinity of St. Augustine.

136. Lt. Col. Albert H. Wilcoxson.

been exhumed. It was found buried in a hole about one and a half feet deep and three *feet long*, the body bent double and crowded in—the skull broken and face terribly disfigured.

Poor Chatfield! little more than a boy! cultivated, refined, and amiable! every one loved him! Only a week before, he, full of life and fun, traversed every part of the old Ft. with me, pointing out what had been and was still being done to make Ft. Marrin [Marion] one of the strongest and best defences in the world. He gathered flowers for us, which were growing far up the wall, and in every way, did all in his power, for our comfort and amusement—and now his terrible death thrills us with horror!

The 17*th* Conn. is so decimated that it is necessary to send a larger force, to relieve them—and so Col. Tillman [Tilghman][137] of the 3rd. has been ordered to the command of that Post and it is quite probable that his regiment will be sent there, also, tho' I presume one or two Companies will remain for our defense. We are very sorriful over their (probable) going for we have made many warm and dear friends among both offices and men! It will take our most interesting class out of school, which I regret exceedingly. I have a fine class just through fractions—which I shall miss, and also my first reading class—but, have had them now, some of them nearly a year! Just one year ago to-day our Regt. arrived here. What a change since then! the town, from a "deserted villiage" covered with dirt and filth—one half, the town in ruins the tall chimneys, alone, marking the spot of pleasant homes or lordly mansions.

Now, all the unsightliness is removed, nice barracks have been built for the soldiers. The forts and breastworks all long ago completed, and among the best we have! The Fts are still man'd by the 3*rd* U.S.C.T's who have become thorough artilleriests'.

A free white school has been established and sustained in part by the Post fund, the rest by taxing the traders. There are about five hundred colored and six hundred white aside from the military force here. The greater portion of the whites belong to the lowest class or 'Crackers' and are miserably poor and degraded—ignorant and filthy it is seldom we find one who can read, and instead of appreciating the free school priveledge, many of them refuse to go, and in visiting among them they offer all kinds of *poor* excuses for not going.

The colored people are far ahead in thrift and industry—tho' many of them are about as dirty—but there is more life—animation—elasticity about them so more hope for their future.

137. Col. Benjamin C. Tilghman.

Sat. 18*th*   Went down to the Yellow Bluff, on the *Hattie*[138] with Miss Jocelyn,[139] Miss Botts, Lt. Barber & Green[140] of 35*th* who were down to get a detatchment of the Regt. stationed there. The day was all that pleasure-seekers could desire. We reached our destination about 11 A.M. espied a boat inside the bar, which we soon made out to be *Delaware*, for Jacksonville. This was pleasant news : We went on shore, met Chaplain Harris of 3*rd* and the officers stationed there. Took dinner on board the boat with Capt. and Mrs. Hyatt, then went with the offices to visit Ft Jones. It was all very nice and we enjoyed it, tho' I was a little *sea sick*. Mrs. McCleane[141] the teacher of the white school, was also along. She is a nice, agreeable lady. Reached home about sunset and I found a nice bundle of letters awaiting me, very much to my gratification. Wrote to Dr. [J.M. Hawks] in the eve. not many in to sing and went home early.

Sun. 19*th*   School very large—did'nt go to church. Went into Mrs. W's [Willard] to sing in the evening. Had an invitation from the Q. M. to go with his wife and a party of offices out with flag of truce tomorrow, if pleasant, to escort a lady across the line; she is from N.Y. and is going to Middle Fla. where her mother and sister are sick and destitute and she hopes to bring them back with her. Mrs. Hyatt will go, think I'll go.

20*th*.

The morning was rainy so party postponed till to-morrow. Spent the morning at Mrs. H.'s [Hyatt] and after school we, accompanied by Capt. Moore, went horseback riding. Spent the evening at Mrs. McCleanes and Willards'.

21*st*   Went down early in the morning to tell Mrs. H. that I had concluded not to go out with the flag of truce as I had head acke—but they were all so earnest for me to do so, that I changed my mind—got ready and at half-past eight we started—us three ladies in an open ambulance, about a dozen officers on horseback—and a cavelry escort ahead with the white flag. It was thought quite probable that we should have to ride out some ten miles but when about three miles out we met a flag from the other side coming down to bring a sick man, who wishes to go to Europe for his health—a resident of Columbus, Georgia. We were somewhat dis-

138. The *Hattie Brock* or "*Hattie*" was a double-decked, shallow-draft light steamer especially designed and constructed in Jacksonville for use on the upper St. John's River. It suffered considerable damage during the war but was later rebuilt.
139. Miss Jocelyn was the daughter of American Missionary Association Secretary S. S. Jocelyn. She taught in Florida until her marriage to N. C. Dennett, then an official of the Freedmen's Savings Bank in Jacksonville. She died after childbirth in 1868.
140. First Lt. George H. Green.
141. Vienna McLean, commissioned as a teacher by the American Missionary Association.

appointed in not having a longer ride. —The lady who went with us, Mrs. Corlis, has just come down from N.Y.—where her husband, who is a Vermonter, is in business—to go over the lines to middle Fla. after her mother and sister who are sick and destitute, and she hopes to be able to bring them back with her. She is a native of St. Josephs, but has lived north quite a number of years.

When the two flags met, our offices went forward to meet the rebel offices, and after conversing a few minutes together an orderly was sent back for a large hamper of provisions and a *'demijohn'* of whiskey: the rebs, also produced liquor of some kind which they called 'skinnings', and they 'stood treat' all round, it had very much the flavor of N.E.R. [New England Rum] of an inferior quality. Soon the officers all came over to our ambulance, and we were formally introduced. Mrs. Curlis, who was to go back with them, found an old friend and school-mate in one of the Capts. so she felt easier about going with them; Capt. Baya,[142] one of the Rebels, whose mother and sisters live in J. [Jacksonville] was with the company, and was allowed to send in for them to come out and see him Their meeting was quite affecting. His mother clung about his neck and begged him to go home with her, but the Capt. is a staunch violent rebel, and has no idea of giving up—though I presume he is quite willing that our government take care of his mother and sisters! The offices are all very nicely dressed, they wear the same buttons as our officers of the line, and Capt. Baya had on a pair of our army blue pants, very nice ones, and must have been taken from some prisoner! —perhaps the ones stripped from the body of the murdered Chatfield!

Capt. Johanagan [C.S.A.], Chief Q. M. of the district, knew and had, not long since, seen several of my old Manatte [Manatee] friends—Dr. Branch[143] & sons 'Bob' Braden and others[144] —. After an hour of pleasant conversation, we spread a cloth and had a nice collation of cold meat, eggs, bread and butter, and pastries, & to which the rebel offices did ample justice, one of them remarking that it was the first butter he had tasted

142. Capt. H. T. Baya, Eighth Florida Volunteers, C.S.A. Descended from an old Spanish family, Baya left his native St. Augustine as a boy to enter business in Charleston. After the war he returned to Florida and headed a steamship line, the chief vessel of which bore his name.

143. Dr. Franklin Branch was a Vermont-born graduate of Castleton Medical College who settled in Tampa in the late 1840s. Before the Hawks' honeymoon in Manatee, Branch purchased land near the Manatee River where he ultimately failed in his attempt to develop a sanitarium. It is possible that Esther Hawks combined the names of the two wealthiest and most prominent residents of Manatee during her residence there to create "Bob Braden." The two were Robert "Bob" Gamble and Dr. Joseph A. Braden.

144. Unidentified.

in three years, adding that they could get no flour but had plenty of corn meal and beef.

Unfortunately, more whiskey was sent back for, and drank by both officers and men, and many of the men on both sides got quite intoxicated. The wind was blowing very hard and heavy clouds admonished us that a storm was at hand so with much hand-shaking and many hearty good-bys, we hastely got started toward home. In exchange for the lady we took out, the rebels had brought a sick man who, wished to go through our lines, to go abroad for his health. It soon began to rain and the Q.M. rode back to us and told the driver to hurry up unfortunately our Ambulance driver had made too free with the whiskey, and was in no condition to drive, but in the hurry this was unnoticed. The horses ran, the driver had no control over them, we tried to get hold of the reins, but they had already fallen from the drivers hands; right ahead, lying directly across the road was a huge pine tree; All through the country we find these obstructions in the roads, a tree falls, no one ever thinks of removing it but a new road is made around it. We saw it and I tried to make the driver turn his horses, but on they went, cleared the tree at a bound, bringing the Ambulance with great force against it—smashing everything and throwing us all, with great violence to the ground. The horses and forward wheels went on spreading consternation among the other horses of the cavalcade, the officers thinking for a moment that an ambush had been laid for the party. I was picked up insensible, but soon recovered; was the only one much hurt—was unable to walk—brought home in the carriage with the Misses Byar's [Baya], Mrs. H. [Hyatt] and the others walked home. Dr. D. [?] carried me into the house—found my hip badly sprained but no bones broken; Dr. Tyrrel[145] called, gave me an opiate which chimed in nicely with my nervous state, making me quite crazy. A great many people in to see how badly I was injured. The colored people heard that I had been shot by the rebs, and all manner of stories were afloat. Did'nt sleep much that night. Just one year ago I came over the road from Camp Finegan

22nd.

I am reminded, as I lie here, unable to rise, of this day here, one year ago! The wildest confusion prevailed—wounded were constantly arriving—every large building in town was in use as a hospital. I was busy all day in, what is now our school house, among the wounded; I remember

---

145. Probably Dr. Henry S. Turill, Assistant Surgeon of the Seventeenth Connecticut Infantry.

that I slept, at Col. Montgomery's Hd. Qr's on an old broken sofa, without even a blanket to cover me, we having arrived, on horse-back at
about midnight, with nothing save what we had on our backs. I remember too, that I went to the hospital breakfast less, and had nothing to eat
till 2 P.M. It was a very busy day: no one thought of it as a day for rejoicing. To-day how different—as I lie here on my hard bed, sounds of re-
joycing and merriment are wafterd in through my open windows—guns
are being fired right across the street at Mrs. Willard's great preparations
are going forward for a grand entertainment this evening. Nature and all
her children seem glad. It is hard to stay here quietly, but I try not murmur. God was very good to spare our lives. May mine be spent in a worthy manner. Three times, since I came I came to this Dept. has it been in
great peril—but my work is not yet finished—May it be well done!

Many of the colored people have been in to-day—bringing me cakes,
fruit, flowers and such other things as they think will please. In return, I
have given many of them a reading lesson, which delights them very
much—so the day has passed pleasantly and I trust not unprofitably. This
eve. Capt. Barker[146] sent me down a rabbit nicely dressed, for my breakfast.

23rd

Feel very lame and tired this morning The noise from the party over
the way kept me awake 'till long after midnight so I did'nt get rested
much. Been a good many in this morning, heard a number of lessons; am
tired.

24th

I thought I should have a nice time to write letters and get rested while getting well but I am beset with company the whole time—and
instead of resting I am getting quite exhausted   High ho! This comes
of being so *popular*!!! There has been a great change in the weather. It is
like June; The children bring me a great many flowers, and indeed they
bring me a great many other things. I think something has been brought
me for every meal since I have been confined to my room; of their stores
they bring me the best—God bless them!—how I love their little black
faces!

The sewing society meet this afternoon—discordant elements are arising. Ladies object to come to associate with the "Nigger Teachers"—This
is quite *humiliating* but like other disagreeables, cant be helped.

---

146. Capt. Edmund P. Barker of the Third U.S.C.T.

Jacksonville Feb. 24*th*/65.[147]

Miss Horatia Ware,

Through the Boston So. I have been informed that an association known as the "Mayhew Society"[148] and of which you are Sec. have adopted me as one of its teachers. I have not heard from this society but presume some of "Uncle Sams" mails are in error, so as I feel that it is important for us to become acquainted as spedily as possible, I do not wait for news from you but, write immediately. This is the third year that I have been in this Dept. as teacher, and I have always felt that it would be a great blessing to me, to know there was some-one at home, personally interested in me and my work here, some one to whom I could look for sympathy and occasionally for help, and I assure you, it is very grateful to me to be brought in communication with those who are interested in helping to smoothe the upward steps of this much abused people—and to be the connecting link between you and them affords me great pleasure, and it shall be my earnest endeaver to make your acquaintance with them as pleasant and as thorough as possible. It is difficult to understand the character of these people from afar off, and every delineating pen is prone to be tinctured with the peculiar temprement and ideas of the writer. A very sympathetic nature, dwells continually on their wrongs and cries over the past. The enthusiast rushes forward and paints most glowingly their future, and insists on their being just what their' fancy paints them—but few take them just as they are; but few bring themselves down, through sympathy, to understand just their needs,—and for myself, many is the time when nicely settled in my mind, that I know them well, all my fine spun theories are upset by some entirely new development of character for which, I find, I had given them no credit. I am convinced, save through love no one can be an efficient laborer among these people; and their intentions are like childrens. Many go out among them as teachers with great ardor to do something, particularly for the souls, of this people, but who keep them aloof as though they were black spiders.

25*th*   Saturday night!—Warm sultry day! Thermometer at 79°—am very tired—Had Dr. Tyrrell [Turill], Capt. Johnson and Mrs. Willard her last eve to play euchre with me, Lts. Wilson and Knight were also here;

---

147. Esther Hawks chose to incorporate the text of this letter in her diary. Hence it has been included in its proper chronological sequence, as though it were a portion of the diary.
148. The Mayhew Society was an independent Freedmen's aid association with headquarters in Boston.

passed the eve very pleasantly, left at ten—but then the girls got into some kind of a glee and I got nervous and wakeful so did'nt sleep much, and today feel the worst for it.

The folks, Mr. D. [Dennett] Miss E. [Eveleth], Mr & Mrs. McCleane Capt. Gates and Mr. Corbit have been down the river a few miles—and they brought me *armsful* of flowers, till my room looks like a garden. Lt. Turner has been in this afternoon. My friends do not mean I shall be lonely. Have been sitting up since dinner. Capt. Gates brought me a cane, from a sweet gum tree, with which I hope to be able to *walk*, before many days; My leg still refuses to do duty but is not so painful as formerly.

26th   Glory to God! Charleston has fallen! I feel like shouting *all over*. A navy supply boat brings us the jubilant news; Our gun boat, the *Hail* is right opposite us on the river, all covered with the glorious news. —And Columbia too, is ours. How can we thank God enough for these victories—brave Sherman and his army have reached the sea, and the war is virtually ended. The whole city is wild with excitement. —Every bit of bunting in possossion of the Post, is afloat, and every gun as well as all the other throats are screaming themselves hoarse! I feel same as old Aunty Brown, who was here when the news came, said she did. 'Why,' said she, if I could get hold of dat Gen. Sherman, and all his brave officers I feel as if I could tote dem all ober dis yer place."

Our Regt. the 21 U.S.C.I s [Infantry] were the first to enter Charleston. As they marched proudly up Meeting St. with flags flying and drums beating, the excitement among the colored people was at white heat—cheer after cheer greeted them at every turn, as they passed out of Meeting St a fine looking black woman sprang out from the crowd, in front of the officers, and pulling her shall [shawl] from her shoulders, spread it in front of the soldiers for them to walk on, it seemed the only thing she could do to show her patriotism The Col. gallantly picked it up and passed it to her, while the soldiers cheered vociferously.

I feel quite smart today, can walk a little though with pain but am doing well. The children have been here in *droves* all day, and most of them bring flowers so I am almost flooded with them. Have written to Milton and to Miss Ware. Hav'nt read a word all day—no time.

27th Monday.

Mrs. Willard gives a grand entertainment to-night in honor of the recent good news; Of course I can't go but staying at home is no cross. I enjoy the thought of a quiet evening quite as much as the others can the danceing noise and excitement. My leg is gaining slowly. I can walk a little on it to-day Not so many in for lessons as usual.

A Woman Doctor's Civil War

28th   Last eve had quite a party here and the noise over the way kept me awake, so I'm not good natured to-day.

March *1st*   About as usual—do'nt see as I get any better. Have had *sixty callers*—Most of them, from among my colored friends. I have quite a class of them, who come daily to read.

Mr. Corbitt[149] came towards night, stayed to tea then stayed to keep me company in the eve the others all going over to Mrs. Willards Mr. C. [Corbitt] is in the last stages of consumption—is a young lawyer of great promise—talented handsome rich—everything to make life desirable—and he clings to it with great pertinacity but Death has most surely marked him. He reminds me so strongly of my friend that I cannot resist the charm of his presence or help liking him very much and pitying him very much too. We spent a pleasant, quiet evening.

Mar. 2nd.   Two of my girls (in my first class) Salina and Rose, came to see last night and brought, one a can of peaches, and the other a half doz-in eggs—they had just bought them out of their own money and of their own accord—dear girls—it is pleasant to be remembered so kindly. Some of them are constantly bringing me something—which they think I shall relish—and the little children are constantly running in with flowers!

March 4th.   To-day 'Father Abraham' renews his oath of office. The man who administered four years ago, 'Judge Taney'[150] has gone to give an account of his evil deeds to a higher tribunal; May the present incumbent of his office live worthier and die older! —I have no record to make. Am still a prisoner. Col. Seaton[151] was to take me out riding in the Gens carriage this morning but the weather proves unpropitious so I stay in my room. It was very warm this morning but a hard shower has cooled the atmosphere very much. My room is sweet with orange blossoms.

6th   Was taken out to ride by Mr. D. [Dennett] in his buggy. First time I've been out of the house in two weeks! I feel like a released prisoner. My ride made me very tired but I got over it better than anticipated. Mr. C. [Corbitt] spent the evening with me—read from Tennyson to me.

7th   This morning the *out door* was too lovely to resist so taking my crutches I got downstairs pretty well, and across the street to see Mr.

---

149. Unidentified.
150. Chief Justice of the United States Roger B. Taney, anathema to abolitionists since the Dred Scott case of 1857 in which he had held that blacks were "so far inferior that they had no rights which the white man was bound to respect."
151. Unidentified.

McCleane [McLean]—poor man! he is in far greater need of sympathy than I He cannot recover, and to leave such a dear wife and little one, with such bright promises in the future if he could only live to gather them! In the afternoon Capt. Moris[?] came for me to go up the river in a row-boat. Went up to Pottsburg Creek—about five miles. The river was just rough enough to make it exhilerating, the air fresh came laden with the sweet scent of the jassamine, which covers all the trees with its beautiful blossoms; sometimes climbing to the top of the big oaks:—Some of the boats-crew landed and gathered a bunch of flowers for us. The row home was quite charming—the river as smooth as a mirror. We stop'ed to look at the little rebel streamer *Sumpter* [Sumter] which has lately been 'raised' and brought up from the bar where she was sunk some months ago. Got home about sunset. Capt. M. and Mr. H. [Hyatt] took me in their arm to the house—then Mr. D. [Dennett] brot me up stairs so I got along pretty well, but right glad to get on my bed again. Dr. T. [Turill] came in after supper, he's smitten with 'Bottsy' staid late, so I was too tired to sleep well.

14*th*   The days go by and I do not get strong, but still go hobbling about on crutches. Sunday morning rode on "Nelly' to school; The children hopped about like grasshoppers in their delight at seeing me out again. Mail came in—the *Canonicus.* got but one letter a few lines from Dr. [J. M. Hawks] desiring me to go to Charleston where our Regt. is garrisoning the city—boat only stayed a few hours, but I was'nt well enough to go on her; Shall go by first opportunity. —Mr. C. [Corbitt] went to St. Augustine on the boat, invited me to go too—wish I had.

Yesterday rode to school, but got very tired. *Wyoming* came in with a larger mail—she remains at this Post.

In the eve; Mrs. Willard gave a big party—was taken over and stayed till 10 1/2,' very delightful to well people, but theres "no 'place like home" when one is sick! The weather is most charming. Of all places in the South, give me Florida in which to live!

15*th*   I have just come from cutting some sacques for two little girls who with their mother and a little brother, came in last evening, and the woman has been telling me her story.

They come from Georgia—eighty miles from here; those little children walking the entire distance through an enemies' country in three days.

The woman, 'Maria' is bright and smart, with fine features and a quick intelligent eye; quite black, as are all the children. She belonged to 'Josh Brown' who has been in the rebel service ever since the breaking out of the rebellion, till laterly he has 'ran away and is home. Her husband belonged to another man and four years ago was carried up into S.C. since when she has neither seen or heard from him.

Her Mistress has been "mighty hard" on her since her master has been gone, and last Christmas refused her any holiday—keeping her hard at work in the field. This was too much for Maria and she run away into the swamp leaving the children in the care of a sister, and all through the long winter she has been trying to get her children and make her escape, but not till last Saturday did she feel safe to make the attempt. She got her children at noon, (it being the only time she could reach them without casting suspicion on her sister.) The creeks were swolen with the late rains but she forded them with her little ones clinging to her neck,—her only guide being a paper given her by a colored man with a map of the road marked out on it by himself—and with this she traversed over eighty miles of strange country, only losing the road once, and that in trying to avoid encountering some people; and to-day she and her little ones are as fresh and hearty as though they had been in a quiet home, during the past four nights instead of fleeing for their lives over an enemies country, where, to be taken would have been almost certain death! Surely the ways of God are wonderful!

18*th*   The day being pleasant and we all in good spirits Mr. D. [Dennett] proposed to take us down the river to his 'Colony' and spend the day at the Bigalow plantation. Mr. D. Miss Evelith [Eveleth] Miss Joselyne [Jocelyn] and I composed the party—got a boat and were off at about 10 A.M. The sail down the river was charming. The new leaves of the trees make a beautiful contrast with the evergreens and the bushes and hanging moss over the rivers edge, many times, covered with the blossoms of the yellow jessamine make pretty pictures. Found Mrs. Breadalbine and her little girl alone on the plantation. Mr. B. [Breadalbine] away at Jacksonville. Went over the place—which very much resembles all the other deserted places.

At noon Mrs. B [Breadalbine] had a cup of tea made, and with our provisions which good Mr. Dennett's foresight provided us with, we had a sumptous repast—Then went down three miles farther to where the colony is located. But few people are yet there, but preparations are fast being made for their accommadation. Houses are being erected by 'Col' Wilson[?] and the men are preparing the grounds for seed. The low descending sun admonished us and we turned reluctantly homeward where we arrived not till the twilight had deepened into evening and the stars were in the sky. I was very weary and would gladly have gone to bed but it was our singing night—so we must be entertaining—how we succeeded *modesty* forbids me from stating!!!

24th   —Went to a ball at Head Quarters, by invitation of Col. Seaton Ch. of Staff—with Q. M. McCoying—an elegant affair. Mrs. W. [Willard] not invited—and violently indignant. Did'nt stay late—only danced a few times—came away at eleven.

25th   We all (that is *us* at the Dennett Mansion" and Mrs. Willard) went up Cedar Creek to-day on the *Sumpter* [Sumter]—to see the operations on the *Mary Benton* which is sunk there, and now being raised. Col. Marple's reg. the 34*th* are on guard there. The *Benton* was taken up there and sunk by the rebels when our forces came to J. [Jacksonville] to prevent it being taken by us,—it is a good boat and not much injured—it will yet do us good service. It is interesting to see the completeness of the arrangements for raising a boat and I was so fortunate as to see the diver put on his marine armor and go down to work nailing on the canvass, to the sides of the vessel, some twenty feet below water. Stout canvas is nailed entirely around the sides of the boat, the upper edge coming above water, the lower, closely confined to the boat This prevents the water from running in while the pumps are throwing it out at the rate of a great many barrells per minute until she floats. This boat is expected to be afloat on Monday and a large party will go up to see the sight. They have been somewhat annoyed by the rebs but no serious harm done. Miner [Hawks] has been promoted to a couple of *bars*—is in good health and spirits. Had a charming ride and good company—got home about sunset——and in the evening had a *big crowd* at the sing, but on reaching the wharf we had learned that a boat would leave the next morning at 10 o'clock for Port Royal and concluding to be in readiness to go on it, I saw but little of the company, but was busy packing up.

Mr. Corbitt came up to see me,—used all his eloquence to persuade me not to leave, and I confess that he is *nearly irresistible*—but *duty* calls and I must go. Went to bed very tired. —Mrs. Copple[152] (Miss Sammis) spent the eve with us; I like her. She is educated, refined—sensible—as usual our folks had to play their silly games—proverbs and the like. I wish we could *possibly* spend an evening here sensibly!

26th—   It is, even now, hard to decide to start for Charleston I have a presentiment that it would be better not to go but most of my things are in readiness and the boat is to start at noon.

Went to Sunday school to say good bye to the children—attempted to do so but broke down entirely. *Cried*—couldn't help it and the children *cried*, for the same reason, I suppose. The little ones clung to me, crying

152. Unidentified.

as if their little hearts would break—several insisted on coming with me—a long string of them followed me home, they brought me flowers and hung about till I was obliged to send them away. At noon word came that the boat would not go till two—at that time we went on board the *Wyoming* which was to take us to the *bar*—where we were to meet the *Petral* which was to take us to the Head.

The children and colored people came to the wharf in *'droves'* to get a last look at their *'dear teacher'*—a great many offices and civilians were on board and many on the wharf to see us away—and my numerous friends, and their grief at my departure seemed to afford them great amusement.

[Charleston]

It was nearly five o'clock before we were off. On reaching the bar, it was to late to go out so we anchored. There were at least a hundred and fifty passengers on board, many offices and ladies, accompanied us to the bar intending to return, on the boat that night, but in this were disappointed. A bountiful supply of 'diamond B.' was carried on board by some of the officers, so they were prepared for a *'time'*—and about eight o'clock the 'ball' opened by Capt. Morse [John H. Moore] coming into the salon—and ordering all the men *out* to give the cabin to us ladies a chance to sleep, there being no staterooms excepting those of the offices of the boat and they were given up to Miss Wilson [?] and the De' Casta's girls, so our chances for rest were rather slim. One of the refugees refused to leave the cabin, saying his wife was sick and needed his care, but Capt. M. [Moore] insisted and he not starting, kicked him out. Capt. M. [Moore] was too drunk to know what he was about! —Then the noise began in earnest on deck—a violin was procured—and dancing, singing howling with an occasional knock down, diversified the entertainment through the night. The stewardess (a white woman from N.Y.) was made drunk, and ministered in various ways to the enjoyment of the crowd—offering her services freely. The Capt. of the boat was too drunk to interfere, so the revel went on. It was the most fearful night I ever passed. I kept Lt. Green close by me and but for him would have gone wild with nervous terror. In the morning no *Petral* was found at the bar so Capt. Snow concluded to venture out with the *Wyoming* but we were hardly over the bar before the shaft of the engine broke and we were obliged to anchor. Our condition was most perilous—the boat totally unfit for sea—the Capt. and most of the offices not over the drunken row, the wind fresh and sea rough and no hope of succor till the schooner which we had in tow could go to Fernandina and sent us assistance. There were at least one hundred and fifty passengers—many of them women and children—under such circumstances how many of us could hope to be saved!! but our sch.

[schooner] met the *Petral* at the bar and she hurried down to our assistance—it was too rough for us to go aboard her so we must be very carefully towed. At one time there was four feet of water in our Steamer; and that was about as much as She could hold. After crossing the bar Capt. Snow came and sat near me, remarking with a sigh of relief—"I have been to sea ever since I was ten years old and I never remember to have entered port with so great a degree of satisfaction as to-day."

On arriving at the dock found no boat to take us on—the *Petral* refusing to go. There were no houses or people to accommodate so many. Capt. Rider of the Sch. [schooner] *Julia A. Rider* offered his cabin, saying that he could accommodate two ladies and a gentleman—so Mr. & Mrs. Hyatt and I went with him. The pleasure seekers, went various ways, but all were accommodated—and immediately set about to have *a dance,* got a hall, and a fiddler and 'went in' for another row. They returned to J. [Jacksonville] next morning. It was raining so, though the Capt. of the *Petral* had engaged to take us to the Head, we could not get out—and we lay there at the dock for two days much to our annoyance. Capt. R. [Rider] was very kind, and did all in his power to make us comfortable and we were as cosy as need be in his little cabin. On the evening of the 29*th* went on board the *Petral* hoping to be at P.R. [Port Royal] by morning but again the "clerk of the Weather" interposed, a cloud of mist settling over the bar so we could not cross; we lay there all night. The accommodations were of the most limited sort—only two staterooms on board and these were given up to Mrs. Corlis' and family and to Mrs. Hyatt and me. They were most uncomfortable—filled with vile oders and filth—and in the morning while dressing, Mrs. H. [Hyatt] noticing a 'speck' on her stocking asked me to look and catch it if a *flee*—when lo! a real "grey back" sleek and hearty—and on further investigations we routed about *fifty* of the enemy and put them to death. Mrs. H. [Hyatt] was in an agony of disgust and terror and I had to laugh at our situation though with no doubts but my own person was *infested.* We passed a most uncomfortable day. The *Petral,* though an excellent sea boat, rocks like a cradle—and the sea was quite rough. Reached P.R. [Port Royal] bar just after sundown. It was very rough crossing and sometimes I could'nt help feeling a doubt as to the *side* of the boat which would come up at its next roll—however we arrived and anchored a little way out, at about 2 o'clock. did'nt go up to the wharf—but lay there over night. Mrs. H. and I refused to go into the state-room again so were allowed a couple of berths in the cabin where we lay down without undressing and passed another uncomfortable night.

Expected to go on shore in the morning but did'nt do so. Capt. Morse [Moore] reported—found no boat to take us to Charleston so determined to go up in the Schooner—which had brought our baggage, his horses &. Took us from the Streamer at eleven A.M. and with a fair wind, we set sail and were off. Everything was favorable and we crossed the bar at Charleston harbor just at dark. The Capt. had never been in her before, but failing to get a pilot concluded to try and take the boat up himself—in which he succeeded admirably with one or two narrow escapes from running on sunken vessels spirles &. As we were near the shore, the wind died away and the tide being strong carried our little craft against the sharp prow of the *Santiago de Cuba* breaking in, a small place on her side and entangling the rigging. It was some minutes before we got clear, then a little tug came out and on learning that the chief Q. M. of the Dep. was on board, towed us up on the dock. Capt. M. [Moore] then went on shore, got carriages and took us off. Mrs. H. [Hyatt] to the 'Charleston Hotel, and I to Dr's [J. M. Hawks] qrs. on Charlotte St. It was hard to realize, as we rattled over the payment that we were *really* in Charleston— quietly living in the rebel palaces—without fear of molestation.

I had no time for moralizing before the coach drew up at the residence of said Dr. H. [J. M. Hawks]. It was near midnight—the house was dark and still. Its magnificent proportions looming up in the darkness like a church or old cathedral. I thought the driver must be mistaken, but he dashed up the steps and thunderd away at the door untill I concluded he had mistaken me and brought me to the Deaf & dumb." Assylum presently a head protruded from the window, soon the door opend and Dr. H. in a very unmilitary uniform, appeared in view—and I went in. Truly the magnificence reveiled by that one little tallow dip was bewildering! I make no attempt to describe it but after our 'pastoral simplicity' in Florida, it is painful to come *suddenly* upon such luxuries! I am tired—worn out by my tedious journey—and a few of days of rest will be very grateful. Can I have them here when so many laborers are needed. Mr. and Mrs. Morse,[153] from Bradford are here with Dr. [J. M. Hawks] also a Miss Butrick [Buttrick][154] from Concord Mass. all in the schools. Mr. James

153. Mr. Arthur T. and Mrs. Louisa A. Morse, pre-war abolitionist friends of the Hawks in New Hampshire.
154. Harriet Buttrick, who was described as "a whole team," by New England Freedmen's Aid Association Secretary Hannah E. Stevenson. Henry L. Swint, *Dear Ones At Home* (Nashville: Vanderbilt University Press, 1966), p. 227.

Redpath has general Supt. of the whole[155]. Chaplain Fowler and wife Miss Dean from Beaufort are here visiting so the house is full—indeed *every body* is here or coming.

All is eager excitement rushing after relics and souvaners of this treason loving city—meanwhile I go to bed and try to rest for the morrow. Dr. tells me that little Edd [Hill]—almost a year a prisoner—has been paroled and is ever now at home. I have a hysterical fit of crying over the good news, and go to sleep.

April. 1865

6th Thursday.   Have been with Mr. James Redpath to select a proper building for an orphan assylum—and we selected a magnificent mansion on East Bay St.[156] owned by Mrs. Ross, who appears to be absent from the city. She is reputed to be a lady of great wealth and her house seems well adapted to the purpose for which we intend it. We go about from house to house selecting such articles of abandoned furniture as we think we can adapt to our Needs. Surely no Orphan Assylum was more magnificently furnished! —We have a fine piano for every floor—elegant mirrors which extend from floor to ceiling—handsome rose wood chamber sets & but a very poor supply of kitchen furnishings.

Visited Gov. Aikens' houses. He is still in the city—claims to be loyal[157]—was obliged to abandon his elegant mansion for one a little out of range of Gilmore's guns.

The city does not show how much it has been battered by our shell,—from a little distance—but in walking about the streets in this part of it we find a great many houses which have been occupied by *our forces* and what is a little remarkable hardly a single *church* has been spared—almost everyone shows a yawning wound. Yesterday Dr. [J. M. Hawks] got a carriage and we visit the 'Alm-house', the Medical School, cemetary and other public places. The Alms-house is an elegant building—large and finely adapted to the purpose—is still in 'running order' has not been interfered with. The same family still in charge. Connected with it is a large and

---

155. When the Federal occupying forces in Charleston took over all school buildings in the city, James Redpath was appointed Superintendent of Schools. Redpath offered jobs to all resident teachers who would take the loyalty oath, and offered to appoint adequately educated black teachers as well. Soon after his own appointment, nine day schools were in operation serving both white and black pupils, with freedmen's societies paying teachers and furnishing textbooks.

156. The home of the fugitive Charleston slave owner Mrs. Ross, at 305 East Bay Street was named the Col. [Robert Gould] Shaw Orphan House.

157. William Aiken, Governor of South Carolina from 1844 to 1846, had been opposed to secession and remained neutral throughout the war.

beautiful garden full of the rarest exotics and the greatest profusion of roses. Mrs. White, the matron gave us a large bouquet, and was *exceedingly gracious*. A little way farther on is the beautiful Magnolia Cemetary, like a great garden of roses, covering many acres. The Cemetary is most charmingly located but in a neglected condition now. It does not, with all its wealth of flowers, begin to compare with Mt. Auburn—still it is capable of becoming one of the rarest sports on earth. The 54 Mass were encamped within its limits and alowed to cut down many of the trees—and otherwise mar the beauty of the place. This is outrageous, still when we remember the cause those boys have for hating this acursed city and all in it, the only wonder is that they have done so little harm.

On our way home visited Noisetts' gardens. The proprietor is a black woman, of great wealth, the widow of a black man—the owner of a great many slaves, and this most beautiful and productive farm. They have cultivated early vegetables for the city markets and also supply the most rare and beautiful flowers. There are acres of land, now neglected, but covered with Japonicas, Oleanders, and great rose bushes. The lane leading from the street to this house, a quarter of a mile or more, is hedged on either side with beautiful rare Cherokee rose bushes. —It is one of the finest places in, this vicinity. The Widow with her large family of children about her, all well settled, gave us a cheerful welcome, and a refreshing treat of fruit and cake!

7*th*   On Sunday after my arrival our regiment was ordered over to Mt. Pleasant to relieve that of the 35*th* who came here and occupy the Citidel where the 21*st* have been ever since our occupancy of the place. This gives us Col. Beecher and wife for near neighbors as they have take Col. Bennetts[158] quarters just below us on the corner of Meeting & Charlotte St. Last night went down to see them and Mrs. B. [Bennett] proposed a horseback ride—it was a charming moonlight eve, so Dr. Marcy got this horse for me and we spent an hour very plesantly.

8*th*   My assylum goes on slowly—it seems as though we should never get it cleaned. I am constantly disappointed about my help. Every body has so much to do it is almost *next* to impossible to *do anything*! Mr. R. [Redpath] came for Mrs. B. [Beecher] and me to ride out to the "Magnolia Cemetary" to select a place to bury our soldiers. We were talking of a visit to Mt. Pleasant but it looked like rain so I went with them instead—rode horseback—saddle turned—girth broke I came to the ground with some

---

158. Lt. Col. Augustus G. Bennett, commander of John Milton Hawks' regiment, had earlier been given the honor of being rowed ashore to accept the formal surrender of the city of Charleston.

violence before we got out of sight of the house—picked myself up changed the saddle, and we went on our way. It rained so we stopped in somebodies cow-yard, till it was over. Selected the finest place in the Cemetery for our "brave and honored" dead" much to the evident disgust of a rebel who is still in charge of the grounds. On our way home rode round the race-course where our prisoners were kept—and out to their holes where they were buried in heaps. In a small inclosure, in *four short rows* are buried 249. of our men—the dead of less than a week! — The colored men are building a fence about it—gratuitously. A monument will soon be erected on the spot.

Our evening schools are doing fairly—the one near us, and in which I have a large class of men is named the 'Saxton' school—it is very interesting and I, although tired through the day cant keep away from it!

9th   Notice was given out in school last night that Mr. French would preach at that (the Zion St.) church today, but it will hardly pay to go so far to hear him! To-morrow I entered upon my duties as principle of the Normal School; Miss Newcomb[159] has been in it for two weeks and on Friday when she left, the schollars made quite a demonstration - made her several very pretty presents &. I expect it will be hard work for me at first, with my lameness, to go up and down so many stairs, besides the long walk to and from school.

The *Delaware* came in to-day from Jacksonville bring the rest of the 35*th*. Mrs. Willard is along with them—got only a few lines from Mr. Dennett, all is well.

April. 10*th*   Went into the Normal School this morning and *assumed command.* There are 600 pupils and 15 teachers, of these 13 are residents of the city, and two are from N.E. [New England] 5 of the native teachers are colored girls—the others are whites. They all seem to meet on an equality. I can detect no shade of difference in their treatment of each-other. These colored teachers belonged to the free people of the city and some of them were educated in Phil. and have taught in private schools before the war. They are intelligent and try hard to give satisfaction as do the others, also. The school is not in very good order so we have been endeavoring to put ourselves in good working trim—have graded the school, and are now ready to commence work.

On account of the great event which is to come off on the 14*th* there will be no school after Wednesday. Great preparations are being made to commemorate the event of raising the old flag over Ft. Sumpter [Sum-

159. Miss Fanny Newcomb of Dedham, Mass.

ter]—by Gen. Anderson[160]—none but invited guests will attend—a great company of illustrious names are expected from the north—and the occasion will be one long remembered.

Thurs.[161] *12th*   Spent the day, in company with Dr. Bennett, Mr & Mrs. Morse, and Miss Buttrick, over with Dr. H. [J. M. Hawks] on Mt. Pleasant where our Regt. is encamped. The sail over was charming. We get a good view of all the Forts as we row along and the approach to the shore is very picturesque—but I was somewhat disappointed in the nearer view of the place. I had pictured Mt. Pleasant in glowing colors— imagining it was to this City what the suburbs of Boston or N.Y. are to those great cities—instead, I find but a few really elegant residences and with all its natural scenery in a state of natural still-wild and unadorned. Rode down to Ft. Moultry [Moultrie] on Sullivan's Isl. Went over it and *under it*. It is very much battered by our shelling but still looks *strong*. In the Ft. is a marble slab erected to the memory of the brave 'Osceola'[162]—a few of the old guns too are there.

It commenced raining as we rode home—which delayed our crossing the river till quite late—and it was dark when we landed on this side— lost our way in coming home—as well *as our gentlemen*. I enquired of a family—the way and a young man came out to put us on the right track, as we proceeded, learned that our guide has served nearly four years in the rebel army, was here at the time the place was evacuated and being tired of the war he, with two others 'skulked'. He was quite young, did'nt seem to have much of an idea as to what the 'fuss' was about. It was quite dark when we reached home. Dr. Bennett [?] had been in search of us but no one had dreamed of three such "straping" lasses as we, being lost.

The news of the evacuation of Richmond, and its occupancy by our troops is to-day confirmed and the still more joyful intelligence of the surrender of Lee's entire army to Gen. Grant. The victory is complete— the surrender unconditional! The army disbanded—soldiers to return home, and all the offices paroled! The city is wild with rejoicing. The colored people go about singing "Glory to God! all our trials seem o'er!" — There is great rejoicing in the city. This will increase, greatly, the enthusiasm of to-morrow's celebration. The boat has arrived from N.Y. bring

---

160. Brig. Gen. Robert Anderson, who as a major had commanded Fort Sumter when the opening shots of the war were fired.

161. The correct day for this entry was Wednesday.

162. Osceola was the Seminole Indian leader who resisted American encroachment into Florida.

such men as never before trod the soil of South. Carolina! First and fore-most on the list stands the name of *Garrison*![163]—God bless him! may he live to enjoy the labor of his hands for many years! Then comes Henry Wilson[164] brave and true son of Mass! —Henry Ward Beecher,[165] Theo-dore Tilton,[166] Dr. Levitt [Leavitt],[167] Judge Killy [Kelley] of Penn.[168] and from across the broad Atlantic, Englands noblest son; George Thomp-son![169]—with a host of lesser lights in the civil world—and from military circles, it is impossible to enumerate the throng that will be present. First of all comes the hero of Ft. Sumpter[Sumter]—Gen. Anderson, around him, centers the interest of to-morrow, and the hand which so sadly and reluctantly 4 years ago—lowered the Emblem of our country, in obedi-ence to the demand of its enemies will hoist the old flag to its old place overe the battered but still staunch old Ft. None but invited guests are to be present. We teachers have all had tickets sent to us by Gen. Hatch—so I suppose we are to be a part of the *show*!

Friday 14*th*   We were astir bright and early. At 9. A.M. a carriage came to take us—(Mr & Mrs. M. [Morse] Miss B. [Buttrick] Dr. Bennett and my-self) to the wharf, where we, with a large company of citizens, visitors and offices went on board the *Canonacus* for the Ft. The day was very rough and unpleasant—and on reaching Ft. Sumptir [Sumter] the brick dust and sand was almost blinding. Long stairs led up over the walls of the Fort. The central, open space was beautifully decorated with flags and flowers—arched over the space for the speakers. Seats were ranged round in a circular form and enough to accommodate a vast audience. The beautiful and novel appearance of the Fort was sufficient to engage our attention until the arrival of the distinguished visitors. The waves were so rough, it was impossible to get over the bar with 'the *Arago* so the *Delaware* went out and took off the passengers and it was after 11.

163. William Lloyd Garrison, editor and publisher of *The Liberator*.

164. Abolitionist chairman of the Senate Military Affairs Committee, Wilson would be elected Vice-President under Grant in 1872.

165. Beecher had for years preached eloquently in opposition to slavery from the pulpit of Plymouth Church in Brooklyn.

166. A journalist who was devoted to women's suffrage and other reform causes as well as abolition, it was ironic that Tilton shared the platform with Henry Ward Beecher. Beecher's involvement in an affair with Tilton's wife, would eventually create a national scandal.

167. Joshua Leavitt, who began writing in opposition to slavery as early as 1825 in the columns of the *Christian Spectator*.

168. Judge William D. Kelley, a member of Congress from Philadelphia, whose opposition to slavery prompted him to help found the Republican Party.

169. Thompson had formed the Edinburgh Society for Abolition of Slavery in 1833 and had worked closely with American antislavery groups.

A.M. before they had reached the fort. Gen. Anderson was the hero of the occasion and headed the procession—he is a tall thin white-haired man, but every inch a soldier—next came Henry Ward Beecher who is the orator of the day, and with him Mrs. Beecher, then Senetor Wilson—Geo. Thompson of Eng. W*m* L. Garrison—Theodore Tilton, Judge Kelly & Kellogg[170] of Penn.—and a great many other distinguished visitors and military and navy offices. It was an imposing sight, enough to stirr the patriotic blood and quicken the heart beat of the least interested among us! Beecher was the orator for the occasion. Any attempt to give an idea of his speach would be worse than useless—suffice it, that he held the vast audience by the spell of his eloquence, bound for more than an hour. Previous to the speach—and just after the prayer by the old Chaplain,—Mr Harris,[171] who was in the Ft. at the time of its evacuation, the Asst. A. Gen. E D Townsend read Maj Anderson's dispatch to the Steam-ship *Baltic*, off Sandy Hook, Apr. 18*th* 1861—relating to the surrender. Then the same old flag went up, raised by the hands of Gen. Anderson, amidst the shouts and tears of the audience. Maj. Gen. Anderson was very much affected during the ceremonies—as indeed was everyone. A salute of an hundred guns was then fired from the Ft. and a national salute from every fort and rebel battery that fired on Fort Sumpter [Sumter]. The effect from the walls of the Ft. was sublime—the boom of cannon deafning! — Then came Beecher with his big gun! —After the ceremonies the visitors looked about the fort visiting the bomb-proofs and hunting up relics to carry away. Everyone had *something* if only a bit of brick. The crowd was so great and the tide having left some of the boats aground, it was quite late before we got back to the city. The affair has passed most satisfactorily to all concerned. It was a scene never to be forgotten! —and we all hope, never to be repeated The glorious old flag floats once more over the spot where it was for the first time humbled!

15*th*   The great day for us 'colored' peoples the day most jubilant and the longest to be remembered by us! At 8. A.M. a vast crowd of the colored people and school children had assembled on the Citidel green to listen to Senator Wilson but his voice being out of tune, after singing "John Brown", and cheering for everybody, we adjourned to Zion's Church, which was soon densely packed: It is a large edifice capable of holding between four and five thousand people—those who could'nt get in stayed as near as possible to the *outside*. In the pulpit were *Wilson*,

170. Unidentified. There is no mention of Kellogg in contemporary accounts of the commemorative festivities at Fort Sumter.
171. Rev. Matthew Harris, also called Matthias.

Garrison—Thompson—Tilton, Judges Kelly [Kelley] & Kellogg—beside several *lesser* lights—among which I *must not* place the gallant Maj. Delaney [Delany] of the 104*th* U S C.T.[172] himself a full blooded black—and master of ceremonies on this occasion. Mr. Redpath introduced the different speakers—with appropriate remarks. Soon as the audience were quiet an old man, once a slave very black and features strongly negro— Saml. Dickerson by name, steped forward with his two little daughters each carrying a magnificent bunch of flowers, and he, with a beautiful wreath of fresh roses in his hands welcomed Mr. Garrison in one of the most touching and elequent speaches I ever heard! It was so wholly unexpected, so admirably done, so appropriate that every one was spellbound. Mr. Garrison was quite overcome—replied at length and in his happiest manner. Then came Wilsons' speach plain, earnest practical: just the best words for the hour, possible to be uttered. The greatest enthusiasm prevailed—and when Gen. Saxton got up to speak to them cheer after cheer rent the air—but it remained for 'old Abe's' name to elicit the wildest and noisest enthusiasm, every one sprung to their feet when our honored President was named as the 'great Emancipator' and hats and 'kerchiefs, swung to the wildest cheers!

Theodore Tilton spoke last. He is an orator—but few surpass him in clear and elegant diction, or eloquence. His manner is pleasing—he was received with great applause. The services closed at 1. P.M. The 'home Guards' formed a procession and all the people 'fell in' to escort the distinguished guests to their homes.

As we came from the church, I could'nt refrain from thanking Thompson, for his *presence* and noble words—and to touch my lips to his hand was honor enough for me. —There was no meeting on the Citidal green, in the afternoon as appointed. The speakers were all too much exhausted to speak in the open air.

16*th* —To-day the children of the Zion Church Sunday School, were to celebrate their second anual aniversary. The church was most elaborately and elegantly trimmed with flowers and evergreens. There were *cart loads* of *roses.* Owing to the presence of so many distinguished speakers the concert was defered 'till evening and Henry Ward Beecher preached, in the morning—to one of the largest audiences I ever saw under one roof—and it was also a very appreciative one as several hearty cheers testified to. In the afternoon all the other speakers—*aired their*

---

172. Maj. Martin R. Delany one of the Union's few black officers received his commission just weeks before the war ended. The "armée d'Afrique" Delany had hoped to raise never materialized, but he recruited many volunteers for the 104th and 105th U.S.C.T. and remained on active duty working with freedmen until 1868.

eruditions—much to our weariness—and I can most heartely say that I shall be glad when the whole party are gone and we can get a little quiet, and go back to our work.

17*th*   —Went to school this morning and learned that the children had been notified to go to the wharf to say 'good bye' to the visitors—almost all carried flowers. Garrison made them a speach and was covered with flowers in return. School didn't amount to *but little*! Went to the rooms where the clothing is given out to the colored people—found a great crowd of dirty and raged waiting ones—with no one to attend to their wants. There was so much to do, that no one pretended to do anything—and with *tons* of clothing in their sight, day after day they come and go away without being served. I began to fit out the school children and in a very short time I had fifteen neatly clad and on their way rejoicing—and with promise to return on the morrow and see to my children's cloths I succeeded in getting away. Went up to my 'orphan assylum' and made arraingements to have the clothing for the little children brought up there and let me give them out, so I shall have an extra duty.

18*th*   School is getting into admirable order—we have no trouble in reducing them to a state of discipline. I like most of my teachers especially the two northern one who I have put each in charge of a floor. One of the "indigenous" teachers I shall get rid of as quietly and as soon as possible—she is nosy and wanting in 'order' so throws the whole school into confusion.

Am getting the furniture moved into our 'Assylum.' It is rather *irregular* and sometimes a little broken, but we are not *over fastideous.*—Took the names of six children who are ready to be taken home—hope to get the house open by the first of next week.

19*th*   School was hardly open this morning before Mr. Hurley[173] came in and told me that President Lincoln had been assassinated—and that Sect. Seward was just alive, an attempt haveing been made to murder him at the same time. It seemed too horrible to believe! When he made the announcement to the school—many of the older children cried aloud. It seemed impossible to go on with school exercises. Soon after Mr. H. [Hurley] had gone several of the large girls who are in classes taught by the white southern teachers, came to me, weeping bitterly and

---

173. Timothy Hurley, described as "a jovial Irishman from Connecticut" and "a shrewd, shameless little scamp, respected by nobody, liked by everybody." Francis B. Simkins, Robert H. Woody, *South Carolina During Reconstruction* (Chapel Hill: University of North Carolina Press, 1932), p. 125. After acting as Charleston's Superintendent of Streets and publishing the radical journal *The Leader*, Hurley served in the South Carolina legislature.

A Woman Doctor's Civil War

begged to be taken out of their classes. I let them go home at the time - and must watch my teachers for any *expression* of disloyalty. The greatest gloom pervades the city. Every native is looked at suspiciously—and I have no doubt but the least expression of gratification at this national calamity will be dealt roughly with. Minute guns have been firing nearly ever since the news came; flags are at half mast. The colord people express their sorrow and sense of loss in many cases, with sobs and loud lamentations! No native whites are seen anywhere on the streets. When the children came to school they all wore little crape rosettes or bows, and in most of the school rooms an attempt to trim with mourning has been made, back of my desk there was hung a lovely wreath of roses tied with black crape—this was all done without any suggestions from us. There are constant complains of teachers expressing disloyal sentement in hearing of the children and I have been obliged to dissmiss one of them for speaking with disrespect of the murdered President. For me, I am begining to be strong in the "fatalistic theory." His work was accomplished and he is removed. I will not doubt but God has other men and means, to finish what is yet undone!

20*th*   Did'nt get to school to-day—been busy at the Assylum. Have given out clothing to nearly 200, babies and little children.

21*st*   Been to school this eve; Hurly [Hurley] made a speach which superseded the usual lessons.

My class of men are quite enthusiastic in their eager desire after learning!

April 22*nd* 1865.

Been at the 'Assylum' most of the day—gave out clothes to over a hundred little ones. Took the name of six orphans who are to come into the house next week In the eve Col. B., [Beecher] wife and Dr. M. [Marcy] came in.

23*rd*   Went to hear Mr. Low [Lowe], agent of the N.E.F. Aso. [New England Freedman's Association][174] preach at the Unitarian Chapel, on Archdale St. Sermon suggested by the presidents death—rather a *mild decoction*—very soothing to secessionist—it could hardly have offended the most rabid of them.

In the afternoon went with Mrs. B. [Beecher] and Col to hear their Chaplin, in the church in this St. Col. played the organ. I and a few other colored brethrin and one sister, did the singing—after church one of the Ladies of the benevolent Society came to me with the *gratifying* intelli-

174. Rev. Charles Lowe of Massachusetts.

gence that she had six more children for us—including a *pair* of *twins* born the night privious. I *commissioned* her to give them *away* as there were two women ready to take them—the other four will come to the house. Went home with Mrs. B. [Beecher] to *tea*. It is very pleasant to go there, everything is cozy and home like. I like them both right well!

24*th*   Only in school a short time to-day—spent the remaining time on East Bay St. Gave out clothes to about fifty children, all I had. They come in *droves* It seems as though we never should get moved in. Every one seems to try to put stumbling blocks in our way. The beds and mattresses which we expected was a sure thing for us—we are to lose. Some secessionist comes in with a prior claim—so things hand along—'till I am sick and tired of this unnecessary delay and wish I could go back to my school and remain their!

25*th*   Mr. Redpath met me with a radiant face this morning, saying "O. Mrs. Hawkes. I believe I'm the happiest man alive'. An *old fellow* by the name of *Hawkes* has given me fifty bed sacks and as many blankets." —I symphathized in his gladness and sent him for a team to bring the boxes to the house immediately. Was so busy did'nt go to school.

Went into St. Phillips' St. for a few minutes to teach Miss Buttricks class 'Rally round the flag". Miss Garland[175] out sick—sent Miss Chase[176] ove to take her place. The teachers report, 650. pupils present to-day. This afternoon—as soon as I was through dinner Mr Redpath came for me to go and look at some things which we are to get for the '*House*'. Borrowed Mrs. Beechers pony and saddle—mounted (with short dress and crinoline)—and off we gaily rode.

Went for the furniture—then called at the Teachers' Home. The ladies were charmingly situated and have got things most home like and comfortable—spent a pleasent hour—then went to call on Mrs. Pillsbury Cor. Montague & Rutledge Sts. Met Mr. & Mrs. John P. [?] and Dr. Brown of the 55*th* there. Mrs. P. [Pillsbury] is now most *charmingly* situated—has a palatial house, elegantly furnished! Got home just at tea-time.

26*th*   Went to school in good season to day—and have been at work 'sorting the books brought down from the Morris' St. school. Find more *french* and *Latin* than we are in need of at present. Our supply of books is very small in all the schools—especially of Primers. My teachers are not the most efficient. I have but two northern ones. Had to turn one out of school last week for expressing disloyal sentiments before the school

---

175. Elizabeth H. Garland of Brattleboro, Vt.
176. Lucy Chase of Massachusetts.

children. Miss Peoples—she denies the charge but I have no reason to doubt the girls who say they heard her say that "Lincoln ought to have been murderd four years ago." I had some idea of sending for a guard to take her away but finally let her go—with the promise to appear before Col. Gurny [Gurney][177] at 3. P.M. It will be a good lesson for the rest of them!

One of the large girls in Miss Chamberlins'[178] class asked, this morning to stay out of school for a few days. She was looking quite miserable on inquiry the following information was elicited. "I feel sick marm," What is the matter, asked the teacher, "Please misses, my baby done come las' night and I feels bad". What! *You* had a *baby* last night? "Yes marm". She was allowed to *go home*!

27th   Grandma' *Peeleg* arrived at the 'House' to-day with her contribution for the 'Assylum'—five little homeless children! The six one a boy baby of a week died last night. The poor old woman has no home and no food so she must stay here and we will do the best we can for them tho' as yet we have no 'rations.'

Got a large box of clothing, sent to me from the Association, for distribution, and have been busy distributing it. Have given out clothes to at least 500 little children and babies within the last ten days. It is tiresome work, and sometimes I do get very cross over it.—Of course I no need do it, but at the rooms they are so slow it will never be done—unless someone does take hold and help!

School is prosperous. There is scarcely a day that we do not have visitors.

28th   Simon Draper[179] from N.Y. visited school. He will speak to the colored people at Zion Church at 4. P.M.—did'nt make a speach to my children much to my relief.

Mrs. Redpath arrived last night—was in the evening school. I like the looks of her very much—rather handsomer than her husband!—Sent off a class of 20 boys to-day—they did'nt like to go but when they found it inevitable, everyone took off his hat—swung it and said "Well good bye ladies, if we *must* leave you!"

177. Col. Gurney was federal commander in Charleston and would remain in that city as a businessman and politician after the war.
178. Melissa Chamberlain of Dover, N.H., soon to be appointed principal of the Ashley Street School.
179. Draper was a Massachusetts-born New York millionaire as devoted to furthering the political career of his friend Daniel Webster and to philanthropy and abolitionism as to his business ventures. He was at this time on leave from his duties as Collector of the Port of New York.

Dined at Col. B's [Beecher] and went there in the evening to a wedding—'gay and festive'! One of his soldiers—a great six footer, and a little bride—both *very black*.

29*th* My family at the Assylum all sick this morning—carried them some bread, tea and corn meal. Hope it is nothing serious. Went down to Col. B's [Beecher] to tea—and spent a part of the evening.

30*th* —Wrote letters all the morning. Dr. [J. M. Hawks] came over from the Regt. Went round to the 'Assylum' in the afternoon and in looking over my animated property there, found it covered with small-pox—so my "Orphan Assylum", turns out a 'Pest-house,' two of the children are quite sick and the others, probably will be. Shall have to send them to hospital
Went back to Mt. Pleasant with Dr. [J. M. Hawks]. Miss Butterick [Buttrick] also along. The wind was against us so had to 'beat' across which took us two hours of charming sailing. It was dark when we arrived. Found Mr. Willey [?] sitting up but quite sick! he was quite joyous over our arrival. Miss B. [Buttrick] will stay 'till Tuesday. I go home in the morning to be with the schools which go up to the race-course at 8. A.M. form a procession thus and march into the little burying ground of the Union prisoners—and with appropriate cerimonies deck thier graves with flowers.

Our May Day Festival!

May 30*th*[180] We have planned for the dedication of the bleak spot where so many hundred of our soldiers were covered in long trenches; in heaps—four short rows containing 249 of our men, the dead of less than a week. These were white soldiers—prisoners of war. The colored men have built a fence about the spot a free offering, and a fine monument is to be erected as soon as we have sufficient means. The cloudless sky and hot sun of an August morning was over us as the school children formed in procession and marched from the Morris St. School, the Club House on the race-course where the opening ceremonies are to be held. We rode slowly up King St. to the race course. There it was thronged with vehicles of every description and pedestrians of all ages, from the baby in arms to the white hairs of bent old age. All faces wore the sweetest smiles and nearly every hand bore bunches or baskets laden with beautiful flowers.

180. The correct date for this entry is May 1.

On reaching the place, found the grounds already covered with a large concourse of people. Among others I noticed Col. Gurney Post Commandant, & wife—Gen. Hartwell—Col. Beecher & wife—Judge Coolery[181] & wife and several other "*distinguished* guests". Mr. Redpath is the animating spirit of the occasion. At 10 A.M. he got the procession formed, the school children in advance. As they passed under the flag which was stretched across the Street which led to the soldiers' graves—with their clean bright faces, neat clothes and hands laden with flowers, all singing "My Country 'tis of thee" it was a beautiful sight. As they entered the little enclosure where our poor soldiers lay, every voice was hushed and with quiet reverent steps they marched around the yard depositing their floral offerings on the new made graves—and Mr. Redpath says the ground all about was covered. It was one of the most touching sights I every witnessed! Mothers whose loved ones lie here—would that your hearts might all be gladened by the sight of this beautiful tribute—to the memory of your precious dead. Would you not bless the black hands which have decked them with flowers—and the noble men whose gratuitous labor has built about their resting place a protection from the rude hands of the thoughtless or jeering! God bless them all and grant to their hearts the prayer of a life time, that freedom which is the inheritance of every child of earth!

The cerimonies in the yard consisted in singing appropriate hymns by the choir of the Baptist Church—prayer by a colored clergyman—and reading of appropriate passages of scripture, none but colored people officiating. It was very impressive and solemn—*and very hot*! We then rode over to the 'Club-house' where there was speaking by several gentlemen of both colors—Col. Beecher among others—but it was to warm to stand outside to listen so I took *it for granted* they were *all right* and went off with some of the ladies of the "Benevolent Society", for refreshments—which, very unexpectedly to us, they had provided. The children danced and played about just as children will at such times and were all very happy. I saw no quarriling or unpleasant feeling anywhere. By 2 P.M. the speaking and eating were over, thus ending the impressive ceremonies of the first Decoration Days[182] and I came home with Col. B.

---

181. Unidentified. Not even the Charleston *Courier*, May 2, 1865, in its detailed account of the memorial observance mentioned a person of this name.
182. The events herein described constituted the first Memorial Day observance, though the Grand Army of the Republic did not officially proclaim Decoration Day until 1868. Some credit the Drs. Hawks with having "conceived, proposed and practiced" the custom of decorating the graves of Union Civil War veterans. Charles H. Coe, "The Late Dr. John Milton Hawks," Daytona Beach *Observer*, August 30, 1941.

[Beecher] and wife—very tired and very glad to get in doors out of the hot sun and rest. At four o'clock went up to the Morris' St. school house to meet the teachers but Mr. R [Redpath] was not there and but few of the ladies, so nothing was done. Went to school in the even. but I was the only teacher there—about 200 pupils present—took Mr. Stevens [?] with me, so set him to teaching a class of women. On my return just heard the good news that Johnson and Beauregard have surrendered with their entire army![183] So the "rebellion" is over! Four long years of the most terrible and bloody warfare any nation every endured, and the old flag floats triumphant over us again—with its glory undimmed and every star brighter than before; "Glory to God! who hath given us the victory!!"

This news winds up the day with a grand flourish—tomorrow the jubilant guns from every fort and Battery will thunder forth the glad news! How thick with events the days come laden!!

May 2nd.   The official announcement of the death of the President only reached us to-day and all business has been suspended by order of the Sect. of War so no schools for today. The public buildings, Military Hd. Qtrs., school-houses and a few other places are draped with black. — The colored people are frightened and apprehensive. They feel a personal loss, and fear the result of it to themselves! —This eve we were to go to the "Teachers' House" to a social dance but some fogyish notion of Mr. Low's [Lowe] prevents the assembly, so some of us will go to have a little social time.

3rd   The party last night was stiff and formal—went late—came home early—went with Col. & Mrs. B. [Beecher]. There has been such a change in the weather that a fan, is positive comfort. Miss B. [Buttrick] came home from Mt. P. [Pleasant] yesterday but returned today to take care of Mr. Willy, who is sick with fever, through the rest of the week.

"Orphan Assylum' not yet in running order—and I am fretting and working to death because everything cannot be accomplished in a moment. Military people are the 'slowest' of aught earthly.

4th   Hon. J. C. Holmes, formerly a member of congress from this city visited my school today. He is a venerable looking old man, and was very 'conciliatory' in speach, and quite anxious to impress me with his strong *union feeling*. This was the *first public* school of the character he had ever visited. He expressed himself as being highly pleased with it.

Went with Dr. [J. M. Hawks] over to James' Is. to visit my old friends who came with me from Florida—Patty and Maria and their families. Pat-

---

183. On 26 April 1865, Confederate Generals Joseph E. Johnston and P. G. T. Beauregard surrendered to General William T. Sherman at Durham Court House, North Carolina.

ty and Tom were over here to sell some black berries so I did'nt see them, but "Aunt Maria" showed me about their house, and field of well cultivated corn and potatoes, and the garden of vegetables, with great pride and satisfaction. They are all doing remarkably well there and feel contented & happy. In going over, our boatman, who an old resident here, pointed out all the places of interest—among other things the big rebel gun known as "The Bull in the woods"—which is still there and in good order, though it is not generally known that this is that famous gun.

5*th*   Been in school all day for the first time in two weeks. Went over to Asylum this morning but found no one there so did'nt stay very long. Felt quite exhausted on reaching home. The wind blew quite hard, and the sand and dust was almost blinding. Mrs. B. [Beecher] came in and found me on the bed. We lay and went to sleep together then I went home with her and stayed till after ten in the Eve, she was feverish and the Col. obliged to be away. Forgot all about the *evening school*!! Dr. Brown has been here for two nights. The Regt. is going up into the country not raiding, as we hope *that* is now *over*—but they are to make stations w[h]ere returning reb. soldiers can come in & take the *oath* and be metamorphised into *good loyal citizens*!!

6*th*   The day is very warm. Have been with Mr. Redpath all this morning devising 'ways and means' for accomplishing our *educational purposes*—also looking out a house for the teachers who continue to arrive. Our association seems insane on the subject of sending teachers to this place at this time of the year. To many, I fear it will be a 'sorry coming.' —We are talking of establishing an 'Industrial School' also a writing school—each to be held twice a week in the afternoon. This, with an additional half hour at our morning schools, will keep us as busy as necessary in order to preserve a good degree of *health*!!

May 1865 Charleston S.C.

13*th*   Mr Redpath has long been anxious that I visit the ajacent Is. and look into the condition of the Freed people on them and last evening Dr. Marcy of the 35*th* proposed to accompany me so this morning at about 8 o'clock he came; the rest of the household having a desire for a good time, proposed being our *escort*. So Mr. & Mrs. Morse, Mr. B. [?] Mr. Willey and Chaplin Hall,[184] started with us. Had no difficulty in getting a boat and crew; A little way from the dock lies a large vessell filled with returning rebles so we rowed round to take a look at them. The *look* was returned with interest. It was ten A.M. when we reached Ft. Johnson. Our

184. Chaplain Thomas A. Hall of the Thirty-Fifth U.S.C.T.

Regt. has but just gone there and are not yet settled, so our reception was not a very *hearty* one. I think they wished us in Castle Pinkney;[185] but after a little fluttering and our solemn assurances that we would'nt be a bother, comparative quiet was restored. Horses were promised and Dr. H. [J. M. Hawks] agreed to be of the party. While an early dinner was in process we visited the Ft. and other works. The rebs, did their work in a most thorough and substantial manner. By an experienced eye, the defences of Charleston are pronounced as the best constructed of any yet examined on either side. It is evident, they were intended to stand a long siege. There is nothing especially cheering in the thought of a summer campaign on James Is. and Ft. J. [Johnson] is barren and desolate looking. Our dinner was a real potluck affair. An old billiard table set out under the trees where Dr's tent is in process of construction—bread and N. H. butter, meat, and fresh berries, with hearty appetites made a capital repast. The horses were at the door. I had for my use, a splendid 'Chestnut' belonging to Col. B. [Beecher] and Dr. M. [Marcy] rode Maj. W's [?] 'Sorrel'. A ride of six miles, with an occasional deviation to visit the 'works' of a few families, brought us to the rebel stronghold, Secessionville. There are but two small framed houses, these were used as Hd. Qrs. and the huts for the soldiers are scattered several acres irregularly. They are built of rough logs and mud, with thatched roofs, a chimny on the side oposite the door, and rough brick floors. A *tent* would be far more agreeable lodgins. There are over 300 people now at this place, and it would take a stout heart to ride unmoved, among them—dirty ragged, *starving* expresses their condition. In my experience, on the plantations among the slaves of Western Fla. I never saw such misery and utter destitution as this—and yet I do believe the people are happier now than then: they seem hopeful, and contented and a little more food is all that is necessary to render them well and happy—and unless this is speedily given them, many must die of starvation. The rations now allowed is not sufficient to sustain life. We examined them. Some of the people who have been here a month, until today have only recieved a few quarts of rough rice—others who have been two weeks had recieved *nothing*. The blackberries are very abundant and constitute the chief dependance: several of the women assured me they had eaten nothing for two days, but berries—and the little children were crying for food. We saw several, especially among the aged, suffering from disease engendered by starvation. One very old woman, was sitting on the ground, because her poor swolen feet and legs could no longer carry her, and as we stoped to speak with the little party,

185. Castle Pinckney was a Confederate prison in Charleston.

she look up with a patient smile, saying "O yes Miss we spects to see hard times for now but when de corn done grow we'll hab enough and be bery happy. I bress de good Lord dat I'se free, and when de crops grow we'll do bery well"[.] Theres faith, philosophy and religion for us. Its pretty hard to *plant* the corn, one is *starving* for and look with patient hope to the harvest. They have done remarkably well with the planting—the lands have been laying without cultivation now for three or four years, at least, and all the tools to be had is a *hoe* and many of them hav'ent *that*. They are also now out of seed. Most of the families have from one to five acres of land under cultivation. God grant them a bountiful harvest!

We promised to help them to seed corn and something to eat—though way to do it is not very clear. We rode around the fortifications, which are of great strength and finely made dismounted and went into the house, formerly head qrs. of the rebs. Our shot and shell have shattered it considerably but it is still in *usable* condition and the people told me they were keeping it for *school*. The wish for a teacher very much and truly, one good missionnary among them could do great good now. The people, especially the women and children are as nearly naked as possible and be *clothed*. Some of the children had evidently once possessed clothing as evidenced by a *shirt collar* with a few tatters attached, still clinging to some of them—but they will not *die* this weather if naked and they are in a far better state of health than could be expected under such adverse circumstances. They have to walk to Mc'Leod's plantation a distance of five miles, to draw rations and as we rode towards home, we met the people returning—and examined what they had recieved.

The ration for the heads of families, we found to be a half *pint* of hommany and *three qtrs pound* of *salt* pork, with a very small *allowance* for *each child*. One man had, on his back the provisions for a week for *nine*—and I would on oath testify that it was not *more* than sufficient to feed them for one *day*—and yet they can get no more for a week! Thousands of rebels who have fought us with all the bitterness of fiends are now feeding freely at the Govt. cribs, and these loyal men and women are starving. It seems as though our military authorities offered a premium for disloyalty. How long O, Lord! how long!

We gave them directions to come to Ft. Johnson on Monday for corn to plant and to bring some black berries to sell, and rode sadly home ward. I have seen the slaves at their unpaid toil on the sugar plantations of western Fla. and heard their tales of grief and abuse—but the hardest cases I ever saw were comfortably cared for in comparison to the condition of these people—and yet I do not believe that one of them would voluntarily return to a state of bondage!

It was nearly sunset when we reached the Ft. and found the regt. under *marching* orders to return to Mr. Pleasant—very much pleased at the change. —Came over to the city in a small boat the water was rough and the boat *leaky*, so we got *wet*—and after the long walk up home I was reasonably fatigued.

Friday the 12*th*   went to hear Salmon P. Chase[186] speak in Zion Church to the colored people. The house was full—Gen. Saxton opened the meeting. He is no orator but what he says generally means something. Mr. Tomlinson[187] made an admirable speach after the Gen. Then Maj. *Delany* "spread himself" tiresomely Chase not having arrived. The speach of the Judge was a model one—and gave the greatest satisfaction to all friends of colored people. Gen. Gillmore [Gilmore] came with Mr. Chase. The meeting was a most enthusiastic one.

Sunday 14*th*   Went to hear Col. Beecher preach at Zion's Church. Had a political discourse and was excellent.

15*th*   Got ready this morning expecting to go to Wadmlaw [Wadmalaw] Is. on a steamer. This is about 20 miles distant, not far from Edisto—but the boat did not come, so Dr. H. [J. M. Hawks] coming over from Ft. J [Johnson], I returned with him to finish up the canvassing of that Island. Got horses and went down to McLeods Plantation about six miles distant where rations are issued. The condition of the people here is far better in all respects save food than at Secessionville—but their rations are about the same. Mr. Hill the Sup. is from Phill. and one of the poorest specimens I have yet seen sent out from the north. His room was more filthy than many of the negro houses. I saw a broom in one corner but it must have belonged to the soldiers which were here, and has been honorably discharged from service, for it certainly has done none lately. Pots and kettles stood about the fire place, for he is his own cook and house-keeper and chambermaid too. I judge by the looks of that room—however, I gained several items of intelligence from him concerning the island. There are 2500 people on it scattered about in the different rebel camps, and their condition is about as I have described at the one we visited. He has given out 50 bushels of seed corn and 7 of garden seed. No doubt much of the *corn* has been eaten—for a man's faith must be very large that could plant corn while suffering the pangs of hunger.

---

186. Mr. Chase was a long-time abolitionist who had been Secretary of the Treasury in President Lincoln's cabinet and was at this time Chief Justice of the United States.
187. Reuben Tomlinson of Pennsylvania, who had originally come south as a missionary. He soon was appointed Superintendent of Education for the Freedmen's Bureau. Tomlinson would fail in his candidacy for the governorship of South Carolina in 1872.

Wherever we have been, the people are very anxious to have a school established but the advanced season, and the necessity for them *all* to labor, with the unhealthiness of the Islands make it advisable not to do so until *fall*! If some good missionaries could be found to go among them to teach them to live and try to make them more comfortable it would be well, or could some one go about and call the people together occasionally and have a talk with them on *little things*—furnish them with a few needels thread &—they would be doing a vast amount of good.

Our ride home in the early evening was very pleasant. Stayed at the Fort over night and Dr. [J. M. Hawks] came over with me in the morning. In the evening Dr. M. [Marcy] came round and invited Miss B. [Buttrick] and me to go and see the rebel ram *Columbia* and the torpedo boats which are soon to leave for N.Y. This ram is one of the most formidable ever built. It is iron plated 6 in thick and then lined with solid oak 14 in. thick—inside of this was an iron net-work to catch the splinters when hit and shattered by shot or shell. She was never used but by some fortunate train of events got sunk, and our navy have just got her afloat and in running order. It is a great curiosity and well worth a visit. We visited every foot of her. She is *enormous* and no one could realize that they were on a floating craft when aboard her. But the torpedo boats are the greatest curiosities. An enormous one eight ft. in diameter and over 250 ft long was about completed, to be used in running the blockade. It looks like an enormous musk mellon in shape and general appearance. We went on to it and looked in. For transportation of freight this form of boat is decided to be the best as a greater quantity can be carried and with less risk than in any other, but no possible comfort could be had on board one save the *poor* one of safety. Several smaller ones of the kind were laying at the dock and we had ample opportunity to examine them.

May 22*nd*.

One of my southern teacher, Miss Branford invited Miss Garland and me to go to Somerville [Summerville] with her on Sat. to visit her Aunt. The railroad is in order and cars running so the idea seemed a pleasant one and we accepted with permission to invite as many others as we liked. S. [Summerville] is 22 miles in the interim, a place formerly occupied by the aristocracy, as a summer resort. Col. B. [Beecher] wife, chaplain and Surgeon—our entire family of five—two of the other teachers and Capt. Pratt Provo. Mar.[188] in all a company of 14 met at the depot at

---

188. Capt. Joseph T. Pratt of the Thirty-second U.S.C.T. Provost Marshal of the Charleston District.

10, A.M. had some difficulty in getting proper accommadations but after hesitating and *almost* starting homeward we finally got off in most excellent spirits our party occupying all the room of one car. A refreshing shower cooled the air—the flowers were rare and many of them new and but for them I could easily imagine myself travelling through N.E. The tall pine forests and level fields of grass had no distinctive marks to remind one of their locality. On reaching the station the most of our party proceded with Miss B. [Branford] to the residence of her Aunt where we anticipated a hearty welcome and plenty of country fare—as we understood Ms. Browining to be "only a country woman" and we were cautioned not to be expecting to much—so my expectations were not up to any great grandeur judging from what I had seen in this and other southern states. What then was our astonishment at being ushered into one of the most elegant and richest furnished parlors I have ever seen in a country residence! MDs were somewhat subdued and sat very quietly while Susy went to inform her aunt of our arrival. For about 15 minutes we were left to amuse ourselves before "My Lady" appeared, in the doorway with a stage curtesy. She sailed into the room and went through with the cerimony of introduction with the airs of a princess—then sank with languid grace, into an easy chair near the Col. and opened upon us a whole broad side of information concerning her losses by the war and the peculiar condition of things as regards servants &—assured us that their house had always been noted for its hospitality—but now, she only had three house servants when she formerly had ten and they were so impudent she would'nt think of asking them to do any extra work—and as their dinner was already over she really could'nt offer us the hospitalities of her house. Our whole party was most effectively 'squelched'. We could'nt utter a *word*—an everyday tone of voice would have sounded *vulgar*. Col. tried to say a few polite things but failed so "my lady" did the *talking*. She felt badly at the new state of things in regard to the colored people she was sorry that they should suffer as they must now— (here she grew pathetic)—for she loved these people—she was reared with them they had played together in childhood & & now *who* would excicise a guardian care for them and more than all beside, (now that they had gone from her fostering care) *who* would lead them to *Jesus*! There was evidence of a profound sensation in the room for me, I nearly choked trying to keep my feelings from over-powering me!

The rest of the party who had rode up to Hd. Qtrs of the 55*th* N.Y. and were staying there sent to enquire if they should come to us, or would we come to them? We chose the latter and were soon breathing from outside madames' hospitable abode and laughing merrily over our encounter with the '*chivilary*'. We had brought sufficient provisions and so taking possession of the gentlemen's dining room we soon had a sumtuous meal. We expected to return to the city at 4. P.M. so early in the afternoon the carriages were brought round and we were taken to see the place which—which rather an unsatisfactory undertaking as it is all in the *woods*—but there are very many elegant, little summer residences like the one we visited and the forest still standing makes the rides very charming. One of the teachers started on the Maj's saddle pony but could'nt manage it so I took her place and had a charming ride.

The cars did'nt come down—so we must stay all night—which was rather embarrassing as our entertainers did'nt *keep hotel* though they were quartered in one, or what was once one, however, they and *we* made the best of it and had a most *jolly* time—danced to grand music 'till nearly midnight—and were then provided with comfortable beds. Sunday went to ride again and soon as dinner was over were informed that the cars were waiting to take us back to the city. It was one of the pleasantest excursions I have taken, arrived home just in time for "dress parade," so as Col. B. [Beecher] came for us to go, we went out to see it and hear his talk to his men. I don't remember ever to have been more thoroughly tired than when I got to my room for the night.

I had just entered my first *nap*, when startled by a peculiar scratching noise and soon Miss B. [Branford] screamed out—exclaiming, "Something is in the room—O, what is it—it must be that '*rac-koon*' (Some of the offices had a tame one)—scream followed scream 'till I got up and searched about in the dark for the animal. Found a small dog curled up near the bed *thumping his tail* to go to sleep by—put him out, amid the suppressed *giggles* of the officers in the other room. This so thoroughly awoke us that it was long after midnight before we got asleep. About 3. A.M. some one thundered up to the door with the gratifying intelligence that the cars had come. I jumped up and ran out on the veranda but as no one else stirred concluded not to make any more disturbance—so returned to the sofa. Miss B. got on her *boots* then into bed again—got up and dressed at five. No cars heard from. Had a nice breakfast and all went over to "guard mount," then round to Capt Cox's office—had the horse saddled and went to ride with Dr. M. [Marcy] and soon Capt. Du Boise[189] came up with us and we rode about town. While we were at dinner the train came down from Orangeburg, and with as little delay as possible we got 'on board and were soon rattling towards the city. We saw many

189. Probably Capt. James J. DuBois of the Fifty-sixth New York Volunteers.

beautiful flowers by the road, but other ways, I could not realize that we were in So. Ca. the scenery was so like much one passes through in NE. We were all heartily glad to be home once more.

Miss Branford stayed, and returned with us without again visiting her affectionate relative. We heard, coming down in the cars, that she made boast of the manner in which she had *snubbed* a lot of yankees; I presume she considered it quite a fine thing—*so did we!*

School goes on after the same way—not great changes now. Mr. R. [Redpath] is not in as often but sends Mr. Allan[190] to attend to such of his duties as pertain to visiting the schools. This is, I think, quite as agreeable to the teachers as having Mr. R. [Redpath] dash in on them as is his custom. Since his wife's arrival he is much more difficult to please—and she is constantly making suggestions and remarks to the teachers, that are quite annoying.

May, 1865.

29th Saturday   the day was so cool we had a fire. Went to market in the morning with Mrs. Beecher, and to school with her at 2. P.M. in the Citidel. She and Chaplin Hall have a large school-room there and a school regularly every day. Soon Mrs. Hyatt came in, announced that her carriage was waiting to take us to ride. Stayed and helped us in school till four, then we rode over to the Arsenal. Capt. Grace of the 54 Mass.[191] is in command and showed us all about, taken great pains to explain to us the different guns, ammunition and other ordnance stores. The grounds are admirably laid out and in excellent order—there is a nice large flower and vegitable garden within the enclosure—so Capt. G [Grace] gave us each a boquet of roses and filled our carriage with *cabbages* and other vegitables—all of which, was appreciatively recieved.

Yesterday (Sunday) by invitation of Dr. [J. M. Hawks] we all went over to Mt. Pleasant to dine with him. On our way to the wharf called at the Orphan Assylum—Mr. R. [Redpath] was there and had the children up on *parade*—as I went in every one of them sprang to meet me, and Mr. R [Redpath], gave up in despair, and went with us, as soon as I could get away from the children, into the house to see the sick. The house is now in good running order and things go smoothly on. There are twenty children now [in] it, and one of the teachers to take charge of affairs.[192] On ar-

190. William F. Allen had been appointed Superintendent of Public Schools for the Port of Charleston in April 1865. After the war he would have a distinguished career as a professor of history at the University of Wisconsin.
191. Capt. James W. Grace, Chief of Ordnance for the Charleston Military District.
192. Adelaide F. Boyden of Leominster, Mass., the temporary matron.

riving at the Dr.'s found him much more pleasantly situated than previously to this morning—he has now very pleasant and comfortable quarters. After dinner a drive out to the picket line (about six miles, was proposed, and about 4 P.M. we got started—I on Col. Bennetts horse and Adj. Dow[193] on one the Drs. the rest of the party in a rickety old two-horse carriage. It was near sundown when we reached the little church where our pickets are camped. The ride out, was most delightful—the air cool and the scenery reminding one of home. These pine lands are very like N.E. After a short call at the *company* Commanders Qrs, we started homeward by way of the beach. had only proceeded a short distance when an unfortunate hitch in the road, broke the pole of the carriage, short off. Lt. Dow rode back to camp to get tools where with to repair damage. It was half an hour before we were on our way, then Lt D. [Dow] and Mr. Morse changed places, & Mr. M. [Morse] and I rode on—after getting some distance ahead, and not hearing anything of the carriage, Mr. M. rode back to see if there was further trouble and I rode liesurely forward. It was growing dark rapidly. Mr. M. [Morse] did not return, so pony and I struck into a canter thinking it best to take care of No. 1. True I didn't have any idea of the *way*, but I thought the horse would go home and I could trust to him which I *did* by turning him in the opposite direction to the one he wished to take when we struck the beach. It seemed so evident that he desired to go wrong that in spite of my boasted faith in his instincts crib-ward I faced about and was proceding at a rapid rate up the beach—when my progress was arrested by some *tall hollering*. I looked right and left for *gorillas* and proceeded a little more quietly. The yells continued and suddenly the thought struck me, it might be some of our party in search of me, so I gave one *terrific yell*, immediately answered by Mr. Morse who soon came up to where I could see him across the marsh, and very quietly inquired when I might be going 'home' I indignantly answered, at which he laughed immoderately. I was soon convinced of my error and facing about my horse showed his appreciation of the change by a satisfied neigh and some of the *tallest* running I care to participate in. Talk about being a road on the beach—why its nothing but the edge of a marsh anyway, and I did'nt see even a line of water the whole way, We were right among the salt-works. Some of the buildings are in ruins so our horses would, every few rods, draw to a sudden halt almost throwing us over their heads. It was now quite dark. We came to what looked like a deep pond of water, Mr. Morse proposed to turn back

193. First Lt., Adj. Charles A. Dow of the Twenty-first U.S.C.T.

but as our horses were ready to go on I urged that we do so—and the stream was safely forded—we soon came to another, deeper and larger but it was also safely crossed. The way now seemed clear and we rode rapidly on. Left the beach and seemed to be on the main road and we were just congratulating ourselves on our safe delivery from the boggs and marshes, when we were brought up suddenly by a rough fence which was thrown directly across the road; we could'nt get round it or over it so hearing a dog bark in the distance, we went in search of the man he belonged to, leaped ditches and rode over an old cotton field till I began to think our adventure would bring us all to a *serious* termination. M. yelled and I screamed and soon an answering yell greeted us from a near plantation, and we got directions from some colored men—to come over another ditch go round the corner of a fence—ride forward a few paces—then go ahead all right, only 'two mile,' from de city'. It all proved as the dark said, and in about a half an hour we rode up to Hd. Qrts, thoroughly tired and hoping to find the carriage had reached them before us—but it had not—so after a nice supper with the Maj. I went down to Drs' [J. M. Hawks], at 10 1/2 went to bed—was just begining to doze when the rest of the party arrived and their adventures were so much more exciting than ours that we hardly had *'the face* to speak" of them. The roads got rougher and the carriage again gave out, so they were obliged to leave it about four miles out and get in as best they could. The Adj. mounted on[e] of the horses and Mrs. Morse on behind him without saddle or blanket but clinging fast to him—while the other horse brought both harnesses and a colard man to guide the party. Dr. and Miss B [Buttrick] came on foot, hand in hand like 'the babes in the woods', and in this style they reached home at a quarter past eleven. They were too much excited to sleep or let anyone so our nights rest was of little good to us, however we were up early and got over to school at little after nine— and I have been suffering from the bad effects of the night exposure ever since—am so hoarse, can hardly speak to-day—but have been to school——and have now just returned from my daily *inspection* of our 'Assylum' which *grows* daily—there ar about 25 children now in it—several have been and are sick—one little boy died to-day. He was brought in from the streets where he seemed to be wandering about with no one to care for him and [how] he has lived or where, we cannot tell. He has evidently been very much abused. Yesterday I ordered a little brandy given him, and the matron carelessly left the bottle with about a pint in it, sitting on the table, when the little fellow awoke, being thirsty and no one near, he got the bottle and drank its entire contents. He was not more

A Woman Doctor's Civil War

than six years old. Never came out of the influence of the liquor, died to-day about noon without waking up. Another boy came in to-day—he has walked from Newburn [New Bern] N.C. and for three weeks has been tossing about in the streets and sleeping on the docks under a boat or on one. To-day Mr. R. [Redpath] picked him up and sent him to us. He is quite sick. Poor little chap! he was so glad to have some one to speak a kindly word and care for his wants a little the tears ran down his cheeks and he kept saying "thank you missis, I'se too glad".[194] Miss Boyden, one of the teachers has gone to take temporary charge of the house, but she is too young and inexperienced for such a place—it needs a good motherly woman, with such a flock!

I have had one of the little girls living with me for about a month took her before we drew rations there and find her so *useful* and *amusing* we don't know how to spare her. She comes the nearest to Mrs. Stow's [Stowe] 'Topsye' [Topsy] of any child I have ever seen. She is constantly 'turning up' in unlooked for moments and places, and often as we sit, in the early twilight she will bob her head in with a comical, "Call me marm" well knowing we had'nt, and quietly curl herself up on the mat offering to sing "Bob Bidly," dance or stand on her *head* and put one foot up "like the boys do marm" if we wont laugh. One day when she was hanging around Miss Buttrick thought best to look a little into her *theology*—so began the catecism with the usual "Who made you!" God marm, "Well Topsy, who *is* God?" With a broad grin and a whirl on one toe "O, he's de fine gentleman what makes all de folks marm." The reply and its delivery so overcame us that, the further queries were indefinitely postponed. She thinks she had a mother once "cos all de boys and girls do, marm!" She is about ten years old—and most devotedly attached to us. She tells me she likes "all de northern ladies no matter what dey does cos they's de ones what made de war and makes we all free". She is shrewd, and cunning—knows quite well how to take care of No. 1—I sometimes talk of sending her over to the 'Home' but she is so desirous to stay with us, I hardly know how to decide!

Sunday June 5th   —sick all last week from the effects of an exposure on the marsh last Sunday night. Came near having pneumonia, now hope to escape but still some danger.

194. Many other children at the Col. Shaw Orphan House had suffered terribly. A five-year-old boy died from a severe whipping he had received before his arrival. Another child who had been roaming about for weeks subsisting on garbage was scrofulous. Cases of small pox, diarrhea and general debility abounded. Drs. Esther Hawks and Henry O. Marcy treated the children. *The National Freedman*, (New York), August 15, 1865, p. 213.

Col. Beechers' regt is ordered up to Branchville about 80 miles, on the rail-road. The Col. is too active a man among the colared people and hates rebs too much to be allowed to remain here longer—then he has been the regular preacher at Zions' Church ever since coming here and some thin-skined individual reports him as using "incendiary language—so Gen. Hatch thinks it wise to get rid of so formidable an advocate of the people. To-day was his farewell address to his people, and it was quite touching. He has won their hearts! Dr. Marcy too, will be greatly missed from among them, he is their most earnest friend and ever ready to work in their behalf. The poor and ailing are constantly at his door. He has also been a good worker in our evening school, which in spite of the falling off of the old teachers and both Superentendants, "still lives" and is a doing good work. The average attendance is more than a hundred and how can we give up while such numbers are eager to come! My class of men come steadily and improve rapidly—they are very earnest with their books and quite devoted to their Teacher. Poor fellows! if they only had something to *give*, I should be loaded with presents. One of them whose little girl comes to school, sent me some ripe figs the other day, the earliest of the season. The boys bring me confederate money in X–XX or 50, dollar bills—Many of my original class have enlisted in Maj. Delaney's [Delany] regiment, under the promise of its being a 'home guard' and so they would not have to leave this Post: then recruiting is stopped and they are uncerimonously "turned over" to fill up the 35*th*—wholly disregarding the promises made them; Many of them are mere boys too young to be allowed to enter the army at any *time*. It is outrageous that no one, especially in the *military* can keep faith with these people! —Shall we ever do so?—

In school, last Friday as I was making my rounds among the classes, on entering Miss Corcaran's room, of girls I noticed that some thing unusual was going on; they were very quiet but their eyes *sparkled*, and they all seemed waiting for me, as I came up to the desk the teacher remarked that "the girls had felt so grateful for my kindness (or something of that sort) that they wished to present me with a slight testimonial of their regard, then a little girl stepped forward and made a neat speach and another said something which I could'nt hear and handed me an elegant gold pencil. Of course I was taken by surprise and with my poor lame lungs could make but a halting reply—but I *felt* very much gratified. Dr. M. [Marcy] tells me that the regiment, he learns, are getting up some kind of a 'testimonial' for him. I am glad, and it is very right they should, for he has been thier fast friend.

A Woman Doctor's Civil War

Dr. M. [Marcy] sent the carriage yesterday so that I could go and hear the Col s farewell address but I had only been there a short time when I was called out to go and visit a patient, one of my pupils who is suffering very severely from the effects of a splinter of wood in her foot. Prescribed and rode back to church—they came for me with a magnificent carriage and horses. This afternoon Dr. M. [Marcy] and I have been out visiting among his patient until tea. It is already very sickly here. What will it be before the summer is through. One old colored woman, I have been with him, to visit, before—and to-day she told us much of her history which is too interesting not to note. The particulars, I have learned from Dr. M. [Marcy] who has known her for some weeks and taken great interest in her condition and that of her family. She is a daughter of Gen Winfield Scott[195] born in or near Washington. —I think her mother did not *belong* to him, but was slave of some friend. He afterwards bought her and two of her children, boys, and took them to Canada and freed them—when the boys became of age to go into business he set them up in some kind of trade in Cincinnatti where they now are (or she supposes them to be) the possessors of considerable wealth. Of course they do not know where or what she is now. She became the property of a wealthy bachelor, shoemaker, by name, resident of Winchester and was his mistress, treated by him as his wife and the head of his house hold, and rendered due respect and defferince as such. She loved him devotedly and lived very happily surrounded by every elegance and luxury which great wealth could furnish. She bore him seven children, three girls and four sons. No jar marred their domestic happiness till the eldest child a beautiful girl, was of age to be attractive—then the inhuman monster desired to

195. Not even the most virulently anti-Scott political broadsides during the General's 1852 campaign for the presidency as a Whig alluded to an extramarital affair, much less to miscegenation. "In an age when drunkenness, profanity, moral turpitude, and ruinous gambling were all too common among men who moved freely in the highest social circles, Scott preserved his character as a Christian gentlemen," wrote his biographer Charles Winslow Elliott. When an eminent phrenologist suggested that Scott had a high level of amativeness the General proclaimed "The professor did not mistake me, but I have always curbed my mutinous appetites. Since my wedding day I have never violated my marriage vow, nor did I ever give a human being cause to imagine that I desired to violate it! I pledge my soul, my honor and my life, that all I now say is strictly true!" It is noteworthy however, that Mrs. Maria Mayo Scott, the General's wife, absented herself from him frequently, including a period of five years from 1838 to 1843, during which she and Scott's daughters lived in France and Italy. Women such as Mrs. Scott, who condemn their husbands to "the unsocial solitariness of a bachelor's bed," wrote a friend of the General, "would have no right to complain if their husbands were to seek in other arms the comfort and consolation which they deny them." Charles Winslow Elliott, *Winfield Scott: The Soldier and the Man* (New York: The Macmillan Co., 1937). pp. 391, 413–14, 643–44.

dethrone the faithful woman who had been his wife in all but the eye of the law for so many years, and give his *own* daughter, her mothers' position. The mother remonstrated, entreated, all in vain the man was determined, and to avoid such an unnatural relation, the girl ran away. This so exasperated the man that he sent the mother to Charleston jail where she was kept a year and a half, then sold, to some one whose name I have forgotten, here in the city—her children, all but one girl that she had with her, were also sold. The Mother fell into good hands and in a few years, with the help of her father, Gen. Scott, she bought her freedom, then worked and traveled collected enough to buy, one daughter and two of her sons, this was fourteen years ago. The other daughter, was a very lovely child and she could not buy her, and at the time of our coming here she was still living with her master in Columbia, as his mistress. A few days ago Mr. Albert Browne, learning this story went to Columbia for this girl and succeeded in bringing her away and she is now with her mother, who is lying at the point of death. The two oldest boys ran away soon after the breaking out of the rebellion and are now, she expects, in or near Washington. The eldest girl who ran away from her own father succeeded in eluding his search for three years, and then was betrayed into his hands, but the place she had been designed to occupy was already filled and she was sold to a negro-trader for the N. Orleans market, and for some years the family heard nothing concerning her. About eight years ago the mother met her at the 'Springs,' she was traveling with her mistress, and seemed to be in good hands, since then nothing has been heard of her. The mother is very anxious about her family and desireous to do something to remove them from the many temptations in their way of an honest life here, and we shall try and get them taken North and protected in some way. Scotts' daugher is a fine aristocratic featured woman, with an eye, and a *head* which does credit to the General. She is possessed of more than ordinary intilligence and powers. Has been keeping boarders since our forces came here, and by over work, brought on disease of the heart, ending in Anasarca. She cannot live many days. They are living in good style—house well, even elegantly furnished; She had amassed considerable property before the war, and spent several thousand dollars, during the war in relieving and aiding our prisoners at this place. Daily I am learning something of this sort. Only a few days since I found a family who had sheltered and fed one of our escaped prisoners for over a year before he succeeded in getting away. They have never heard from him since—Does he live! and can he have forgotten *such* benefactors!

June 1865

Susan Black—

8th.

I have in school a woman of this name whose history has greatly interested me. She is about thirty six years of age, quite black, but with good
features, bright and intellegent. She was born of pure African parents and
has always lived in one family, to whom she is still greatly attatched. The
first notice taken of her, which she remembers, by her old master, was
when she was about twelve yrs old. One day he called her to go into the
shed with him—saying jocosely that he was afraid, but his eldest daughter hearing it said to Susan "You keep away from Pa don't go in there",
however, he called again soon, and she went after him. When there, he
caught hold of her, held her and in spite of her frightened resistance—
with his handkerchief stuffed in her mouth, committed *rape* on such a
child. She was sick for three weeks after. On her recovery he used her as
he liked. When about thirteen she gave birth to a son. She wasn't going to
nurse it or care for it and [it] was placed in the hands of her sister to bring
up. This is the only child which she has ever had which greatly enraged
her master and he whipped her several times, saying that she destroyed
her children and he liked the breed to well "to allow it to run out"

He had daughters older than she and when one of them married, Susan
was a part of the marriage parties. Susan lived quite happily with her
young mistress, married a fellow-slave, had a "real wedding" in church
as she expressed it, and until the breaking out of the rebellion had no serious troubles. Her husbands master was quite indulgent to him, and gave
him many privilleges, so one night when out fishing with two others, the
temptation to go out to see the yankees was too great to be overcome—
and he went; Susan, meanwhile was living up in the country. Her Master,
now Maj. Henry Rivers [C.S.A.], on learning that her husband had gone,
undertook to console her by offering her joint stock, in his affections
with his wife. Tried entreaties, money, which she threw in his face, and
lastly whippings and threats. Susan would'nt tell her mistress of her per-
secutions fearing to make her unhappy so poor Susan bore in silence his
abuses, till one day, after exhausting all his powers to make her yield to
his desires, he had her stripped naked, tied up and then with his own
hands beat her 'till the feaver of passion had subsided. Susan said he
would take particular pains to beat her over the pubis; until she was terribly swolen and the blood run down her legs and stood in pools on the
floor. She showed me her body and limbs and they are now covered with

frightful great white scars. As soon as she was sufficiently recovered she resolved to endeavor to make her escape and if possible join her husband somewhere. She succeeded in reaching this City and was secreted in a small room, by her father, great search was made for her—but she remained in security—twice dressed in boys clothes, she attempted to cross the water to Morris Is. but was frightened back. This was about two months before the fall of Ft. Wagna [Wagner]—and from that time 'till the occupation of this place by our troops, she was confined to one small room, only daring to venture out in the evening. When our soldiers marched into the city Susan was wild with delight—which she hardly knew how to express. As the troops marched through the street, coming opposite to her she pulled of [off] her shawl and spread it down for them to walk on. The officers gallantly stepped aside and raised their hats in recognition of her delicate compliment. —Susan's husband came over to Port Royal and enlisted in the 1*st* S.C. Regt, was a good soldier, got disabled was discharged and came back here with the "Yankee soldiers" to find his wife, which he was not long in doing and they are now living here as quietly and happily as though they had only lived prosy ordinary lives like other people.

Susan goes to school—her husband goes a fishing. She is very earnest to learn, and I take pains to give her extra instructions—and altho' four months ago she could only read her alphabet which she had picked up in Slavery, now she can read understandingly in the Sec. Reader—and is learning to write rapidly. The devoted attachment to us northern ladies is wonderful—she feels that she cannot do enough for us—and if we would let her, would use all her time, out of school, in our service. She is very neat and capable.

June—

15*th*   Miss Allan [Allen],[196] who has been sick with fever for only a week died on Sat. morn. at 5 o'clock. She was only about sixteen, came down with her uncle, to be a companion for him in his lonliness, he having just burried his wife.[197] It seems like losing a member of the family to have one of the teachers taken away by death—and we all share in the common grief. Had funeral services at the house, quite a number of friends and offices including Gen. Hatch were present and went to the grave. We burried her in the little yard of the Unitarian Church. The scene at the grave was very impressive. Many of her school class had

196. Miss Gertrude Allen.
197. Mrs. Mary (Molly) Lambert Allen.

learned of her death and followed with the procssin. They brought beautiful flowers to put on her coffin. The hushed and awed expression on their faces as they stood among the corn, which is growing close up among the graves, and pouring through it into the grave was a picture, once seen, never to be erased from the memory.

This sad event has cast a gloom over us, and we look at each other with inquiring eyes, mentally questioning—Who will be the next victim to this terrible South Carolina. It will be strange, if many remain here, if there be not many more for the season gives promise of an abundant harvest for the Destroyer. The schools are to be closed on the first of July and we shall all need rest by then. The average attendance in mine now is 6.75 larger than at any previous time. The labor is great, but they make such good returns for the pains taken with them that it is great pleasure to work. There is much sickness in the city at this time, among the children. Two have died at the Assylum, but in both cases there had been great abuse and starvation before the children came to us. We are constantly having cases of small pox break out but this seldom proves fatal.[198] We have now over thirty children at the house. Miss Boyden who has been in charge as matron has resigned, owing to undue interference from Mrs. Redpath, who really is a great nuisance among the teachers—picking a continual fuss. All will be rejoiced when she leaves.

June/65

16th   Thought of going up to Orangeburge this morning with Miss Lee[199] and Gen. Hartwell—but last night went up to call on Mrs. & Mr. R. [Redpath] who leave for home on the next steamer, and found them so dejected and blue over the attempt of yesterday to get up a demonstration among the colored people to show their appreciation of his services among them that I immediately determined to give up the trip and stir up the children, to give him a meeting this afternoon which would obliterate all other sensations of failure—for in fact the fault was not in the least owing to the blacks, but to some few of Mr. R's [Redpath] white friends who are jealous of his popularity among them and, no doubt Mr. Hurley is at the bottom of it. This morning Mr. Morse and I gave notice in school of the meeting and to have our schools reassemble at 3. P.M. and march in procession to Zion Church. Two-thirds of the children were there—A thousand children, or more and they made a goodly line—and collected a

198. John Milton Hawks had charge of the smallpox hospital in Charleston during this period in 1865.
199. Miss Ellen M. Lee of Massachusetts.

large crowd to see what was going on The church was quite well filled when we got there and we ran it over. We waited, the children sang, and got tired, still Mr. R. [Redpath] didn't come—and at last we had to send for him, when he arrived the wildest enthusiasm prevailed among the children. They yelled and hurra'd to their hearts content. Then Mr. Pillsbury was chosen chairman and Saml. Dickenson [Dickerson] offered some resolutions, intended to be complementary to Mr. R. [Redpath] but some colored brother took exception to their wording, and at one time it seemed quite likely our meeting would break up in a mob—but the thing blew over, (under a compromise), and after some remarks from Pillsbury, Redpath addressed the children. Whatever else may be said of him, he is no coward—and I do not believe any power could deter him from uttering his honest convictions, when he chose to do so. The children cheered most vociferously. He alluded to the remarks of our '*Southern friends*' and their sympathizers to the effect that he was demorilizing the people, especially the children, so to test the matter, he put the questions to the school boys. "How many of you boys expect to be governors of the State of S.C.—How many expect to go to congress? How many expect to be Mayor of Charleston? How many mean to be president of the U.S.? and it is wonderful how unanimously *determined* all the boys are, to occupy these positions[.] Every hand went up and every boy said *I*. It was a novel way of settling the question of demorilization and must have satisfied the most exacting pro-slavery.

Mr. R [Redpath] then bid them "good bye" and thought to slip out before the meeting broke up and get off without a *rush* outside, but the children, divining his purpose, made a rush for the door, also and the scene in the yard beggars description. The children surrounded him, clung to him and for some minutes it was impossible to move, then a buggy came along, he got into that, leaving his wife behind and got away,[200] and then the children went quietly home!

18*th*   Dr. Brown came down from Orangeburge last night. He make his home with us when here. We all like him, so it is pleasant for him and us. Mr. & Mrs. Morse went up to Somerville [Summerville] with Mr. Stevens this morning, to spend the day—so we are having a quiet time. Col. & Mrs. B. [Beecher] came in, to call early. Col. is in the bluest possible mood. thinks he has been wronged out of his position here and now they are trying to cheat him out of a Brevet-star—which report tells him has

200. James Redpath subsequently devoted most of his energies to another cause, the famous Redpath's Chautauqua or Lyceum Bureau. Emerson, Thoreau, Horace Greeley and Henry Ward Beecher were among his clients. Redpath was killed by a streetcar in New York in 1891.

arrived from Washington for his shoulders and he imagines that Gen. Hatch is withholding it till by false representations, he can get it withdrawn—so all this frets and chafes the dear Col. till he is ready to resign and go home in disgust. —We got up a nice dinner and invited them up to it, and so had a nicy cozy time all to ourselves.

Mr. M. [Morse] returned in the eve but his wife remained at S [Summerville]. It has been one of the quietest and most happy Sundays since I came here. I wrote a long letter to L.D. [?] enquiring about the petition sent to Gillmore by the colored people to have Col. B. [Beecher] reinstated, in command of the city when Gurney leaves.

June—Charleston S.C.

20th   I have been intending for some weeks to have my teachers here to spend the evening and, give them a little entertainment so invited them, for last evening. Mrs. Willard knowing of it desired to come too— then I invited Dr. Briggs[201] and he asked permission to bring some few offices of the 54*th*, which I readily gave providing none were brought under 'false *pretenses*'. The teachers came early as they came alone and by eight o'clock the parlor was full; my northern teachers all came and all but three of the others, fourteen in all, four of them colored girls, Dr. [Briggs] and his Asst. Surg. [Dr. Baseman] (Colard)[202] [colored] were over. Mr Allan [Allen] came to tea, then the offices of the 54*th* in all, we had over thirty present. I confess to feeling a little *nervous* as to how the thing would go on, but it was unnecessary—for *one* evening, at least, a company of ladies and gentlemen treated each other as such without regard to *color*—and the most observing critic could not have noticed the least prejudice—or unpleasant feeling of any kind to-wards each other[.] My colored teachers drove up to the door in an elegant carriage—the white ones came *on foot*. Dr. Baseman is a cultivated and refined gentleman thoroughly educated and of elegant manners. He and Mrs. Beecher promenaded the veranda in earnest conversation for a long time much to the amusement of Mrs. Willard—who then began to banter Dr. Briggs, on the subject of visiting in company with, and treating as equals their colored people—just then I came near them and she said laughingly, O, Mrs. Hawks do introduce Dr. Briggs to that lady of color, he wants to promenade with her. I looked enquiringly at the Dr. "Certainly Mrs. Hawkes' I should be pleased if agreeable to the lady, to be introduced to her". So

---

201. Dr. Charles E. Briggs, Surgeon of the Fifty-fourth Massachusetts Infantry.
202. Unidentified.

saying he rose, gave me his arm and bowing to Mrs. W. [Willard] we crossed the room and I 'presented' him to Mis Mary Westrum [Weston], the most thorough bred lady in the room; she took his arm and they walked to-gether for a long time—an honor which he *did not* confer on Mrs Willard. The party went off admirably no disagreeable hitches in it. Several of the ladies played and sang. Mis Buttrick read a beautiful poem from Mrs. Herman's [Hemans][203] and all seemed well pleased. Had refreshments of cake and lemonade. Dispersed at Midnight.

June. Charleston. 1865

26*th*   The past week has been one of almost constant rains, (which still continues to fall). On Friday it fell so heavily at the time for school that but few of the teachers, or scholars were able to go. At our school, most of the teachers came, I rode down as usual, and we had nearly 150 children. All the classes were gathered in one room, and we had general excercises, such as singing, speaking calisthenics and the like performances-much to the evident delight of the children. The carriage came for us, and we came home at about 11 o'clock. In the evening, at about five, it not having rained for about an hour, Maj. [Eliphas] Smith of the 55*th* N.Y. came round with his pony and I went to ride on it—but before we got on the race-course the rain recommenced and we were obliged to come homeward.

Stayed all night with Mrs. Beecher. The Col. is up to Branchville but she expects him home today Sat. Came up home 'between the drops', intending to get my sewing and return, but was sent for from the Assylum; so did'nt go down till after dinner. Col. came, tired and blue, and I came home. Sunday—hav'nt been to *service*, though we have all, that is Col. & Ms. B. [Beecher] Miss Lee, Miss Chamberlin Lt. Batchelder [Batcheller], Lt Rice[204] and self, been into the church across the street where there is a fine organ; and had a great sing. Lt. Rice is a superior organist and singer, so we have had a charming time. The old Aunty who, for fifty years has kept the keys of this church, came in and begged us to sing "joy to the world"—for her—which we did,with right-good will. She is very supranuatred, bent nearly double, and gave till one the whole history of Charleston. Took dinner with the Col's folks: and we had a most extra one; roast turkey and all the necessary fixings, which is really an episode worthy of note. Last night got a reply from Hd Qrs in regard to the pe-

---

203. Felecia Dorothea Hemans, poetess, 1793—1835, author of "Casabianca" ("The boy stood on the burning deck . . .").
204. First Lts. Holland N. Batcheller and Marshall N. Rice of the Thirty-fourth U.S.C.T.

tion. Could'nt get it returned as it was already on file—must make further enquiries in the same quarter for Frankie [Beecher]!

27th   School's hard this week. We have everythings to do to get ready for examination on Friday. Shall not make a *great* effort but we shall invite in the childrens' friends and such offices as are numbered among our *favored* friends and do the best we can!

Charleston July 12*th* 1865

Our examination passed off well; no breaks or haltings on the part of the children. They did much better than the teachers who seemed to me exceedingly dull and stupid. The day was quite hot and the rooms well filled with visitors. Col. Holloway,[205] Drs Briggs and Hawks, Lts. Rice & Barber Mrs. Willard and a few other officers were among the number. I felt proud of the school as a whole, but the Primary Dept. did not do as well as I could wish. Mr. Tomlinson was greatly delighted with some of the *original declainations*. They were the most wonderful of literary productions. The children sang well and many of them recited very prettily the boys especially did remarkably well with their declainations— and everyone seemed quite delighted with the entertainment offered. Miss Tannis Holloway's class of little ones presented me with a box of *goodies*—cakes, candies &. The children were all prettily dressed and I was grieved to part with them—and they were loud in their expressions of regret at my going.

Monday morning Mrs. Beecher and I started out to ride (Mrs. B. is staying with me till she leaves for Somerville [Summerville] where the Col. is making ready for her)—we rode out the entrenchments, and it looked so pleasant out in the green woods and the bordering fields of waving corn, that we felt urged to go on—did so and had a most charming excursion— went out about five miles. It got to be very hot before we reached home, —Mrs. Moore[?], Miss Buttrick and Dr. Brown had arrainged to go to Hilten [Hilton] Head to spend the fourth and they urged me very hard, to go too, finally I consented and we were very busy in getting ready, went on board the *Clyde* at 4 P.M. Left the harber at about 5.—It was a lovely evening, though very warm. Mrs. M. [Moore] and I went into our stateroom about elevan. Miss B. [Buttrick] and the Dr. stayed on deck all night and had far the more comfortable time. We were obliged to sleep with open doors it was so sultry—but the pilot was our next door neighbor and promised to see that we were not annoyed. I did [not] sleep. It was too hot. Made fast to the dock at about sunrise of the *4th*. It seemed like Sun-

205. Unidentified.

day, everything was so still, not a gun, not a boy with a snap-cracker to indicate the "day we celebrate. I could'nt help contrasting this with every place in the north, where, from midnight to midnight again, the air is filled with rejoicing and gunpowder and especially *this* year, how everything in the free north will go mad with joy over the day. It would be pleasant to look at Boston, in contrast with Charleston to-day. There isn't much heart here for rejoicing! We went first to a Restaurants near the Port Royal Harbor and, joined by Col. Kosley [Kozlay?][206], all breakfasted together—then got a carriage and went out to Miss Liller's [Lillie][207] at the Freedman's Home; There is to be a gathering of the colored people from all parts of the Island at Draytons's where Gen. Littlefield is to address them, and probably some other gentlemen after which then come back to Miss Lillers [Lillie], where refreshments are provided for them on a grand scale. Lemonaid in barrells—watermellons by the cartload bread and cheese and crackers in abundance. Tables are set in front of the house and partly shaded with bushes. At about 2. P.M. the people returned and the *scramble* commenced. "Bro Murchinson" [Murchison][208] much to the annoyance of Miss L. and everybody else, took it upon himself to say, that the feast was ready, and they had nothing to do but help themselves. This was wrong, and contrary to the intentions of all. They should have been kept away from the tables and *helped*, then all would have been served, but a grand rush was made and they acted more like wild animals than human, beings. It was a most revolting sight but after the word was given, there was no help for it. It was long before the crowd could be dispersed.

Gen. Littlefield and several other notables called at the house to see us, and were very gallant and complimentary to us ladies. The Gen. was particularly satisified with himself and everything else. He goes North on the *Arago* which sails this evening. So with a sweet word to all, he bounced himself away—after dinner several of the ladies went out riding—and in the evening we all went in an ambulance out to 'Marchland' [Marshland] to see the "Lesser School." There are two teachers there, Miss Fowler and a beautiful German girl with an unspellable name.[209] The dwelling and school are in one house, and both are admirable. A cosy little parlor—and a comfortable sleeping room for the teachers, and a nice airy school room back of these. The location is very pleasant—though somewhat

206. Probably Col. Eugene A. Kozlay.
207. Miss Sarah P. Lillie of Hopedale, Mass.
208. Abram Murchison, a black who doubled as an army cook and a most influential preacher.
209. Miss L. Fowler of Mt. Kisco, N.Y., and Miss Selma Wesselhoeft of Dorchester, Mass.

lonely but the ladies are provided with saddle and horse—their leaves are plenty so they do not suffer for society. The people near were having a 'shout' so we all walked down, in the moonlight, to *see*, we could *hear* at the house. The ride home was charming, Then we all went to *bed* on the floor. There were no mosquitoes to trouble us—but my bed was too *hard* or I too tired, I didn't feel greatly refreshed in the morning. Dr. White [Wight] of the 32*nd* C.Ts.[210] came out with Dr. B. [Brown] and took dinner with us. We passed a quiet day—towards evening went out to ride— Mrs. Morse Dr. White [Wight] and Miss Lillie on horseback and I in buggy. Mr. Alvored [Alvord][211] called and offered to take us to the boat in his carriage. We went on board the *Ann Marina* about half past eight and at 10. were on our way to Charleston. There are no berths in this boat so we sat on deck all night in most uncomfortable positions. Reached the city soon after sunrise, and the long walk to Charlotte St. was very tedious—and a cup of hot coffee was very grateful to us.

Dr. B. [Brown] did not succeed in being 'mustered out' (which was the business which took him to P.R. [Port Royal]) so has to return to Orangeburg to get some papers signed—he hopes to be able to go on the *Fulton* next week. Most of the teachers go at that time. Miss B. [Buttrick] and the Dr. are having a desperate flirtation, which they seem greatly to enjoy.

July 7th.   Came over to Mt. Pleasant on a 'Steamer' with Dr. [J. M. Hawks] Mr. & Mrs. Morse—very hot and we were a long time in coming. It is cool and pleasant here. A constant breeze keeps away the mosquitoes so that we actually sleep without 'bars'—which is a great comfort.

8*th*   Capt. Sharpe[212] came early this morning, and while the rest slept Dr. [J. M. Hawks] & I went to ride with him, out about six miles. A very pleasant ride through dim woods where the early sunlight had not yet penetrated. Stoped at a plantation for water and to enquire after one of Ds. [Doctor's] patients—got served water for ourselves and horses. The sick man was dead so Dr. went in to see if he had small-pox, and Capt. [Sharpe] & I rode slowly onward. By the time reached the water's edge and the end of our road the sun was up to a scorching height, so we made but a short stop, but hurried towards home, as fast as possible. I like my new horse very much and she is ambitious not to be outdone by any other on the road. A very good understanding exists between us, and in spite of D's [Dr. J.M. Hawks] fears I dont believe she will run away with me! — Mr. M. [Morse] has gone over to the city. Hav'nt got up our bed yet, so

210. Surgeon Charles M. Wight.
211. John W. Alvord, General Superintendent of Schools for the Freedmen's Bureau.
212. Capt. Henry Sharpe of the Twenty-first U.S.C.T.

Mrs. M. [Morse] has the Drs, and we sleep on the floor. The sun is hot but the breeze is so strong, right from the sea, that we do not realize that it is too warm.

9th   Went over to Charleston to see the girls before they leave for the North. Mrs. M. [Morse] Dr. [Hawks] and I went in a little boat of our Q.M's and it was 11 A.M. before we started. I do not think I ever suffered more from sun and heat than during trip—scarce a breath of air rippled the waters which our boat slid across as over a mirror—and on reaching the dock the heat seemed too intense to live in, but we were obliged to walk up to the house in it—and on reaching there Mrs. M. [Morse] and I both felt that we had narrowly escaped sunstroke. I do not remember ever to have suffered so severely from heat—and that night we got no sleep, as our mosquito net was over to Mt. Pleasant and the infernal howlers came near eating us up. I took up my quilt and tried the veranda but they soon found me. O it was a horrible night!!—

10th   In the morning went with Dr. [J. M. Hawks] to call at the Teachers Home. It was very warm. The girls in demi-toiletts[213] making violent efforts to be comfortable—had'nt fully decided to go to the 'Head' tonight with our folks but rather expect to do so. On our way home sought in vain for 'ice cream'. I went to call on Mrs. Barnett[?]. S [she] has been ill and still looks so—then went to see Miss Western [Weston] but she had not returned from school, went from there over to Orphan Assylum. Stayed a long time in hopes to see Redpath[214] but he didn't come. Poor Amy (our Topsy) is in disgrace—accused of stealing money of the matron—and in close confinement, up in a little attic, living on bread and water. I went up to see her—the poor things heart is nearly broke at such a terrible accusation and after a very long talk with her I believe her innocent. What seemed hardest to her was that Mr. R. [Redpath] had "made her tell a lie on herself" by threatening all sorts of punishment—he had made her say she took the money but she declared he could'nt frighten her into saying so again. She had cried 'till her eyes and face were so swolen as hardly to be recognizable. I comforted her as best I could but could do nothing though I made Dudly [Dudley Redpath] violent by protesting against the treatment, and saying I believed her innocent of the theft. My connection with the Assylum now ceases. It has been a great fret with me and I had to leave it in such incompetent hands. Mrs. Barker[215] is a vulgar

---

213. Demitoilets were dresses that were somewhat elaborate but less so than full dresses.
214. Dudley C. Redpath, superintendent of the Col. Shaw Orphan House.
215. Mrs. Barker, a woman from the North, had been engaged as permanent matron of the Col. Shaw House, replacing Miss Boyden.

uneducated Irish woman, and Dudley is a mere boy. They both do as well as they can but neither are fit for such a position!—

Received invitation this morning to Fanny Holloway's wedding, to take place this eve at seven o'clock. So concluded to stay over another night. Dr. B. [Brown] Miss Buttrick and Miss Boyden left for the Head on the boat at 8 P.M. and we went to the wedding. Mr. & Mrs. Morse, Dr. [J. M. Hawks] and I were the only *outside*, or *white* guests, present. It was a very elegant little affair and everything went off in the most approved style. Mr. Lewis[216] pronounced the ceremony. I do wish our ministers had a little more delicacy! Where is the appropriateness of talking to educated and refined people who have always been free as though they were plantation negroes and needed to be enlightened in regard to civilized usages and customs? Yet so it is, and not one of them can marry a couple, the least tinctured with Negro blood but they dwell on such topics as no delicate mind would think of in connection with many of these people. Our cake and wine was of the nicest and a large slice of cake was given us to carry home. The house seemed desolate enough, when we returned to it and found it empty. We shall miss the loud cheery tones of Miss Buttricks pleasant voice, and her good, healthy presence in and about the house, but we too, shall soon be gone!—

10*th*   Came back to Mt. Pleasant this morning. It is good to be here out of the noise and unhealthy atmosphere of that dirty city. Have'nt done much but rest to-day. Took a short ride in the cool of twilight then early to our luxurious bed on the *floor*, yet but we need no mosquitoe's net that's one comfort!

Charleston, S.C. July 1865

11*th*   The morning being cloudy and cool, I concluded to visit the Dr's [J. M. Hawks] colony with him. It is out about six miles, a little beyond the saltworks on the beach. Dr. had brought a couple of bbls of meal and one of pork to be distributed to the people. We got there a little before the cart, and spent the time in visiting the different cabins. They are quite comfortable buildings—better than the average—very few of them have any articles of furniture save such as are made from rough boxes or boards, and it is curious to see the primitiveness of cooking and *table* furniture. Occasionally we would find one or two plates and in one cabin, a *knife*, and *fork* and spoon. I talked with the women about keeping their houses clean—and instead of buying things to eat right up—trying to save

---

216. Rev. J. W. Lewis, an organizer of Sunday Schools who had earlier provided most of the books for the library of Esther Hawks' Jacksonville school.

a little and get a few dishes. One old woman asked very earnestly why she should buy a plate. Why said she, "I's lived mor'n fifty year and never had an earthen plate in my life—reckon I can live de rest of my days without one." The people were delighted with our visit, and swarmed around us like flies. We visited every cabin speaking words of encouragement or advice to all. Their fields of corn wave in luxuriant growth quite up to the doors. I hav'nt seen any better anywhere. The people were loud in their regret that nothing was ripe, to give us—but the melons soon would be and then we should have some.

The cart had now arrived and we went back to the porch of Scipio's house—to see its distribution—the people all following with bags or boxes. One of our soldiers who was there on a visit measured out the rations. The most hearty good-will prevailed and the pleasant duty was soon over and after shaking hands all round, kissing the babies and promising the elder ones, to assist them to some clothing, if possible, we rode away followed by the blessings of the whole company. It was now past noon and the sun was very hot. My head ached and my temper somewhat *ruffled* by *heat and* fatigue, to say nothing of the hard work of holding "Miss Topsy" who was anxious to get her dinner. Then my hair came down and I lost my net—then it commenced raining and we rode home through the woods instead of by the beach. The trees intercepted the breeze and the heat was nearly sufficating—so we were right glad to reach home and get our dinner. At high water we all (Mr. & Mrs. M [Morse] Dr. [J. M. Hawks] Dr. B. [Brown] and I) went in bathing. By the way, Dr. and I went in last night after everyone was a bed, and enjoyed it very much. Today I made great efforts to learn to swim, but my courage fails— my head goes under and I come up on my feet blowing like a porpoise. We stayed in the water about half an hour—then hurried up to the house where our good Susan had all in readiness for us to wash and dress.

12*th*   We spend the time in a very listless and unprofitable manner. Went in bathing again and this eve took a short gallop over to the landing, then up round Camp. Mrs. M. [Morse] and I have done little but read *novels* and *frolic*, since coming here.

13*th*   We all called on the Col. [A. G. Bennett] and wife at Hd. Qts. Mrs. B. [Bennett] is "fat and fair" but I couldn't see wherein lay her irristisble fascination for the gentlemen. She has a voluptuous form (no doubt *that* is it)—to me she looked irishy. She said but little, and not particularly well. Two dirty-ill-favored children, were presented as the "heirs". The Col. seemed embarrassed or under some constraint—not at all like his usual fresh, genial self—did'nt make any long call. Went riding afterwards—only a little way.

14*th*   The Regt. is ordered to Hilton Head—to go immediately—so we must soon say farewell to all our anticipated enjoyments of Mt. Pleasant. It's too bad to think of returning to the old camp ground in the sands of that forsaken island! All is bustle and activity in camp—tho' none will get away before the first of the week. The officers leave these pleasant scenes with regret but most of the men have families at Mitchelvile[217] and will be glad to go nearer home.

16th   Three Companies left on the *Loyalist* today but didn't get off till midnight on account of the tide[.] We are all busy packing up.

17*th*   Everything is packed and down on the wharf—but no boat has come for them yet—our bed and furniture is all away—but there is no prospect of a boat—so we must get back the bed to sleep on to-night, which we do; after considerable talk and some trouble. We Mrs. M [Morse] & I, went in bathing. Dr. [J.M. Hawks] & Mr. M. [Morse] over to city all day.

Mt. Pleasant July 1865.

18*th*   The Regt. those that were here have all gone. left this afternoon and Mrs. M. [Morse] and I have full sway. It is lonesome. Mr. Allan [Allen] came over about noon to visit the school. Calld on us for a few minutes—after he left I went up to visit the school; have been meaning to ever since I came. It is in good order—I was greatly disappointed in it, as the teachers are very slovenly looking. I did'nt think they could manage a *school* very well, but the younger one appears to much better advantage in school than out. It is exceedingly hot, though here on the beach we do not know it, but the sun is scorching.

19*th*   Slept on the floor with Susan, with only a blanket, and feel lame this morning. We are to go over to the city with all our 'traps' today. Such frequent moving is very hard, this weather. The *Loyalist* came back for the other Co. from Ft. Johnson and as we went to the wharf to come over in one little boat, she was just getting ready to leave with the last of the 21*st* for P. [Port] Royal. Saw Dr. Roberts[218] a few minutes. The sail over was most charming. We were right glad to get to the house and by the time our things came and were brought in, we were all very tired.

22*nd*   Went up to Sommerville [Summerville] to see Col. Beechers' folks and get out of the heat of the city. Car riding is very tiresome—Not a decent car in the Dept and they are always crowded with

217. Mitchelville named for deceased Gen. Ormsby M. Mitchell was an all-black village near Hilton Head.
218. Assistant Surgeon Nathan S. Roberts of the Twenty-first U.S.C.T.

filthy people! —Chap. Hall was at the depot when we arrived, and took us over to his pleasant quarters to await the carriage which he sent up to Hd. Qrs for. We did'nt wait very long. The Chaplain went up with us, and we were soon most cordially welcomed and made comfortable by dear little Frankie, the Col's sunbeam, as I love to call her! It was school time, so I went in with her and assisted till the boys all had their lessons. Lt. Batchelder [Batcheller] was there. He is sick and Mrs. B. [Beecher] has taken him home to rest and recruit. The Col. is away on official duty and may not return for a day or two. Dr. Eldridge[219] and wife called with Maj. Bogle[220] in the eve. We went to ride in the carriage before dark.

23rd   Did'nt any of us go to church—read some—went to ride towards night Mrs. B. [Beecher] driving. Col. did'nt come much to our regret.

Summerville July 23/65

23rd   Gen. Scammon Gen. Hallowell[221] and Maj. Willoughby came up this morning. They are the 'Examining Board' and came to examine the offices of the 35th They were very pleasant and social so the day passed very happily. In the evening we tried to get up a little 'time'[.] Maj. Bogle and I went over to the Drs' [?] to enlist their sympathies, which was easily done and at 8 o'clock we were all to go up to Capt. Daniels'[222] quarters where there is a piano, and have some music and dancing. We had had a heavy shower during the afternoon and about the time for us to start it began raining quite hard. Then the offices sent for the ambulance but when it arrived, it was so late we concluded not to go, but have a game of Euchre instead. So the ambulance took home the Dr. and wife and we played cards till eleven, Gen. S [Scammon] & I playing against Gen. H. [Hallowell] and Maj. Bogle.

24th   The offices left on the cars for Orangeburge [Orangeburg]. Mrs. B. [Beecher] and I took the carriage and rode over to the Hospital, and then through the pleasant woods about town for two hours. She then left me at the school-house where I went to see about starting a school for the colored children. Miss Parker, one of our colored teachers from C. [Charleston] is here and wishes to teach—so I went to see Maj Bogle and got him to allow us the school-house which is occupied by families of colored people. This he has done, and the house has been cleaned. No

219. Dr. William H. Eldridge, Surgeon of the Thirty-fifth U.S.C.T.
220. Maj. Archibald Bogle of the Thirty-fifth U.S.C.T.
221. Brig. Gen. Edward N. Hallowell.
222. Capt. Edward S. Daniels of the Thirty-fifth U.S.C.T.

one was there when I arrived but by sending out little messengers with the news that *school* was ready, and Maj. P. [?] arriving, we soon had quite a room full. I put them into running *order*—classed them, heard them sing, and after about two hours work left them in Miss Parkers' hands. We had twenty-five children to begin with, which is quite admirable. I have no doubt there will be seventy five before the end of the month.

Col. [Beecher] got home about three P.M. much to Franki's delight. He looks tired and as brown as a native but after a bath, a nap and refreshments was he old self full of jokes and witicism. We enjoyed the evening very much. Towards dark Franklin Mrs. M [?] & I drove out. It is one of the queerest, stillest places I was ever in, one can have no idea of being in a village for the houses are entirely hid from each other by the intervening forest, no part of which, save enough to dump a house on has been removed and this is what gives the place its healthiness.

25*th*   The morning train brought Dr. H. [J. M. Hawks] and Lt. B. [?] who went to the city Monday. We gave them a cordial greeting and accepted with gratitude the '*goodies*' which they brought, for breakfast. The day passed quickly away and at 2 P.M. we were rattling on towards the sweltering city again. It was very hot and we felt tired on reaching the house—but there was no immense amount of work in the way of *packing* to do. I had sick headacke but the work must be done as we learned it quite possible that a boat would go to Port Royal at ten o'clock. Happily for us it didn't go. We slept on the floor in the parlor, the furniture was taken away to-day so our room looks most forlorn. A great many were in to see us and say good-by.

26*th*   Another long day before us. Soon after nine I went in spite of the heat, to visit the schools. Mr. Cardozo[223] has several teachers and himself in the Normal Building, but everyone looked tired and worn, and the teachers especially were looking with great eagerness to its close. Visited Miss Pages'[224] class of young ladies in the St. Phillips—don't think it amounts to much. Went on our way home, with Miss Western [Weston], to call on Mrs. Clausen. At 8 o'clock we and all our goods were on board the Sts. [Steamship] *Loyalist* en route for Hilton Head. There were a great number of passengers and no accommodations whatever. The *deck* was

223. Francis L. Cardozo was a mulatto descended from an intellectually gifted family of Charleston Sephardic Jews and a graduate of Edinburgh University. Cardozo would eventually become head of the Union League and would serve during Reconstruction as South Carolina's Secretary of State and later as Treasurer.
224. Miss Octavia Page of Massachusetts.

our only bed or we might go below into the steerage. This after much investigation we chose as the most comfortable place. The men fixed up some boards, put our bed on it and so far as *that* went we were really quite well provided for—but we were surrounded by a most motley crowd of all colors, ages and sex—horses, cows and dogs, men women, babies and 'crackers'[.] these latter, smoked, then talked and eat *red herring* till late into the night—and began again very early in the morning. Mr. & Mrs. M. [Morse] Dr. [J. M. Hawks] & I all lay on the same mattrass—but none of us got a great amount of sleep and were glad of the morning dawn—hoping soon to be on shore—but we had come very slow indeed and it was near eleven when we reached the wharf. Came up to our boarding place on the beautiful beach and Mrs. M. & I were soon divested of all extra clothing and a bed—only rising in time for dinner at 4. o'clock. No boat leaves for N Y. till next week. Mr. & Mrs. M. [Morse] went out to Freedman's home in the eve. Will stay there. I rode out there with [. . . .]²²⁵

225. The conclusion of this sentence in the original diary is faded and illegible.

[The Sea Islands]

Hilton Head So Ca 1865

27th   It is a delightful rest of mind and body to breathe this fresh sea air and listen to the incessant hymning of the waves! We are right on the beach, only a few feet from high tide there is a constant breeze which relieves us from flies and mosquitoes so I have nothing to do but to take life easily and grow strong and healthy during the next two months. This eve rode over to see Mrs. Morse. She is freting over their detention but, better than yesterday. There is nothing to disturb her there—home and abed before nine o'clock.

Monday 31*st*   The days are all alike. In the morning I ride up to camp on Topsy—then over to see Mrs. M. [Morse] home and dress for dinner— then out riding either on the beach or over to Miss Smiths', towards evening. There are no women at the house, only six or eight young men, clerks in the Custom House all pleasant enough but no society. There is a Secesh lady and her three children here now, they came down from C. [Charleston] with us. She is a widow of a Spanish consul. He died before the war. She is Spanish but has lived here over twenty years—is strong in her secesh sentiments and very bitter at the idea of not having slaves to do her biding. She goes north by next boat. Is trying to save her property.

August

4th   The boat sailed at 2. P.M., was quite crowded and many were denied, fortunately, Dr's [J. M. Hawks] influence got Mr. & Mrs. M. [Morse] off much to their satisfaction.

Went on board the boat—saw quite a number of old friends going home. Mr. & Mrs. Hinny [?] and two children, among others. They all looked in need of northern air. It made me a little homesick—still I am glad not to go—the journey is so tedious.

It is my birth-day. How often such days come round now! Last year I was on Morris Is' within hearing of the heavy cannon that were pelting

A Woman Doctor's Civil War

old Sumpter [Sumter]. This is the *third* birth-day I have passed in S.C.
Where will the next one be? Let me try to make it a better and a happier
one than this!

I have been up to camp to try and start a school but there are many difficulties in the way. In the first place, Camp is liable to be moved farther
back, to the ground now occupied by *9th* Conn. which is to go home on
next boat; so I must do what I can till that is settled. Had school a few
times in the hospital tent, but that does'nt amount to much so I have giv-
en it up till we get moved, then I will begin in earnest. Col. B. [Beecher]
seems willing, even anxious to assist me in any way—and I shall impres
the Chaplain as an assistant.

11*th*   The days go by, one so like another that the marks of difference
are not worth recording. In the morning I go usually, to camp: Have now
my school organized so intend to spend two hours in it every morning.
Have only the non-commissioned officers, as it is more essential that they
learn to read and write and I shall have but little time to give them.

Almost every evening, we ride on the beach or out to some plantation.
Col. Marple spent the evening with us Monday. He has just returned from
the North and stops here on his way to Jacksonville. Dr. [J. M. Hawks] is
trying to get leave to go there. I shall perhaps go too. Yesterday Gen.
Hartwell called. I like him—he is genial, kind, and true-hearted. His regt.
the 55*th* Mass. are to be mustered out immediately. Gen. says he likes the
service and would rather stay in it for the present at least! Called at Gen.
Woodfords'[226] to see Mrs. Capt. Hunt.[?] Gen. W. [Woodford] went north
on last boat—out of the service.

Hilton Head—August 1865.

Dr. [J. M. Hawks] has asked for twenty days leave of absence to go to
Florida. The object of his visit to see the country in the vicinity of Smyrna
and on the Indian River. He is intent on the orange culture. This has been
a pet idea with him for many years; it was the object of his desires when
we went to Fla. ten years ago and is now stronger than ever. He is desireous for me to go with him to J. [Jacksonville] but there are many reasons
why I would rather not do so—and two of the strongest are 1*st* the excessive heat and 2*nd* the idea of going on one of these little, hot dirty steam-
ers is almost intolerable. I am sea-sick all the time. I shall not go if I can
avoid it without too much hard feeling.

226. Brig. Gen. Stewart L. Woodford had briefly acted as Military Governor of Charleston.
A career as Republican lieutenant governor of New York, Congressman and diplomat awaited him.

School flourishes finely just now. We have taken one of the Co. met [meeting] houses and I have impressed the Chaplain in as assistant. He isn't much of a worker and preferbly won't come much! —It is very hot riding over and back from camp and sometimes I fear my *zeal* will *melt*. Go over to Freedman's Home to see Mrs. Smith[227]—have no other acquaintance here.

Aug. 15*th*   Dr. [J. M. Hawks] has obtained his furlough and we are only waiting for the *Louisburge* to come over from 'Lands End' to start for Fla. I have no good excuse for remaining so must go along. Mrs. Miller, one of my Charleston teachers and her little nephew, are waiting to go[.] She had no place to stay, so I invited her here——The boat is, and has been expected hourly for several days. We have everything ready to start, but she does'nt come. We came near having a conflagration last night. Mrs. M. [Miller] who is provided with all the paraphanalia of housekeeping on a small scale, and who gets tea or coffee at all sorts of unreasonable hours—in attempting to refill her alcohol lamp when it was burning, set fire to the liquor and in her fright through [threw] bottle and all on the floor, scattering the alcohol about; it was soon in a blase, the boy screamed, Mr. Weldon [?] saw the fire, rushed in and it was extinguished without much damage—only a serious scare.

227. Jane B. Smith of Hanson, Mass.

[Florida]

Jacksonville Florida August 1865.

Left Hilton Head on the *Louisburge* on the evening of the 17*th*, in a heavy shower. I most reluctantly—and I must, confess, in a very disagreeable humor. If Dr. Hawks was'nt one of the best men in the world he would have thrown me overboard for I was most unreasonably cross. The boat was wet and *dirty*—the staterooms without ventilation—the cabin small! My idea of comfort does'nt include *Steam boats*. Arrived at Fernandina next day about noon—and remained till next morning. Went on shore and walked about town. No business going on here. Called at the Assylum to see Miss Merrick. The boat woke up a few of the colored people, who came lazily down to the boat, but everyone looked as if walking in their sleep and needing a good shaking. This place is decidedly in the *rear* and until the R.R. is in running order, must remain so— while this and some of the other places, is getting a fresh start! Before I had reached Mr. Dennetts' several of my old scholars had espied me and I had quite a body guard by the time we reached the house. Mr. D. [Dennett] came down to the boat. He seemed glad to see us—is full of business—kind and cordial as ever [.] Before night a dozen or so old friends, officers of the 34*th* and 3*rd* were in to see us. It seemed quite like old times. Minnie is looking well and in good spirits. Col. Apthorpe [Apthorp][228] and wife came down on horseback They are living up where Col. Beecher had his Hd. Qtrs. Many of the colored people and children have been in to say 'howdye'.

Sunday 20*th*   Haven't been out all day. There has been a constant rush of visitors—mostly colored, and the first question is "Are you come to keep school?" —They seem delighted to see me back. Mrs. Brown, my special old friend, has got three of her children and is as proud and happy

---

228. Lt. Col. William Lee Apthorp of the Thirty-fourth U.S.C.T. Mrs. Apthorp had assisted Esther in teaching at the Odd-Fellows Hall school in Jacksonville.

as a mother can be. They are nice girls, and she lays great stress on bringing them up "like white folks". I had to go over and see them last night. Mrs. B. [Brown] hasn't made much progress with her books since I left. Says she must leave that to the girls now. She does'nt need to "worry her mind so much". Mr. Dennett has concluded to go north on the *Louisburge* on his return from Augustine and leave me in charge of affairs at this 'Bureau'—during his absence! It will be, to say the least, quite a novel position but I think I can *fill* it!! (Of course)

Monday 21*st*   Began my official career this morning. Feel quite consequential. Placed my official signature—E. H. Hawkes A.A. Com. Fred. Bureau & A L. [Acting Assistant Commissioner Freedmen's Bureau & Abandoned Lands] to a request for transportation for a soldiers' family. I feel quite the business *man* after'd! At noon five little boys came in, brought from Lake City by a soldier of the 3*rd*. Sent to Mr. D. [Dennett] for disposal and he "turned them over" to me to provide for their wants and learn their histories. We shall send them to the Assylum at Fernandina. They are all about twelve years old, and each has a history a few facts of which I gathered from them which I will transcribe in the order in which I learned them. George Wolf born in Tallahassee where his father and mother still are, was hired out by his master who refused to let him visit his mother but drove him away with threats, so falling in with a party of our soldiers he left his place and was sent here by them.

Charlie Turner is a native of Penn. born in Harrisburge [Harrisburg]. He is a bright active little fellow, and was stolen by a rebel soldier named Tom Watson, on one of their raids into Penn. He was carried to Columbus and there sold to Gen. Lee,[229] who Charley says, was very kind to him. He was with him several months and at last taken to Richmond and then sold to a man named Bob Shepherd with whom he went to Tallahessee where he was at the close of the war, when he ran away, in company with another little boy about his age, and came in with our troops; the other boy went to his master's for his clothes and was shot by him and his fate is a mystery! Milton Chambers, born in Sumter Co. S.C. belonged to Rev. Mr. Chandler, who sold him to a Mr. Sheffield in Madison Fla. when he was about six years old He has never seen any of his friends since. Poor little fellow! he cried bitterly when he found he was to be sent to Fernandina—said he wanted to go to Sumter to find his mother.

229. There were several General Lee's in the Confederate Army. This was probably not Gen. Robert E. Lee, who owned no slaves at the start of the war and voiced his opposition to slavery during the conflict.

Mark Johnson—a yellow boy born in Va. sold into Ga about seven years ago—when his mother died—he knows of no friends of relatives, since the war broke out—his master has abused him and one day after being whipped "just for nothing Miss" he ran away, got to Tallahassee and eventually came off with our soldiers.

Anna Curry born in Marion Co. sold up on the Swanee [Suwanee River]. Run away from her mother when she was a little child and has never seen her since. She ran away from her master Ben. Kile—"before freedom" sometime about Christmas because he was "too mean for anything" and went back to a former owner who took her in and was kind to her "till freedom" then drove her off. She found friends among some colored people who eventually sent her here. She had fitts which have injured her senses.

Charley Jessims and Jake Marsh both raised in this state and driven away by their masters who "didn't want any niggers about who were free and could'nt work for what they got to eat" so they came with our soldiers and all will find a pleasant home with Miss Merrick.

The *Louisburg* has returned and goes out early to-morrow morning. Mr. D. [Dennett] goes on her. I have been helping him pack and make ready his things to be left behind in my charge.

22nd   Business comes in with a rush. I think the natives must have learned that the 'head of the Bureau' is absent and so are trying the metal of the new functionary. White and black come for all manner of things. I have been alone and very busy all day. Lt. Hammond[230] has'nt yet reported for duty but I have no trouble in managing affairs. To-morrow the *Hattie* goes up the river—have'nt thought of going with Dr. [J. M. Hawks] but may conclude to do so. Thermometer stands at 97°—not much company to-day Lt. H. [Hammond] came in this eve and will be here to-morrow ready for duty. The work to be done is mostly in settling differences about abandoned lands between the freedmen and the old owners, who are returning and trying to claim them lost property on which the negroes have been settled and are raising crops and it gives rise to much talk and the passing of many papers between the Military heads and this office—but so far the Bureau has got the best of the matter and no property has yet been given up. It is wonderful how *loyal* these old rebels have always been!!

Aug 23rd   St John's River on brd Steamer *Hattie*[.] As we sat lazily about the table pretending to read or write, a messenger came to the Dr.

230. Lt. David M. Hammond of the Thirty-fourth U.S.C.T.

A Woman Doctor's Civil War

[J. M. Hawks] saying the *Hattie* would start in half an hour. Nothing had been said about my going and I had given it no thought. Dr. said "well Nett, will you go along—and I said "do you wish me to?" "most certainly I do" said the Dr. so I arose, put on my cape and hat and we started at 9 ½ A.M.—The idea did'nt occur to me that we were to be away over forty eight hours so I had no getting ready to do and no baggage to carry only, Mrs. Childs new book *Looking towards sunset* to read on the way. At the boat we found all ready to start. There were a few other passengers—one lady—and her brother going to Craven Cove. Dr. Applegate[231] going the entire route. It takes a great while to get the *Hattie* under way", but she was, at last, got off and we watched Jacksonville fade gradually in the distance till a sudden bend in the river hid her entirely from view and we turned attention to the wide beautiful river over which we are passing. The *Hattie* would hardly be called a *swift* boat, so we have ample time to wander and exclaim and admire the broad stretch of level bordering of tall pines or moss hung oaks on either side of us. We passed Magnolia about noon—there is *one house* at this celebrated place. Just after dinner we tied up to the rickety old posts and loose boards dignified by the name of wharf. At Green Cove—This is quite a settlement of a dozen or twenty houses. Facing the river and near the wharf stands the new hotel, but the war interrupted its builders and it has never been completed. Tow headed youngsters and baby faces with an occasional sable visage showed themselves at the doors and windows showing that the deserted looking houses were inhabited. We walked up the principal street on the broken planks of what was once the *sidewalk* which is the only indication that there ever was a street here for it is so overgrown with coarse weeds and rank grass as to be undistinguishable. This walk led us to the spring from which the place derives its name. It is the most beautiful I ever saw. A large bowl, a couple of rods across, hollowed out of the sand and lined with emerald and pearl, studded over with diamonds, which sparkle as the dim rays of sun light penetrate the dense overhanging foliage, the water so clear as to induce the wish to handle the pretty jewels at the bottom. At the head, the waters boil up with great force, so much so that no one has yet been able to reach the bottom at this point. The whole appearance of the spring is lovely and picturesque—the tall oaks with their hanging mosses gives a tropical look to the scene not to be met with in any other part of the country. The water is clear rather warm and so strongly impregnated with sulphur as to be perceptable in the air long before we gain sight of the spring.

231. Probably Dr. Lewis Applegate of New York.

The beauty of the place is greatly marred by a number of unsightly, de-lapedated huts built for bathing houses and now fast rotting back to a state of nature. We stopped long enough to drink of the water and take a photograph of the lovely picture on our brains, before the wheezy voice of the *Hattie* called us on board.

It required a great deal of pushing with poles and much loud talking on the part of the gentlemen to get Miss *Hattie* started—but she was eventu-ally got off without injury but being in a wayward mood she insisted on running her head straight for the upper end of the cove with the evident intention of *crossing* the next point instead of going round it and not un-til the mud was well stirred could she be induced to go aright. Science tri-umphed and we are again on our way rejoicing—but is'nt it hot! At Lacoi our next stopping place several of our passengers get off. This place is even more in ruins than the ones below. There are several skilleton houses in view. The wharf extends far out into the water but is in a very uncertain state. A railroad was just completed from this point to St. Au-gustine, just as the war broke out but had never had an engine on it—had been run by horses a little while—the track is mostly destroyed—the men who stopped here are starting a sawmill and have brought up the laborers and rations to-day. There was formerly a good mill here. The river is wide and deep. As the sun declines heavy, black clouds roll up the sky and as the darkness thickens, we get brilliant illuminations from the black cloud with an occasional low muttering of thunder and just as we reach the wharf at the stately city of Palatka the storm bursts upon us with heavy rain and wind. Capt. Websters[232] Co. of the *3rd* USCTs are stationed here. The Lt. in command a bright handsome young man by the name of Allan [Allen][233]—came on board for the mail—just before stopping, we run into a cloud of blind mosquitoes filling the boat—almost putting out the can-dle. I brushed them from the table and sides of the cabin by hands full. They do not sting Our staterooms are miserable affairs. The stern of the boat has settled so much that none of the doors will shut. The rooms have nothing in them but a straw mattrass and one coarse blanket. On asking the steward for a wash-bowl and pitcher was informed that there was but *one* on board. I obtained the use of this for a few minutes each morning a towel was also handed me but it looked like such a *veteran* in the service I had'nt the heart to use it. Luckily we had towels of our own. Did'nt sleep much—Mosquitoes were troublesome.

232. Capt. Frank W. Webster.
233. Second Lt. Joseph N. Allen.

24th   The wharf presents quite an animated scene this morning. Lt [Allen] came on board and breakfasted with us. We have nothing to eat but *army rations*—the butter so strong as to be unendurable. Henry Bony & Steve Rivers stood on the wharf with outstretched hands to greet me as I seped ashore. Wherever I may go I meet the friendly faces of some of my old pupils. We went up through the town, which is not very large and would hardly be dignified by a special name in the north. There are several large houses but they all looks as the are, deserted—the streets are entirely obliterated by the rank grass and tall coarse weed, and only a little foot path shows the way There is a pretty little Episcopal church which is in good condition the trimings and chairs in the alter are of cedar which fills the air with its sweet odor. We wanted to *steal* one of the chairs but *better thoughts* prevailed and we left them in the dirt. Many of the houses are empty—the others mostly occupied by colored families— but few whites have yet returned. Went out to see the old camp ground of the 21*st* but it is quite overgrown with weeds—and looks like a very forlorn field of poor soil. As I walked along while Dr. stoped to take a longer look at the old camp ground, the weeds were so tall as to quite hide me, in the road, so I was obliged to *call* in order to be *found*. Met Johny, Jim and Fred Rivers going to the boat to see me, John had a tame *quail* and the others each a little *chicken*. I didn't quite see how I could minister to their comfort but couldn't disappoint the bright eager eyes of the boys, so they held on to them till I should go to the boat—but first showed me the way to their home. Rose has grown coarse and fat—isn't pretty as she used to be.

They all seemed delighted to see me. On the way back, met Dr. [J. M. Hawks] with a boy, carrying a big watermelon, which he had succeeded in buying off a colored man who kept a store. It wasn't open at 9 A.M. and when it was, had nothing in it but a few *melons!* The boat whistle now called and we were soon off. The river above this place grows suddenly narrower and we begin watching for alligators. Strange birds become more numerous and the fish more plenty—it is fun to watch them; they sometimes leap out of the water as high as five or six feet. We are greeted by an occasional clearing—perhaps a rude cabin from which human faces peer forth at us, formerly *white*—showing that the race of '*Crackers*' is still extant. At "Horseshoes landing" an old man was building a flat-boat, this is the only sign of industry we have yet met.

At Welaka is two or three small huts which look inhabited. The bank of the river is high here, and at the landing a nice flight of steps lead to the top. There are a couple of tall chimneys, all that is left standing of somebodies pleasant home! Welaka is the Indian name for this river and a most appropriate one—"A chain of lakes' and this is just what it is a little way above Welaka, we stoped to fill the watercasks, there being a nice brook of excellent water, the plank was put out and while the men "toted" the water, we spend the time in admiring the varid tangle of vines, insects and flowers, till at last the undivided attention of us all was chained by the most diminuative of huming birds as it flirted among the flowers. It was the cuningest little thing, not bigger than a honey bee with a body of black velvet and wings and tail of the brightest of crimson and green and gold. It darted about as swift as thought running its long bill and little head into the wee blossoms, in a most entransing manner. A tall lily-like blossom of bright scarlet won my covertous gaze and I sighed so hard for its possession that Capt. Mixer[234] went and gathered it for me.

Near Welaka we passed the wreck of the old *Columbine* which was captured and sunk in the Spring of /64 with a Co. of the 35*th* on board.[235] About five miles above Welaka, is little Lake George. The entrance is narrow, then suddenly rounds out into a broad beautiful basin—from three to five miles wide—five miles further on is big Lake George, 15 miles wide and 20 across. The shore on the farther side is not discernable, soon after entering, a fresh breeze sprang up making the waves quite rough—and before we were half way across we had a heavy storm of rain and wind rocking the *Hattie* and making her a little unmanageable so that we were quite anxious for a sight of the river again. It was half past four when we reached the lake, and we were over three hours in crossing. Just before we again enter the river, we pass an old wreck of a rebel steamer sunk by them to prevent its falling into our hands. When the river was reached the rain was over but the clouds were still dark and heavy. A little way on, we run into a school of fish, a very large on [one], and so thick that the water as far as we could see looked as though it was *boiling!* The wheel knocked them about and one was thrown out onto the shore, high and dry.

Volusia is five miles above the lake: We wish to reach it for the night.

The river is more narrow—the white cranes are going to roost, and in the dim twilight they look, on the trees, like large white flowers As we near them they get restive and fly on for a few rods, to another tree a few

---

234. Capt. Mixer had recently been appointed Master of the *Hattie*.
235. The *Columbine* was perhaps the only naval vessel ever to be taken by enemy cavalry. Proceeding up the St. John's River for an assault upon Enterprise in May 1864, it was fired upon and damaged by Capt. John J. Dickison's mounted troops. The following day, attempting to withdraw down river the *Columbine* was again fired upon by Dickinson's guns a mere sixty yards away at Horse Landing. The *Columbine* was quickly disabled, struck a sand bar and surrendered after a prolonged fire-fight.

A Woman Doctor's Civil War

rods in advance: this they do several times till at last the darkness covers them and we go by, no doubt, greatly to their satisfaction for in the dim uncertain light the *Hattie* must look like some huge monster trailing itself along over the smoothe water! It was nine o'clock when we reached Volusia and so dark as to prevent us seeing how much of a place it was [.] a light glimmered on the shore and on reaching the little relics of a landing we found a man with a lanthorn, attracted hither by the whistle of the boat, so there must be people living in this vicinity! The Capt. promises that we shall be off by 3 A.M., which none of us believe so we retire to our hot, uncomfortable berths—but not to sleep till the "wee, small hours" begin! It is wonderful, this power of adaptation, possessed by nature! People living in comfortable homes, surrounded by all the luxuries of life would hardly believe they could live amidst the privations and discomforts, which we soon accustom ourselves to! until they are as easily borne as our former lives!

25/   We got started at an early hour—and by the time I got on deck, were gliding over a smooth dark, glossy stream, so narrow that occasionally the long limbs of the trees would brush us as we pass! The trees and bushes covered over and interlaced with thick clinging vines, forming pictures of fairy grottoes, gothic arches and sylvan retreats, covered with the most delicate tracing of leaves and vines, needing only a loose rein to Fancy for her to people them with syliphs and wood-nymphs, in a most appropriate manner—and the reflection of the beautiful picture in the inky water, so smoothe and mirror like, is so perfect as to induce the belief that it is but its continuation. I sit entranced for hours watching the lovely scene. Not a breath disturbs the placid water or riffles the foliage on the banks, while the only variation in the picture is made by the different arrangement of the branches and their thick covering of vines—occasionally a little prairie land runs up to the river, looking like a great garden of rare and gorgeous flowers; great honest-eyed cows with their friskey calves at their heels scamper off at our approach or stand gazing at us in stupid wonder. As the sun gets higher my river reflections disappear. The woods are full of strange birds as is the river banks. Alligators are very numerous and some of them very large—the shores re echo the sharp creak of the rifle. The Capt and Dr. Applegate keeping up an incessant fireing at the simple denizens of wood and river. A large flock of beautiful little green and gold parroquetts, flew up from the trees startled by our rifles and flew screaming away. They are very numerous here. The river grows more tortuorus and narrow, the boat runs her stubborn nose into every turn sadly defacing the vines and trees. At one place where the turn was very abrupt we were at least half an hour in getting round it. Three times the boat run into the same spot—the fourth we had advanced about *four feet*—but good natured perserverance won the day. I heard no swearing and but little *loud talk* during the entire trip.

It was about 5 P.M. when we emerged from the little twisted stream into another broad lake—its rough waves rock us but we rejoice in plenty of sea room and go on our way with increased speed. This is Lake Monroe at the head of which is Enterprise, on the one side and Mellonville on the other; we stop at Enterprise where a couple of passengers get off. The wharf is in a very delapidated condition [.] It was once a very good one. This place was started by a yankee from Conn. (who has been here long enough to get the yankee all sucked out of him).[236] He build a nice large house for the accommodation of boarde[r]s, and had a boat to run between here and Jacksonville. This boat which we are on was his; he had just completed it at the beginning of the war and named it the *Hattie Brock,* for his daughter. It was captured by our forces at the last anual conquest of Florida. This house and its outbuilding comprise the whole, visible of Enterprise. It is now occupied by Capt. Watson of the C.S.A.[237] who married Hattie B. [Brock] he came down to the wharf—is a fine looking young man, and no doubt fought well for the cause he was in.

Now we go across the lake to Ft Reed where Capt. Adams[238] and his Company are. This Ft. was built during the Indian troubles and is a mile back from the landing. Our whistle woke up the boys and by the time we were fast to the few parts that are left of the wharf, the beach was swarming with them. A small boat went ashore, and Lt. Steward [Stuart][239] came on board. Told us Capt. A [Adams] and Lt. Rogers [240] had started overland for J. [Jacksonville] three days ago—horse back to Gainsville then down in the cars. This is quite a disappointment as we are to stay here all day tomorrow. Dr. [J. M. Hawks] is full of his Indian river scheme—means to start in the morning, get a horse here—and return by way of St. Augustine, I to return by the boat. It commenced raining so Lt. S. [Stuart] stayed on board. We had a game of Eucher—and passed the evening very pleasantly. He invited us to breakfast.

236. Jacob Brock, the steamboat line pioneer of the St. John's River.
237. Capt. William B. Watson, First Battalion, Florida Special Cavalry, C.S.A., who would later manage steamship lines on the St. John's and Indian rivers.
238. Capt. John M. Adams of the Thirty-fourth U.S.C.T.
239. First Lt. John J. Stuart of the Thirty-fourth U.S.C.T.
240. First Lt. Andrew P. Rogers of the Thirty-fourth U.S.C.T.

26th   Capt. Mixa [Mixer] Dr. A. [Applegate] Dr. H. [J. M. Hawks] and myself, went ashore in the small boat at about 8 o'clock this morning to breakfast with the Lt. at Ft. Reed. He sent a two horse carriage, (two mules and a cart) to the landing for us. The road out to camp is charmingly *picturesque*. The branches of the live oaks on either side add much to the beauty of the scene and very much to the difficulties of *travelling*. Somewhat to our surprise we reached our destination *with* our heads on. The Lt. gave us a cordial reception and what was quite as grateful to our feelings a most delicious breakfast of sweet corn bread, new butter, fresh eggs, fresh pork, venison sweet potatoes, an excellent cup of coffee with *real milk,* to all of which we did ample justice greatly to the delight of the sable cook who prides himself on being "de bes cook in de company Miss!" After our poor rations of bread and bacon on the boat these luxuries were most welcome and delicious [.] As soon as breakfast was over the gents started off with their guns in search of game, Dr. [Hawks] to learn what he could of his Smyrna trip The men of the Co. came about the door with their spelling books and primers. I knew immediately what this meant and soon had quite a school agoing—but soon others came up with paper and envelopes to get letters written to go down by the boat. The first was a brotherly affair easily dispatched[.] The others were more complicated, one being a "pop the question" missive which, of course, must be done with delicacy and skill, another a business question begging the fair enamaretta to name the day when she would make him "the happiest of men." I succeeded to the satisfaction of all parties in my difficult task. The cook, for whom I had written a most tender epistle, prepared me a delicate and tempting dinner to which I applied myself with commendable ardor—. After eating all I well could, cook very considerately *tied up* what was left, for me to take on board. The *carriage* was not brought to the door and we returned to the boat. Many of the men begged me to stay and give them a months schooling but I felt compelled to resist their tempting offer to build me a nice *cabin*—feeling that I have already neglected my *official business* in J. [Jacksonville]. I little thought when we came on board of being absent so long, indeed I supposed the boat was to return on the next day, not knowing the distance we were to come, which the Lt. tells me, is not less then 300 miles by way of the river. Between the beach and camp is one of the largest orange groves I ever have seen, it contains over a thousand trees of the sweet orange, and a large number of same, besides some lemons. The trees are set out in straight wide rows, there is a good show of fruit on them but the orchard looks yellow and uncultivated like the inhabitants. It belongs to a secesh by the name of Spear [Speer].[241] He has not yet returned to it but it is carried on by a cracker family living on it. The boys brought me some sour oranges of last years growth, still hanging on the trees. The new fruit is not beginning to turn yet. At 3 p.m. the *Hattie* got up steam and we waved an adieu to Ft Reed and Enterprise, crossed the lake, which was quite rough and entered the river about sunset but only went a couple of miles before stopping for the night—as the Capt. proposed supplying the boat with fresh beef—and the cattle being plenty here, thought this a good place to stop, so the men shot a fine steer, and while it was being dressed Capt. M. [Mixer] and Dr. A. [Applegate] went across the river turkey hunting. I sat on deck watching the deepning shaddows in the beautiful mirror beneath us, listening to the drowsy hum of insect life, mingled in with an occasional sharp note from some late bird—weaving all sorts of fancies, wild and fantastic. How the dreamy hour witches one—till the past with its stern, unpoetic realities slips away, the present is but a point to rest the feet on, while poised, we gaze at Fancies' bright imaginings for the future.

I wish I could paint the picture spread out before me! The water so perfectly still as to reflect every branch and leaf of the trees on the opposite bank. Occasionally the head of an alligator appears above its surface as he floats slowly homeward, or the whirr of some of the numerous waterfowls stirs the lazy air as they seek their friendly sorts! As the night settles down and the stars peep tremblingly forth the shaddows on the shores deepen. The line of dank weeds and coarse flowers becomes thin and vapory till at last they are but a part of the shore—which is no longer thick with trees and hung with vines and mosses. Just opposite me is a heavy, frowning fortress: It stands out distinct and well defined against the sky. In the centre is an arched sallie part, on either side of which are pondrous columns and from the top of one is a ship's flag staff. As the night grows darker the gloomy ft. comes close up to us and we rest under its shaddow. Just below the Ft. is a long street with tall buildings on either side which resemble stately residences, but they seem deserted, no lights flash from the darkened windows; no sound of hurrying feet or eager voice reaches me, but the picture is so real that I instinctively reach forward to gaze up that long quiet street, half expecting to be quieted by the familiar sounds of busy life! A little lower down; is a beautiful church with a gothic outline. The great door is open and from out its darkened portal a long

241. Dr. Sidney Speer, a grower who had earlier tried to have Fort Reed made the seat of Orange County but had lost out to the Orlando forces.

possession, dim and shadowy winds into the depths of the night. Close by my church, sadly out of place the gaunt spectered outline of a gallows comes out sharpely defined against the sky—and from it swings some unsightly object. I know it's only the tall, bare cedar which I admired before their metamorphosis—but now it looks so real that I shudder! Memory recalls some of the horrible tales of the attrocious acts commited against northern men by the infuriate demons of this very State. I try in vain to turn to the other pictures but the horrid gibbet holds my gaze. The splash of oars and the sound of cheery voices break the spell and I shake off the sad denied thoughts and go to my forlorn stateroom for the night—to lose them in wilder dreams!

27th

Sunday morn—The night was cold and damp towards morning the rain fell in torents. I was obliged to close my window which made the room very disagreeable. We got under way by light and when I went on deck my fancy pictures were left far behind! The Capt. and Dr. were already dealing death to alligators. We had fresh beef for breakfast, and a promise of *roast turkey* for dinner! It rained nearly all day. I sat on deck wrapt in my shawl, and dreamily watched animals and inanimate nature! it was 3½ P.M. when we reached Ft. G. [George]. It was not quite as rough crossing as when we went up but the wind was "right fresh". We stopped at Volusia about noon to take on a big boiler, and this delayed us an hour or more—then the rain will make it dark early so our hopes of reaching Palatka to-night grow beautifully less. While waiting at the landing I went on shore to reconnoiter and see if I could discover where so many *natives* had come from. There was a half dozen men women and children on the shore—more white faces than we had seen on the whole journey.

Went up to the old fort—overgrown with weeds and grass; built against the indians—found several groves near—but as there was no one to enquire of concerning them learned nothing of their history. Struck on the road leading back into the country—followed it till I came in sight of a couple of rude houses which I concluded to visit—but as I drew near, three frisky dogs sprang out at me barking furiously. Then I remembered what Lt. Stewart [Stuart] had told us, that it was'nt safe to go up to a country house on foot on account of the dogs so I beat an inglorious retreat. On my return found an old orange grove but the fruit, like many of life's pleasures, was bitter-sweet, and though satisfied of this with the first taste of bitterness, yet woman like, I was tempted to try another and yet

another 'till my lips and mouth burned with the pungent juices! Went
back at the call of the whistle and we were soon off.

28th   Only reached Welaka last night; tied up to the wharf at about 9
o'clock. It was too dark to venture further. Soon after midnight I was
awakened by tramping and loud talk in the cabin, and soon the noise of
the pumps below [.] I drowsily wondered if we were starting so early and
as the noise continued, concluded that we were, taking on wood at Palatka, so dropid again to sleep. Imagine my surprise this morning, to learn
that the boat had leaked so as to settle her stern so low in the water that it
was running in over the guard of the rudder box. —The noise briskly
awoke the Capt. or he says another half-hour would have sunk her—and
it required lively work from all hands to keep her afloat. The crazy old
thing! to sink tied up at the wharf—It would have been a sick joke for us!
It seems the roughness of the lake st[r]ained the boat badly and made her
leak, then she was not pumped out as usual, before the men "turned in"
for the night. It rained hard before morning and we are having a through
north-easter. It was raining very hard when we stopped at Palatka, but
my boys were all there to say "howdy" to me. Johnny had the quail
which I lost overboard, and gave it to me, this time I held it fast; and gave
it in charge of the colored woman for me. Made a short stop at Locoi [La-
coi]. Passed the wreck of the "Maple Leaf,[242] at about 4 P.M. It has rained
hard nearly all day; it will be late when we reach J. [Jacksonville]. When
about ten miles above the city the Engineer stuck his head into the pilot
house, with the startling intelligence "I reckon, Capt. we'll be short of
wind afore we get to the city" adding "I can't get over sixty pounds of
steam now" the boiler leaks so it puts the fire out"[.] The night was setting in dark and foggy—the prospect was not animating but Capt. M.
[Mixer] Laughed away our fears and a little before 9 P.M. we tied up to a
big schooner, which was as near as we could get to the wharf. It was too
dark and rainy to attempt the perilous feat of going ashore over that
schooner, so after being assured that the boat wasn't full of water so liable to sink during the night, I retired to my downy couch—(that is to say,
my bed is an inclined plane!).

29th   Obliged to come ashore in a small boat—so took breakfast with
the Capt. and got home after 8 A.M. tired, hungry and dirty! how good

---

242. The *Maple Leaf* was a Federal transport ship on the St. John's which was blown up
after colliding with a log filled with explosives in 1864.

A Woman Doctor's Civil War

fresh water clean clothes and a comfortable room look—after such a rough week. Busy all day in assisting Lt. H. [?] in affairs of the office, attending to the wants of the people, &.

This Eve, several offices in to see and congratulate me on my safe return. It is good to be home and comfortable again!

Jacksonville Florida 1865

30th   Had sick-head ache all day. Went in to see Mrs. Shepherd [?]. She sent for me, being sick. She has some uterine trouble and wishes me to treat it. While there Mrs. Brown came in bringing an *ice-cream* for me, it was in quite a liquid state but real nice [.] Miner [Hawks] and Adj. Welch[243] spent the eve with us. M. [Miner] is in excellent health and spirits. Right glad to have them go, so as to go to bed. Finished reading *Great Expectations* to-day. The *Louisburg, St. Johns'* and *Fountain,* all in to-night—got a letter from Mr. Dennett, informing us that he is relieved at this post and that Col. Osburn[244] would assume immediate command. This is unexpected news and will be a severe blow to the colored people, for they have the firmest faith in Mr. D. [Dennett] and with the best of reasons for he has been their faithful friend for a long trying year. Instead of going north as he anticipated he goes to Savannah to relieve Capt. Ketchum,[245] who is sick.

Sept 1st   Col. O. [Osborn] came on the *Louisburge* yesterday, called here this afternoon. He is rather prepossessing in his personal appearance. Looks keen and intelligent—but is cautious and reticent. Not particularly enthusiastic no great talker, but systematic—business like—sincere and honest. I trust for the sake of these poor people whose welfare is now, in so great a measure in his hands! Maj. Hoyt,[246] Miner [Hawks] and several other officers in this morn, *business driving!* It is rather a *hot day* for fall. I hav'nt been out much only to see the colored folks, hav'nt made any calls yet, indeed the most I do is to hear my girls say their lessons.

The *Louisburg* goes directly back to the Head taking Gen. Hydes [Vogdes][247] who is relieved at this Post. Col. Marple assumes command

243. First Lt. John B. Welch of the Thirty-fourth U.S.C.T.
244. Col. Thomas W. Osborn, who was appointed Assistant Commissioner of the Freedmen's Bureau.
245. Capt. Alexander P. Ketchum who following the capture of Savannah was sent there to reorganize home guards and to supply emergency needs of the populace.
246. Maj. Augustus A. Hoit of the Thirty-fourth U.S.C.T.
247. Brig. Gen. Israel Vogdes, whose signature appears to look as if it were spelled "Hydes".

'till the next arrival. The more I see of Col. O. [Osborn] the better I like him! He has come to stop with us so we have a good chance to become acquainted which I make the most of so as to know what manner of man is to have the interest of these people in his hands.

3rd Sunday
At home all day—read *Adam Bede* commenced it last night and finished it to-day. I like the book. Adam is a man after my own heart" but it requires all my knowledge of men to reconcile such a character with the love for that simple girl Hetty, however it only proves the assertion that "love makes men both *mad* and blind" and a pretty face bears a stronger charm than any other attribute of womanhood! I don't believe that a man in love ever admitted to himself that the woman of his choice was other than beautiful! What a blessed hallucination!

4th   Started out early this morning to make some calls, stopped at Mrs. Reeds, then went up to Col. Apthorps—dined with them, Chaplin Moore[248] & Col. Marple mess with them. At table the conversation turned on the recent refusal of the chaplain to marry a couple because the woman *was white*. It seems that Jesse Brooks of Co. E. was formerly owned by a young woman out beyond Lake City. He came off some time during the rebellion and enlisted in the 34*th* [U.S.C.T.]—not long since this woman came to J. [Jacksonville] having worked for the money to pay her passage, met Jesse here, and somehow, they have struck up a bargain. Jesse went to the Provost, got a permit then went to the chaplain to marry them which he refused to do, on the ground that she was white. the parties were greatly disconcerted and pled hard for the ceremony but he was inexorable! It could'nt be done, they may live together without marriage, if the[y] choose, and they certainly will, but matrimony is not for such— so says the Chaplain. Col. A. [Apthorp] and I took the ground that he had no right to refuse to perform the ceremony *simply* on account of color. If a white woman *chooses* to marry a black man who can say her nay? Col. M. [Marple] sided with Moore, so the discussion grew quite animated but I do not think we made the Chaplin see the *foolishness* of his position.

Chap. M. [Moore] is looking for the position Supt. of Schools for this State.[249] Got a riding skirt and promised to go riding with Col. & wife this eve, but was'nt ready when they came round, so sent them along promising to overtake them by the time they reached the cemetery but before I

248. Homer H. Moore, Chaplain of the Thirty-fourth U.S.C.T.

249. Chaplain Moore's hopes were not in vain. He was soon appointed Superintendent of Education for Freedmen in Florida, though he held this position only briefly.

got there it began raining and I presume they went home. Had a nice little ride alone, got quite wet before reaching home. "Nellie" was in excellent spirits!

5*th*   After breakfast took Nellie and rode out a few miles on the Augustine road visiting all the families I came across. At one house I found a woman and two children who claimed to be the wife of Jesse Brooks— her youngest baby, she said was his child the other, a little pale faced one, she didnt feel disposed to say who *its* father was. She had only come in lately and on claiming her husband he refused to recognize her rights on the plea that they were never *lawfully married;* so she has come out to this place to keep house for another man and his children, who wife is dead! It would puzzle a wiser than Solomon to straighten the matrimonial tangle of these people! It was very hot before I got home! In the eve Miner [Hawks] came in and it being such splendid moonlight we proposed to enjoy it by taking a stroll down to the river. So we invited the ladies who are living in the other part of our house, Lt. H. [?] and Col. O. [Osborn] to join us, and went down to the wharf just back of the house. The river lay like a great sparkling gem without a disturbing ripple. We laughed and chatted Col. and I through [threw] coal into the water on a trial of skill. A lot of Fiddlers were disturbed and ran across the wharf. Col. O. [Osborn] had never seen any before and in my explanation of their peculiar mode of locomotion I said they were a sort of *stern wheel crab.* The idea tickled the Col. exceedingly—He did'nt get over it for a long while. As we stood on the wharf the *Wyoming* came up the river and stopped here, Capt. Beech got off and we all went up to the house.

6*th*   No news yet from Dr. H. [J. M. Hawks] but the *Wyoming* has gone to Augustine with Gen. Foster[250] and staff, so he will probably return on her and be in season to return on the next boat to the Head. Agreed to get up to-morrow at sunrise and ride with Col. O. [Osborn] down to Drew's Plantation, to visit some families and see if all the houses are inhabited.

4*th*   We got started in good season—the sun was just peeping up and the grass and bushes were heavy with dew, the road was a most uncertain one, being merely a briddle-path and sometimes ending in a very unsatisfactory manner—however it was a merry ride and we came out at the Plantation all right and before most of the poeple were up; we made a stir among them, asking all sorts of questions about gardens and modes of

250. Maj. Gen. John G. Foster, military commander of the Department of Florida.

life—found the houses were all occupied and so we talked to them about winter gardens and I promised to send for some seed for them—on our ride home, we went over to the brick monument, and cemetery. Got back with good appetites just in time for breakfast. Maj. Hoyt [Hoit] came in and asked me to ride out to the Panama Mills, about six miles, with him, to see how the people were getting along there—promised to go. The *Wyoming* came in about 3 P.M. bringing the Dr. [J. M. Hawks] looking pretty well but thin and black—and in excellent spirits. About 5 P.M. Maj. [Hoit] came with his horses and we started. The one I rode was a fine large sorrel mare, spirited and strong—she went over the ground like a bird. The road is beautiful—through the tall pines. The Mills were burnt some time during the rebellion; but the houses, some twenty in number, are standing in different stages of decay, they are not all inhabited. We found room for at least twenty families—talked with the people about winter gardens and promised them some seed. It was quite dark when we reached home, and the supper was awaiting us. The evening passed pleasantly in listening to the recital of Dr. [J. M. Hawks] adventures across the country.

8*th*   Col. Osburn [Osborn] leaves tomorrow morning for Tallahassee. He has offered me the position of Asst. Supt. of Schools for this state—adding that it's only because I am a woman that he gives me a choice in the matter, for if he *could* he should have me detailed and put on *duty* at *once.*" I wish I could take the place. It would be full of work, but that is just what I should like—but I don't expect Dr. [J. M. Hawks] will consent.

Jacksonville Fla. Sept. 1865

11*th*
    Dr. Benton[251] invited us to visit a plantation on the other side of the river with him. It is in the Stone place and has a fine orange grove on it. He has leased the place and is going over to get some oranges (which are nearly grown), to take to Beaufort on his return. We took a lunch—ice and sugar for lemon aid and settled down to a regular pic-nic feeling. The sun was very hot—but umbrellas kept us from suffering—the row over delightful. A large family of "Crackers" occupy the plantation house. Two or three great strong looking men and boys sitting lazily about the door—while the yard was overgrown with coarse rank weeds, and accumulations of rubbish, breeding dissase. The woman complaining that the

251. Unidentified.

children were all sick—and they looked so, their colorless faces and tow colored hair gives them all a sick look—otherwise the children were bright and smart looking enough. One of the peculiarities, I noticed in this family, was that the three youngest children were without names. I enquired of the mother, the reason for such an ommission. "Wall" she said "they took to calling of 'em *whity* and *blackey* and sich names when they was little and it seemed like they never would call 'em anything else." So the poor things go without names!

We had quite a hard shower on our way back but did'nt get much wet. The *Louisburg* lay at the dock when we arrived and will leave tomorrow at noon for the Head. Went round to say good bye to Mrs. Brown family—and a few others. Mrs. B. [Brown] is in great perturbation has got to move out and give up her pleasant little home to its rebel owner. She will try and build herself a little house this fall. They are all working like bees getting ready to move.

12*th*   Worked hard all the morning getting things in readiness to go and putting away Mr. Dennetts things—quite a number of the people in to see me. Came on board at noon—go in to Fernandina where we shall remain to-night. Dr. Hausen [?] & Chap. Hobbs [252] along going north. On reaching F. [Fernandina] it commenced raining so did'nt go ashore, but Dr. went up and called on Miss Merrick.

252. L. M. Hobbs, former chaplain of the Third U.S.C.T., a minor official of the Freedmen's Bureau who would be appointed Superintendent of Florida's Negro Schools in 1866.

[The Sea Islands]

13th   Arrived at Hilton Head about 3 P.M. I had been sick all day, didn't get up till we got into the harbor. —Rode up to the house with Mr. Williams[253] of the Sea Island House. The first person that came running out to meet me was Albert G. Brown, the Treasury Agt. with the exclamation, O, Mrs. H. [Hawks] you don't know what you have lost by not getting her[e] sooner! Col Beecher has just gone from here this morning and he came to get you to go home with him"! I assured him it was a disappointment not to see the Col. and then he gave me time to enquire after the rest of the household! Severance[254] has not yet returned and Hancock [?] is away in Ga. so the family is small.

16th   Went up to Beaufort on the *Spaulding* which has just been released from quarantine—she having lately returned from Aspnwall [Aspinwall, Panama; now Colón] with fever on board. It was some time before we could find Dr. Durant's residence but when we did our welcome was sufficiently cordial.

Hilton Head—Sept. 1865

20th
Returned from B. [Beaufort] to-day. The aquinocted storm came on and has raged with great fury all the week, so I couldn't get away sooner and this morning had to come down on the little tug *A. Getty.* It was quite rough especially at the dock, and it took us a long time to get ashore. Dr. Roberts was along.

22nd   Dr. [J. M. Hawks] has gone up to visit the sick on Paris [Parris] Is. and will not return till tomorrow so I have come over to the Freedman's Home to stay with Miss Smith—we are to stay here the rest of the

---

253. Mr. E. T. Williams.
254. Clarence M. Severance, a federal customs collector.

193

vacation and mess with her which will be much pleasanter than where we now are.

23*rd*   Early this morning Andrew Bastrom (Mr Atwood's[255] clerk) came for us with a horse for Miss S. [Smith] and we went over to Marshland to breakfast with the teachers—had a charming ride and on our return went over to Mr. Atwoods' and spent the day—which was very pleasant.

Freedmen's Home

24*th*   Got our things moved over here to-day and are now quietly domiciled. Chaplain Fowler, came over with Dr. to dinner, and during the afternoon Mr. Dennett, arrived from Savannah. In the evening Mr. Purdie just returned from the north, came in so we had a right merry party. The men talked-Florida most of the time[256] but we managed to get in a word now and then. Fowler stayed with us over night.

25th

This eve, Mr. D. [Dennett], Mr. P. [Purdie], Miss S. [Smith] and I, rode out to Marshland. Miss S [Smith] rode Nellie and she ran with her several times so coming back Mr. D. [Dennett] took the little imp and Miss S. rode Jim. Fowler is still here.

26*th*   The ladies from Marshland, walked in this eve, just as we were finishing our tea. Mr. Purdie was here so we had had a merry time. The girls stay all night. They are planing a visit to Savannah and anxious, or seem so, that we go with them Mr. Dennet [Dennett] returns tomorrow. No boat yet for Charleston so the Chaplain is still our guest.

Freedmen's Home. Sept. 30*th* 1865

30*th*   Sunday, Fowler didn't get away till yesterday. Mr. & Mrs. Gage from Beaufort dined with us on friday. We have been very busy with our

---

255. Unidentified.
256. More specifically, John Milton Hawks, his long-time friend James Fowler, and G. A. Purdie talked about the feasibility of establishing a colony of black army veterans and freedmen on land in Volusia County, Fla. This land, situated along the Halifax River near Mosquito Inlet, on the north side of Spruce Creek and at Dunn Lawton, had impressed Hawks when he had seen it a few weeks earlier in August 1865.

Hawks would officially form the Florida Land and Lumber Company, in conjunction with Fowler, Purdie, Brig. Gen. Ralph Ely, and officers of the Twenty-first and Thirty-third U.S.C.T., stationed at Hilton Head, in October 1865. Hawks, *East Coast* (Lynn, Massachusetts: Lewis and Winship, 1887), pp. 49, 72.

sick and with looking over and putting things to rights." Affairs here have been very poorly managed both in the construction of the house and its *internal* management.

This morning before I was up, Mr. Atwoods' team was at the door to take us over to his house to breakfast. Miss J. [?] and I went, and stayed *all day.* Dr. [J. M. Hawks] came over to dinner, we read the speeches of [Gen. Benjamin F.] Butler and Sumner[257] aloud, and enjoyed them. Wrote some letters and had a right good time generally. Promised to go again next Sunday when the Marshland ladies will also be there. Mr. A. [Atwood] is like an indulgent father to all the teachers here, generous and genial—always ready to assist them in every possible undertaking, with his horses, or his purse, or what is as good as either and sometimes far better, advice! —We are to spend the eve at Marshland on Tuesday—and plan about the Savannah trip which is to come off this week.

Freedmen's Home Oct. 1865

Oct. 2nd   We rode out to Marshland after tea. I rode Nellie consequently arrived about a half hour before the Dr. and Miss Smith. A couple of naval offices were there, but they did'nt make a long stop. Miss F. [Fowler] and W. [Wesselhoeft] go to Savannah to-morrow morning. I do not go—had rather go alone some time—the girls are too gay. 'T.D.' [?] came up just as we were starting away. Our ride home in the moonlight was delightful. I enjoyed it wholly and *alone*, as my horse would not keep with the others.

3rd   Col. Bennett and his wife are both sick with fever. Mrs. B. [Bennett] sent for me to come and see her, to-day. She has no nurse so I tidied them up a little and left them feeling much better. The Col. looks the sicker of the two. They are both on one bed—and the room is small and close.

4th
  4th   Rode over to Col's to-day. He is some better, she about the same. Got him up on to the lounge, which is better for both, combed her hair— no slight job—made their gruel &. A box of seed, which I asked for, has arrived and I rode out to some of the plantations, near, and told the people to come for them and plant some winter gardens.

257. Charles Sumner, the Radical Republican leader in the Senate.

5th

5*th*   Mrs. B. [Bennett] not so well to-day. Col. doing nicely. Had a delicious goblet of milk to drink. —Rode round on the beach and called at Mr. A's [Atwood] on my way home, it was near dinner hour, so I stayed. Dr. [J. M. Hawks] came in and he stayed too.

7*th*   Mr. A. [Atwood] sent for us this morn, but Dr. didn't wish me to go, so I have spent the day alone, Miss S. [Smith] went. Mrs. B. [Bennett] sent for me about noon. She is no better. Says it does her good to have me come in, and no one but me can comb her hair. Col. is able to be out now.

8*th*   Col. sent down early this morn for Dr. to see his wife—had a "bad turn"—is'nt so well to-day. Rode over to the Saw-mill and to Cherry hill on Jim, alone, this afternoon. I enjoy these rides exceedingly.

10*th*   Have been at Col's all day. Mrs. B. [Bennett] died about noon. She grew alarmingly worse since yesterday. Her sister arrived Monday Eve. —She was *enciente*. Dr. and I will go up to Charleston with them tomorrow! —

[Charleston]

October 1865

18th

18*th*   Went to C. [Charleston] on the 11th. Had a very smooth passage. Went on the *Canonicus*. I was *sick,* as usual. We rode up with the Col's folks, to her mothers' then went from there over to Wentworth to Mrs. Clausens', where we boarded during our stay. They were delighted to see me—and I received a most cordial welcome from all my old friends. Mr. Cardoza [Cardozo] has possession of my school in the Normal School building for the Am. Mis. Asso. [American Missionary Association]. Went in there on Friday morning—met a noisy welcome from my old pupils most of whom are back there and all were anxious to know when I should take charge of the school again. Mr. C. [Cardozo] is a mulatto, educated in England, and well fitted so far for the position he occupies but I think He is lacking in discipline.

It commenced raining before we left the school, and rained very hard all day. —Sat. morn. it was fair. —went up to the office of the Bureau and was so fortunate as to meet Mr. Tomlinson, the School Supt. there, had a long talk with him on school matters, but nothing definite could be determined. Mr. Williams the Supt. for the N.E. Society came in—had a long talk with him. They propose that I go to Columbia and organize the schools there nothing has yet been done in that place. Mr. W. [Williams] will write me soon. Mr. Sumner,[258] who has charge of the Morris St. school, came in—talked with him a short time—don't like him—he is arrogant and egotistical—but has the name of being a fine scholar—an excellent disciplinarian—makes great use of the *rattan.* Went *shopping* and went up to our old home on Charlott [Charlotte] St. Mr. Cardoza [Cardozo], brother to the teacher, with his family are living there, it seemed

258. Arthur Sumner of Cambridge, Mass.

home like to go there. Did'nt see Harriett—but the rest in the yard seemed glad to see me. Had many callers. I am so sore footed and lame from much walking as to be hardly able to step.

Sunday didn't go out till evening. Susan came to see me, the girl is my most devoted and faithful *slave*. She would lie down and let me walk on her without a murmur if she thought it would give me pleasure. Wrote a letter for her to her son—who has gone to live in Michigan with an officer of one of the State Regts. After tea Dr. and I walked down to the Orphan Assy. It is on this St. (Wentworth) in the house owned by the rebel Sect. Memminger.[259] It is one of the most costly and aristocratic houses in the city. The grounds occupy a whole square. The garden full of trees, flowers and shrubbery, laid out in fine walks and lovely arbors, the whole surrounded by a great high fence which one can neither see through or over. We were a long time in finding our way in but at last succeeded in rousing the house and one of the little boys opened the gate. A fire blazed in the grate giving the room a bright cheerful look. Two teachers from the N.F.A. [New England Freedmen's Association] had arrived the day before and were in a delightful state of uncertainty as regards a home or a *school*—no one has any idea of the policy to be pursued. Mr. Tom Hinson says he doesn't know what to do—has received no instructions from the northern societies. Mr. Williams, a young man sent out by the N.E. Asso. is in the same delightful state of uncertainty as regards matters; so my visit here will not be productive of much good.

Mr. Hurley is here in C. [Charleston] has started an independent paper *The Leader.* He was in to see me this morning—is very bitter against Redpath and recaptitulated all their grievances and told me he had reported certain things done by R. [Redpath] while here, to the Boston Society. He is determined to ruin his influence among the people of Charleston—and thinks he can do it. He also told me that reports derogotary to the character of Col. Beecher, were freely circulating in the city, brought by the people of Somerville [Summerville]—reports to the effect that Beecher had turned against the colored people and that he was becoming disipated—all of which I beg leave to doubt till it comes from a more authentic source!

We thought to leave C. [Charleston] Monday at 10 A.M. but the boat was delayed to take the 56*th* N.Y. (which is mustered out) to the Head on its way north—so we came on board after tea but did not leave till mid-

259. Christopher G. Memminger was the German-born Secretary of the Treasury of the Confederacy.

night, waiting for the officers to come on board. The *Coit,* the Genl's boat, brought us down. It is the most comfortable boat I have been on in the Dept. We had had a nice visit up to the city. It was pleasant to go right to Mrs. Clausens and find a home. Mrs. C. [Clausen] is a nice, bright mulattoe woman, was a teacher in my school. Her husband is doing a good business in a livery stable on St. Phillips St. Set up for himself since our forces came here; He rents a fine large house, has it comfortably furnished and they set as good a table as I ever desire to eat at. Mrs. C. [Clausen] is a capital housekeeper and excellent cook. We had nice homemade bread which was a great luxury. Mrs. C. was formerly a slave, owned by a family of Jews, who live near. She was a favorite house-servant and allowed to obtain sufficient education to be able to teach the less fortunate, even among the free colored children, and for fifteen years she taught a little school, built a little house in the yard; of course this was not allowed, so the school went in the name of her masters' sons. The boys, two in number, are very fond of her and she now does much for the family. The youngest son, a young man of 18 yrs. comes in to see her every time he goes to or from his work, always greets her, and says good bye with a kiss, no matter who is present, his pet name for her, is *"sugar"* which, she says, he has always called her, from a baby. Mr. C.s [Clausen] father and mother live with him. She is a fat old negro, woman, he is a white man, a German—married this woman when he first came to Charleston, and has always lived with her. I don't know how she became free. Mrs. C. [Clausen] married when quite young, the brother of her husband by whom she had one child; he went north on business of some kind and on his return found his wife married to her present husband, his brother——the poor fellow died in a few years of a *broken heart so they say!*

Mrs. Clausen is quite intelligent and takes great interest in political affairs——takes several papers and *reads them*—and is, with all, a very smart woman. She told me, (what I did not before know) that no free colored person could teach a school or enter into any kind of business unless some white person was present to countenance the affair. Miss Mary Westen [Weston] my best (colored) teacher, taught school in her fathers' house for several years, and was twice taken to the police station for so doing—and *obliged* to *hire* a white woman to sit in the room where she taught—then she was allowed to go on with her school. So, in regard to property—it must be held in some *white persons' name.* It is hard to realize the truth of such statements—knowing these people and how well able they are to care for themselves!

I heard very unfavorable accounts of the Assylum from the colored people. Mr. Lee,[260] an intelligent man, in the office of the Bureau, told me that the children were dying "like rotten sheep" for want of care and proper attention—and many others said the same. Mrs. Barker is, they say, a southern woman, and has all a southern woman's hatred for freed negroes; Dr. Jenkins[261] who attends them medically is also a secesh, and the people have no confidence in either—indeed they go so far as to say, the Dr. is poising [poisoning] them—eight died during the past month— some have run away. My dear little Rosa and her sister Sarah both dead— buried while I was there. Mr. Hurley says that Dudly [Dudley Redpath] can be found, at any hour, at a drinking saloon on King St. If this is true, I don't wonder the institution is not flourishing. Mr. [James] Redpath is coming out by the next boat—then I hope these affairs will be righted if he is the man to right them——which is very doubtful, if Hurley can be believed!

260. Unidentified.
261. Unidentified.

[The Sea Islands]

On reaching home, Tuesday morning after a nice breakfast at Mr. Atwoods', I found the Augustine teachers domiciled with Miss Smith waiting a boat for Florida. They had been here since the day we left. Miss Botts goes there this year with the Misses Smith. It was good to see "Botsy" again and we have enjoyed life right well during the past few days. The dear girl insisted on helping me with my sewing so we have been making the nice dress sent me as a present from the Mayhew So. The *Louisburge* is laying at the wharf waiting the arrival of the northern steamer so as to take the mail.

Sat 21*st*

The *Louisburge* went out last night and the *McClellan* came this morning bringing a load of teachers, twenty one, in all, sixteen of them come from the N.E. Society and are staying here at the Home waiting transportation to their different localities. Miss Buttrick's genial face and cherry voice greeted me, on my return from Marshland where I had been to see Miss Fowler who is sick yet. Many of the old Charleston teachers have returned, Miss Garland will not be sent out, her flirtations have reached the ears of the prim ladies at the "Rooms" and they decide that she is too young to be sent so far without a protector—and she, poor girl; has lost the one she thought she had secured last Summer. Maj. Pratt,[262] after devoting himself to her all the time she was in C. [Charleston] and giving her every assurance of devotion, save a formal offer of his heart and hand, has, as soon as he was mustered out of the service; *gone and married* another girl, to whome *he was engaged* all the time.

The girls are all in good spirits and all ready to enter any grand campaign in Charleston which may open to them. All are eager to go to the city—and most of them have made up their minds that they will go there

262. Major Joseph T. Pratt, Provost Marshal of the Federal garrison at Charleston.

and no where else. —Only a few of the teachers had got out to the Home so I rode down to see who had come and *escort them up,* and also to try and see Mrs. Pillsbury who goes right to Charleston on this mornings boat. Was too late to see her, but met the ladies—two *ambulance loads,* down on the row. It was a pleasant meeting! their faces looked fresh and good! Maj. Delaney [Delany] and Mr. Williams, (the Supt. sent out by the N.E. So), were with them. *Four loads* of baggage came over, and a delightful scene of bustle and confusion permeated every part of the house, *outside* and *in,* all day; At night we spread beds along on the floor in the big room and put them to bed. The room looked very like a grave-yard with its row of mounds, after all had retired. Dr. [J.M. Hawks] went to camp and I took three in my room. —Of course no one could be over comfortable but the girls all seemed to take things in good spirits. Miss Buttrick and Miss Smith slept with me and Miss Knight,[263] who is suffering from a severe cold, took the lounge. A Miss Hosmer[264] comes from Concord with Miss B. [Buttrick] and she hardly thought it possible to sleep away from her. She is a queer, little, homely, pedantic old maid, and if first impressions are to be relied on, not especially lovable—another fussy one is one of the Knights. She seems to have a very confused idea of her own identity and every thing pertaining thereto judging from the manner in which she leaves her things about, loses them and then bustle about in search—but aside from these little personalities this is a fine looking set of noble women!

22nd

The girls are not greatly refreshed by their nights rest, but all are astir and out in the balmy air, with a lively sense of enjoyment about the tedious sea voyage, —I thought I would ride out and see Miss Fowler so, Miss Pattrick [Patrick][265] wanted to go with me and Dr. [J.M. Hawks] sent Jim for her to ride. We started and Jim finding himself with a timid rider, pranced about in a coltish manner rather disturbing to ones' equalibrium,—then took it into his head that he must go to the stable, at last the saddle turned and she came to the ground, but nothing daunted, got some men, who were passing to refasten the girths and help her mount and we started anew; the next *dash, dislodged* her *net waterfall* etc— and all landed in the sand, so she concluded to give up and I rode back to

---

263. Probably Miss A. Jane Knight of Lancaster, Pa.
264. Jane Hosmer of Concord, Mass.
265. Miss Ellen M. Patrick of Hopedale, Mass., who would become a life-long friend of Esther Hawks.

the house with her, and then Miss Chamberlain wished to try the horse, so she mounted and we rode off, without further trouble, leaving poor Miss P. [Patrick] searching for her *waterfall*. Miss Fowler is much better; was dressed, and rode a few yards on my horse. Miss C. [Chamberlain] and I had a delightful ride, the day was as perfect as natures' self and the singing birds made vocal the woods:—As usual I lost the way going out; the coming home is always plain sailing.

Mr. Williams came out to see us, and decide the locale of the teachers. He has a trying position for a boy of his size to fill. Miss Buttrick and Miss Page are greatly exasperated by being told that they are to go to Edisto— and Miss B. [Buttrick] declares she 'wont' go. In my conversation with him, relative to school matters, I asked why the societies had sent men at a salary of a thousand a year to fill places which we women occupied creditably this spring and summer.[266] Why not, I asked, send these men off into the interior or on the islands where it is so difficult of access and lonely for women and where in the same positions men would be furnished with horses and other comforts. So Mr. W. [Williams] went on to explain that in the interior it was quite unsafe for teachers and much more so for *men* than women, so women were sent to such places! I could'nt help saying that I was glad to know definitely, what the women were sent here for, although I had'nt supposed, previous to this that they were sent as the protectors of the men. This sally pleased the girls, and rather disconcerted Mr. W. [Williams] he, evidently is in an uncomfortable position. I offered to go up to C. [Charleston] with the teachers and start them at house-keeping which offer he eagerly accepted, so I shall make my plans accordingly. He goes to Beaufort to-day and the girls stay here till called for!

23rd   Took Miss Pattrick [Patrick] to ride over to Marshland this morning. We enjoyed it very much. She is a bright enthusiastic little thing and we had a long, delightful, *school-girl* interchange of sentiments and thought. She is a girl of more than ordinary culture and refinement—one of the best specimens among the teachers.

The girls ramble off like a pack of school girls just let loose; to all of them this delightful weather is a revelation, and the vegetation is most

---

266. Esther Hawks' salary of $40 per month was substantially higher than the $10 per month she had been paid in her original contract with the National Freedman's Relief Association but lower than the salaries of her male counterparts. Contract between National Freedman's Relief Association and Esther H. Hawks, October 30, 1862, Hawks Papers. "Let me advise you to change your sex," wrote James Redpath to Esther, "if you expect to be paid the full value of your labors." James Redpath to EHH, July 5, 1865, Hawks Papers.

strange and curious, to *new* eyes. Today Miss Lilly [Lillie] has changed the beds from the floor to the room occupied by the colored people, they going into the wards, kitchen or anywhere, that there is room to lie down in; some of the girls turn up their noses at the thought of sleeping in the "negro quarters"—but there seems no remedy for it, so they submit with as good a grace as possible. Miss L. [Lillie] is a good manager, and has taken the reigns of government into her soft white hands with considerable firmness already. The people will find her a different mistress from Miss S. [Smith]. She is very *economical*—tells me that during her stay here, she not only lived from her rations but saved *forty dollars* out of what she sold! How it is possible that anyone could do this and not suffer for proper and sufficient food is beyond my ken! The ladies are already grumbling at the poor and meagre fare,and when I expostulate with them on the injustice of such complainings they tell me I have been out here so long that I have *forgotten what decent food is!* and I presume there is some truth in such a statement! —but I dont like to hear them complain of these little things it shows a *hankering* after the "flesh pots of Egypt" not compatible with *missionary labors!* I cant feel that these girls are here, many of them, with extensive ideas of self-sacrifice. It seems rather that they are bound on having a *good time!*

23rd No news yet, from Mr. W. [Williams] the ladies are becoming impatient—and so is Miss Lilly [Lillie]. We have quite a number of sick and I take entire charge of them now, to relieve Miss L. [Lillie] during the stay of the teachers. Mr. Green[267] a colored man from Ohio, here buying cotton, called today and as he was going out on some of the plantations, offered one of the ladies a seat in his buggy if she liked to go: Mrs. Stoddard[268] accepted and they didn't return till quite late in the evening, came laden with oranges and flowers; Mrs. S. [Stoddard] is enthusiastic in her praise of Mr. G. [Green] and her ride, and all the other ladies are envious of her, meanwhile we eat of the oranges and are satisfied. One or two officers of the 21st called and the eve passed very pleasantly.

24th Took a long ride with Miss P. [Patrick] on the beach this afternoon. I rode Nelly and she Sally—they go finely together, and we enjoyed the time very much—did'nt get back till quite dark. The folks were at tea.

25th It is very tedious waiting Mr. Williams movements—but the wind has been so strong for a day or two that I doubt if any boat has been

267. Unidentified.
268. Unidentified.

able to go out for C. [Charleston]. This afternoon we planned another ride but while we were getting ready Dr. Roberts and Lt. Dow came with two extra horses to take some of the ladies out so Miss Boyden and Miss Pattrick [Patrick] went; and I promised, if I could get Miss Fowlers' saddle which was at Mr. Atwoods', to overtake them on the beach with Nellie. —They started but the girls were timid and they had considerable trouble before they got out of sight but did'nt give up. Nelly came for me about an hour after they had gone, and I rode up to camp to get the Dr. but he was away, so I rode over to the beach. Nelly was in excellent spirits and we over took the party a little way above the *creek*—rode till nearly dark before turning about; the ride home was very lovely—our horses would'nt keep together so I enjoyed a *solitary ramble!* When we reached the entrenchments I turned there and Lt. Dow and Miss B. [Boyden] did also but the others did not see us so they went round by the beach. We stopped a little way from camp, at a cabin where the people were having a shout. It was a new sight to Miss Boyden, and I wished Miss Pattrick [Patrick] there too, it would have interested her so much! —I got home sometime before any of the others. Nelly goes over the ground like a bird, and when in good humor is a most charming *little beast!*

26th

26*th*   I have decided to go up to Charleston before the girls do, and try and get things in readiness for them, so to-morrow morning I go. Miss Buttrick wishes to go with me; I guess, she thinks if she only once gets to C. [Charleston] they will let her stay and say no more about Edisto—so she goes with me. We hear nothing from Mr. W. [Williams]. This eve two or three of the girls went over to Lands End with Mr. Green to spend the night. Miss Fowler came in to go to Beaufort, but went with them. After dark several of our officers called, and some of the girls proposed having a dance which was eagerly accepted by all present. So Adj. Dow wrote up to some of the other offices to come down and bring some music—which they did and we had a jolly time till near midnight. Our sable musicians were, apparently, much pleased with such an opportunity to display their talents. One professed himself fully equal to call off especially for a "Squad-drill" which he '*did'* greatly to the delight of the party.

27*th*   The boat would leave for C. [Charleston] at ten so we got ready. Miss Sargent[269] concluded to go too, as her baggage had been sent on by express and she was uneasy about it. Mr. Atwoods' team was to

269. Letitia Sargent of Gloucester, Mass.

come for us but as the minutes flew, we got fearful and impatient and took our traps and started. Miss B. [Buttrick] and I had made provisions for housekeeping on a *small scale*. We had tea, condensed coffee, sugar crackers, with a few *sweet* potatoes which someone gave Miss B., a few candles, to light us over the dark places, and some oranges to serve as *dessert*. These were all packed in Harriett's *travelling basket*, which was *quite heavy*—as we soon found. As we neared the stockade, we met Dr. who told us the boat had left for C. [Charleston] but the *John Adams* was in and ready to take the ladies who were to go to Edisto—so we turned back—just then a big wagon with Mr. Williams along, came up, going for the baggage—we put our traps in and it went on. When we reached the piazza all was bustle and confusion. I explained my idea to Mr. W. [Williams] who heartily approved the two Knights, Miss Paige, Boyden & Cogswell, and also Miss Buttrick, who is refrustory, are booked for Edisto. They were soon got ready, a carriage came over from the hotel for us and in a little while we were all aboard the *John Adams*. It was 11 o'clock when we got started and about one when we reached Beaufort. The *John Adams* is an old ferry boat, only fit to paddle about river, and very *slow* so our chances for *seeing* the country were excellent. At Beaufort Miss Figitty Knight discovered that she had left her *trunk behind*. I couldn't sympathize with her as all had received fair warning to see that their "plunder" was aboard. Met Mr. Tomlinson on the wharf, the Capt. of the boat wished to lay over till morning, because as he said there was no accommodations on board for us ladies, but as we must stand out by 4 A.M. and it was very doubtful about getting places to stay and as we *should* have to *stay* on *board anyway* in order to be in *season* to *start* at that hour I could'nt see the point to be gained by waisting so much time and I said so as emphatically as I knew how—and as the final decision rested with Capt. Low[270] we, that is Mr. Williams and I joined Mr. Tomlinson on the wharf and went to Capt. Low, to settle the matter. He had decided to let the boat stay there till morning on account of the discomforts to the ladies. Capt. Low said I, if that is your only reason for this delay—I, in the name of all the ladies, protest against it. We are willing to suffer the inconveniences but not an unnecessary delay, particularly as our comfort would be about the same whether we go on or stay as in order to start in season, we must remain on board. This view of the case decided him and he ordered the Capt. to be in readiness to go in an hour. Met Dr. Durrant, as I left the office. He had an ambulance at the door so I got in and rode up

270. Unidentified.

to the house with him, had a cosy little chat with Mrs. D. [Durant] got a bit of cake went out to see the *puppies,* then rode back with the Dr. The girls were taking dinner on the boat so went and joined them, after arrainging with Tomlinson for the use of some blankets for the night. Mr. T. [Tomlinson] assures me that the house in C. [Charleston] is in readiness for us to go to. We had a pleasant trip up the river and just after dark anchored off St. Helena bar. We had on board, between decks, about a hundred and fifty colored people, with all their 'goods and chattels'. In passing up or down the gangway the stench was almost intolerable. I do not think I could have lived an hour in the place. It was as open as it could be, but so many dirty people crowded together would poison any room. In the evening I went up to the opening, and got them to sing some of their native 'shouts' "Nobody knows the trouble I see" is a great favorite of mine and they sang it well, also "Roll Jordin roll" and "Wrestling Jacob," and many others, greatly to the delight of the audience below.

Going to bed was rather a novel performance. We got out our blankets, on a piece all round; two of the girls took up their quarters on the benches in the little room where we took our meals, two occupied the mates' room. The Capt. hung up a couple of hammocks, right across the deck, I occupied one, Miss Paige the other, and Miss Buttrick spread her blankets on the deck and lay down to her peaceful slumber, in quite a *domestic* way—just beyond us, on the same floor, a couple of honest eyed cows switched their contemplative tails, a young horse, watched us from a pair of scared eyes, two pigs squealed discordantly of the discomforts of their position, and several boxes containing domesticated *birds* kept up an uneasy flutted suggestive of minds ill at ease. The uneasy swaying of the boat kept off the drowsy god, but I was obliged to keep very quiet in my unstable bed, and as it was I lay with the pleasant anticipation of rolling out onto the floor at every motion. Before morning we three were quite sea sick—but we early got into the river again and soon got over the extreme nausea. Reached Edisto about 9 A.M. Miss B. [Buttrick] and I walked up to Seabreaks [Seabrooks] where there are four supts. and teachers—Mr. Alden[271] & Whittemore,[272] Miss Bliss & Ames.[273] It is nearly a mile from the wharf—but we enjoyed the walk—after our close quar-

271. John Alden, General Superintendent of Freedman on Edisto Island, S.C.
272. B. F. Whittemore of Massachusetts, a Methodist minister who would be appointed Assistant Superintendent of Education of South Carolina.
273. Mary Ames of Springfield, Mass., would record her experiences and those of her friend Emily T. Bliss, also of Springfield, in *A New England Woman's Diary in Dixie in 1865,* (1906) (reprinted, New York: Negro University Press, a division of Greenwood Publishing Corp., 1969).

ters. Found the people at this plantation very pleasantly situated and very comfortable. M[r]. Alden and the ladies were getting ready to go to C. [Charleston] on the boat, so we didn't see much of them at the house— but we wandered about and over it after the manner of *this country,* and without let or hinderance. The house is one of the finest plantation mansions I have seen, large, roomy and well finished. The gardens surrounding it were formerly much noted, and even now the grounds have preserved much of their beauty. Miss Bliss is a lady of means, working without salary. She is a small, yellow faced prim old maid, pleasant and affable enough but not over companionable, to us. Miss Ames is tall and *red* but both are cultivated in manners, and very worthy ladies. Mr. Alden the Supt, is little more than a pretty faced boy, in appearance, and Mr. Whittemore his assistant, is a "prig". A carriage and two horses was ready to take them to the landing. They seemed to have a dim idea that politeness required them to offer us a seat in the carriage, but their inclinations so warred with politeness, that we preceiving the strife declined discommoding them, and walked on. The boat whistled and soon the carriage passed us, one of the young men remarking as they went by "hurry up ladies or you will be to late for the boat." —At the landing there is a sort of rude camp where the people stay on their first arrival or when waiting for a boat to leave, this was a scene of great activity now—many of the people who had come with us stopped here: On reaching the landing we had only time to say good bye to the girls, who all stood, with a disconsolate air, on the bank—waiting our departure. As the boat got under way the last tableau was rather startling The five ladies stood up in a row on the landing Miss Paige with Her 'kerchef to her eyes and the others waving theirs directly back of them, stood a pile of *five rough coffins,* which we had brought up from Beaufort: I called the attention of Miss Buttrick to the picture so suggestive of the fate of many of our number who have come out with warm hearts and eager hopes to work in this part of the vineyard. God grant that it be not typical of their fate!

Mr. Williams remained on the Is. It was nearly eleven o'clock when we got away: and now we go outside and it is rough so Miss B. [Buttrick] and I are sea-sick and stay in the Captains room. The Capt. is a bluff, kindhearted Cape Cod man and did all he could for our comfort.

[Charleston]

It was 5 P.M. when we reached the wharf at Charleston. Our coming up the Harbor was very pleasant. The old Fts [forts] frowned on us like the faces of old acquaintances—and the city itself looked smiling and happy in the sinking sunlight As soon as the boat was fast, I went on shore to look for a cart to carry our plunder up to the house, leaving Miss B. [Buttrick] in charge, till my return; I met a couple of colored soldiers belonging to the 33rd and *impressed* them into my service, and we soon got a cart; they went with it to the boat and I went on up to Mr. Pillsbury's office to see the house and getting some meat for us *to eat* with our 'hard luck' which we brought along with us. I also instructed the man with the team to come round by Mrs. Clausen's and get our bedding and other things from there. I was delayed, by losing my way when I came on to Meeting St. I turned and went down towards the Battery, for several blocks before finding out my mistake—so when I reached Mrs. Clausens' Miss B. [Buttrick] had already arrived—and she and Mr. Redpath stood talking in the 'porch'. Mr. R. [Redpath] had only been in the city a few hours, came by the overland route. He is looking finely, and in excellent spirits. After seeing the things loaded, Mr. R. [Redpath] walked up to the house with us. It was nerely dark when we reached there, and we were some time in deciding *which* was the house, but, at last we decided that it *must* be the 'Rhett house'[274] so, though the exterior was rather unpromising we made bold to enter and were met in the door by a colored women, living there, Mrs. Chaffers and on interrogating her, she assured us that nothing had been said to her about moving and that the house was inhabited by *ten families.* This we found to be the case—so after holding a 'council of war' we concluded to leave the goods in an empty room in

---

274. Robert Barnwell Rhett, leader of the pre-war secessionist movement, had temporarily abandoned his Charleston home to cultivate Castle Dismal, a plantation he rented near Eufala, Ala. Rhett returned to Charleston in 1866.

the care of the woman, and we wended our way—*boiling* over with indignation at this piece of stupidity, back again to Mrs. Clausen's leaving word for the girls to go to the Hotel should they come there that night. Mr. Redpath advised us to go the Hotel and teach the Boston So. [Society] a lesson by sending in a good round bill of expenses—but I have no desire to put them to any unnecessary expense so we go back to Mrs. C's [Clausen] and she soon makes comfortable room for us. Mr. R. [Redpath] stayed to tea and at about half past eight he and I walked down to the hotel in quest of the ladies—greatly to my relief no boat had come from Port Royal that day and I went back with a lighter heart. It is curious to note the changed manner of these Charlestonians' toward us northerners. This Spring they were all servility, they couldn't be polite enough or do enough for us, but they are now, very far from that state of mind. They stare at us with insolent familliarity and often make some lighting remark in a tone which reaches our ears, or a curl of the upper lip and slight elevation of the nose expresses more than words would dare; Mr. R. [Redpath] and I were comfortably stared at as we went in to look at the books for the arrivals but we bore it with christian meekness!!—

Sunday 29*th*   Went early in the morning, in search of Mr. Pillsbury, to learn what had been done as regards the matter of a house. Found the house without much trouble, on Rutlege St. All at home, Hurly & Redpath both there, Mrs. P [Pillsbury] is looking much better for her visit north. Mr. Jenks' who is Rental Agt. says nothing can be done about the house before Wed. by that time the families will be moved, then it must be cleaned, which will surely take till Saturday and if we get in by that time we may congratulate ourselves of our good fortune—the great lesson of ife is "*wait*". Mr. P. [Pillsbury] was taken sick with colic—helped get him to bed. Went out in the kitchen where Mrs. P. [Pillsbury] and Jenny were cooking and had a long talk with her on school matters. She will not go in as Mr. Sumners' Asst—is there now for a few days helping him "classify". Says she would like to take charge of the "old folks' home," and have nothing to do in the schools! While we were there Misses Ames & Bliss called and we learned from them that the teachers were at the hotel, arrived after we were there, last eve, so we hurried down to see them. They are in good spirits and say they enjoy living at the 'Charleston' very much—are glad to get something to eat & . They had a rough time yesterday. The boat was loaded with secesh and they treated them with great insolence. They were not told when dinner was ready or invited to have any, tho' all the others on board were—no accommodations whatever were furnished them and if they asked for any were refused. It was after dark when they reached the wharf, no one knew what to do, so they sat down in a *row* on a log and waited till a 'hackman' came up and offered his services, they then rode direct to the Rhett house, expecting to find me there. Their reception was something like ours. Getting the message I left for them, they returned to the hotel—and here they are contented to stay till other provisions are made for them. We all went down into the parlor and had a pleasant time. Lts. Barber and Rice called. Miss Green went off with them to dine, and we went home, quite as well pleased with our more quiet quarters. There are two gentlemen from the N.Y. Asso. Mr. Meacham, an old English presbyterian minister and Mr. Wright[275] a young man, who was sent by the Society to take charge of the Morris St. school, but Mr. Tomlinson has him booked for Columbia; neither of them have done anything here yet though they have been here a week or two. I cant help feeling indignant at seeing such men sent down at salleries of a thousand a year to usurp (they don't fill them) the places which we occupied last year! It is so unjust to us and to those whose means support these schools!

30*th*   Mr. Tomlinson returned to-day, was quite *horrified* at finding the teachers at the hotel and 'flew round "right smart" till he had found them more humble accommodations. Mr. Cardozo offered to take three and Mrs. Clausen takes the other five if they can put up with sleeping three in a bed and *one* the floor; as nothing better offers, they are obliged to acquise and before *tea* they are domesticated with us—to our grief and great discomfort; the drivers who brought them from the wharf, only charged the modest sum of $24.00 for their services, but Mr. T. [Tomlinson] being of an ungrateful turn, did'nt reemploy those worthies but got a team from Uncle Sam, to do the moving so the girls didn't come away with quite as much *style* as they went there! —We visited the school this morning. The children evinced great delight at seeing us. My old school continues crowded but the Morris St. is thin and poor! for several unexplainable reason the children do not return to that school, as to the Normal.

Charleston, October, 1865
31*st*   I go to Mr. Pillsburies office every morning and then up to the house to hury up the *workmen,* and least to see if any are there. The people are moving, but nothing in the way of preparation is yet begun. —Mr.

---

275. Mr. Theodore G. Wright of Huntingdon, Mass.

Shaffer, the colored man who hired the house, is sick over on or near Meeting St. and sent for me to come and see him so the little girl led the way and Miss B. [Buttrick] and I went over to the place. It was a long walk—found Mr. S. [Shaffer] in bed; he talked very reasonably about the house. Said Gen. Saxton had told him he should'nt be disturbed, but have a part of the house still, so we talked the affair over pleasantly and agreed that, at present, till he could recover and have time to look about for another place, he might stay in the lower part of the house and perhaps his wife could work for us. This matter settled, he treated us to some nice oranges which grew in Rhetts yard, and we started for home. On getting opposite the Meeting St school thought it best to make a "clean thing" of all the schools, so went in to visit it. It is under the care of Rev. Mr. Randolf [Randolph] (colored) formerly the Chaplain in the *32nd*.[276] He is a northern man and may be educated, but his mission is not school teaching for, as one of the colored men more strongly than elegently expressed it—"he is'nt fit to take charge of the training of a lot of pigs.' I suppose he meant that class of pigs who are supposed to be *minus souls*! —The school is a disgrace to the Supt. and an injury to the pupils—every day of such schooling is detrimental to the pupils. I couldn't help being amused at his apparent unconsciousness of the disorder which reigned, and the air with which he would occasionally, when the din got too much, strike the bell, and with finger uplifted, in an inquiring tone say, "Do I hear a whisper? I think someone is whispering". Had it been so no one could have told for so many were talking out loud, a whisper would not have made the least impression.

We were well tired on reaching home and glad of the nice dinner in readiness for us. Didn't go out again, but Mr. Tomlinson came in and we had a long talk over school matters! He is much troubled to know what to do with Miss Buttrick has no place here for her, and was quite determined to send her to Edisto or *north*, when he came in, but I think he has concluded to set her at work at something here, now, so much for a friendly influence! I also told him what I thought would suit Mrs Pillsbury, and that also he was pleased to learn as they do not wish or need her in the school, so that is satisfactorily arranged. Then Mr. T. [Tomlinson] said that if I would take it I might have charge of the Meeting St. School, as he should turn out its present incumbent and that soon—but I declined, telling him he had more teachers here now than he knew what to do with which was no news to him. This conversation was held out on the veran-

---

276. Rev. B. F. Randolph, an Oberlin graduate who served as chaplain of the Thirty-fourth U.S.C.T.

da; then Mr. T. [Tomlinson] went in and said a few words to the ladies, congratulated himself on being able to avail himself of Miss B's [Buttrick] valuable services in the city, & &

The weather is changing—it grows colder fast and this eve we have a fire in the grate, Miss Pattrick [Patrick], Meacham [?] and I have animated talks on the *woman* question!

Charleston November 1*st* 1865

Mr. Tomlinson came round this morning to say that he had made ar-raingements with Mr. Cardozo, to take charge of the house and all the Boston teachers to go in with them, so this ends my mission there and I am at liberty to return to the Head as soon as I choose; but I go in and tell the girls after he has gone and they all protest. They never will consent to live so, and so there is great commotion, new plans are made and reject-ed, again and again still they all protest "we never will go in and live with Cardozo's family and pay a dollar a day for our board"—so I promise to see Mr. C. [Cardozo] and state the facts of the case to him and make some different arraingement. About noon Mr. C. [Cardozo] called and we dis-cussed the matter and as all he wants is house room, and will be most hap-py to get it without such an addition to his family we had an amicable chat, and settled things in a satisfactory manner to us all. Mr. C. has one half of the house and we the other. This crowds us a little but is far prefer-able to all living in one family!—

Nov. 2*nd* Thursday

The men are farely at work in the house with white wash and scrub-bing brushes. I do'nt think Mr. Bimms the boss of the job, likes to have me about hurrying up the men, but it must be done; He shakes his head in a very negative way when I tell him the house must be ready for us to move into on Saturday, and says it cant be done, but I *know* it *can* and mean it shall be: Met Mr. T. [Tomlinson] and told him I know of a good place to confiscate a few chairs—he was anxious to know too; told him the St. Phillip St. school house, had a dozen or more in it which might well be spared as there was no school there and not likely to be, and the house all open, and everything being destroyed. He said he could'nt give me any order to take the chairs but if I should take them without his consent or knowledge he should say I did "a smart thing"—so with this encourage-ment I made sure we would be able to take enough for *present use.*

It is cold and cloudy today. A storm is brewing [.] Ellen Lee and Miss Chase arrived from the Head last night. Miss Lee is at Merchants hotel and Miss Chase is at Capt. Smiths. Miss Sargent has gone down there with her.

Mrs. S. [?] and Miss White[277] are to go up to Georgetown. A part of the 35*th* Regt. is there under command of Col. Willard. Mrs. W. [Willard] is also there so they will have gay times, at any rate!

3rd

It has been rainy all day. Lt. Barber came up about dark, so I told the girls and him my plan for securing a *chair apiece,* and invited him to join in the expedition which he agreed to do, providing I'de be Captain—so as soon as it got quite dark we sallied forth. Miss Clausen, Buttrick, Patrick [Patrick], White, Lt. Barber & myself. We entered the back way and groped our way over the first floor without finding any chairs so I told them we must go up another story. I went first, the chairs were way across the room, it was very dark and I expected every minute to run across some old fellow or other who had come in to spend the night but nothing of the kind occured and we each started home with our chairs; on reaching the outer gate, concluded it was best to separate and not march through the St. in a body so telling each to look out for no. 1. we started, and in a few minutes were all safely back in Mrs. C.s [Clausen] quite parlor as if nothing had happened, but with *eight* nice chairs piled up ready for transportation on the morrow. Found *Gen* Beecher, at the house, he came down this afternoon. Spent the evening with us. Capt. Batcheller was also in. We moved a part of our traps up to the house to-day and meant to have stayed there to-night but I feel too tired to go up so we do the best we can without our bed—and the *formal* possession to-morrow though the men are not nearly through with the work—the windows are all broken and there are no fastenings to the doors but these but these little things will be rendered better after we get into the house than while no one is there to see to it[.] No one but Miss B. [Buttrick] and I go up to-morrow. The others will stay here till we can get ready for them.

Rhett House—

Sat. Nov. 4*th*

Took *formal* possession this eve. It has rained so all day we could do nothing and there being no hopes of its holding up we concluded to come in *spite* of rain—so here we are, and too tired for anything but the *bed;* no wood with which to make a fire so we go supper less to bed—in confidence believing that breakfast will not be so difficult a matter. I rumaged over the rooms at Pillsburie's office and found quite a lot of old iron

---

277. Miss Almira P. White of Exeter, N.H.

in the shape of *pots* and kettles—and our household goods left in Har-
rietts care, are on hand, furnishing us with a *tea pot*, so we feel quite
cheerful over the prospect. Owing to the open state of the house below, I
allow Miss B. [Buttrick] who has a great horror of midnight adventures,
to barricade our door with her biggest trunk, and we are soon revelling in
the luxury of a comfortable *bed* and *enough of it* for the first time in a
fortnight. Mr. Cardozo moved in today so we do not feel quite alone in
this great shell. We are both feeling the effects of an attack of diarhea,
which Miss B. [Buttrick] affirms is but the natural result of the dry meal
she ate at the home last week!—

November—1865

Sunday 5*th*   Getting breakfast possessed the charm of novelty, at
least; I broke up an old barrel and made a fire, boiled some sweet potatoes and water for our condensed coffee, this, with a few 'hard tack'
(which we found to be very wormy) constituted our first meal, and it being Sund. our dinner and supper was only varied by the addition of a little
strong bacon which I got at Mr. P.s [Pillsbury] when we first came. The
day passed, wet and cold. We kept busy as long as possible in arrainging
such things as we had, the girls trunks were brought yesterday—they will
come tomorrow. Mr. T. [Tomlinson] gave me $20 to begin housekeeping
with, and we would *like* to spend a little of it for our *dinner* but cant, so
we sit down to our potatoes and coffee with what relish we can muster.
Miss B's [Buttrick] appetite has returned and bids fair to exhaust the supplies—but their being nothing very inviting on hand we agree to go without supper.

About dark Miss Lee and Capt. Thorne[278] came up and seeing us in such
a dreary state, insisted on our riding down to Capt. Smiths to get warm.
Miss B. [Buttrick] was feeling too unwell, but I gladly accepted the invitation and we were soon before a cheerful fire. Gen. Woodford came in
and we had a nice social time—while good Capt. Thorne bustled about
and got a cart and had some wood carried up to our place, with instructions to the boy to cut some up and build a fire. After getting well warmed
the Capt. carried me back and did'nt leave till he saw a good fire burning
in the grate. He has my warmest thanks for his goodness!

Monday 6*th*
Left Miss B. [Buttrick] to 'do up' the work and I went down to the office to see about supplies. It is very aggravating to go to those whose busi-

278. Unidentified.

ness it is to aid you be met smilingly and assured of all possible assistance, again and again, and yet feel that they won't budge an inch, or accomplish a thing one minute sooner—than as if you were not hungry and tired and worn out with waiting! I begin to think they *hate* to see me come into the office, I badger them so much and make them do things in a hurry and after all I have to go do them myself, as for instance I want a cart to go to the Commissaries. Capt. Wall[279] sends one on order to Capt. Low, after waiting a couple of hours, I go myself and find they have forgotten all about it, so I see it sent off and then walk down to the foot of Broad St. with my list or articles needed; get snubbed by a little secesh clerk, (formerly in the rebel commissary) till I assure him that I have a right to come there for these articles and unless he can attend to me and the business in a respectful manner I will ascertain from Hd.qrs. where the trouble is. Seeing I was not to be frightened, he changed his tactics, and was mighty kind, and ever afterwards treated me with "*marked consideration*".

It was 2 P.M. when I got back to Mrs. Clausens, with a loaf of stale bread (all I could get at the bakery) under my arm and a little pail of butter in my hand [.] They urged me to stop to dinner so I did and it *tasted good* too— but my conscience reproached me for leaving Miss B. [Buttrick] with such a scant supply so I hurried home, the girls going up with me. I have succeeded in getting a few little bedsteads for the girls and during my absence the straw arrived so I set them to filling the bed-sacks—a long counter has also come from Mr. P.s [Pillsbury] for us a dining table—this with our *chair* and marble slab (set up on a barrell) with out immense mirror mounted on it quite furnished the dining room, and Mr. T. [Tomlinson] promises to send us a *sofa.* Mr. Sumner & Williams are coming to supper. The girls have got out there odd dishes, I got a doz. tin plates at the rooms so supper will be a *grand* affair! Susan has arrived and when I got back *every*thing was waiting for me to decide *where* they were to be put. Miss B. [Buttrick] has'nt the executive ability of a *hen.* I never saw a woman of her mental capacity with so little management! She is no more assistance in work like this, than a child!

We are really quite comfortable this eve; a nice fire in the grate shed a cheerful brightness over the rough furnishings—and to our surprise we find the gass in order, and the room is now flooded with its brilliancy. Our supper was a success—that is everybody got a place knife *or* fork and something to drink out of, with nice hominy and syrup, bread, butter &

---

279. Capt. O. S. B. Wall, one of the army's few black officers; he was quartermaster of Charleston.

tea! So we are all in the best of humor. Lt. Rice and Col. *Gen.* Beecher took tea and spent the eve. Gen. stayed all night and slept on the sofa which arrived just in season. No wood has yet arrived, so we have to forage on our neighbors and on the outbuildings. As Mr. W. [Williams] has arrived I shall leave the getting of wood to him and may he have as 'sweet' a time at *getting,* as I have had. Mr. Cowens came in and we bargained for a lot of table furniture which he has to dispose of.

Tuesday 7*th*   The work goes bravely on. We are getting underway. Gen. Beecher is invaluable in keeping the fire going. Susan manages the culinary with a skillful hand, and I hold the reigns of government with greater ease than I anticipated after my long abdication. Furniture for the girls from Capt. Smith's arrived to-day and they are all quite comfortable fixed—and if none of them ever have to live in a poorer home in this their lot in life will not be over *hard!* Much of the glass is broken and we have all taken colds, but Gen. B. [Beecher] is fast remedying the windows—so when *that wood* arrives we shall be proof against wet and cold! —Maggie & Lizzie Wynne called to see me today (two of my Charleston teachers) I have succeeded in getting places in school for them. They beg leave to send me a pair of chickens which I *permit.* (they arrived about tea time and will make a nice dinner for to-morrow). Went to the depot to meet Mrs. Beecher at 4 o'clock but the train did'nt get in till five. It is good to have Frankes' loving little head nestle against me again! and her arms to clasp me and lips to kiss—but I cant help wishing, for her own sake that she was less childish!

Wed. 8*th*   Miss B. [Buttrick] and I have been out shopping—getting necessary housekeeping articles—and got home a little before dinner, very tired—visited the schools and also called at the Orphan Assylum—had a pleasant chat with Mr. Redpath—"that bird of evil omen" as the Clausens affectionately style him. Miss Brown,[280] one of teachers, is sick there and I went up and prescribed for her. She has intermittent fever. — Housekeeping goes on bravely. I rather like it. Susan is a jewel of a cook and with such a girl the whole thing is made easier. Our dishes came this after-noon—so now if we only had table cloths we could set a nice table enough for *any*body—as it is we do not feel ashamed of it.

Thurs. 9*th*   Mr. Redpath spent the eve with us. He goes north the first of next week. Capt. Thorne sent up his horse and buggy to Mrs. Beecher so we went shopping again. Sandy, his colored boy, sat between us and

280. Minnie L. Brown of Watertown, N.Y.

drove and the attention we received from the Charlestonians in the streets was quite flattering. Evidently, the sight was a novel one to them, and we enjoyed their astonishment very much as did '*Sandy*' too.

After Mr. Redpath left us we had a quiet game of Eucher. Gen. B. [Beecher] and I against Miss Chamberlain and Miss Buttrick:—The Beechers thought of returning to-morrow but the court martial did'nt close as expected to-day.

Friday 10*th*   My work here is about finished. The girls are comfortable and everything in good running order. They groan over my leaving them but Miss Hosmer will come up and take my place so that is all right. To-day is the first leisure I have seen but we slept *three* in a bed last night, and Frankie kept me awake with her peculiar trials that no one but me can soothe, till after midnight, so I do not feel very *workish* this morning. Went down to see Miss Brown—and Mrs. Barker kept me a long time with a recital of her trials and complaints. I ca'nt endure that woman; she is snaky and bad tempered without enough native talent to hide it! I do not understand how Mr. Redpath can allow such a woman to be at the head of that Assylum. —The Gen. and Frankie go to-morrow morning— Read in the paper to-day of Wirtzs [Wirz][281] execution. Thank God for this bit of justice!

Sat. 11*th*   Got up at 5. this morning to see the folks off, tried to get into the kitchen so as to make them a hot cup of coffee but everything was locked, and so they had to start out with empty stomachs but they will reach home by 8. o'clock.

The locksmith came yesterday and took the locks from all the doors, so now not one of them can keep shut—which is annoying considering the *low* state of the wood pile and the change of weather. Miss Chamberlain & Miss Chase are suffering severely with cold on the lungs—Mr. Willis [?] is reported on the sick list this morning. Had Lizzie [Wynne] wash the dining room and hall floors—and also clear out one of the little out buildings for a store-room. Miss Lee and I rode down to Commissaries and got in another stock of provisions. Were gone all the forenoon. Rummaged over an empty house and found some large demijohns, just what we wanted for syrup—vinegar &. Sandy carried them all up to the house for us. Called at the School-house on our way home and got a *nice* rug,

281. Capt. Henry Wirz, the Swiss-born commandant of the Andersonville, Ga., prison camp, was executed in November 1865 for his part in allowing intolerable conditions at the camp. Wirz was the only former Confederate to be executed by the federal government.

which I was afraid *might* get *stolen!* —Got a new dining table sent us by one of the offices from Hd. qrs.

Sunday 12*th*   Some of the girls went to church—some over to Magnolia Cemetery. Capt. Batchelder [Batcheller] stayed here last night—is here to-day. Gen. Hartwell dined with us. Capt. B. [Batcheller] is expecting his wife—she will come here. Mr. Willey [Wiley][282] is here—came in on the "northern boat yesterday. Mrs. W. is with him—Went out a little while after dinner. It is warmer and our roses show their appreciation of it by blossoming. We have a beautiful yard!

Charleston November, 1865

Monday 13*th*   Intended to go to the Head to-day but no boat went. Gen. Hartwell assures me one will go to-morrow and he will send me word at what hour, in the morning. Saw by the paper yesterday that Capt. John H. Moore was dead. Poor fellow! He died of delerium tremors at a (colored) house of ill fame. His course has been rapidly downward during the past year—a real generous hearted man—but of no principles—an excellent officer and wel liked by all who knew him! —A large procession of military, followed him to the grave. Service at Grace Church——I tried to go in but the crowd was too great. "Peace to his ashes!"

---

282. Probably I. W. Wiley, an official of the Freedman's Aid Society of the Methodist Episcopal Church.

[The Sea Islands]

Tuesday 14*th*   The *Sampson* a miserable little boat but staunch and strong, goes to the Head this morning. Met Genls Hartwell and Woodford on board. I was very sick and during the latter part of the day it was exceedingly stormy and rough, at one time there was some danger of our being *swamped* the waves came over the boat so. There were several women on board and they kept up a dismal howling praying, during the danger. It was 4 P.M. when we reach the wharf. I went with Gen. Woodford to the Port Royal house. The rain must have been very heavy here for much of the way the water was over my boots along the wharf—so I was quite drenched on reaching the hotel. Find some wood in the fire place so I built a little fire and puting my wet clothes before it to dry went gladly to bed.

Wed. 15   Met Genl's Littlefield and Woodford at breakfast—had a good-natured chat with Gen. L. [Littlefield] who has but lately returned to the Dept. with a view to having his affairs straightened out. Gen. W. [Woodford] is his counsel and Gen. Hartwell is to prefer the charges.

Mr. & Mrs. Willey [Wiley] are here. Came down on the *Rockland* and did'nt get in till this morning, laid in the river over night—they came the inland route. Dr. [J. M. Hawks] came over for me and I rode out to the 'Home' just before noon. The people were all glad to see me and I am glad to see home.

Miss Hosmer has become so much attached to the place that she does'-ent care to go to C. [Charleston] now that she is wanted there. She goes by the first boat. Miss [Jane B.] Smith is still here, but is teaching with Miss Breck[283] at Mitchelville they have a large school.—

---

283. Miss Elizabeth P. Breck of Northampton, Mass.

Hilton Head Nov. 1865.

Sunday 18*th*   Miss Hosmer, went on Friday—and we are getting ready to move up to camp. Miss Lilly [Lillie] would like to have me stay here with her, but she doesn't wish to give up this room, so if I stay I must go into that big room to sleep and live which would be quite disagreeable, besides we live very poorly and she charges us ten dollars per week board, which I presume is as cheap as we can get board anywhere but we should get better fare. She charged Miss H. [Hosmer] for board all the time she was here, and she, poor girl; worked hard all the time and besides taking the whole care of the sick and wards, did considerable sewing for Miss Lilly [Lillie]. We were invited to breakfast out at Marshland this morning. Miss S. [Smith] & Mr. Atwood, Mrs. Webster[284] and Bastrum Dr. [J. M. Hawks] and I. —a delightful party which we all enjoyed. I went out on 'Nellie' and as soon as I dismounted she took "French leave," so I had to ride home in Mr. A's [Atwood] waggon with the Marshland ladies, and we all went in and spent the day at Mr. A's [Atwood] not coming home till dark. There is one of the densest foggs to-night I ever saw, it is so heavy that the water runs from the houses as though it was raining. The air is close and sultry. It has been warm all day.

20*th*   The weather changed in the night, and we have a cold fierce driving north-east storm. The rain beats in everywhere; and we have yet no stoves up. It is too stormy to think of moving to-day, but shall go to-morrow.

Sunday 26*th*
Again living in a tent! It brings back old times—two years ago I came here to live in a tent—but how different the condition of things from now! We are camping quite near the old "camp ground, only further back from the beach. Came up Tuesday. We have a hospital tent for living room and a wall tent to sleep in so we are quite comfortably off—have a *carpet,* sofa, *two* rocking chairs, and a centre table—relics of our Charleston living. The rest of the furniture consists of boxes, trunks &. I dont think I shall know how to keep house without a trunk in the room hereafter; it has got to be a *necessity* in the way of furniture! Dr. [J. M. Hawks] went up to Beaufort Friday. I visited the schools in Mitchelville. We mess with Capt. Davis[285] & wife who live in a house close by. Sat up

284. Unidentified.
285. Capt. Mahlon E. Davis of the Twenty-first U.S.C.T.

last night writing. Wrote Chaplain Hobbs that I would come to Fla. Get a letter yesterday from Mrs. Loring[286] offering to pay expenses if I go to Fla. so answered that, and wrote Mother & Annie [?]. It must have been very late when I retired. It certainly *was* when I woke this morning—breakfast was over, and the people all away and I had but just got home when Mr. Atwood and Mr. Webster called on their way to Marshland, to get the ladies over to spend the day—and invite me to go too. They are to call for me on their return. Spent the remainder of the day at Mr. A's [Atwood] very pleasantly. Miss Smith, Miss Breck, and the Marshald [Marshland] ladies there. Came home about dark. It seemed a little lonely to come into the tent and spend the night alone!

27*th*   Dr. came in early this morning. Stayed on boat the *New Hampshire* (navy supply boat) last night, came down on a tug to that late last night.

Didn't make much of a beginning in school to-day but hope to do better to-morrow. Rode Nelly a little while—not very far.

28*th*   School opened quite flourishingly to-day. None but men from "Co A." present, as they were the only ones we said anything to on Sat. We wish to make the school self-supporting.

Hilton Head Nov. 1865.

Sunday Dec. 3*rd*

School goes on bravely. The men are earnest and as eager as ever to be taught. We have only about thirty each day—but that keeps us very busy—as each one has a different book and lesson. Most of them write. They have made great improvement, since my first school in the Regt. On Friday morn, soon after the opening of school Mr. Dennett, with Miss Joselyne [Jocelyn] & Everleth [Eveleth]—so I went over to the house with them leaving Miss Cogswell[287] in my place. (She came down from Edist[o] last eve) and stayed over night with me. Dr. [J.M. Hawks] went over to Capt. Davise's to sleep. Dr. Burdett [Burdette],[288], came for him in the night to go to a case of strangulated hernia; this roused me, and I didn"t get to sleep again till nearly morning. After dinner we had the saddles put on Jim & Nilly and I took Miss C. [Cogswell] out to Marshland. Jim capered about some when we first started and managed to upset Miss C.

286. Mrs. Charles B. Loring, an official of the New England Freedmen's Aid Society.
287. Miss Catherine A. Cogswell of Foxboro, Mass.
288. Dr. James F. Burdette, Assistant Surgeon of the Twenty-first U.S.C.T. under Dr. Hawks.

who came to the ground with more haste than dignity—but not much *hurt*. So she mustered courage and again mounted and we rode serenly but Miss C. was full of fears which had their usual result on the horse, who was'nt on his *best behaviour* but we go on very well by going slowly. When but half way there I espied a ladies' hand kerchief in the road and being desirous to test my ability to mount and dismount alone, did so, greatly to my own admiration. The girls were not at home so we rode back and went down to Mr. Atwood's in search of them; they were just sitting down to dinner so we dismounted and dined with them. Miss Baker[289] has come in from 'Lawtons' and is staying at Mr. A's [Atwood]. Sat. rode down to wharf to see if a boat was going to C. [Charleston] as Mis Cogswell is anxious to go on—none going. She stayed at Mr. A's [Atwood]. I came home and have had some head ache all day. Got my hair down and dress in disorder from lying down, then Lt Hall of Navy called soon after Gen. Littlefield came in—and afterwards another naval officer. Miss C. [Cogswell] was here, and helped *do* the ceremonies. Mr. D. [Dennett] took dinner with us. Miss C. goes out to spend the night with Miss Fowler. She came in early this morning thinking a boat might be going to C. [Charleston] but none goes. A telegram from Hd. Qr's at C. [Charleston] came this morning that Gen. Grant would be here to-day, so I hesitated about accepting Mr. D's [Dennett] invitation to go out and ride a little while but the day was too enticing so we started about 10 a.m. intending to be gone an hour or two, but prolonged our ride to Storry Plantation where Miss J. & E. [Jocelyn & Eveleth] are and did'nt get home 'till nearly night. Had a charming ride and very pleasant visit. Mr. & Mrs. Fowler seem very kind and pleasant people, and treated us most cordially. About dark the firing of guns announced the arrival of Gen. Grant, and all the officers of the Regt were invited to meet him at Post Hd. Qrts. so immediately after tea all went down to do honor to the "conquering hero," arrived at Col. Green's[290] but *he had gone*—however the boat had not left the wharf so they went on board and just *passed* in *review* before a "small spare man in citizens' dress shaking hands with him", and this they suppose to have been Gen Grant, but I think the question is involved in some obscurity. It is hard to see what object he could have had in landing here at all. It could'nt have been much gratification to him and certainly not to any one else. I confess to being greatly disappointed!

---

289. Mary F. Baker of Hopkinton, Mass.
290. Unidentified.

Dec. 4th

So Dr. [J. M. Hawks] is no longer an officer in the Army! His resignation has been accepted and he notified of the fact.[291] I confess to feeling very badly for this. It would have pleased me to have had him remain in the service till the 21st [U.S.C.T.] are mustered out. Again, I do not think he has treated me fairly in the matter—by not consulting me in reference to resigning—but I did not know that he had done so till some two weeks after it had been sent in. I know his only reason for this secrecy was to avoid my arguments against it and this, I think, was somewhat cowardly so I feel quite justified in being unhappy about the matter; and nothing has made me feel more so for many months. He gives up a good salary, an easy position, and one in which his influence for good might be immense and his sphere of activity was large; and when, it seems to me, he could have done about as good service for this "Land & Lumber" company which is so engaging to his mind.[292] I wish I could feel that he is the man to manage the complicated machinery of such a concern as he imagines himself to be! I wish I had more confidence in his business capacities and judgement but it is impossible for me to feel sanguine of success in any business enterprise requiring judgment and practical ability, which may engage his attention! His past life has not been one to qualify him for the position of manager in such affairs—and I predict that this enterprise, if begun will be a *failure* in that, instead of making fortunes in a *few months* or years, they must wait through many before they realize in profits the amount of outlay at the begining—but if the colored men who go into the company are not losers and if a colony is founded there for them, where they can have safe and permanent homes—it cannot be a failure—though it *fail* to make its founders *rich*. However, it is all right. I am fast settling into the belief that "whatever *is* is right.". It's a blessed consolation, when we are desirous of overthrowing some of the wrongs and outrages arrising from outraged justice and so called *laws*—to fall back on the assurance that "all things work together for good," and drift

---

291. The official date of John Milton Hawks' resignation was November 21, 1865. Hawks later requested that his resignation be revoked and that he be permitted to be mustered out with his regiment, but to no avail. JMH to Brig. Gen. Jos. K. Barnes, Surgeon Gen. U.S. Army, December 18, 1865, JMH Military Service Record.

292. Many soldiers assigned to the Twenty-first and Thirty-third U.S.C.T. signed statements indicating their intention of settling upon the lands of the Florida Land and Lumber Company and of investing their capital in the association. List of Men of Company "B" Thirty-third U.S.C.T. who intended to Purchase and Settle Upon the Lands of the Association being formed by Surgeon Hawks, Twenty-first U.S.C.T., undated, Hawks Papers: Florida Land and Lumber Company, Prospectus . . . (Hilton Head, South Carolina, 1865?)

along blindly with the current! After all isn't it just as well as this constantly freting over what is inevitable? now for instance, I have made myself and the good Dr. very unhappy by what I have said in regard to his resigning. The sting left by bitter words can never be effaced and how foolish to utter them in a case like this. What a pity that a *curb-bit* cannot be devised with which to bridle the tongue! I suppose good Professors would tell me there was one all ready for use but I have seen so few successful applications of it that my faith in its efficacy is too weak for trial!

The *Cosmopolitan* which came to bring Gen. Grant was only here about an hour—took the party right on to Savannah and returns here tonight and leaves sometime in the night for Charleston. Dr. [J. M. Hawks] will go up on her—so will Mr. Dennett and Miss Cogswell. Rode over to the 'Home just at dark then round to Mr. Atwoods' to see Miss C. [Cogswell]. As they were just setting down to dinner, went in and took a cup of tea with them. It was quite dark when I reached home, and the air was heavy with fog—took cold in my face and was kept awake by neuralgia all night—never had anything like it before and can't say I enjoyed the sensation. Had sick head acke 'till sunset.

5*th*   Haven't felt like work to-day so after coming from school read *The Atlantic* till dinner time—and soon after, had 'Nelly' brought up and rode over to get some books at the 'Home' and then carried a pattern to Miss Smith. On my return took Mrs. Davis out to ride on the beach and then rode down to Mr. A's [Atwood] to see Miss Smith, who had gone over there but she had left before I got round. So came directly home, to escape the damp night air.

Hilton Head 1865.

Dec. 8*th*   Yesterday was our 1*st* National Thanksgiving Day. There was no demonstration of festivity among the whites here; Indeed since the removal of Hd. Qts. everything is at a stand still and though there has been no winter when ladies were so plenty as this, there has been none when gayety was at such a low ebb. It may be because so many of the offices have *their wives* and families with them so home pleasures take the place of more questionable excitements, if so it is well. Many of our offices have their wives here this winter—but Mrs. Davis and one Lt. wife and myself are the only ones living in camp. This reminds me of a little joke we have on Capt. D. [Davis]. When Miss Cogswell was here, Mrs. D. [Davis] talked of going out to ride with us but could'nt get a horse. So Miss C. [Cogswell] and I started alone, she on "Jim" who is such a knowing beast that he has a most hearty contempt for all timid riders of the female persuasion, so his first efforts were used to convince Miss C. that she could'nt manage him, and just as we got opposite Capt. Silva s[293] tent he gave an extra twist and she fell off. 'Jim' meanwhile trotted off to the stable, of course everybody ran. The Regt was on 'battallion drill' and one of the men said to Capt. D. [Davis] "The horse has thrown Mrs. Davis," so he dashed away rather uncerimonously from his company, and came up with a rush to see "Where's Mrs. D. [Davis] he exclaimed breathlessly." Miss Cogswell had just risen to her feet and was shaking the sand off—"Wheres Mrs. D.? Somebody said she was thrown from the horse." No, I said, this is the lady that was thrown. "All right" said the gallant capt. and back he hastened to his company—without a thought of poor Miss C. so we laugh at the Captain a little. But this has nothing to do with Thanksgiving. We didn't have breakfast till nearly eleven, and as I went supperless to bed the night before my appetite was in excellent order. We had no 'extras' but I think all felt thankful. Soon after my return, Mr. Atwood's team with several of the teachers aboard came for me to go there and spend the day—and though I had determined to stay at home I allowed myself to be persuaded, and we had a very quiet, pleasant time, with a most excellent dinner. It was dark when I returned to my lonely tent. Mrs. Webster insisted on coming in and waiting till a candle was lighted to be sure that the 'bug bears' were in hiding but I never feel any fears, when surrounded by our good, faithful colored soldiers. Sat up and sewed 'till quite late as there was a big dance in the Co. Mess tent right opposite, so I could'nt get to sleep on retiring—and when at last I slept my dreams were filled with all sorts of dangers by sea. In the first place I was in some swift river, alone, and with all my clothes on trying to swim—my hat and scarf I lay on top of the water, and soon an eddy caught them and they were whirled beyond my reach. I made frantic efforts to reach them and found myself close to some high falls, and the water so deep that I could'nt reach the bottom, so I struggled back and found on reaching shoal water that all my clothes save a little sacque, had been torn off me in my struggles and I felt very much ashamed, in getting back to the house—but some good friend stood before me. In my joy at my escape I awoke, but soon slept again and now all manner of perils beset me on board a steamer—so I again awoke in a violent perspiration and fright and didn't sleep again till light. And I suppose this is all the result of a *good dinner!*

293. Capt. Charles Silva of the Twenty-first U.S.C.T.

Hilton Head Dec. 1865.

10*th*

Yesterday morning Mr. Dennet [Dennett] came, arrived from C. [Charleston] the eve. before. Dr. [J. M. Hawks] will come on the next boat. Mr. D. [Dennett] informed me that Mr. Todd[294] was at the Port Royal Hotel, just arrived from N.Y. so I ordered Nelly and we rode down and called on him, then I rode over to the 'Teachers' Home in Mitchelville and called. They are a very pleasant family. Promised to send a horse and saddle for one of them to ride this afternoon. Didn't get home till dinner was ready.

Did'nt go out in the afternoon—and at tea time stayed over to Capt. Davis' about an hour for a game of Euchre—played with Adj. Dow against Dr. Burdett [Burdette] & Mrs. D. [Dow] but they were too *sleepy* and dull to make the game interesting. On my return brought 'Tip'— Capt. Seller's little white poodle, with me, found Mr. D. [Dennett] and Miss Evelithe [Eveleth] just at the door with the horses. Miss E. [Eveleth] and '*Tip*' both stayed all night. It commenced raining soon after we retired and rained hard all night. I was kept awake by my teeth and face "too much for anything". Took "Tip" to breakfast and he refused to return. It is a rainy day but not cold—yesterday was very bright and warm. Friday was cold and very windy. I rode over to Seabrooke with Dr. B. [Burdette] and Mrs. Davis.

11*th* Dec. It is reported that the *Cosmopolitan* goes to Jacksonville, leaving the dock this evening and I am quite undecided as to whether I can get ready to go on her. it is now past noon. I dont feel much in the spirit of going at all. We are so comfortable here—and it would be so nice to have a quiet winter! But as that is among the impossibles I must make up my mind to roughing it again. I hav'ent yet heard either from Boston of [or] from Chaplain Hobbs—so I am in a state of uncertainty as regards what I am to do—but I must go to Florida anyway and there circumstances will determine the next step. It is raining hard and I do not believe the boat will go out to-night and if it does'nt go till tomorrow we shall probably go on her—as Dr. [J. M. Hawks] has determined that he will go down, in hopes of meeting either Fowler or Purdie at J. [Jacksonville]. I will go over to the Home and get those books in order so as to take them along should we go. I don't feel any strong *impression* on the matter of going to Fla. on this boat.

294. Unidentified.

[Florida]

Jacksonville Fla. Dec. 1865.

18th   We concluded to come on the *Cosmo* so Tuesday was a very busy day and it was quite dark when the last load of things left the tent for Mr. Willey's—he is to take our furniture and keep it till called for, all but three cane seat dining chairs and my stuffed rocking chair which I leave with Mrs. Davis. The boat was to leave at 8 P.M. so right after supper I got on 'Nellie' and started for the boat. We called at Mr. Atwoods' not thinking to stop but there was quite a 'surprise party' in waiting to see us there, so we alighted and went in for a last friendly half-hour. Misses' Smiths, Breck, Lillie, Evelithe [Evelethe], Baker and Joselyne [Jocelyn], and Mr. D. [Dennett] were all there; the time passed rapidly and pleasantly and the last good byes were said sadly on my part, with many promises to write soon. On reaching the boat, we found one load of our furniture, which the blundering driver had taken, and left there instead of at Mr. Willey's and there we were obliged to leave it. I presume it will all be stolen or spoiled as it came in raining hard before morning. It rained hard all day Wednesday. We arrived off the St. John's bar about 10 A.M. and had to lie there 'till 2 P.M. for high tide so it was past 4 o'clock when we landed at J. [Jacksonville]. Dr. went ashore and came back with the intelligence that our old 'home' had been given up and the teachers are all at another house farther up town. Chap. Moore was out of town and, the Hotel was full so the best we could do was to remain where we were, on the boat till morning which we did. Mr. Todd and Charlie Tucker who came down got boarding places somewhere so we saw no more of them. The two Beaufort ladies, with their babies stayed on board, as did several offices and in the evening the men gave us a 'concert' (!), Thursday morn. Dr. [J.M. Hawks] again went up town, called on [?] Hayat [Hyatt] whose family is here, and they agreed to take me into their family while I remain in J. [Jacksonville] so about 10 A.M. a cart came for our things and we walked up to their quarters in the rain. They are living in the old regimental head quarter occupied by Col, Montgomery when our forces first came here in Feb./63. It is the house where I spent the night on our return from Finigan [Camp Finegan]! I can have a place to put my 'plunder' and a chance to sleep on the floor, for all of which I am duly thankful!

In the evening Dr. Hanson[295] came in and invited us to walk up to see the teachers, and so, though it was very dark, we all went. I walked with Dr. H. [Hanson], Col. Marple and Chap. Moore & Capt. Salvage[296] were there when we arrived, and soon after, Dr. Donalson[297] came in so we had quite a party; Two of the teachers were out. Miss Stowe,[298] one of the ladies, was down in Missippi last year, and I tried to talk with her something about the schools there but she only answered briefly or in monosyllables so I soon gave up the attempt—and as all were engaged in an animated talk with the gents, so I turned my attentions to Col. Marple, who came and took a seat near me. He told me about the rough times the people were having out at Gainesville and how insolent and overbearing the whites were, so we talked for an hour or more on subjects pertaining to the Freed men and the 'Bureau.' There is great dissatisfaction felt and expressed at the course taken by Col. Osborn in regard to the affairs of the 'Bureau' this late 'order' of his turning over the affairs of the Freedmen into the hands of the civil authorities, is felt to be premature and ill advised—but it may be merely an experiment to see how the *thing will work!*

It was late when we returned, and Dr. [J. M. Hawks] was in very uneasy state of mind on account of my exclusive attentions to Col. M. [Marple]. He was pleased to be in a state of jealousy very difficult for me to understand or "see the point" of—and Friday morning he felt no better, about it. He must see *charms* in me which other gentlemen do not appreciate to be troubled with jealousy! It is certainly most foolish for a man to take offense because his wife is capable of carrying on an animated conversation with other gentlemen of intelligence! The boat was to leave for the Head at 4 P.M. so he went off in the morning. I expected he would be back again before the boat left but he did'nt come, and, I suppose, went away in a huff. I do not feel that I did anything to provoke it—and I am glad to record that for once at least, when I felt myself unjustly accused I kept my temper! It rained all day Friday but Mrs. Hayett [Hoit] and I went out

295. Dr. Daniel D. Hanson, Surgeon of the Thirty-fourth U.S.C.T.
296. Capt. John W. Selvage of the Thirty-fourth U.S.C.T., the Acting Assistant Adjutant General in Charleston.
297. Unidentified.
298. Miss Emily C. Stowe of New Haven, Conn.

and visited the different schools. My visit was most unsatisfactory as there were so few children present. In White school, when Mrs. McLeane [McLean] had 150 children last year, there are now but about 30, and two teachers employed. There are eight teachers now at work in this place, where we found four to suffice, but then now we have a school Supt. and of course the thing is done according to *orders*. I am surprised to find that the schools here have not been '*graded*' and that the matter is not considered of sufficient importance to be agitated or thought of! —In the evening the teachers come down here attended by the Chap. Dr. H. [J. M. Hawks] and Capt. Salvage [Selvage], we tried to start some singing and to talk about starting a reading club, but could'nt do it so we just rattled on. There seems to be two parties at the teachers' home, and a part did not come down. Saturday I went down to our old home to see about the teachers things but took the wrong key and so could'nt get in. My colored friends are just finding out that I am here and they come in squads of from two to a dozen to see me. A great many of the old residents have returned and the streets are full of new faces. Business is reviving and many new buildings are going up so that the place is hardly recognizable. Col. Sprague[299] is in command of the District and as Col. Marple has gone on the *Cosmo,* to go north, Maj. Hoit is in command of the post. Miner [Hawks] came down from Palatka this morning. He is looking finely and in good spirits. Mrs. Hoit and I rode out to the Jewdan plantation this forenoon—lost way and went out to Carmichael's, two miles beyond. The roads are very wet, and in many places the streams so swolen that we were somewhat in doubt about crossing but our noble horses carried us through in safety. It was past noon when we reached Jewdan's. I got the people and children together and talked with them a little on their prospects and what they proposed doing when the owner returned, as they expected he would about Christmas—but few expect to stay there so they are doing nothing on the lands now, and are very short of provisions, but they look quite comfortable and cheery. We went into the large house to see an old woman who is sick with fever and ague. She and her daughter live there together, all the men are in the army and they are rather destitute just now owing partly to this sickness. They are both very smart women. The younger one told us that she and her mother had cut nine cords of wood, about a mile from the landing and brought it all down to the water on their backs and were now waiting to get a boat to take it to Jacksonville. The younger one takes it down, unloads it and cords it up on the wharf herself and then finds purchasers. They are

299. Col. John T. Sprague.

smart women. The young one is a bright mulatto, and one of the smartest ones I have yet seen.

Sunday we did'nt go to church. It was cold and rainy. We got Mr. Hull,[300] a young Rev. who is here *missionarying* interested in our colony and he went out to give them a *little preach* and see what he can do for *their souls.* I confess to being more seriously troubled about their *bodies* just at this time and so between us both I trust the poor creatures may be cared for. Miner was in several times during the day but I didn't see very much of him alone. Monday I cut a riding habit for Mrs. Hoit and that occupied us all day, only the time I spent looking over our things and getting those that belonged to me moved over here. The rats have made havoc among the loose papers and dry goods. Miner came round in the evening and we walked a long time on the board walk while he told me his plans and asked my advice in regards to some matrimonial entanglements which he has got into. The family with whom he boards is from N.E. the father and sons were engaged in starting a saw-mill and Miner has invested with them. The old man was taken sick and died a few weeks since—leaving his wife a daughter and son and son-in-law. The daughter, Mary, it seems is very much in love with our young Captain, and all the family are trying to get him married to her; the young folks have talked over love and marriage and unless something occurs to take M. [Miner Hawks] away from them I am afraid he will be a 'benedict before he realizes what he is about. I don't think he is very violently in love, but he likes her very much and thinks her the *essence* of *perfection.* It is very evident that she is in love with him. She is two years older and altogether to[o] well versed in love matters for such an unsophistacated boy as Miner. I hope something will happen to prevent them marrying, at present;—but I hav'nt much hopes and sha'nt be surprised to hear that the thing is consummated at any time! He talked very freely with me on all the pro's and con's of the affair and acknowledged the weight of my reasons and seemed inclined to take my advise which was to leave that boarding place and wait a *couple* of *years,* then if both are of the same mind, marry—but I am afraid, when he gets back, their influence will prevail and our first news will be that he is married. "All things work together for good." I hope *this* may! Wrote to Chaplain Hobbs this morning and shall stay here 'till I hear from him.

Miner returned to Palatka Tuesday morning—carried up some books and slates for the school in his company. In the afternoon Mrs. H. [Hoit] and I rode out to the Panama Mills, visiting all the families there and on the way. There are not so many families at the Mills as when I visited them last Summer, but I was glad to see the seed which I sent them had been planted and now supplied them with garden vegetables. They all remembered my former visit and seemed very much pleased at my return. This place is six miles out, so it is too far for the children to go to school but several of the people send their children in here to stay with some 'aunty' so as to give them a chance at school. (We learned that many of the children came in from the Jewdan's place which is more that four miles—bringing their dinners every-day—).

Col. Bardwell spent the evening with us. He has just returned from the North out of the army and is going into business in this state.

The weather is very unsettled. There has'nt been a good fair day since I came here.

Wed. Eve. Capt. Johnson [?] and Mrs. Copell spent with us. She is the most intelligent and best appearing lady I have seen in this Dept. among the natives—but she has received her education at the north end and only lived here a short time. Capt. J. [Johnson] is going into business with Col. B.[?], and will I presume, if she ever gets her divorce, marry the lady which is rather remarkable as he is a Virginian of good family and of means and she is sufficiently *colored* to be evident to the most casual observer.

Friday afternoon Mrs. H. [Hoit] and I rode out to St. John's Mills. We have never been there before so the way was new to us. The distance about four miles. There are but two houses on the road and not feeling in the mood we left them thinking to call, on our way back. These Mills have been destroyed by fire, since the Union forces occupied Jacksonville whether by accident or not it is hard telling but it is supposed it was done by the rebs. We found two men at work among the ruins and they informed us that the mills were to be rebuilt by some men from Mass. There is one dilapedated, windowless and doorless house still standing and in this we found one of the men's families, a forlorn looking place and people! On our way back we stopped at the first house—a little colored boy came to the door and on enquiry we learned that his mother was dead and the father in J. [Jacksonville] at work and he and a little Sister were there alone. As the door swung open, I noticed that the house was full of smoke, and also a smell of burning cotton. I asked the meaning of it and the little boy said his sister was burned. I immediately alighted and on entering, found the child curled up in the bed and on the floor close to it her clothes were all on fire just ready to flame up. I tried to put the fire out but found I could'nt, so put the things into the water pail and then turned to the child. As soon as I had uncovered the girl, she exclaimed "Oh! Miss Hawk, I'se so glad you come." The children were some of my old pupils and knew me immediately. She was badly burned in the back and arms. The little boy, who is not more than eight years old had got the clothes off so quickly that the burn is not *very* deep. I could find nothing in the house to put on it—so Mrs. H. [Hoit] rode over to the next house and they sent some oil. I dressed the burns and we left them alone. It was quite dark before we got away; As we were invited to take tea with the Hogan girls [?] we rode there before going home. They had made great preparation for us and we enjoyed the occasion very much. It was about eight when we reached home and soon Mr. & Mrs. Robinson came in to call; she is lately arrived from Vt. where she has been during the war!

Sat. 23*rd*   At eight this morning a large company left here for St. Augustine on a pleasure trip. Several of the teachers went along. I did think I would go too, but they do not return till next Wed. and that is longer than I wish to stay, so I remain here. Got a letter to-day from Chap. Hobbs. He wishes me to go to Quincy and take charge of the schools at that place—but will telegraph to me when he wishes me to come. So *that* is settled. Don't know whether I desire to go there or no, but will go out and see. Rode over to see how the little girl was doing. It was raining hard all the way so I got a thorough drenching. Carried out some clothing to her and some dressing for the burns, which look badly to-day. Wrote to Miss Joselyn [Jocelyn]. Mr. Todd was in, in the evening.

Sunday 24*th*   Went to Sunday School and stayed to hear Mr. Hull. Went round to call on Mrs. Brown, who is very happy in her new home! Mr. Purdie was here last night. goes to the Head tomorrow.

Jacksonville Dec. 25th, 1865

Christmas! A year ago to-day I was here, in J. [Jacksonville] only just arrived from Port Royal. The evening we teachers all spent with Mrs. Willard and had a right merry time; To-day everything is quiet and there is no demonstration of festivity among the white inhabitants. They hav'nt much heart for merry-making. The colored folks seem to be having a good time generally. The Maj.s' two little girls and I went up and took *refreshments* with "Aunty" Brown. The girls had quite a party of the better class of girls and younger men; Their table was a very artistic affair. A nice great frosted, pound cake graced the centre and oranges, apples, nuts and raisins with several varieties of cakes and meats loaded the board; to all of which we did ample justice Then we stayed a while to see the plays and antics, and returned to a quiet evening at home; Maj. and wife went out to ride and did not return till late in the evening. Mr. Purdie came in and I sent letters to the Head, to be mailed; besides writing to Dr. [J. M. Hawks] a long letter rather expressive of my state of mind, and not very amiable, I am afraid he will think.

26th   Spent the evening at Col. Samine's.[301] Col. Bardwell and Capt. Johnson[302] were there; Capt. J. [Johnson] is just recovering from the effects of the assault on him out at Gainsville [Gainesville] last week by a couple of ruffians, one, the *clerk* of *the* court, the other his son; and I believe assisted by a *friend*. The young man accuses Johnson of insulting his mother while he was provost Marshall there last Summer. The insult consisted in his refusing to listen to her complaints of some colored people who had walked across her yard without permission, even after she had ordered them *not* to do so; this was sufficient to enrage the chivalrous young man, and so he took this way of avenging *the wrong!* Capt. Culluman [Cullen][303] of the 7th Regulars, in command of the Post, refused to interfere or give any protection to Capt. J. [Johnson] and the murdurous band was not molested 'till a telegram from here ordered their arrest, and they were then sent down under a guard but without being in anyway confined, so one of the men jumped off the cars and escaped—they making no effort on the cars for his recovery. The remaining prisoner was greatly exasperated at being put under guard of the colored soldiers and in the same guard house with colored criminals—besides having a 27 lb. ball attached to his legs.

Dr. Hanson came in during the evening but did'nt stay long. We had a very pleasant time—and are invited to spend evening there with the teachers next Friday.

27th   The *St. Marys* returned today from Augustine. I got a large mail from the [Hilton] Head this morning—a long letter from Mrs. Loring but she doesn't mention my coming there, so I am left at my own discretion. In the evening we went up to the teachers Home to see the returned company and also some who have come from Fernandina and Lake City. The room was full, eighteen or twenty ladies and about a dozen offices. They are a fine looking set of women, most of them of superior intelligence

301. Unidentified.
302. Captain James W. Johnson of the Third U.S.C.T.
303. Captain James Cullen, commanding officer of the Gainesville U.S. Army garrison. The Seventh U.S. Regulars, as a white occupation unit which had replaced a company from the 34th U.S.C.T., was very popular among the white citizens of Gainesville, none more so than Capt. Cullen who had married into one of the town's leading families.

and refinement—of this class, more especially are the two from Lake City, Mrs. Campbell and Weld [Wildes][304]—both ladies who have lost their husbands in the war; When the cars came in we had new arrivals in the persons of the Tallahassee ladies, Misses Swift & Dewey.[305] So with the exception of the Gainesville two and one or two at Fernandina and four at St. Augustine, all the teachers in this State were present—but all were too tired to be very agreeable so the evening passed rather dull, after all. Capt. J. [Johnson] and Mrs. R. [?] went with us.

28th   Spent a very restless and uncomfortable night. The weather is very warm and sultry and has been all the week. On Christmas Day the thermometer stood at 83° in the shade, and I should think it had been quite as warm ever since. To-day it is rainy and the air seems quite exhausted of its oxygen. I feel as though if I only had a room I could call my own and a bed if ever so *rough* I should be glad to shut myself into the one and occupy the other for a good part of the day, but such rest is not for me! By invitation of Chaplain Moore, I dined at the teachers'—and then spent an hour with them very pleasantly. They are not *exactly harmonious,* but we dont notice the discordance and so steer clear of the difficulty. We had a nice dinner and *that* was what I was invited to. I am meditating going out to Tallahassee with the teachers from that city on Sat. The only trouble is, I have nowhere to stay on arriving there and they seem to think a place cannot be found—but I guess I shall venture. I will try and find some good respectable colored family and get board with them if I can do no better.

We left J. [Jacksonville] Sat. morn, Dec, 30th at 4 o'clock—of course got but little sleep through the night. The morning was warm and rainy, and we all felt decidedly uncomfortable—which couldn't be entirely owing to the disagreeably crowded state of the cars. Reached Lake City (formerly known, and down on the maps as 'Aligator' owing to the great number of these creatures in the ponds in that vicinity) at about 8 A.M. There are no depots at any of the stations, but at this place there is quite a large storehouse, close to the track and into this we all went to get out of the rain: It is a very dirty place, piled with bags of grain and cotton, interspursed with all sorts of freight—we hunt for an unoccupied spot or box on which to sit and at last sucseed in poising ourselves on the edges of various articles and here we *begin* to *breakfast,* on what we have

304. Maria L. Campbell and Mary T. Wildes both sent to Florida from their Portsmouth, N.H., homes by the New York based National Freedman's Relief Association.
305. Susan A. Swift of Bridgeton, Me., and Fanny H. Dewey of New Hampshire.

brought with us; the cars stopped at Bowldwin [Baldwin][306] for this ceremony and several deluded individuals were victimized but *we* knew better so here we sit and are just beginning to grow amiable and merry over
our situation, when we are politely asked to *move*, as they wish to put
that freight aboard". The man *looked* vicious and I verily believe he had
been watching his opportunity so as to disturb us at *just* the moment
when we were getting comfortable so we picked up our baskets and he
took our seats. As the car was not far away we adjourned to it—and then
finished our meal; the two teachers for this place came up with us. They
are nice, pleasant women: widows, who have lost their husbands in the
war; they have both been hospital nurses in Virginia and now they come
out to teach. Lake City is hardly what its name implies. A few scattering
rough built houses with one or two more pretensious ones is all that is to
be seen. The colored people flock down to the station when the cars
come in, with careless listless looks; no stir of business greets one at any
of these stopping places. It was half-past ten before we got started
again—on enquiring as to this delay, we were gravely informed that they
were trying "to force the other train to start earlier!"

It was too dark when we passed the battle field of Olustee to see any of
the marks of that sanguinary fight—and as the woods on both sides of the
road seemed but a continuation of the miles before. I could'nt wake my
sleepy thoughts up to the occasion. We made frequent and long pauses
for no seeming purpose only "to save time" as some of the officers said.
Reached Madison about noon and had a half hour for dinner—quite a
number of the passengers got off here, but more got *on* so we kept
crowded; We dined from our baskets sumptuously; Our offices all went
to the *hotel* and they reported favorable. I had sick-head acke so it did'nt
matter much what we had to eat. Soon after we got started some ladies
got to talking about the war; one pert Miss said *she* had two cousins in the
Yankee army, that is, they *were* relations but she didn't *own* them now;
no relation of hers could be a traitor to his country so she had disowned
them;—She said they sent her folks a large box of *dry goods* which were
very acceptable, at the time. I wanted to ask her if southern ladies were in
the habit of receiving *presents* of value from strange gentlemen—but
didn't *dare risk* the *snub* which I was sure to receive. It was mentioned as
something remarkable that we arrived at Tallahassee without meeting
with any disasters. The cars didn't *run* off and nothing broke but what

306. Baldwin, Fla. (near Jacksonville), the juncture of the Florida Railroad and the Atlantic
Gulf Central Railroad.

A Woman Doctor's Civil War

could be easily mended. It was 6 P.M. and dark. There was no ambulance in waiting as we hoped to find so we walked up to the house, nearly a mile—over a rough hilly road which was quite refreshing after the sandy sameness of Jacksonville and Port Royal. Found Capt. Websters' folks, with whom the girls are living, living in a pleasant little cottage and in a quiet cozy style. The house is small and they have little enough room but willing hearts could easily find a spot, for a friend without any great inconvenience, so I shall stay with them. Sunday it continued to rain, but we all went to church with the colored people. Had Sunday school, then Mrs. S. [?] went away and I stayed to meeting. Owing to the rain, the house was not full. After the benediction, I talked to the folks a little about forming a benevolent society for the purpose of aiding the destitute of their people & They listened with close attention and seemed well pleased with what I said; In the evening Col. Osborn and Lt. Col. Apthorpe [Apthorp] and wife were in. Col. O. [Osborn] was very cordial and pleasant, and seemed glad to see me. The teachers here have the impression that he and indeed all the offices here and also those men in the Bureau, treat them with indifference not to say *disrespect* because they are *teachers* of *"contrabands"*—but I imagine the reason of the neglect is because the girls hav'nt made themselves agreeable and have acted in a manner to carry the belief that they had such ideas and felt a little *lofty* over it!

Early this morning I went into the kitchen to wait for the others to get up, so after making the acquaintance of all the inmates I got a book and commenced a *small school*—three boys, who had just come in from the country. They were delighted with the book and made great efforts to remember the letters; one, the last one in, is bright—he learned all the large letters through the day. The others are not quite so quick. Chap. Hobbs' is away at Quincy and will not return till to-morrow, so I have his bed and sleep in a lumber room quite comfortably.

Monday went over to Col. O's [Osborn] office to look after the books which have but just arrived. Miss Swift went with me—had a pleasant call; he is kind and genial—wanted to know *why* I did'nt come directly to that place instead of stopping in J. [Jacksonville]. Went with Chap, Hobbs down to the church where he addressed a large audience of the colored people; He made them an excellent speech and they listened appreciatively—played Euchre in the evening with Mr. Reed [?], Mr. & Mrs. W. [Webster].

Tuesday morn went to school with the girls. Only about twenty pupils present. It is rainy and cheerless. I have been looking about this wonderful capital. It is quite a pretty place, but there are no nice stores and but few first class houses; I think the Capitol is the only brick building in the place. It is a very good building for this part of the country (!) Towards night Miss L. [?] and I walked down to the P.O. and then down to a very pretty enclosure called the "Lovers Retreat,". I believe it is private grounds but it is much frequented.

In a store, learned that Dr. Branch,[307] our old neighbor of Manatee was in town staying at his son Orsan's who it seems is the local Methodist preacher at this place: So on my way home I called to see the good old Dr. He looked as of old, and was most cordial: I did'nt go in as I heard Orsan and family were violent secessionists and knew, of course, they would'nt be *very* glad to see me—even if they pretented to be.

Tuesday morning I was up be times. It couldn't have been later than midnight when I got up and dressed; the moon making it so light that I thought it must be morning. Lavina had a nice cup of hot coffee and some biscuit and butter for us—and at 6 A.M. we, (Mr. Reed [?], Lt. Sumner [?] and I were steaming away for Jacksonville. It was still raining and dreary—. We had no adventures till night. Stopped at Madison to dinner. This is quite a pretty place—and very aristocratic so much so that no colored school has yet been established in that place they utterly refusing to *board* or rent rooms to teachers. Didn't make much pause at Lake City only to change cars. The cars were crowded and uncomfortable: *Judge Long*,[308] a villianous secesh, sat near me, with his family and once, after we started he requested permission to close my window, as the damp air was too much for that *precious baby* and I being amiable, let him do it, but when I found that he was the man who said, on our way up, when there was so many of us, that if one of the teachers should call at his house to get board, he should "order her into his *kitchen*"—so I put up the window again and when, he again requested it shut, I politely told him that I was sorry to discommode him but as I was feeling sick must keep the window raised; (all but the *sorry* was *true*) and I kept it up.

We passed Olustee before dark. It is wonderful what a correct knowledge of the location of this battle field every Floridian has; they glory in it, gloat over it—and swear by it. The only way it is marked is by the cutting off of the tops of the trees by the balls and shell. One of the rebs who sat in the seat in front of me, remarked that "that field would be a bright spot in history"—and one which all true southernors would be proud of!

307. Dr. Franklin Branch of Vermont became a pioneer physician and druggist in Tampa during the late 1840s. At the time of the Hawk's honeymoon, Branch was attempting, unsuccessfully, to develop a sanitarium in Manatee. He later returned to Tampa where he resided for the rest of his life.
308. Probably the local magistrate Judge Augustus Long.

When not far from Camp Finigan [Finegan] we came to a sudden stand still. It was sometime before we learned the cause of delay. A freight train in front of us had run off the track and obstructed us: after waiting nearly an hour the conductor told me we should be obliged to walk past the other train and that the engine had gone down to the Station and would return with a car for us; so we all scrambled out and walked on through the bushes and mud over a deep brook and through a marsh for quite a distance till we got on firm track again and as no car was in waiting as we anticipated, some of the men soon had an old pine knot wood stump burning and we crowded round the fire waiting—waiting. A colored man gave me a part of his trunk to sit on: about midnight the wind blew up cold and the stars came out: It was a half hour after midnight when the engine returned with an open flat car to take us: and only two of them, every inch of the room was occupied, bodies and baggage piled on in rather a promiscious manner: I shivered with the cold and damp, and was right glad to get here at 1 ½ A.M. The house was not fastened so I had no difficulty in getting in but there was no fire and no way of making one, no bed and no way of getting one without rousing the family so I lay down in my clothes on the sofa and shivered till daylight then went out and walked to get warm. —The air was cold and bracing and it *did me good.* Got home just as the family were sitting down to breakfast and all were wondering what had become of me, as nothing but my *hat* and carpet bag was visible. It is a cold day and everybody looks and *acts blue*—big fires are in demand!

A letter from M. [Dr J. Milton Hawks] awaited me, informing me of my appointment as guardian of a little colored girl whose father died in the army, leaving a little money which goes to this child.[309] I am appointed by Gen. Saxton—also a letter from Mrs. Stevenson desiring me to visit all the schools and report their condition as soon as possible, this makes it necessary for me to go to Port Royal, which I shall do by the first boat. Dr. [J. M. Hawks] comes here in a few days—to look after the interests of the Land & Lumber Co.

Jacksonville Fla. January 1866

Sunday 7*th*
The cold is quite severe. It is seldom we have a harder spell in this locality than this one: We have had ice several mornings and the frozen ground is crisp under our feet. It is all we can do to keep comfortable. The room in

---

309. The Freedmen's Bureau had appointed Esther Hawks legal guardian of Lizzie Gillison, whose father Pvt. George Gillison had been killed in Charleston.

which I sleep now is our common dining room on the floor. One window (sash and all,) is gone, and the others are but little protection from the cold they are so broken; but I do not take cold very easily from such exposure: Went with the children to Sunday school; Nobody else came till about half an hour after times so we sat on the steps and waited—but few were present: This doesn't seem much like our crowded school of last year, when we had a regular attendance of about 200. The teachers show but little interest in anything pertaining to the colored people and the result is they are losing their interest in the schools. The teachers quarril among themselves in a shameful manner. There are two parties and one will not speak to the other. —The house in which they are living has been given up to the owner, and it is very difficult for them to get another. The church has also been turned over to the trustees so the school there will soon be broken up. Dr. Mitchell[310] who is at the head of church affairs, has returned, to remain and is fixing up this office. He is as urbane and courtly as when in Beaufort, three years ago, he made himself so irissistable to us all at Dr. Durrants'. His family has not returned. The boat from the Head is not yet in, but is expected. I shall return on her.

   8th   It was a charming morning, sun clear and warm. Mary and I walked down to the P.O. before breakfast and we were all congratulating ourselves on the delightful change in the weather, but before nine o'clock, the sky was overcast, the wind blew, the sand whirled and eddied about like snow, and we had the most uncomfortable day of the season; no one stirred from the fire who could avoid it, at night the water pails all froze over and the ground froze quite hard.

   9th   Colder but still. Went up to the barracks to see how the poor people got on through such weather: The poor little children were standing out on the sunny side of the buildings, rolled up in their rags, shivering with the effort to keep from freezing. I picked up a few clothes for some of the most needy.

   10th   The sun shines warm again greatly to the delight of us all. Miss Jocelyne [Jocelyn] and Eveleith [Eveleth] came on the *Fannie* from the Savannah and they report the *Cosmopolitan*, as being at Fernandina on its way here. I went with the ladies to the 'Home' but they were so "up in a hub bub," that they concluded not to stay there and so we started to go to Mr. Swaims in hopes they could get board with them, and on our way came across Mrs. Reed and she invited the ladies to go home with her

---

310. Dr. J. Mitchell, a native of Maine who had settled in Jacksonville before the war and remained loyal to the Union.

A Woman Doctor's Civil War

which was not an agreeable solution to all our difficulties now there was only Miss Dearborn, a N.H. girl, who has come out at the request of Capt. Robinson [?], and is to go on to Tallahassee Sat. morn., so I took her down to the 'Home' and told them they must make room for her to stay there and left her.

11*th*   Miss J. & E. [Jocelyn & Eveleth] came this morning and we went up to Mrs. Browns' then its school, then back here to see the Chaplain; He wishes the girls to go to Pilatka [Palatka] to open a school there— but they would rather stay here, so I dont know what will be the result of it all. Miner [Hawks] was down from there last Sunday. I wish for his sake the girls might go up there; it might keep him from getting caught in the matrimonial noose this winter. —It is still warmer to-day.

12*th*   It is one of the most lovely of days, and we have made much of it. Mrs. Hoit, Lt. Welch[311] and I went out riding early in the afternoon: The horses were in good spirits, so were we, and we had a gay gallop.

In the evening several teachers and their Capts. came in. Mr. Fowler, and Purdie, arrived on the *Cosmo,* and we had quite a merry party. Mrs Dearborn was here, to be in readiness to go out on the cars in the morning: Mr. & Mrs. Greeley [?] and Chap. Moore, also swelled the party, so our room was *full* and they stayed till almost midnight.

Sunday Eve. 14*th*   Chaplain Fowler preached in Moor's [Moore] place and he gave us a 'good preach.' Chose for the foundation of his remarks the parable of the 'talents.' His talk was practical and close fitting both to the white and colored of his hearers, and was listened to with close attention. Chaplain Moore sat by with rather an abstracted and wearied look as though he thought such good plain talk, rather out of place, or he might have been calculating the profits of his investment in Canals on the river, as immediately after meeting was over I observed him in close conversation with an old black woman, urging her to go over and settle on some land which he wishes her sons to buy, but she, (it was old Mrs. Smith from Jewdan's place, the one who cuts so much wood) wanted to know who would support her and family 'till things could be raised. She is a shrewd old woman!

This evening have been reading Carl Shurtz's [Schurz][312] report of his tour through the Southern States. It is an able article and must have weight with Congress if the President ignores it. It is plain talk and right

311. First Lt. John B. Welch of the Thirty-fourth U.S.C.T.
312. Schurz was a German-born former Union general assigned by President Andrew Johnson to report on conditions in the Southern states. He was later a Republican Senator from Missouri and Secretary of the Interior.

to the point, and *any*one who has been here since the war could bring corroberative evidence of the truth of his experience as he states it: There is no exhibition of expression of loyalty among the people of the south, and any one who should venture to indulge in such expressions would be frowned down: The bitterness of the women is remarkable. One of those here who was obliged to take the oath in order to be allowed to open a boarding house for union officers says she only did it because she was obliged to, and I don't believe one of them ever took it for any other reason, yet this woman on her arrival here, was perfectly destitute and one of our officers advanced her the provisions with which to open house with, and she; has not only made a good living but quite a fortune out of it. There is nothing to[o] mean for them to say of the teachers and no inducements could prevail on them to offer us any civilities or take one as a boarder—and every impediment is thrown in the way of the schools and their success. How can they be so blind! and so neglect their own interests? I hope Schurtz's [Schurz] Report will be the means of opening the eyes of Congress to the folly of the present policy of the government, and be the means of keeping the States in their present unenviable political position. It would be very disasterous to all northern men and to the negroes to have the hand of the military removed now: It cant be done with safety for at least a year or two. These 'reconstructed' rebels must learn a few lessons before they can resume their relations among loyal states, they must at least commit the alphabet of loyalty to heart before *all* the rights of citizens can be safely confided to their hands. To be a *rebel* must cease to be a virtue. At present the poor men who have remained true to the Union are the most unfortunate, they are despised by the rebs and their lives only safe so long as the military are in power; They are not sought for offices, and strict surveilance is kept over them. They know they are *marked men*, and only tolerated for a season: The bitter reflection must often come to them that it would have been better for them to have been *traitors* than loyal to their country if this is the return she makes for what they have suffered. And much of the military which we have here, is no protection. We are hearing reports, every week of the shooting of negroes by infuriated white men, and no account is made of it. An officer of the [Freedmen's] Bureau will be sent to *investigate'* but no arrests for these murders takes place, several such cases have lately been reported and the murderers are at large.

One or two of the planters in this vicinity have tried the experiment of *white labor*; bringing irish and german emigrants from N.Y. One man near Gainsville by the name of Lewis (called Col.)[313] a very great *'blower'*

313. Col. Edward Lewis, C.S.A., who had ridden with Dickison's Raiders during the war.

had ventilated the question considerably among our officers, and at last really did get 14 irishmen, and two of their wives out to work on his plantation—gave them his negro quarters to live in and "hog and homony" for rations. In (less) than a fortnight the experiment came to grief by all hands leaving for this place to await transportation to N.Y. Not one of them could be hired on any terms to remain and work here; One of the women stopped at Mrs. Shads' boarding house awhile and her virtuous indignation was great against the man who wanted to make "nagers" of them, and thus ends the first great trial of introducing *white labor*: The men who were brought out on the *Clyde* under Col. Titus[314] and were wrecked on the coast below here, have also all found their way to this place and are begging chances to work their passage back to N.Y. This company was going to colonize on Indian River and start a big fishing business tho' it is shrewdly surmised that the old blockade runner *Clyde* would be used in running negroes over to Cuba, where they would be beyond the trials and temptations incident to a life of freedom! —It is'nt supposed that Col. T's [Titus] morals would be in the way of such adventures!——

It is very warm to-day and this evening mosquitoes are quite frisky. There is a great change in the weather since *last* Sunday. It probably will not stay so pleasant long.

---

314. Col. Henry Titus, C.S.A., who after the war operated the New York and Indian River Preserving Company, which was mainly an oyster factory.

[The Sea Islands]

Freedmen's Home

Hilton Head Jan. 23rd 1866[315]

Left Jacksonville on the 16th a week ago today on the *Cosmopolitan*. Chaplain Moore and Lt Elliot[316] & wife were companions in misery. It was nearly dark when we reached the bar and though the tide was all right still our over timid pilot refused to come out so we lay there till morning: I was quite seasick through the day. It was half-past eight when we reached the dock and as Dr. [J. M. Hawks] didn't hear of the boats arrival I remained on board till morning, then went up to Mr. Atwoods where I took breakfast and then Dr. found me about 8 a.m. Took dinner with him at Capt. Abels [Abeel][317], and at night went over to the Home, and took up my quarters, there indefinitely. About dinner time an officer from the *New Hampshire* which is still the 'receiving ship' and lies on the other side the harbor called to invite us to join a party in visiting her this afternoon; this was especially agreeable to me, & about three o clock we got started: a dozen ladies & half as many gents. On board, we were most pleasantly entertained by the offices—visited every part of the ship very like going over a well regulated villiage of moderate extent—had some singing, a dance and wound up with 'colored performance' of singing & dancing. Two boats full of us home, so we had a little *race* and our crew got beaten, which didn't make anyone feel very badly. At the 'Home' found Miss L. [Lillie] as pleasant & agreeable as usual and all the old inmates glad to tell me 'howdye' [.] Fanny & Wilson especially, expressed themselves as most glad to have me back. I think they all, *love* me rather more than they do Miss L. [Lillie]!

315. This entry is out of chronological sequence.
316. Second Lt. William R. Elliott of the Thirty-fourth U.S.C.T.
317. Capt. Edgar Abeel of the Twenty-first U.S.C.T.

19*th*   Visited Miss Breck & Smith at their school, thus *dashing* into my new duties with *old friends*.[318] Miss B. [Breck] seemed rather *fluried* at the *business* character of my visit—but Jenny remained her usual calm, unruffled self—dined with them, and we had lots of pleasant gossip. Captain Dickinson[319] in to spend the eve with Miss L. [Lillie] not *over* pleased at finding me domiciled here. To-morrow a party are to go to the Lawton Plantation and Dr. [J. M. Hawks] & I will join it. This is one of the few places that I have never visited but have always had a strong desire to do so—so I anticipate the trip with pleasure but I commiserate myself beforehand on the effects of the 24 miles of horseback riding after my long rest from such exercise. The Mitchelville teachers are to be of the party.

Sat. 20*th*   Owing to the clouds, we were late in getting started. Nobody was ready in season, but about 10 1/2 A.M. we finally got off. Dr. & I, Mr. Atwood—Miss Turtshell & Allender[320]—Capt. Dickinson & Miss Lillie. I had Col. Bennett's splendid horse and consequently was best 'mounted' of the party. We were a merry party and made *good time*. Several times I was supposed to be run away with but pursuit being useless I generally 'turned up' riding at a sober pace—very much accelerated, however by their approach, in fact I found it nearly impossible to keep within speaking distance of any of the party. I am sure I never rode so *fast* or so far at one time before: and was pretty well tired when we arrived at Lawtons'. The teachers had'nt returned from the 'Head', and for awhile we were somewhat disappointed at not being able to get into the house; but we that is Capt. D. [Dickinson] and I set up to work to try and *break* open some door or window but everything was most securely shut

318. Esther Hawks' new duties involved visiting several freedmen's schools. She wrote the following account of a visit on a loose sheet of paper inserted in a volume of her diaries:
I get some amusing answers to my queries; Said a proud and exultant teacher the other day, when I was visiting her school, class of primary children numbering 40: Wont you go round and look over my writing class—at the same time holding up two slates for my inspection, very nicely covered with printing and neatly copied drawings—straight lines—curves—parrallels &. Their teacher was quite anxious for me to test their knowledge so I do so, and many of the answers were quite satisfactory—pointing to the 'spiral' at the end of the lesson I asked a bright little woolly head what it was—he looked very hard at it—eyed it side ways like a chicken—then flashing up his bright eyes, quickly he said "Its a *spider* Miss"—he seemed so thoroughly to enjoy his knowledge that I refrained from correcting him. The next little fellow—went through the chatechism evin better—and on coming to the intricate spiral boldly affirmed it to be a "*squirrel*". The teachers eyed me suspiciously—but I could not refrain from smiling at this second deffinition—so I had to expose the ideal hallucinations of my little friends—this provoked an explanation of what the twisted scrol really meant, and I retired during the process.
319. Capt. Joseph W. Dickinson of the Twenty-first U.S.C.T.
320. Probably Miss S. J. Twitchell and Miss A. E. Allender of Connecticut, both of whom were teachers of freedmen.

against us and I gave up, not so the Capt. and we soon heard a persevering shout from the back of the house, he had forced an entrance, then we were all pulled in through a window, then the Capt. set to work to pick the other locks and we were soon in full possession The teachers not coming, our appetites got the better of our politeness, so we set about getting dinner. Mr. A. [Atwood] built a fire, then someone bought some oysters, which all concluded to eat raw; and with the good things we brought with us and found there we soon sat down to a most appetizing dinner—and a more uproarous crew never gathered about *that* table. Seated on trunks, boxes, sticks or whatever could be made available we were in the 'high tide of enjoyment' when some of the curious outsiders who had been gazing open mouthed at our audacious selves shouted "the teachers are coming." They were still a long way off, so we protracted our dinner—profound silence reigned as they came in and there succeeded such a babel as seldom occurs now adays among people of *refinement*, which we 'colored schoolmarms' hardly dare claim *being* at all times. Just as we thought of starting for home, the state of the weather claimed our attention. The heavy clouds hung black and threatening, and a few large drops spattered down on the steps admonishing us of a kind of sprinkling *not* set down in the book—and before the horses were well under cover the rain came down splendidly—as soon as the heaviest was over we felt that we must start in spite of a wetting which looked highly probable. We went home by way of the beach. The tide was low and the breeze invigorating—so in spite of the clouds which occasionally made a dash at us our ride home was decidedly pleasant. Just as we turned off the beach it began raining in earnest so giving my steed the rein we dashed on through mud and wet over bushes and logs, and were home at least twenty minutes before the rest of the party. Capt. D. [Dickinson] went over home with Miss T. [Twitchell] and on his return came in and spent the evening with us. From his manner, he must be quite a familliar visitor here; he is certainly quite at home. I am very tired and sore, my arms are lame trying to hold that fiery horse: he has a reputation for running away and I have had hard work to consider myself *entirely* safe, several times to-day. The Col. said he would'nt *dare* lend him to *any other lady*, which is intended for a compliment to my equestrianship!

21st   Too lame to move unless *absolutely* necessary—so stayed at home all day very quietly, had a nice little time with the children just at dark, to their great delight. They are not very tenderly cared for here!

22nd   Visited the school at Marshland. Took lunch with the Ladies and Mr. Dennett, who came out to call, then rode part way home with

A Woman Doctor's Civil War

him. Capt. D. [Dickinson] and Col. Moore of 6*th* Reg. is to spend the eve. —Dr. [J. M. Hawks] went into parlor to write and we stayed in Miss L's [Lillie] room and had some "table-tappings"—very uninteresting performance.

23.   Went again to Mitcheleville to visit the school and teachers. Took dinner at Mr. Atwood's—rode out to the Wright's plantation on 'Jim' with Miss Lillie. This is one of the loveliest rides on the island. We came out on the beach called at the house and rested a short time thus home by the inland road: It was almost dark when we arrived—and being so late we came home at a "spanking rate." Capt. D. [Dickinson] again here this eve.

24*th*   Expected to start at 10 A.M. for Charleston but boat did'nt get off till 10. this eve. Came over to Capt. A.'s [Abeel] where Dr. boards, then went up to see Mrs. Davis' and dined with them—spent the day very pleasantly. Came down to Capt. Abeals' [Abeel] where we took tea. At 9 o'clock came on board the *Canonicus*. The wind blows hard. Dr. [J. M. Hawks] goes up with me. How sick I shall be!!

Editor's Note

During March, 1866 Dr. Esther Hill Hawks was in charge of quartermaster stores in Charleston, South Carolina. In this capacity she distributed needles, cloth, finished clothing and other items to needy freedmen.[321]

Dr. John Milton Hawks meanwhile was increasingly active on behalf of his Florida Land and Lumber Company. Passage of homestead legislation specifically enacted for the benefit of blacks affiliated with the company enabled Hawks and his partners to move from the planning phase into actual operations.[322] Milton purchased with company funds a portable second-hand steam engine and other related machinery from a company in Bangor, Maine. He spent more company money on equipment needed for a saw and grist mill, and still more to pay skilled craftsmen to integrate these components into a newly constructed two-story building. Dr. Hawks mortgaged the company's land to obtain capital to complete these transactions, and to buy the company's first shipment of logs in March 1866.[323]

Within months however, Esther Hawks' earlier prediction that "this enterprise, if begun will be a failure," was proven accurate. A combination of poor management and even worse luck contributed to the rapid failure of the company. Excessive capital was expended on a mill which had, according to Milton Hawks' later estimate, three times the capacity needed. Several of the mills' parts were lost while they were being brought through Ponce de Leon Inlet. And the firm's treasurer absconded with company funds.[324] Mill workers were understandably angry when the Florida Land and Lumber Company was unable to meet its payroll in the fall of 1866, and subsequent production of lumber diminished drastically.[325]

Even as the company's mill was struggling to remain in operation, three shiploads carrying some five hundred black families from the Columbia, South Carolina, area arrived at Mosquito Inlet, having sailed

---

321. List of quartermaster stores transferred to control of Esther H. Hawks in Charleston, list of items distributed by Mrs. Dr. Hawks to the freed people of Charleston, Hawks Papers.

322. J. H. Hawks, M.D., ed., *The Florida Gazetteer* (New Orleans: The Bronze Pen, 1871) p. 127.

323. Ibid., pp. 127–28.

324. Ibid., p. 128.

325. Lt. R. B. Patterson to Col. Sprague, November 15, 1866, Letters Received, 1865–1869, Box 35, Records of Department of Florida, National Archives, Washington, D.C.

from Charleston under the auspices of the Freedmen's Bureau. But the hopes of the newcomers were quickly dashed. The majority, whose settlement was promoted by the Florida Land and Lumber Company, according to Milton Hawks' later account, "were displeased with the light, sandy soil of the homesteads that were selected for them," and soon departed.[326] White planters from the interior, seeking cheap labor, induced most emigrants to trade their palmetto huts, uncleared lands, and fish and palmetto-cabbage diets, for permanent homes, broad cultivated fields, and hog 'n' hominy."[327]

While Dr. John Milton Hawks was struggling in vain to make the Florida Land and Lumber Company succeed, Dr. Esther Hill Hawks continued to teach and otherwise serve freedmen in and around Charleston. And in the summer of 1866 she was most optimistic about the prospects for improving the lives of former slaves through education. Her heart, she reported to Miss Hannah Stevenson of the Boston based freedmen's society which sponsored her, was "full with rejoicings, which must be shared with *some* one who is interested in this grand work." "I am quite alone here now; and to be so *glad*, and say nothing about it, isn't in my nature!"

[Letter to Hannah Stevenson]

We have got our school-house started in Summerville: isn't that good news? —we have been so much troubled to get land. Several places have been offered, but on investigation we found good titles could not be given; but at last, two single ladies with more land than money, have been induced to sell us an acre for the modest sum of $200. The Methodists also get an acre with us at the same price, and we shall have the church and school-house on the ground, but not under the same management. We shall keep the school in our own hands.

Gen. Scott[328] has given us enough of the confederate barracks to build both houses, and a teacher's house besides, all of which we shall try to do! I went up there last Saturday week; Miss Buttrick went the day before; and she and Mr. Parker[329] had seen and conversed with many of the people, and appointed a meeting on

326. Hawks, *East Coast*, p. 71.
327. Hawks, *Florida Gazetteer*, pp. 127–28. Pleasant Daniel Gold, *History of Volusia County, Florida* (DeLand, Florida: The E . O. Painter Printing Co., 1927) p. 95.
328. Maj. Gen. Robert Kingston Scott who succeeded Maj. Gen. Rufus Saxton as the Freedmen's Bureau's Assistant Commissioner for South Carolina, Georgia and Florida. Scott would resign in July 1868 to become Governor of South Carolina.
329. Mr. J. W. Parker, an official of the New England Freedmen's Aid Society.

Sunday. Summerville had no free colored population, and those here now are of the destitute class, so we can hope for but little aid from them. On Sunday, the barracks-chapel, where our meeting was held, was crowded with as eager and enthusiastic an audience as I care to meet. I told them the object of the meeting; and then, as well as I could laid the plan of what we wished to do before them,—told them *we* would pay for the land, and Government gave them the lumber,—and asked what *they* could do towards getting a house ready for a school and teachers in October; money and work were both needed. The first man to speak was a good carpenter by the name of Dunmeyers; said he, "I is a plain man, and alers does what I agree, and I say that I will stan' by the good work till it's done finished." The next man that spoke said, "I is called a good carpenter; I has no children of my own to send to the school; but I want to see the house built and I gives two weeks work on it." So they went on, some giving work, some money, as they could best afford, until twelve weeks' labor and $60 in money was pledged,— the women doing their part, offering to board or lodge the workmen as best they could. Every one, even the children, seemed alive to the importance of having the work done, so as to have the house ready for the Northern teachers in October. A little boy, about eight years old, came up to Miss B. as we were leaving the meeting, and said, "I got 55 cents; I'll give *that* for the new school-house; it's all I've got to give." Others were sorry they had no money, but they could work and earn some. One of the school-boys, a young man, now at work, promised to give $5. I often think, when participating in such a scene, how much richer is *our* reward, who are simply almoners of your bounty, than you can receive, who have to see such scenes through others' eyes! These destitute people, living, some of them, in rude huts made of mud and palmetto, one might suppose that all their interest was necessary to keep them from starvation; yet they are all ready and eager to do *all* and more than is required of them, that they may have a school for their children. I hope nothing will interfere to prevent the accomplishment of this object. I shall go up to P. again before the close of school, and if I find that the work drags for want of money, we must try and raise some for it. Now that we are really at work I feel as though I could *beg* with a good will, that they may not be disappointed in what we have undertaken. Advise me what it is best to do. Shall I wait till I come North, and then try and raise some money outside of the Society.[330]

330. EHH to Miss [Hannah] S. Stevenson, *Freedmen's Record* 2 (August, 1866) no. 8, pp. 149, 150.

Editor's Note

A few weeks after composing the preceding letter Esther Hawks returned to New England for a visit and presumably made efforts to raise funds for freedmen's schools, such as the one under construction in Summerville, South Carolina. Then in November, responding to her husband's appeals that she join him at his colony, Esther set out for Florida.

[En Route to Florida]

November 1866—

Left Manchester on the morning of the *6th*—for Boston on my way South. Was undecided whether to go by Steamer to Charleston, or to Savannah, and dreaded eather route very much. My mind was filled with gloomy forbodings of shipwreck and all sorts of disaster by sea! The way looked long and dreary and I left home feeling exceeding loneley and forlorn—and my delight was proportionate, when, on reaching Studio Beams' I found a note from Dr. M. [Marcy] saying that he and wife had concluded to go on to C. [Charleston] "and would be most happy to secure" my companionship;" I went directly out to Cambridge and we made arraingements to start Tuesday Eve. the *7th*. Then I went out and spent the night at Joe DeMeans. It was election day and the cars were full of eager excited men wondering, guessing and prophesying on the elections. Coming into the city in the morning saw a very amusing sight at depot, a *man* laboring under an accumulation of band-boxes—no woman along so he alone was responsible—they dropped—the covers came off—and rolled about—the poor man looked hopelessly about, but no one offerd to assist him so he strung them on his arms and disappeared. Its the first '*band box*' I've seen for a long time!

Went up to No. 8. —no one but pretty little Miss Fortin [Forten][331] and Mr. Walcut [?] there, but Mrs L. [?] soon came in. Closed up business with her and then went with Dr. M. [Marcy] to get our tickets—through to C. [Charleston] had no difficulty in doing so—price $37. Dr. [Marcy] went home we agreeing to meet at Providence depot at 5 P.M, then I went up to call on Miss Green. She was away but I dined with her mother and spent a couple of hours, till time to go to depot. The carrs leave at 5 1/2

331. Charlotte Forten, granddaughter of the black sailmaker and abolitionist James Forten. After teaching in the public schools of Salem, Mass., she came to Port Royal in 1862 and commenced a long career of teaching freedmen. Miss Forten described her experiences in "Life On The Sea Islands," *Atlantic Monthly*, 12 (May, June, 1864).

p.m. and as 20 minutes past—Dr and Mrs. M. [Marcy] had not appeared. I think that last half hour was one of the most anxious of my life—but just as I was giving up in despair—they came panting along, the street car having been detained by some obstructions.

Off at last and we proceeded to make ourselves comfortable—with our numerous bundles and shawls. . Crossed the Sound from Stonington—and arrived in N.Y. without incident of note—finally concluded to go directly on without stopping—so crossed over to Jersey—and at 8 A M were comfortably seated and ready for breakfast which we proceeded to take—nice fresh sandwiches—cranberry sauce and every thing complete save a cup of hot coffee—and this we managed to do without. The day proved to be one of unsurpassed brilliancy—clear and cold—even here we noticed a change from our N.E. severity of climate. The rich autumnal dyes still flooded trees and vines—and as we got into Pa. the grass looked green—fall flowers still clustered about the doors, apparently untouched by frost—and we seemed to have turned backward several pages in Times' Ledger!' we hurried along making but short pauses! at noon we were informed that there would be time for dinner—but we just managed to swallow a cup of hot coffee—before we were off again. The way looked familiar and most of the villiages to have changed but little since /61 when I was last on the road—but as we got into Maryland we encountered no soldiers and the road was'nt pickited as then.

We were delayed at Baltimore—and had time to admire its broad streets and fine monuments The cars are drawn through the city by horses—a man stands on the forward car with a trumpet which he blows as we near each corner. I saw very few colored people in the lower part of the city It was dark when we reached Washington—and we rode directly across from Rr. to the boat which was to take us down the Potomac. as far as Aquia Creek. Penn. Av. was brilliantly lighted with gas and moonlight—and as we crossed, above Willards [hotel]—The Capitol gleamed on us clear and serene like a benediction—after a tedious prayer!—the boat was comfortable—and the evening too chilly to stop outside so we lost most of the beauties of this river trip. At about 11. p.m. we again took the cars—and "off to Richmond" is the cry. The cars were very comfortable and we tried to go to sleep but the excitement had been too much, so it is a long time before we could get quit—and not till the good little Dr. [Marcy] repremanded us severely for disturbing his, and the other passengers, rest! —a couple of offices in the seat front of us were quite as restless as we. Before morning it got very chilly. At 5 1/2 A.M. we reached Richmond. Everyone got out but us and as it was so near light we got permission to remain, which was readily granted—a light, colored boy staying to take care of the cars. We ate our breakfast, and at 7. o'clock the depot was opened so we deposited our bundles there in the care of an old colored man, and sallied forth to see the sights. First went to the 'Spotswood House'—found a comfortable parlor—and Mrs. M. [Marcy] and I got warm and rested while Dr. [Marcy] 'recornoirted'. On the same train with us, came news of our elections—so the city was in an agitated state of mind this morning. In the bar-room discussions ran high and much of the more inflamable material was already to explode in another war—and loud and deep was their expressed contempt for poor Mass, over her colored representatives—tho' one regular fire-eater declared that "she ought to be entirely represented by 'niggers!'"

We went first to visit the grounds about the Capitol. The sun was up but the heavy dew kept us somewhat chilly. The court house, burned by the rebs, to prevent their papers from falling into our hands stands as the fire left it a monument of their folly. Close by is the Gov's house, and but a few rods off is the residence of "President Davis", and 'Gen Lee'. The grounds are ornamented with fine statues of eminent men—conspicuous, for its truthfulness, stands Henry Clay. The monument, surmounted by an equestrian statue of Washington is one of the finest I ever saw far surpassing the one in the Park in Washington—on the pedestal, about one third way, and on which the shaft rests, are Patrick Henry, Mason and Jefferson. It needs four other figures to complete the monument; I presume these will be, Davis, Lee, Stonewall Jackson & Wirtz [Capt. Henry Wirz].

The sky was too hazy—for a good view of the city from the top of the Capitol, so we, concluded to visit Libby and then return. I never had any clear idea of *what* this prison *was*, 'till I saw it. I presume everybody else knew it was a large tobacco warehouse—with the sign of Libby & Co. over the door—but I had a vague notion of a vast dungeon made up of filthy cells in which our men were incarserated, instead I find a great open room—cheerless and barren enough but *roomy*. The heavy iron grating over the windows are but the repetition of other warehouses; the walls have been whitewashed—floors cleaned and in both the lower and upper rooms partitions put up—making comfortable rooms for the soldiers who now use it as a guard house. The officer in charge, a *2nd* Lt. of Reg. In. [infantry] was *polite*, but not *cordial*, so we refrained from many questions—as he was evidently *bored*, by our curiosity. He showed us, with some appearance of gratification a frightful machine over a trapdoor—used as a *gibbet*—both by the rebs—and since the war, by our soldiers.

On the opposite corner, across the street, stands 'Castle Thunder' a counterpart of Libby. It is a wonder to me how our soldiers could have resisted demolishing both these dens of iniquity. I should have thought not a stone would have been left standing "one upon another," when it first fell into the hands of our outraged soldiery! but instead of *injury*, the buildings have been benefited by our occupancy of them!

In this part of the city are all the large warehouses and most of the business-men caused them to be burned rather than have them fall into the hands of our Govt, but they are fast rebuilding, and it would be difficult to tell now the extent of the disaster! —The city is built almost wholly of brick. —Street-car tracks are being laid in some of the streets, and business seems in a more thriving condition than in the cities further south. 'Northern capital reaches her easier, I suppose—or the energies of the people are not so prostrated!

Went across the bridge over the James River to Manchester but had'nt much time to spend there, stopped on a little island, to rest, and went up into an enormous live-oak tree which has been fitted up with seats. The view over the river, the canal and the cities, with a birds eye peep of Bel-lisle, interested us here for a long time—till we were admonished by the sun that, 'Time' could'nt tarry for us—so we walked slowly back to the Capitol—and our friend of the morning showed us over the building. A statue of Washington, in the lower vestibule, said to be one of the most lifelike resemblances, struck me as being decidedly below the average in intelligence of expression and intelectual developement, it has the stiff awkward look of a country bumpkin who, is making his first appearance in company in new clothes! and a bust of LaFayette, in the same room, looks almost idiotic. If these are correct likenesses we ought to *thank* the artists who have idealized them for us!

Our guide, who has been here during the entire war, told us many little anecdotes of the various grandees of the Confederacy—pointing out the 'secret committee'-room, in which [Jefferson] Davis' met his advisors—and where the oiling of the machinery, and the plans for its work, was all done! The room looked as though it had been long and faithfully used. From the top of the building our guide, pointed out—on one side of the Park, the church where Davis' worshiped. It was here that he first learned of the surrender, and he hastened to make good his escape with his gold bags. Then he showed us the position of the rebel soldiers and their strong points—also the point of enterance of our army, and the direction in which McClellan[332] advanced on the city.

---

332. George B. McClellan as commander of the Army of the Potomac had failed in his campaign to capture the Confederate capital in 1862. Two years later he again failed as the Democratic presidential nominee against Lincoln.

I got a few *leaves* and a little twig of myrtle from the yard before Davis' residence, as mementoes, as we walked back to-wards the depot. We were heated and tired so went into a nice Restaurants and called a cup of tea and oyster stews, all of which was furnished us in excellent style and of the best quality—and for the modest (?) sum of 15 cts each—however we consoled ourselves with the reflection that we could'nt eat oysters in Richmond every day—or *get* such *nice* ones in *any* city!

We visited several fine book-stores, and looked into an occasional dry-goods establishment, on our way back to the depot. In many of the windows were photographs of all *southern* men of note in the Confederacy—but no one is yet bold enough to exhibit union *offices*—even if any have desire to do so. The depot offered facilities for *washing faces*, which we improved—grateful for the opportunity—and one of which we stood in great need.

We were soon "all aboard" and off for Petersburge [Petersburg]—which we reached in time for supper. The cars stop an hour there to wait for some other train—so we had as much time to look about as we cared to improve. The city is larger and far more imposing than I expected to find—having lived so long in Fla. & S.C. where *names* only are imposing. I have got into the habit of being surprised at a *name* with a *city* to back it. One way lay right through the entrenchments and over the well fought grounds of a less than two years ago—line after line and earthwork—trenches—obstructions and fortifications of various kinds—we rode slowly through—leaving them behind us with the last hues of the setting sun, resting on and hallowing the grave of many a true and noble heart!

We reached Welden [Weldon, N.C.] at 8 1/2 P.M. (on the Roanoake River), and here the passengers are expected to sup—so we produced our basket of provisions which holds out wonderfully—and made a show of eating but those Richmond oysters still asserted themselves in my stomach, so it was *only* a show with me—but the Dr. seems always blessed with a capacity for *more*!

After we got seated in the cars from R. [Richmond] an ex-reb soldier, still in uniform who has the management of the express on the road as far as Welden [Weldon], came along and demanded $1.50 for taking care of our trunks and seeing that they were on board &—which Dr. [Marcy] refused to pay as it was an unjust charge, our tickets being paid through—also insured transportation for baggage without further charge [.] The young man got very violent and used some rather saucy language but Dr. kept cool and he did'nt get the money—but he creates quite an excitement, a young southern lady traveller expresses herself and her sympathy by declaring that she "always *did* and alway shall hate yankees!". —

The cars was nearly empty from this place: the night was chilly and we got but little rest or sleep tho' the car was a tolerable one—reached Wilmington [N.C.] about 5 A.M. crossed the Cape Fear R. [river] on a ferryboat—with but little delay. There was a heavy frost. We reached Goldsboro in time for breakfast, which according to report was but a poor one—but we "eat and were filled" from our wonderful supplies; but this meal finished the *cranberry sauce* !

I have'nt said much about the natural scenery, and in fact there is but little to say—level, uncleared lands, with marsh and cane brake interspersed makes up the sum—since leaving Richmond. Like the people, *flat* with a more luxurient growth of weeds and vices than virtues—in both cases, cultivation is the necessity! From some of the *names* without places, in the woods, a unique specimen of the genus homo, was added to our company—he chewed tobacco most vigorously and squirted the juice about him with the fearless indipendence of a true son of the 'Chivalry'. Our little Dr. found no difficulty in drawing him into conversation—and we soon learned that he was a Dr. Surgeon Dentist—and *local preacher*—being now on a tramp *plying* his *trade*—had been down to some *large* place in the woods to *preach*, and so took his medicine chest along in case of accident. For a man of his size, he could *chew* more tobacco than any one I ever saw—our seats were fast being swamped in the flood and would soon have been afloat but for the timely suggestion of the Dr. to change seats so that he could make use of out doors as a spitoon! —He left us at Florence, which we reached just at noon. There is no depot at this place—tho it is the junction of the Georgetown & C. [Charleston] R.R. but there are several small houses in the vicinity and we stop opposite a fine (for this country) hotel—but it is to early an hour to dine so we find the landlord in a most ungracious humor with the R.R. Conductors who thus deprive him of a fine business. We went into the house, and walked about the place for an hour or more. The stockade where the union prisoners were kept is only a short distance—a bleak open field—mute-witness of agonies never to be written. —The hot sun sent us into the car to rest and so we took our last dinner from the bandbox and there was still enough left for another day. Since leaving Wilmington we have found rough roades—slow travelling and missed the luxury of comfortable cars—but one car goes over the road and that is but poorly filled—not quite so much travel as in the more northern part of the States.

We opened the door and windows, turned back our seats and enjoyed balmy air and green far stretching forests of pine intermixed with a few old moss-hung oaks—hardy vines—and palmettoes, all teeming with a verdure which is not changed by times or seasons. The Santee trestle work is a wonderful work of art. The low marshy bed of the Santee makes it necessary to build up a frame from 30 to 50. ft high at which to lay the rails and this is five miles long. The cars go very slowly across it and to sit and look back on this mere thread in the air across which we had come was almost enough to make one dizzy! The view of the city as we approach it from this side is not so fine as from the ocean—but we were very glad to see its tall spires against the evening sky just as the short twilight was fading into the dusky night. I gave my baggage into the hands of an honest faced old woolly-head who carefully repeated my address several times to "make it out straight—" he said, and we walked up to the teachers' home. There was no one in the sitting room but Nellie P. [Ellen M. Patrick] and she gave me a most rapturous welcome. Susan heard the commotion and greeted me with tears of delight. It seemed just like coming home after a dreary absence among strangers! and if I could only remain here through the winter I should be quite happy. The house is full as usual. Miss Coggswell [Cogswell], who is to teach in our new school-house, at Summerville, and Miss Knight who has remained on at Edisto all summer are here. Mr. Sumner is the same eccentric compound of wit, impudence and genial sociability. Tom's place has been supplied by a smaller boy from the assylum—a bright active rogue who can steal the food from your plate and lie you into a belief of his innocence!

We improvised beds for our party, and after a warm cup of tea—and a good bath I felt tired enough to make an early acquaintance with mine—but my most tender embraces failed to soften or elicit much warmth.

I remained at home all day Sat. looking over and putting my possessions into form for a removal. Sunday eve Mr. S. [Sumner] Nell [Ellen Patrick], & I, walked down to the foot of Calhoun St. where the 'emigrant ship' the *Granada* I think is making ready to sail for Liberia with a company of 500. colored people, under the auspices of the 'Colonization Society".

We did'nt go on board as it was too late but the wharf was crowded with eager visitors, and I met many old soldier friends tho' none among those who had determined to go.

Dined yesterday at the Assylum, Mr. P. [Pillsbury] was in one of the gracious moods and gave me a cordial invitation to visit here, and make that my stopping place which I partly promised to do, but Mr. S. and Nellie vetoed the plan,

Monday as Nellie was'nt feeling well I went into school and let her rest at home. The teachers and children were all glad to see me—and I enjoyed the day very much. Mrs. M. [Marcy] went in too & as Sue Branford was, out took her class. Miss Knight was taken sick on Sat. with fever so she will have to stay for several weeks perhaps. Miss C. [Cogswell] tends her. Mr. Everett[333] is also here sick, so we have enough to do. Tues. Nellie was better but I thought it best for her to rest so went again into school. Miss Sharp[334] came in to see me. She is one of the most offensive females I ever chanced upon tho' she makes considerable sho of liking me and I ought'nt to say so. Invited me to go to Secessionville with a party from the "Baker Theological Institute" (which is under Rev. Lewis'[335] hands, consequently very efficacious), to take up the teachers at Mt. Pleasant on the way. I had already concluded to visit them in the morning so I told her, and that if they went I might go too. As she is in bad repute with Mr. S. [Sumner] & Nellie [Patrick], did'nt invite her to dine—but promised to meet her at the boat at 10 A.M. to-morrow.

Wed. 16*th*   Fixed my trunks—nailed on hinges straps &—and packed in articles left here—by this time it was near ten o'clock and I had hardly thought of our trip, but just at the last minute Mrs. Marcy concluded to go with me and we started—walked very rapidly and arrived just as the boat was about to push off, so for once we were in luck. Met Mr. Webster and Mrs. Lewis Mr. & Mrs. Chipperfield [?] anxiously waiting the appearance of Miss Sharp, but the boat left without the appearance of that interesting 'fair maid' and the party were all afloat in their calculations—however decided to visit Sullivan's Is. and have a picnic. I got off at Mt. P. [Pleasant].

Found the girls in school and much pleasanter situated than last year—they have a large house—live in the upper part and have their rooms for school—each having a room by themselves. Miss Hancock[336] is pushing her class ahead rapidly—and with the same restless energy as of old. I spend a delightful morning with them. They were quite glad to escape the presence of Sister Sharps party—and at noon Maj. Corbin—Mr. Byron [?] & Esger Bowen [?] came in to take us over to James. Is. so our dinner was hurried into a basket and we set out—the wind blew so fresh that Mrs. Marcy was afraid so she went over to Capt. Bachellers' (his family are living here now) to await our return or go back alone to C. [Charleston] in case we did'nt get back in season.

---

333. Mr. Albert Everett of Groton, Mass.
334. Mary A. Sharp of Rockville, S.C.
335. Rev. J. W. Lewis who had earlier organized the racially integrated Sunday school in Jacksonville taught by Dr. Esther Hawks and had sent upon his return to Beaufort the books that formed the nucleus of the library at the school Esther operated in Jacksonville in 1864.
336. Cornelia Hancock who taught at Mount Pleasant, S.C., on behalf of the Pennsylvania Friends Association.

The water was rough and our dinner taken under difficulties, but it was quite a sumptuous affair and what was lacking in style we made up in merriment. No-body knew exactly where to land so we got into the marsh—stuck in the mud—and then onto an oyster bed—but at last found our way to the landing—and on reaching it learned that, the villiage was still seven miles off (Maj C. [Corbin] and the other gents. were going there to appoint court) so they bustled about and learned that at a cotton gin about a mile away we could probably get a mule cart and horses for the men—so we walked on visiting one cotton gin on our way. This is the first time I have ever seen a gin in opperation. This plantation is carried on by an enterprising colored man from the north, and he feels much pleased with his success. As our *coach* was in one place, harness in *several*, and mule to be hunted for, we had ample time to visit this last mill, and also the cotton field near so we gathered a fine handful of the nicest cotton to take home. It was 4. P.M. when everything was in readiness for a start. Miss H. [Hancock] & P. [?] sat on the front seat and the Taylors' back of us, all on boards put across the cart. Mr. Bowen and Lee sat up with the driver with such a load our mule could go no faster than a walk. The wind had switched up a sky full of clouds and now blew raw and damp with every indication of its growing *damper*!

The first start of the mule precipitated our little *Taylers* out *behind*— and then Mary declared that she would ride behind the Maj. so she mounted, and we go underweigh without further mishap. It was nearly dark when we reached S. [Secessionville] and a drizzly rain had somewhat cooled our mirth—so we went into the house. —the same that I visited on my inspection of the Is. when we first came to C. [Charleston]. — It has been made habitable and is occupied by a family of natives who gave us warm seats at the fire and treated us most civilly, tho' how they could do it through all their dirt was a marvel. We only stopped long enough to get warm as the darkness admonished us of the necessity of returning—so the business was soon disposed of—and we got started on our way at about dark. Carry rode behind the Maj. this time and Mr. Bowen got a horse and buggy belonging to a Dr. who is stationed here, and Miss H. [Hancock] rode with him so Mary & I had the cart all to ourselves.

Reached Lees, at the landing about 8. o'clock and he soon had a nice lunch prepared for us to which we did ample justice. The wind was against us, so our homeward way was long and crooked—stopped at the Battery for Mr. B. to get out, and then I went home with the girls—when we arrived about midnight it was raining quite hard and the laughter & jokes & merry songs were quite washed out of us.

Thurs. 17.   It continues to rain and looks likely to, so I visited Capt. B. S—and spent a pleasant hour—met Dr. M. [Marcy] & Chap. H. [Hobbs] there—came over at noon. It commenced raining quite hard so I went into Cardozo's school in Military Hall and waited, but it did'nt stop so walked up with one of the teachers.

Friday 18*th*   Several of the teachers called to see me in the morning. As we were at dinner Miss Lincoln [?] came for us to go down and visit the 'Emigrant ship' again. A party of 15 was made up—two loads in the ambulance.

We went on board—climbing up a ladder over the high side—visited every part of the ship under the Captains escort.

Friday at 9. P.M I went on board the *Dictator* for Pelatka [Palatka], via Savannah. Miss Betume [Botume][337] and Miss Langford[338] arrived, last evening—they started on the *Wagner* and lost all their baggage and $300 in money—so we got a graphic description of the burning of the boat and rescue of the passengers.

Reached S. [Savannah] early Sat. morning after the best nights rest I remember ever to have experienced on a boat. This is my first visit to the "forest city" so I am anxious to improve it with all the sight-seeing possible. I noticed a hale whiskered old man, in the cabin, as I came out to go on shore. He was talking with a gaunt looking 'cracker' woman, in a 'log-cabin' bonnet who was returning from a visit to a brother in Ga. and noticing that I was alone very courteously offered to be my escort about the city—adding that 'Mrs Frink' (the cracker wished to go shopping and we would take her along and return for her. There is a see [sea] wall 20 or 30 ft high with a long flight of steps leading up to the street. It is quite too early for anything but business men and teams. The shops are being opened. We entered a pleasant square around which the various dry goods shops are located—visited several of them. There is a good display of articles and I am surprised at the difference of prices between this city and C. [Charleston]. No wonder the business here is more brisk. I should think every thing was at least ten per cent cheaper. We traversed the entire length and bredth of the city. It is very lovely—the broad streets lined on either side with fine old shade trees, with not unfrequently a *row* up the center making a pleasant shade, but I should think too damp and dense for health. In the course of our ramblings I learned that my escort was 'Col Boyd' C.S.A. formerly of Price's Missouri Cavelry.[339] Was living

337. Elizabeth H. Botume of Wyoming, Mass., who would later write *First Days Among the Contrabands* (Boston, 1893).
338. Fanny S. Langford of Wyoming, Mass.
339. Lt. Col. John R. Boyd, C.S.A.

at St. Josephs' when the war broke out—lost his property—a strong secessionist—and bitter against the Govt. but pleasant and loquacious. He was on board the old *St. Mary's* when she came near falling into the union hands and to prevent it she was run up into a creek on St Johns, and sunk. He spoke with much feeling of the loss of his property saying with strong emphasis, "I should'nt wonder if I should be obliged to *work* with my *own hands*, for a living yet!" —It sounded so rediculous I could'nt help laughing telling him that "where I was raised" that was'nt considered derogatory to ones character or standing. We visited the 'Pulaski Monument' and the old reb waxed eloquent as we rehersed the daring exploits of the brave Pole, who lost his life in the defence of a liberty which he could not hope to enjoy in his own country—The monument stands in the centre of a square, is a Davis Oberlisk erected to the memory of Greene & Pulaski[340] by the citizens of Savannah—built of marble about 55 ft high—the pedistal occupying about 12 ft of it. It stands on a platform of granite about 3 ft above the ground, and is enclosed by an iron railing—on one face of the pedestal is an equestrian statue of Pulaski representing him just as he was falling, from the effects of the fatal shot— on the opposite face are some heraldric designs but my knowledge of the subject is too meager to understand it. The whole is surmounted with a female figure, representing the goddess of liberty. The whole design is most admirable and the material and execution good. Gen. Lafayette laid the corner stone during his visit in 1825. Just beyond the Monument square is the 'Park' a lovely 'forest' of luxurient growth of vines, trees and flowers, with rude seats invitingly placed among the trees. In the centre are some of the prettiest water-workes I ever say. A centre fountain sorrounded by twelve bronze figures each spouting a colum of water into the air. The enclosure contained many beautiful flowers, roses and Chrisanthemums in great profusion. A surly irish was cleaning up the leaves; after some coaxing he gave me a boquet of late blossoms, which I preserved as a mento of the Forest City! —Col. B. [Boyd] now went back for Mrs. F. [Frink] not caring to visit the "nigger schools" asserting that it was "all thrown away to try to make anything but slaves of them"—so I continued my walk alone quite out of the city limits before I found the school, which is an old barrack remoddled and very well adapted to the purpose. The teachers also live here, and it being Sat. I had the pleasure of seeing them all. They are very comfortably situated—have a Matron, Supt, Asst. Supt. and but eight teachers. The whole number of children

340. Revolutionary General Nathaniel Greene and Casimir Pulaski, a Polish-born patriot cavalry officer.

registered is not more than 600, according to the statements of the teachers. I do not think the school system here is to be compared with that of Charleston—either in system or discipline. In fact these pious Am. Mis. [American Missionary Association] are not the best people in the world to organize or conduct public schools whatever they may be able to do in Sunday-schools,—however they do a great deal of good hard work and are far more consciencious in the discharge of what they consider their duty—than are the teachers of any other organization! —But they did'nt *ask me* to dine with them so I walked slowly back to the boat. Calling at the Freedman's Bank as I passed, learned from Mr. Bleinkerhoff—Cashier, that Mr. Dennett went through the city the day before on his way north to be married.

Savannah is a beautiful city. It is pleasant to wander through her shaded streets into which the fierce rays come mellowed to almost twilight softness—but the walls of the houses and the trees covered with dank mould and lichens is too suggestive of malaria to be a desirable place of residence. The streets are not paved and the deep sand reminds me of Beaufort, only these are much wider. At 3 P.M. we go down to the beautiful river—rimmed with its broad savannahs and vast rice plantations. It is 18 miles to the mouth of the river, where Ft Pulaski frowns at us from its grim port holes; and I look curiously for the wonderful enchantements of the Thanksgiving Eve, we danced away, there in '64.

[Florida]

The ocean was as smoothe as the river. Everyone, even the rough Capt. remarked the unusual placidity. I was'nt in the least sick. Run into Fernandina. The Assylum has been removed to Magnolia [.] Gen. Finnigan [Finegan] has secured his property.

Several passengers get off her. I have made the acquaintance of a very pleasant couple by the name of Wintringham from Jersy [Jersey] City—on a pleasure trip. Will go as far as Enterprise—we walked over F. [Fernandina] but the sun was too hot to enjoy it much. Left at 10. A.M. reaching Jacksonville at 3 P.M. learned of Col. Apthrop [Arpthorp] that Dr. [J. M. Hawks] had gone on the *Sultan* which was wrecked near the Inlet, so I could'nt expect to go on her—my best course was to keep on up the river and get across as best I could. Called at the [Freedmen's Savings] 'Bank' and wrote a note to Dennett. Called at Mrs. Thompsons' to carry a shawl to one of the teachers, boarding there—saw several of my old pupils, who danced about in great glee at the thought that I had returned to teach in J. [Jacksonville]—the boat only stopped in J. [Jacksonville] half an hour—so I was quite exhausted when I got on board with my long rapid walk in the hot sun. We reached Pilatki [Palatka] at 9. P M. and found the *Darlington* with Capt. Brock[341]—awaiting our arrival to go on in the morning. Coming up the river, after the Capt. found out my destination he and several of the passengers told some "powerful" yarns about the country, its people and espicially of the insects and wild animals but I persist in not getting frightened somewhat to their disappointment, I think.

Monday morning at breakfast, I recognized with pleasure an old Charleston friend, Maj. *now* Col. Hixon[342]—and we renewed our pleas-

---

341. The steamer *Darlington*, captured by Federal forces in 1862, was returned to its owner Jacob Brock shortly after the war.
342. Lt. Col. Noah H. Hixon.

A Woman Doctor's Civil War

ant acquaintance with mutual good-will and pleasure—as it helped to shorten the hours.

The beautiful vines and gaudy flowers along the bank which added so much to the pleasure of last Summers' trip, are all dead and the notes of the mocking bird are silent now—then the boat travelled along without stopping at every bend of the crooked river so just as the last rays of the setting sun lingered lovingly on the bosem of beautiful lake Monroe—we stopped at Ft Reed opposite Enterprise. I noticed that a good wharf has taken the place of the ruin of my former visit. We all spent the night on the boat. Col. H. [Hixon] went up to camp to pay off the troops and we walked up past the hotel and looked about a few minutes. I was anxious to see the mail courier from New Smyrna to engage a passage back with him—so we walked out on the road and soon a quaint little cart drawn by one of the patient long eared tribe, with a driver so near the color of the evening as to be undistinguishable—and a dolorous looking passenger pearched up in a camp chair, which brought his head in close proximity with the canvas covering of the cart. The whole turn-out seemed in a fatal sincope on the last stages of a collapse and it was with difficulty that the driver comprehended the nature of my request, however he promised to come to the boat for me early in the morning and I retired after biding my new friends 'good by' as my early start would prevent my seeing them in the morning. I was early aroused by the patter of rain on deck and my spirits sank with barometer like rapidity at the thought of the lonely ride of 34 miles in the rain—but to my great delight the rain ceased with sun-rise but the sky continued to look lacrymose and it was evident that it could rain at a moments notice. About 7. A.M my friend the driver, crawled down to the boat—looked about in a hesitating undecided sort of way for a few minutes, and retreated. I went up to the hotel to expedite matters—tried to get a cup of hot coffee—one was brought, but my roving life has'nt yet enabled me to overcome my love of *milk* and right fresh sweet cream I could'nt swallow that cup of coffee without it. So returned to the boat and got the stewardes to put me up some sandwiches for lunch—by this time everyone was astir and all came out to rally me on my *early start*—returned to the hotel with Mr. & Mrs. W. [Wintringham] and Col. H. [Hixon] to see me off!

The Lt. in command, somewhat more sober than last night told frightful stories of the impossible nature of the road over which we had to pass—to *enliven me* as the Col. said. Stage is ready announces Mr. W. [Wintringham] and there stood the queer, ricketty concern, on two-wheels—at a slant of 45 degrees—the mule looking innocent of grain and in a quiet subdued humor in fine accord with everything but my state of mind. How was I, to get into the 'vehicle'. I tried the *back way* but the thing tipped up—so that would'nt do—if I had been *alone* there would have been no difficulty—but with *such* an audience a certain amount of decorum was to be maintained. At last the Col. brought a chair and I got up to the tills very nearly unharnesing the mule by the opperation and to save myself caught hold of the top rigging which gave way—and hurried me rather ungracefully into the *cart*. A camp chair was placed for my accommodation and in it I seated myself—with what dignity I could rescue from its last fall—alas! the seat was too high for the other arraingements and brought my head into unpleasant relations with the canvas—but I took off my fashionable bonnet, and hurried the driver into starting thinking that if we could only get out of sight of all that company I could soon adjust myself to circumstances. After considerable *pulling* at the bridle and sundry smart kicks by the driver the mule consented to move—this brought a hearty laugh from the audience and I was assured by Hixon that my Charleston friends should have a graphic description of the scene. I waved them adieu heartily rejoiced when a friendly palmetto bush hid them from sight—alas! had run its rough root across the street and the jolt of the cart over it upset my camp chair precipitating me to the bottom of the *cart* but right *atop* of my bonnet. A young man in the rear, who now first attracted my notice, rushed to the rescue or I should have certainly tumbled out of the vile dog-cart most ungracefully. On being righted I, seated myself flat on the bottom, and by sitting corner-wise was enabled to stretch out my *legs* full length—and this I found far more comfortable. The man who came so opportunely to my assistance proved to be going to the same place—*in search of his fortunes*! —had come from Michigan—allured by the glowing accounts of Mr. Mitchell, the Dr. [J. M. Hawks] and other enthusiasts. Will he reallize his bright anticipations?

Our driver is on his guard and non-committal—evidently expects me to complain of the roughness of the way—but my temper is unusually placid and no amount of rough jolting can disturb its serenity. I enjoy the warm hazy atmosphere—the quaint palmettoes and moss hung oaks—which occasionally brighten the landscape—and the long stretches of prairie covered with coarse weeds and grass, with an occasional white or golden aster peeping through it—and when tired of my position get out and walk long distances till mud and water in the road compel me to take to the cart again. So the slow hours drag themselves along. I munch my hard bread—and regale myself sumptuously on delicious oranges with which I am bountifully supplied—thanks to Col. H. [Hixon] and that abominable old mule never once surprised us with a *trot—slow-walking* is what he could be recommended for!

A Woman Doctor's Civil War

Mr. Williams, the driver, entertained us with the unprecidented abuse which has been heaped upon him by the Govt. and confided to us that he "allowed a man could'nt do better than to get out of such a derned country as soon as he could" and that he contemplate a removable to *Brazil* at no distant date, but I doubt if he ever gets round to it.[343]

It was 9 P.M. when we reached Mrs. Sheldons tired and hungry. A little crowd of women and others stood on the porch as we rode up and all gazed curiously at the newcomer but no one spoke—so I made my way through them to a lighted room—and just then the mail was brought in which created a diversion. An appology for supper was soon on the table and after a slight attempt to partake, I gave up and as soon as I got warm went to bed—Mrs. Mitchell kindly offering to share hers with me as her husband was away.

[Here abruptly end those diary entries of Dr. Esther Hill Hawks which have thus far been discovered. As indicated in the Foreword, it is likely that Mrs. Hawks completed another volume of her diaries, covering the period from 1866 to 1870. Pending the possible discovery of that volume, the present editor has provided a brief account not only of that period but of the remaining years of the Drs. Esther H. and John Milton Hawks as an Afterword.]

---

343. Mr. Williams may not have gotten around to it, but other former Confederates did. They established a colony in Sao Paulo, Brazil, where slavery was still legal.

Afterword

Esther H Hawks

Esther Hill Hawks, M.D., in later life.

On the proper training of the children
rests the hope of the world.
EPITAPH

By 1869 only nine black families remained at what John Milton Hawks, as the first postmaster of the community, had named Port Orange.[1] By that time too, the Florida Land and Lumber Company had failed. Creditors had long been pressing in local courts for payment of the firm's debts. In October 1867, Dr. Hawks and other company officials were able to prevent Justice of the Peace Christopher Sutton from selling a load of the company's mahogany logs, but within two years a public sale of the company's property had been forced by irate mortgage holders.[2]

Years later, Milton Hawks, contemplating the failure of his colonization effort, took solace in that the Florida Land and Lumber Company

led the way to the settling up of the country on the coast and the enhancement of land values from the government price to about $50 an acre. But to most of the stockholders who so liberally subscribed their money in aid of this experiment, the fact that so many freedmen were started on the way to material prosperity will be more gratifying than large dividends of money alone. It may also be a pleasant reflection, that in the failure of the company, its managers, who were also its largest stockholders and creditors, never made a dollar out of it, and never tried in the least to secure

1. Michael G. Schene, *Hopes Dreams and Promises: A History of Volusia County Florida* (Daytona Beach, Fla.: News Journal Corporation, 1976), p. 80, citing Jacksonville *Florida Union*, September 26, 1868. The name Port Orange was chosen by Dr. Hawks because there was no similarly named post office in the United States. "If a person forgot to add the state on the envelope, it would come to Florida all right. Several times the department at Washington addressed me at 'Orangeport' but I corrected them until finally letters came correctly addressed, "Milton explained. Charles H. Coe, "The Life and Works of Dr. John Milton Hawks," New Smyrna Beach (Fla.) *Observer*, April 16, 1948.

2. Christopher C. Sutton to Colonel John Sprague, October 19, 1867, Letters Received, 1867–1869, M-2, Box 53, Letters Received, 1865–1869, Records of Department of Florida, National Archives; and Schene, *Hopes Dreams*, p. 80, citing (Volusia County) Chancery Order Book 1, pp. 10–13, 15–18; "Civis," Jacksonville *Florida Union*, September 14, 1867.

themselves from loss, but paid out to those who had furnished labor and material to the company the last dollar of the company's property.[3]

These seem to be noble sentiments, but the record of the Florida Land and Lumber Company in its dealings with blacks was not without its blemishes. Allegations were made of misappropriations of Freedmen's Bureau rations by General Ely and indeed at the Port Orange store of Milton Hawks himself.[4] And so much dependent upon rations distributed by the Freedmen's Bureau were blacks, who had been settled in Port Orange by the Land and Lumber Company, that the Freedmen's Bureau stopped issuing such rations in August 1867 and instead began offering blacks free transportation to other parts of Florida.[5]

The blacks who did remain in Volusia County, however, were assisted by the Freedmen's Bureau during the summer of 1867 in their efforts at establishing a school. The Port Orange and New Smyrna members of the First Union Freedmen School Society of Volusia were repeatedly thwarted in their efforts at constructing a new schoolhouse.[6] But they rejoiced when in the fall of 1867 Esther Hawks opened a school at New Smyrna. Forty young freedmen attended the school out of a total black population of only slightly more than three hundred.[7]

The following year Dr. John Milton Hawks was appointed Superintendent of Schools for Volusia County by Florida's radical Republican administration.[8] Given Dr. Hawks' long-standing commitment to improving the status of freedmen there is no reason to doubt that a heavy emphasis on black education in the county continued during his tenure.

Esther Hawks, meanwhile, did not restrict her activities to teaching. She also resumed her medical practice, and "gave her services and medicines as physician and as teacher without money and without price."[9]

Presumably Esther assisted Milton in clearing and cultivating his extensive orange groves.[10] She was also an active member of the Women's Loyal National League and vice-president of the Equal Rights Association of

3. Hawks, *The East Coast* (Lynn, Massachusetts: Lewis and Winship, 1887), p. 72.
4. Purman to Woodruff, April 13, 1867, Assistant Commissioner, Letters Received, 1866–1868 H-W, Box 4 Assistant Commissioner, Letters Received, Freedman's Bureau Records, National Archives, Washington, D.C.
5. Schene, *Hopes Dreams*, p. 81.
6. Ibid., p. 82.
7. Synopsis of School Report for October 1867, Freedmen's Bureau Records, National Archives. Esther Hawks was the only teacher in Florida whose activities were supported by the Mayhew Society at this time. *The Freedmen's Record*, III, November, 1867.
8. Oaths of Office, Volusia County, 1860–1877, Records of Secretary of State, Tallahasee.
9. "Esther Hill Hawks, M.D.," *Lynn Historical Society Register* (1906–1907): 42–43.
10. *Daily Mirror & American* (Manchester, N.H.), November 2, 1867.

Florida.[11] Milton Hawks is credited with having introduced through Senator William J. Purman the first petition in favor of women's suffrage ever put before the Florida legislature,[12] but it is likely that Esther also influenced Purman's decision to submit the controversial suffrage petition.

The Hawks' had befriended William Purman while he had maintained an office at the Port Orange property of the Florida Land and Lumber Company in his capacity as Special Agent of the Freedmen's Bureau, despite Purman's unfriendly reports about the company to his supervisors.[13] One writer Michael G. Schene has gone so far as to suggest a "dubious relationship" between Purman and Esther Hawks.[14] This suspicion is without foundation and is based on the joshing style of a letter written by Purman in May 1867 to "Mrs. Dr. Hawks" in which, along with pledging to send both religious and school books to Port orange, Purman wrote, "Since my departure from your tropical *fleasy* and mosquitoey country I have felt like a new Yankee," and added "I expect to visit your *imaginary* town next Fall—."[15]

For all of Major Purman's kidding tone, fleas and mosquitoes indeed thrived at Port Orange.[16] So too did deadly snakes, one of which provided Esther with still another narrow escape from a premature death.[17] Tropical storms were frequent,[18] but religious services were rare. When the Rev. Mr. Reynolds asked a blessing at table in the winter of 1867, the event was as close to a religious service as Port Orange had enjoyed or would enjoy for a long time to come.[19]

All of these drawbacks conspired to make her stay in Florida in the years after the war less than gratifying for Esther Hill Hawks. Neither her professional and charitable pursuits nor her continued labors for such reform causes as women's suffrage could alleviate her discontent. Not even the charms of the Hawks' "bathing yard,"[20] helped; nor did reminders of

11. Elizabeth Cady Stanton, Susan B. Anthony, and Matilda Joslyn Gage, *History of Woman Suffrage* (New York: Fowler & Wells, 1882), vol. 2, pp. 381, 765.

12. *Makers of America,* Florida Edition (Atlanta: Florida Historical Society, 1909) vol. 2., p. 386.

13. Purman to Woodruff, April 13, 1867, Assistant Commissioner, Letters Received, 1866–1868 H-W, Box 4, Assistant Commissioner, Letters Received, Freedmen's Bureau Records, National Archives.

14. Schene, *Hopes Dreams*, p. 81.

15. Maj. Purman to Mrs. Dr. Hawks, May 13, 1867, Hawks Papers.

16. Purdie to EHH, August 3, 1867, Hawks Papers.

17. Ednah D. Cheney to EHH, October 23, 1867, Hawks Papers.

18. Ibid.

19. John M. Hawks, "Report From Volusia County," Jacksonville *Florida Union*, June 18, 1868.

20. Purdie to EHH, August 3, 1867, Hawks Papers.

the warm Florida sunshine as contrasted with the bitter cold of New England winters, like one she received from a friend from Warner, New Hampshire: "We are in the middle of an intensely cold 'snap' stinging cold. If you were here you would wish yourself back in the land of flowers again."[21]

Despite her envy about Florida's weather, the writer of the above epistle also observed to Esther, "it seems an isolated life for you."[22] And Esther's loneliness and sense of isolation were intensified by Milton's frequent absences. One such absence occurred in May 1869 when Dr. Milton Hawks, temporarily insolvent following the collapse of his Florida Land and Lumber Company, was persuaded by Florida's Lieutenant Governor W. H. Gleason to make a trip mainly on foot down the coast from Port Orange to the vicinity of present-day Miami.[23]

Within months after returning from his journey, Milton Hawks began to concentrate his attentions on land promotion. In April 1870, he met Mathias Day, an entrepreneur from Ohio, in a Jacksonville hotel. Hawks persuaded Day and his companions to come to Port Orange to look over the country. With Milton as guide, the party spent several days aboard the schooner *Rover* looking over land along the Halifax River.[24] Day became especially interested in an old sugar plantation called the Samuel Williams grant, which he soon purchased for the reputed sum of twelve hundred dollars. The community that Day established on his land and quickly peopled through his promotional efforts would be named for its founder: Daytona.[25]

It was around the time that her husband was occupied with land promotions that Esther Hawks decided to return to New England. By early September 1870, Esther had entered into a partnership in the Lynn, Massachusetts, medical practice of Dr. Lizzie Breed Welch, who had been a friend and classmate at the New England Female Medical College.[26] Along with Dr. Mary J. Flanders, they were the first women physicians in Lynn,[27] a shoe manufacturing center with a population of some 30,000.

There was ample competition for Dr. Esther H. Hawks and her colleagues. Lynn was also the home and focus of activity of two other

21. Miss Harris to EHH, February 3, 1868, Hawks Papers.
22. Ibid.
23. Hawks, *East Coast*, pp. 23–50.
24. Ibid., pp. 59, 60.
25. Schene, *Hopes Dreams*, p. 100.
26. Lynn (Mass.), *Transcript*, September 3, 1870, pp. 2, 4.
27. "Esther Hill Hawks, M.D.," *Lynn Historical Society Register* (1906–1907): 43.

prominent lady healers both of whom emerged from obscurity as Esther was commencing her practice. One was Lydia E. Pinkham of Vegetable Compound fame; the other, Mary Baker Eddy, founder of the Christian Science Church.[28] There is some small question as to whether or not Esther knew Lydia Pinkham personally, despite their similar pre-war abolitionist backgrounds and the Hawks' periodic production of their own elixir. There is *no* doubt that Dr. Esther Hawks was personally acquainted with Mrs. Eddy since the latter bought and lived in a house across the street from Esther's office in 1875.[29]

Despite competition from patent panaceas and faith healers Dr. Esther Hawks' medical practice flourished.

Most of her patients were women; most of her cases gynecological. But those seeking her aid were not merely residents of Lynn. From Poughkeepsie, New York, in November 1871, came a letter from an old friend, Colonel James Beecher's wife Frankie, to her "Darling Essie." Mrs. Beecher, suffering from a uterine inflamation and fever, implored Esther to come to Poughkeepsie and doctor her. "Will $40,000 be any compensation to you for coming and spending a week with me and curing me? Because if I had it I'd give it to you and then you could go down and make the Dr. [J. M. Hawks] rich with it. Anyhow I'll pay all your expenses and more." "I love you better than I do any feminine of my acquaintance," Mrs. Beecher concluded.[30]

In 1874 Esther Hawks terminated her partnership with Dr. Lizzie Breed Welch and began an independent practice in a new office at 81 Broad Street in Lynn, to which she moved after her return from a visit to Milton in Florida.[31]

This visit was not paid as earlier ones had been to the Hawks' old home in Port Orange, scene of so much previous frustration for the two. Esther's winter was spent instead in a new community, called Hawks Park, some miles to the south.[32] Hawks Park had its origins in the summer of 1865 when Surgeon Major John Milton Hawks, while on leave from his

28. Robert C. Washburn, *The Life and Times of Lydia E. Pinkham* (New York: The Knickerbocker Press, 1931), p. 77.
29. Ibid., p. 79.
30. Frankie Beecher to EHH, November 21, 1871, Hawks Papers.
31. "Esther Hill Hawks, M.D.," *Lynn Historical Society Register* (1906–1907): 43.
32. The reader will seek in vain to locate Hawks Park on present day maps of Florida. An act of the Florida legislature in 1919 abolished Hawks Park as an incorporated town. It then became part of Edgewater and to complete its disappearance the Edgewater post office absorbed the Hawks Park post office in 1923. Barbara Miller, Florida Collection, Florida Department of State, to me, January 9, 1981.

regiment,[33] had obtained an old Spanish land grant, the 500-acre Alvarez Grant situated two miles south of New Smyrna.[34]

Following Esther's departure from Port Orange in 1870, Milton had interspersed his medical practice with service as engrossing clerk of the lower house of the Florida legislature,[35] had been appointed a notary public,[36] and had served as assistant assessor of internal revenue for District Number 5, comprising the eight western counties of Florida.[37] In the latter capacity Milton had lived briefly in Pensacola where years earlier he had acted as Collector of Customs.[38] While in Pensacola, Dr. Hawks had called a meeting of interested citizens for the purpose of establishing a public library, had headed the subscription list, and had personally collected both books and money for the project.[39] Milton had written and published the first directory of the city of Jacksonville[40] and the *Florida Gazetteer*, which after its publication in 1871 was long considered the definitive county-by-county guide to the state of Florida.[41] Dr. Hawks was also surgeon in the Marine Hospital Service in Jacksonville.[42]

As for the settlement of Hawks Park, Milton (who had once dreamed of establishing a cooperative community in which there would be no temptation to steal or do wrong)[43] was no longer quite so idealistic. When he founded upon his 500 acres the town that bore his name, he was as much bent upon personal enrichment as upon public service.

The first map drawn up by the Hawks Park Company showed thirty orange groves, some of which were owned by Milton himself. It also showed two major thoroughfares, the Strand and Ridgewood Avenue, and eight additional streets. On one of these there was a hotel, Bayview House, that boarded visitors and was the center of the town's social life. In addition there was a store and a schoolhouse.[44]

33. Hawks, *East Coast*, p. 49. Twenty days leave to "visit the St. John's River, Florida, on private business," was granted Surgeon J. M. Hawks on August 9, 1865. Hawks Military Service Record.
34. Original Spanish Land Grant to Geronomo Alvarez, with subsequent record of changes in ownership to John Milton Hawks in 1865, County Courthouse, Volusia County, Florida.
35. *Makers of America*, p. 384.
36. Ibid., p. 386.
37. Ibid.
38. Charles H. Coe, "The Late Dr. John Milton Hawks," *Daytona Beach Observer,* August 30, 1941.
39. *Makers of America*, p. 386.
40. William Richard Cutter, *Genealogical and Personal Memoirs Relating to the Families of the State of Massachusetts* (New York: Lewis Historical Publishing Co., 1910), p. 359.
41. John M. Hawks, *The Florida Gazetteer* (New Orleans: Bronze Pen, 1879).
42. *Makers of America*, p. 385.
43. Ibid.
44. This map may be viewed at the Hawks Collection, Edgewater Public Library, Edgewater, Florida.

Here Hawks practiced medicine, tended his orange groves, and served as postmaster. His public spiritedness was legendary. One day while the doctor was calling on a patient, the mail carrier accidentally took the Hawks Park mail to Oak Hill, ten miles beyond. Upon learning this Milton rode to Oak Hill to retrieve the mail, brought it back, and personally carried it to local residents.[45]

Milton Hawks promoted Hawks Park as a "New England Village on the Atlantic Coast of South Florida."[46] He sought to persuade people in New Hampshire, Massachusetts, and other northern states that the land was rich and fertile and the air was so healthful that invalids could often be cured of their ailments without taking medicine.[47] Milton hoped to people his town with "industrious, intelligent and moral citizens."[48] But for a land promoter he was surprisingly frank about some of the drawbacks of life in Hawks Park, as when he wrote Daniel Marshall who contemplated moving there, "neither you nor your wife would be contented a day (here) after she gets well. It is a frontier town, rough and rude in appearance and everybody poor. And yet the people do get money enough to pay for clothes and provisions."[49] On occasion Dr. Hawks complained openly about how dull life in his town tended to be.[50]

Still several of the Hawks' friends and relatives, along with strangers fetched by promotional brochures and flyers, settled in Hawks Park either permanently or as winter visitors. Some of these grew oranges or lemons, others kept bees or raised poultry, still others simply retired to bask in the Florida sun.[51]

By 1887 the town had a population of 120, residing in 41 houses. A new boardinghouse for transients had been added, and so had a Congregational church, a post of the Grand Army of the Republic, and even a literary society.[52]

Dr. Esther Hawks' 1874 visit to Hawks Park was not her first, nor would it be her last. She frequently left her medical practice in Lynn to spend the winter months in Hawks Park, sharing with Milton a modest but comfortable two-story, four-room house, replete with cellar and

45. *Makers of America*, p. 386.
46. Hawks, *East Coast*, advertisement, unnumbered page.
47. *Daytona Beach Morning Journal*, March 31, 1877, p. 3.
48. Ibid.
49. JMH to D. R. Marshall, May 1, 1879, Hawks Collection, Edgewater Public Library.
50. JMH to D. R. Marshall, Esq. September 18, 1879.
51. *Florida State Gazetteer* (1886–1887 Edition), p. 184.
52. Ibid. Pleasant Daniel Gold, *History of Volusia County Florida* (DeLand, Florida: The E. O. Painter Printing Co., 1927), p. 126.

A Woman Doctor's Civil War

kitchen pump and sink, all of which were rarities in late nineteenth-century Florida.[53]

For his part Milton Hawks not only spent most of his summers with Esther in Lynn, but was also absent from Hawks Park for other prolonged periods. In 1872 he opened a drug store in Allston, Massachusetts,[54] and the following year added another in Hyde Park, Massachusetts,[55] where "popular Family Medicines" were "given out on trial, sold on credit or given away" and "Homeopathic, Botanic, and Eclectic Medicine in variety" were always available.[56]

Milton practiced as a physician in conjunction with the operation of his pharmacies[57] until he sold out his holdings in both stores. He later resumed medical practice in Lynn while living with Esther between 1882 and 1888.[58]

All this while Dr. Esther Hill Hawks was an increasingly successful practicioner and revered public figure in her adopted city. She was a member of the New England Hospital Medical Society,[59] of the Boston Gynecological Society,[60] and of the Lynn Medical Fraternity.[61] In recognition of her medical service during the Civil War she was elected unanimously an honorary member of the New Hampshire Association of Military Surgeons when that organization was formed in 1899.[62] Moreover, Esther Hawks, who had once while waiting to deliver the baby of a poor black woman in an old barn collected a bundle of old rags to make garments for the expected arrival,[63] could not let a single progressive reform cause intended to better the human condition go by without making some contribution.

Esther was one of the founders of Lynn's Associated Charities, and an officer in that organization for as long as she lived.[64] She struggled to im-

---

53. JMH to D. R. Marshall, Esq., September 18, 1879, Florida Vertical File, Florida State Archives, Tallahassee.
54. Cutter, *Genealogical Memoirs*, p. 359.
55. Ibid.
56. Elizabeth H. Freeman, Sec., Hyde Park (Mass.) Historical Society to me, October 20, 1980.
57. Ibid.
58. Ludovine Hamilton, Lynn (Mass.) Historical Society to me, October 25, 1980.
59. *Lynn Historical Society Register* (1906–1907), p. 43.
60. Ibid.
61. Ibid.
62. Myra Allen Ruppel, M.D., "Address," *Tributes of Respect and Love From Associates and Friends Read at the Remembrance Service Held at the Friends Meeting House on Silsbee Street, Lynn, Massachusetts, May 30, 1906, In Honor of the Late Dr. Esther H. Hawks* (Lynn, Mass.: Boys Club Press, 1906): 19.
63. Ibid.
64. Cutter, *Genealogical Memoirs*, p. 361.

prove the hygenic conditions of slum tenement dwellers both as a physician and as a philanthropist.[65] She was a patron of the city's boys' club
and of its day nursery, and contributed generously in time and money to
the local vacation school and kindergarten.[66] She was a charter member
of the Lynn Historical Society.[67] Along with her membership in the Lynn
Woman's Club, Esther was a promoter, activist, and officer of the Woman's Rights or Suffrage Club.[68]

Dr. Esther H. Hawks was elected a member of the Lynn School Board in
1889 and served for several years.[69] During one election Esther received
the most votes of any candidate of either party since her name was placed
on the ballots of both the Republican and Democratic parties![70] Esther's
belief in the perfectability of man, and especially of the young, led her to
frequently test the patience and skill of teachers, even when they were
confronted with incorrigibles. Her battle cries were: "Try him again!
Never give him up!"[71]

Drawing upon her experiences as a school administrator during and directly after the war, Esther Hawks frequently visited classrooms as a
member of the Lynn School Board. Her first words, after a bright salutation, were typical of a physician and active member of a society for the
prevention of tuberculosis: "Throw open the windows; let us have some
fresh air; these children look drooping!"[72]

"There would follow a story," one teacher recalled, "or some shrewd
questions to test their comprehension of the lesson under way, and she
would leave us all wide awake with renewed energies and interest in our
work. Yes, a visit from Dr. Hawks was always an inspiration."[73]

Dr. Esther Hill Hawks was stricken by a malady that incapacitated her
from February 1906 until her death.[74] As her illness grew worse the child-
less Esther took an even greater interest in the well-being of young people and in their futures. Much beloved by small children she was visited
almost daily by a troop of little ones.[75] And one of her final enthusiasms

65. Lummus, *Tributes of Respect*, p. 27.
66. Mrs. Hannah T. Carret, *Tributes of Respect*, p. 5.
67. Cutter, *Genealogical Memoirs*, p. 361.
68. Lummus, *Tributes of Respect*, p. 28.
69. Estelle Williams, Secretary, Lynn Historical Society, to me, March 23, 1981.
70. Ibid.
71. Lummus, *Tributes of Respect*, p. 29.
72. Ibid.
73. Ibid.
74. *Lynn Historical Society Register*, May 7, 1906, p. 1.
75. Undated clipping, *Lynn Item*.

was the school-city government idea, which she felt would develop sturdiness of character and an appreciation of citizenship.[76]

Esther Hawks' will contained generous bequests to Milton, to her surviving siblings, and to others. The bulk of her estate, however, was willed to the Hawks Park Free Library and Village Improvements Association, to assorted scholarship funds and charities, and for annual prizes to Lynn students who wrote the best essays on the subject of peace, "it being my intent and hope that the study and thought necessary to the writing of such essays may impress upon said pupils the wickedness of war and strife, and may tend to their moral improvement."[77]

On May 6, 1906, Esther Hill Hawks died in her home at 16 Newhall Street, in which, save only for her winter trips to Florida, she had lived for twenty-two years.[78]

A member of the Universalist and Free Religious Societies,[79] she had hoped for a simple burial, and received one. But posthumous tributes were numerous, transcending the maudlin and accurately reflecting the quality of her life. Dr. Esther Hawks, one friend recalled, "never became a mere physician to the body; she has been quite as active in the treatment of the soul and the development of character."[80] Another claimed, "Scarcely an effort has been made in our city since her coming among us for moral mental or civic progress which her hand has not touched if not inaugarated."[81]

The ultimate tribute to Dr. Esther Hill Hawks, was spoken by the minister who presided at her funeral service. "She has been doing God's work in the world."[82]

*　*　*

In Florida, Dr. John Milton Hawks, while he continued his medical practice, his orange grove tending, and his land promotion, worked on behalf of many of the same causes as his wife in distant Massachusetts.[83] In addition Milton was a member and, for some years, post commander of the Hawks Park post of the Grand Army of the Republic.[84] The doctor

76. Lummus, *Tributes of Respect*, p. 30.
77. Will of Esther H. Hawks.
78. "Esther Hill Hawks, M.D.," *Lynn Historical Society Register* (1906–1907): 43.
79. Ibid., p. 44.
80. Carret, *Tributes of Respect*, p. 4.
81. Lummus, *Tributes of Respect*, p. 30.
82. *Lynn Historical Society Register* (1906), p. 44.
83. *Makers of America*, p. 387.
84. Cutter, *Genealogical Memoirs,* loc. cit., p. 359.

did not allow nostalgic military fanfare to becloud his firsthand aware-
ness of the horrors of war and was especially active in the American
Peace Society.[85] He was a member of the Free and Accepted Masons, of
the Free Religious Association,[86] and, of course, of the Village Improvement Association of Hawks Park.[87]

Milton's innovative mind also led him to devise and have published
two albums for the keeping of records of births, marriages, deaths, and
other vital statistics. The "Hawks Personal Record Tablets" were entered
according to an Act of Congress in 1876, by J. M. Hawks, in the Office of
the Librarian of Congress in Washington. These record tablets were fore-
runners of present-day records of vital statistics required by law throughout the United States.[88]

One of Dr. Milton Hawks' most time consuming and most gratifying
pursuits was writing. In 1887 he completed and had published *The East
Coast of Florida*, a descriptive narrative that combined regional history,
geography, travel yarns, recreational tips, data on flora and fauna, and
numerous suggestions on how to make money.

Dr. Hawks wrote a number of professional articles as well, the best
known of which was "The Cause and Prevention of Yellow Fever,"
which appeared in the *Boston Medical and Surgical Journal* in 1872, and
was frequently reprinted, even after the Spanish American War. "The
specific cause of yellow fever," he conjectured, "is a malaria arising from
the decomposition of human excrementitious matter in an atmosphere
of a constant high temperature. Moisture and stillness of the air contribute toward rendering an epidemic more intense and fatal; the latter by allowing the poisonous miasm to accumulate, and the former by
facilitating its conduction to the lungs."[89]

This theory was subsequently invalidated by the research and experi-
ments of Carlos Finlay and Walter Reed. But Hawks' article, which summarized earlier theories of yellow fever causation as well as presenting
his own, served as a valuable jumping-off point.

Much of Milton Hawks' nonprofessional writing centered about his
long-time devotion to racial justice. As late as the winter of 1909, in fact,

85. *Makers of America*, p. 387.
86. Ibid.
87. Ibid.
88. A set of these tablets, on which Volusia County records were maintained, is preserved
at the Edgewater Public Library, Edgewater, Fla.
89. Dr. John Milton Hawks, "The Cause and Prevention of Yellow Fever," *New England
Journal of Medicine* (October 30, 1872): 441.

Milton contributed an article to the school newspaper of Hampton Institute, a black college in Virginia.[90]

In his last years, Hawks enjoyed the status of patriarch. When this mild-mannered, good-natured joker and storyteller, noted for his sweet and courtly manners, spoke or wrote, people listened to or read his opinions with respect, even such controversial opinions as these:

> Through all my professional life, it has been my conviction that in nine-tenths of the cases where people recover from acute disease under the various systems of medical practice, they would recover anyhow without any medicine whatever, if they only had proper nursing, attendance and dieting. Consequently, the true mission of the medical fraternity is to prevent disease by the timely teaching of the laws of health. The highest state of public health can not be attained under the fee system as practiced at present.[91]

> Questions needing attention in the interest of happiness and prosperity are the moral, intellectual and industrial training of the young, and habits of industry inculcated and enforced; "if a man will not work, neither shall he eat"; greater respect for the laws of the land until better law can be established. This is the best training for all races of men.[92]

In late March 1910, Dr. John Milton Hawks came down with what appeared to be a routine cold. The cold did not prevent him from calling on an old patient who was dying, a former soldier named Sawyer who had bought his place from Dr. Hawks years earlier. But Milton's cold became increasingly worse, preventing him from attending Sawyer's funeral. Later Milton Hawks took to his own bed, certain that he would himself die within days. Calmly, Dr. Hawks made plans to be buried in Hawks Park, and reviewed with the executor of his will the provisions he considered most important, those appropriating money for a concrete library building on the corner of his land just west of the alligator pond.[93]

Milton's death on April 2, 1910, prompted one Hawks Park resident to write, "Well I can truthfully say that one of the best men living has gone and how we are going to miss him."[94]

90. John M. Hawks, "The First Freedmen to Become Soldiers," *Southern Workman* 38(1909): 107–9.
91. *Makers of America*, p. 386.
92. Ibid., pp. 386, 387.
93. Mary Jane Marshall to "My Dear Children," (Daniel R. and Vilona L. Marshall), April 2, 1910, Hawks Collection, Edgewater Public Library, Edgewater, Fla.
94. Ibid.

BIBLIOGRAPHY

This Bibliography is limited to sources of Dr. Esther Hill Hawks and Dr. John Milton Hawks documents and to the more important references used in the preparation of this volume.

Ames, Mary, *A New England Woman's Diary in Dixie in 1865,* (1906). New York: Negro Universities Press, 1969, orig. publ. 1906.

Anderson, Bern, *By Sea and By River: The Naval History of the Civil War.* New York: Alfred A. Knopf, 1962.

Annual Reports of the New England Female Medical College. Boston: Published by the Trustees, 1856, 1857.

Billington, Ray Allen, ed., *The Journal of Charlotte Forten.* London: Collier-Macmillan Ltd., 1953.

Blake, John B., "Woman and Medicine in Ante-Bellum America," in the *Bulletin of the History of Medicine,* 39 (March–April, 1965).

Boston, Mass., *The Liberator,* May 17, 1861.

Botume, Elizabeth Hyde, *First Days Amongst the Contrabands.* Boston: Lee & Shepard, 1893.

Brocket, Linus P. and Vaughn, Mary C., *Woman's Work in the Civil War.* Philadelphia: Zeigler, McCurdy, 1867.

Brown, William Wells, *The Negro in the American Rebellion.* Boston: Lee & Shepard, 1867.

Bureau of Refugees, Freedmen and Abandoned Lands Records, War Records Office, National Archives.

Cabell, Branch, and Hanna, A. J., *The St. John's: A Parade of Diversities.* New York: Farrar & Rinehart, 1943.

Charleston *Courier,* 1864–1866.

Civil War Naval Chronology, 1861–1865. Washington: Govt. Printing Office, 1971.

Coe, Charles H., "The Late Dr. John Milton Hawks," Daytona, Fla., *Daytona Beach Observer,* August 30, 1941.

Coe, Charles H., "The Life and Work of Dr. John Milton Hawks," New Smyrna (Fla.) *Observer*, April 16, 1948.

Conn, Granville P., *History of the New Hampshire Surgeons in the War of Rebellion*. Concord, N.H.; Ira C. Evans Co., Printers, 1906.

Conrad, Earl, *Harriet Tubman*. Washington: Associated Publishers, Inc., 1943.

Cornish, Dudley Taylor, *The Sable Arm: Negro Troops in the Union Army, 1861–1867*. New York: W. W. Norton & Co., 1956.

Cornish, Dudley Taylor, "The Union Army as a School for Negroes," *Journal of Negro History*, 37 (October, 1952).

Cutter, William Richard, *Genealogical and Personal Memoirs Relating to the State of Massachusetts*. New York: Lewis Historical Publishing Co., 1910.

Daniels, Jonathan, *Prince of Carpetbaggers*. Philadelphia: J. B. Lippincott Co., 1958.

Davis, William Watson, *The Civil War and Reconstruction in Florida*. Gainesville, Fla.: University of Florida Press, 1964, orig. publ. 1913.

Daytona, Fla., *Daytona Beach Morning Journal*, March 31, 1877.

Departments of Florida and South Carolina Records, National Archives, Washington, D.C.

Dickison, Mary Elizabeth, *Dickison and His Men: Reminiscences of the War in Florida*. Louisville, Ky.: Courier-Journal Printing Co., 1890.

Elliott, Charles Winslow, *Winfield Scott: The Soldier and the Man*. New York: The Macmillan Co., 1937.

Emilio, Luis F., *A Brave Black Regiment: History of the Fifty-Fourth Regiment of Massachusetts Volunteer Infantry, 1863–1865*. Boston: Boston Book Co., 1894.

"Esther Hill Hawks, M. D.." *Lynn Historical Society Register*. 1906–1907.

Farley, M. Foster, *An Account of the History of Stranger's Fever in Charleston, 1699–1876*. Washington: University Press of America, Inc., 1978.

Fitts, James Franklin, "The Negro in Blue," *Galaxy*, 3 (February 1, 1867).

Forten, Charlotte, "Life on the Sea Islands," *Atlantic Monthly*. 13 (May, June, 1864).

Franklin, John Hope, *From Slavery to Freedom*. New York: Knopf, 1956.

Freedmen's Bureau, *Reports of Generals Steedman and Fullerton on Condition of Freedmen in the Southern States*. 1866.

Freedmen's Record, 1865–1867.

Gerteis, Louis S., *From Contraband to Freedman: Federal Policy Toward Southern Blacks, 1861–1865.* Westport, Conn.: Greenwood Press, 1973.

Gold, Pleasant Daniel, *History of Volusia County, Florida.* Deland, Fla.: E. O. Painter Printing Co., 1927.

Goodrich, Marie S., "Dr. and Mrs. John Milton Hawks," unpublished manuscript, 1962, Hawks Collection, Edgewater Public Library, Edgewater, Fla.

Hanna, Alfred J. and Hanna, Kathryn A., *Florida's Golden Sands.* Indianapolis: Bobbs-Merrill, 1950.

Hawks Collection, Edgewater Public Library, Edgewater, Fla.

Hawks, Esther H., "Freedmen's School in Florida," *The Commonwealth.* (Boston), September 9, 1864.

Hawks, Esther Hill, "War Reminiscences—1861," unpublished journal.

Hawks, Dr. John Milton, "The Cause and Prevention of Yellow Fever," *New England Journal of Medicine.* October 30, 1872.

Hawks, J. M., M.D., *The Florida Gazetteer.* New Orleans: Bronze Pen, 1871.

Hawks, John M., "Report From Volusia County," Jacksonville, Fla., Jacksonville *Florida Union,* June 18, 1868.

Hawks, John M., "The First Freedmen to Become Soldiers," *Southern Workman.* Winter 1909.

Hawks, John Milton, *The East Coast of Florida.* Lynn, Mass.: Lewis & Winship, 1887.

Hawks Papers, Library of Congress.

Heitman, Francis B., *Historical Register and Dictionary of the United States Army, 1789–1903.* Washington: Govt. Printing Office, 1903.

Hendricks, George Linton, "Union Occupation of the Southern Seaboard, 1861–1865," unpublished Ph.D. dissertation, Dept. of Political Science, Columbia University, 1954.

Higginson, Thomas Wentworth, *Army Life in a Black Regiment.* Boston: Beacon Press, 1962, orig. publ. 1869.

Hildreth, H. C., *A History of Gainesville, Florida.* Unpublished Ph.D. dissertation, Dept. of History, University of Florida, 1954.

Holland, Rupert Sargent, ed., *Letters and Diary of Laura M. Towne.* New York: Negro Universities Press, 1969, orig. publ. 1912.

Hurd, Duane Hamilton, *History of Merrimack and Belknap Counties, New Hampshire.* Philadelphia: J.W. Lewis, 1885.

Jacksonville *Florida Union,* September 14, 1867.

A Woman Doctor's Civil War

James, Edward T., et al., eds., *Notable American Women, 1607–1950.* Cambridge, Mass.: Belknap-Harvard University Press, 1971.

"John Milton Hawks, M.D.," *Lynn Historical Society Register,* 1910.

Johns, John E., *Florida During the Civil War.* Gainesville: University of Florida Press, 1963.

Johnson, Allen, *Dictionary of American Biography.* New York: University of North Carolina Press, 1928.

Johnson, Guion Griffis, *A Social History of the Sea Islands.* Chapel Hill: University of North Carolina Press, 1930.

Johnson, Robert Underwood and Buel, Clarence Clough, eds., *Battles and Leaders of the Civil War.* New York: Appleton-Century Crafts, 1956, orig. publ. 1887–1888.

"Letters of Dr. Seth Rogers," *Massachusetts Historical Society Proceedings.* vol. 42, 1910.

The Liberator. (Boston) May 17, 1861.

Lopate, Carol, *Women in Medicine.* Baltimore: John Hopkins Press, 1968.

Lynn, Mass., *Transcript,* September 3, 1870.

Makers of America, Florida Edition. Atlanta: A. B. Caldwell, 1909, vol. 2, 1911, vol. 4.

Manchester, N.H., *The Daily American,* August 27, 1861.

Manchester, N.H., *Daily Mirror and American,* November 2, 1867.

Mansfield, Edward D., *The Life and Military Service of Lieut.-General Winfield Scott.* New York: N. C. Miller Publishing Agent, 1862.

McPherson, James M., *The Negro's Civil War: How American Negroes Felt and Acted During the War for the Union.* New York: Vintage Books, 1965.

Meltzer, Milton, *Tongue of Flame: The Life of Lydia Maria Child.* New York: Crowell, 1965.

Military Service Records of Edward O. Hill and John Milton Hawks. National Archives.

Montague, Ludwell Lee, *Haiti and the United States, 1714–1938.* New York: Russell and Russell, 1966.

National Anti-Slavery Standard, June 14, 1862.

The National Cyclopaedia of American Biography. New York: J. T. White & Co., 1898.

National Freedman, 1865–1866.

New York Times, 1861–1866.

New York Tribune, April 1, 1864.

Oaths of Office, Volusia County, 1860–1877, Records of Secretary of State, Tallahassee, Fla.

Official Army Register, 1861–1866.

The Official Atlas of the Civil War. Washington: Govt. Printing Office, 1891–1895.

Pearson, E. W., *Letters From Port Royal at the Time of the Civil War.* Boston: W. B. Clarke Co., 1906.

Pearson, Henry Greenleaf, *The Life of John A. Andrew, Governor of Massachusetts, 1861–1865,* 2 vols. Boston: Houghton, Mifflin & Co., 1904.

Pease, William H., "Three Years Among the Freedmen: William C. Gannett and the Port Royal Experiment," *Journal of Negro History.* 42 (April, 1957).

Peirce, Paul Skeels, *The Freedmen's Bureau.* Iowa City: State University of Iowa Press, 1904.

Perkins, Frances Beecher, "Two Years with a Colored Regiment, A Woman's Experience," *New England Magazine.* 17 (January, 1898).

Pierce, Edward L. "The Freedmen of Port Royal," *Atlantic Monthly.* 12 (September, 1863).

Quarles, Benjamin, *The Negro in the Civil War.* Boston: Little, Brown & Co., 1953.

Randall, J. G., *The Civil War and Reconstruction.* Boston: D. C. Heath & Co., 1937.

Redpath, James, *A Guide to Hayti,* 1861 edition. Boston: Haytian Bureau of Migration, 1861.

Reynolds, John S., *Reconstruction in South Carolina, 1865–1877.* Columbia, S.C.: The State Co., 1904.

Richardson, Joe M., *The Negro in the Reconstruction of Florida, 1865–1877.* Tallahassee: Florida State University, 1973, orig. publ. 1965.

Rollin, Frank A., *Life and Public Services of Martin R. Delany, Sub-Assistant Commissioner Bureau Relief of Refugees, Freedmen, and of Abandoned Lands, and Late Major 104th U.S. Colored Troops.* Boston: Lee & Shepard, 1868.

Rose, Willie Lee, *Rehearsal for Reconstruction: The Port Royal Experiment.* Indianapolis: Bobbs-Merrill, 1964.

Rosen, Fredrick Bruce, *The Development of Negro Education in Florida During Reconstruction: 1865-1877.* Unpublished Doctoral dissertation, University of Florida, 1974.

Schene, Michael G., *Hopes Dreams and Promises: A History of Volusia County Florida.* Daytona Beach, Fla.: News Journal Corp., 1976.

Shofner, Jerrell H., *Nor Is it Over Yet: Florida in the Era of Reconstruction, 1863–1877.* Gainsville, Fla.: News Journal Corp., 1976.

Simkins, Francis Butler and Woody, Robert Hilliard, *South Carolina During Reconstruction*. Chapel Hill: University of North Carolina Press, 1932.

Skyrock, Richard Harrison, "A Medical Perspective on the Civil War," *Medicine in America: Historical Essays*. Baltimore: John Hopkins Press, 1966.

Smedley, Katherine, "The Northern Teacher on the South Carolina Sea Islands" unpublished Master's thesis, Dept. of History, University of North Carolina, 1932.

Stanton, Elizabeth Cady, Anthony, Susan B., and Gage, Matilda Joslyn, *History of Woman Suffrage*. New York: Fowler & Wells, 1882, Vol. 2.

Steiner, Paul E., *Disease in the Civil War: Natural Biological Warfare in 1861–1865*. Springfield, Ill.: Charles D. Thomas, 1968.

Swint, Henry L., *Dear Ones at Home*. Nashville: Vanderbilt University Press, 1966.

Swint, Henry Lee, *The Northern Teacher in the South*. New York: Octagon Books, Inc., 1967.

Taylor, Susie King, *Reminiscences of my Life in Camp With the 33rd United States Colored Troops Late 1st S.C. Volunteers*. Boston: Published by the Author, 1902.

Tributes of Respect and Love from Associates and Friends, Read at the Remembrance Service Held at the Friends' Meeting House on Silsbee Street, Lynn, Mass., May 30, 1906, in Honor of the Late Dr. Esther H. Hawks. Lynn, Mass.: Boy's Club Press, 1906.

Waite, Frederick D., *History of the New England Female Medical College, 1848–1874*. Boston: Boston University School of Medicine, 1950.

Waite, Otis F. R., *New Hampshire in the Great Rebellion*. Claremont, N.H.: Tracy, Chase & Co., 1870.

Wallace, John, *Carpet-Bag Rule in Florida*. Gainesville: University of Florida Press, 1964, orig. publ. 1888.

The War of the Rebellion: Official Records of the Union and Confederate Armies, 128 vols. Washington: Govt. Printing Office, 1880–1902.

Warner, Ezra J., *Generals in Blue: Lives of the Union Commanders*. Baton Rouge: Louisiana State University Press, 1964.

Warner, Ezra J., *Generals in Gray: Lives of the Confederate Commanders*. Baton Rouge: Louisiana State University Press, 1959.

Washburn, Robert C., *The Life and Times of Lydia E. Pinkham*. New York: Knickerbocker Press, 1931.

INDEX

(previously 1st S.C.), 194n, 209,
225n; 34th U.S.C.T. (previously 2nd
S.C.) 95, 121, 175, 189, 235n; 35th
U.S.C.T., 93, 95, 103–4, 112, 127,
140, 151, 167, 214; 104th U.S.C.T.,
132
religion of freed blacks, 39–40, 70,
103–4, 230
Republican Party, founding of, 130n
Reynolds, Rev., 102–3, 273–74
Rhett House, 209, 211–12, 214
Rhett, Robert Barnwell, 209n
Rice, First Lt. Marshall N., 159–60, 211,
217
Richmond, Va., 254–57
Rider, Capt., 124
Rivers, Major Henry, C.S.A., 154
Rivers, Fred, Jim, Johny, Steve (former
freed black pupils of EHH), 180
Robert, Christopher Rhinelander, 102
Roberts, Asst. Surgeon, Dr. Nathan S.,
66, 166, 193, 205
Robinson, Capt., 242
Robinson, Mr. (Sunday School
Superintendent), 73
Rockland, 221
Rogers, First Lt. Andrew P., 183
Rogers, Dr. Seth: praises Drs. Hawks for
getting hospital in order, 47n
Rosa (freed black orphan), 200
Rose (freed black), 180; brings food to
EHH, 118
Rose, Willie Lee, calls JMH "fanatical,"
23
Ross House, Charleston, converted into
orphan asylum, 126, 126n, 156
Rover (schooner), 274

St. Augustine, Fla., 7, 71–73, 83, 104–5,
110, 119, 176, 183, 190, 235–36;
description of, 107; teachers, 201
St. Helena bar, 207
St. Johns, 188
St. John's bar, 108, 229
St. John's Mills, 233
St. John's River, Fla., 44, 59, 177, 181n,
183, 187n, 263, 276n
St Marys, 235, 263
St. Mary's expedition, 43
St. Marys River, 43
Salem, Mass., 253n
Salina (freed black) brings food to EHH,
118
Sammis, Miss. *See* Copple, Mrs.
Sampson, danger aboard, 221

Sandy (freed black), 217–18
Sanitary Commission, 50–51, 63, 70, 86
Santee trestle, 259
Santiago de Cuba, 125
Sao Paulo Brazil, confederate colony in,
268n
Sarah (freed black orphan), 200
Sargent, Letitia, 205, 213
Savannah, 101, 188, 188n, 194–95,
226, 241, 253, 262; description,
263–64; monuments to Greene and
Pulaski, 263
Saxton, Brig. Gen. Rufus, 23–24, 40–
41, 99n, 132, 143, 212, 240, 250n;
defends blacks from abuse, 34;
organizes 1st S.C. Inf., 26
Scammon, Brig. Gen Eliakim P., 104,
106–8; praises black scout, 109;
supports efforts to improve refugee's
lives, 108–10
Schimmelfennig, Brig. Gen. Alexander,
92, 92n
school program, 159
schools for freedmen, 39, 42, 45–46
Schurz, Carl: report on conditions in the
South, 242, 242n, 243
Scott, Maj. Gen. Robert Kingston, 250
Scott, Gen. Winfield, 152–53;
allegations of miscegenation against,
152n
Seabrooks, S.C., 207, 228
Sea Island House, 193
Sea Island Negroes, 38
Sea Islands, 18; living conditions on,
26n
Seaton, Col., 118, 121
Secesh lady (Spanish), 171
Secessionville, S.C., 143, 260–61;
destitution of freed blacks in, 141–
42
Selvage, Capt. John W., 230–31
Severance, Carolina M., 72
Severance, Clarence M., 193
sewing school, 102, 109–110
Seymour, Brig. Gen. Truman, 61, 91
Sharp, Mary A., 260
Sharpe, Capt. Henry, 162, 162n.212
Shaw, Col. Robert Gould, 50n, 51; death
of and tributes to, 52, 52n, 54
Shaw, Col. James Jr., 77
Sheldon's, Mrs., boardinghouse, 268
Sherman, Lt. Col. George R., 83, 85
Sherman, Gen. William T., 95, 117
Slave narratives: Black, Susan, 154–55;
Chambers, Milton, 176; Curry Anna.
177; Foster, Mrs., 70; Jessims,

DATE DUE

PRINTED IN U.S.A.